The Fashion Retail Academy
Library
15 Gresse Street
London W1T 1QL
library@fashionretailacademy.ac.uk

TI1493590

365

habits of
successful
graphic
designers

First published in the United States of America in 2011 by
Rockport Publishers, a member of
Quayside Publishing Group
100 Cummings Center
Suite 406-L
Beverly, Massachusetts 01915-6101
Telephone: (978) 282-9590
Fax: (978) 283-2742
www.rockpub.com

Library of Congress Cataloging-in-Publication Data available

ISBN 978-1-59253-737-2

Digital edition published in 2011
eISBN-13: 978-1-61058-144-8

10 9 8 7 6 5 4 3 2 1

Design: Rockport Publishers

Printed in Singapore

365

BEVERLY MASSACHUSETTS

ROCKPORT PUBLISHERS

Laurel Saville
Steve Gordon Jr
Joshua Berger
Sarah Dougher

habits of successful graphic designers

Insider secrets from top designers on working smart and staying creative

CONTENTS

INTRODUCTION

Designers' days are filled with wrangling in those isolated ingredients of type, color, form, image, and copy into something ordered, arresting, and compelling. It's a strange brew of art and commerce, what designers do. Many of the tools of the trade—from PMS and CMYK, to grids, palettes, picas, and pixels—are an expression of a designer's requirement to corral the creative into some kind of service.

This need to control the artistic impulse also expresses itself in designers' proclivity for maxims, precepts, and rules. Use sans serif type for headlines. (Unless, of course, you're designing for the Web.) Make every client think they're your only client. (Except when you're trying to show your industry experience.) Stay focused on your career. (But taking time off is pretty grand, too.) And herein lies the rub: for every design decree, there is a counter commandment as well.

However, as we set out to collect the most cogent and helpful of all of the above from a wide range of highly opinionated designers—big names in large firms, to solo practices and up-and-comers—we were struck by the overall consistency of good advice and successful practices. We were struck by another thing as well: the generosity of designers in their willingness to share their hard-won lessons. The best designers are united in their passion for the beauty and necessity of what they do and follow habits only because they contribute to the larger good of design, designers, and the clients their work serves. So whether you're starting out or well established in your career, we think you will find everything from helpful hints to deep wisdom in the following pages. You may choose to break the rules you find here, but as they say, it's always best to know them first.

–Laurel Saville

avantgarb

ONE OF FASHION'S QUIETEST ACHIEVERS, LONDON DESIGNER HUSSEIN CHALAYAN CREATES CLOTHING WITH A SCULPTURAL AESTHETIC, DRAWING FROM ARCHITECTURE, ENGINEERING AND EVEN POLITICS.

37 // SOCIAL FABRIC
WORDS // CAIA HAGEL
PORTRAIT // JULIAN ANDERSON

Pol Oxygen is an Australian-based international magazine of design, art, and architecture. As art directed by Marcus Piper, its pages reveal the designer's appreciation for the form, function, and dimensionality of publications.

industrial

AT THE KORTRIJK INTERIEUR BIENNIAL, VISITORS HAD TO PEER THROUGH TO SEE KONSTANTIN GRCIC

CONTRIBUTORS

DAVID ALBERTSON, ALBERTSON DESIGN
WWW.ALBERTSONDESIGN.COM

David Albertson founded Albertson Design in 1995. There he leads a diverse range of projects from new magazine launches to large-scale identity and brand communications efforts. Albertson Design developed the launch of Make and Craft magazines as well as created the identity for the Aspen Art Museum and an annual report for HP.

ALAN AND AMANDA ALTMAN, A3 DESIGN
WWW.A3-DESIGN.COM

A3 Design is a family-owned design studio specializing in the most important asset to your company: your brand. With a focus on value, clear communication and company culture, we build visual experiences your company can grow from, your audience relates to and your employees are proud of. We feel the dynamic of a husband and wife team creates a devil's advocate approach that benefits every project. Every decision is questioned, debated and justified. Amanda and Alan Altman head a team that continues to add value to their client's businesses with wow! experiences.

ANDY ALTMAN, WHY NOT ASSOCIATES
WWW.WHYNOTASSOCIATES.COM

Andy Altmann and David Ellis are the brains of Why Not Associates, a twenty-three-year-old firm that has left its mark across a wide swath of projects in the United Kingdom and beyond. Their unorthodox style of working, their varied client list, and their experimentation in a variety of media give their work a distinct—but never predictable—look. Their monograph, Why Not, was published by Booth-Clibborn Editions in 1997 and in 2004 *Why Not Associates 2: Graphic Design, Film, and Photography* was published.

DOUG BARTOW, ID29
WWW.ID29.COM

id29 is a brand and communication design studio driven by intelligence, hard work, common sense and the understanding that exceptional design and creative is a competitive asset. Our capabilities include brand identity, communication design, web design and development, and creative technologies. Our clients are household names, multi-billion dollar internationals, mid-sized companies, institutions, organizations and entrepreneurs. We work with remarkable people who demand remarkable results and loathe mediocrity.

DONOVAN N. BEERY, ELEVEN19 COMMUNICATIONS, INC.
WWW.ELEVEN19.COM

Donovan N. Beery oversees all creative development at Eleven19 Communications, Inc., in Omaha, Nebraska. He previously served as the Web designer at Union Pacific and the corporate identity and Web designer at Nexterna. He teaches visual communications at Metropolitan Community College, has lectured on Web design at Creighton University, and proudly served seven years on the board of directors for AIGA Nebraska. He currently co-hosts The Reflex Blue Show with Nate Voss and Donovan Beery, www.36point.com/the_reflex_blue_show.html.

JAMES BENNET
WWW.THEATLANTIC.COM

Before joining The *Atlantic* staff, James Bennet was the Jerusalem bureau chief for the *New York Times*. During his three years in Israel, his coverage of the Middle East conflict was widely acclaimed for its balance and sensitivity. Bennet, a graduate of Yale University, began his journalism career at the *Washington Monthly*. Prior to his work in Jerusalem, he served as the Times' White House correspondent.

NICOLE BLOCK, NICEVENTS
WWW.NIC-EVENTS.NET

Nicole Block is a designer and illustrator, living and working in Brooklyn, New York. She works mostly with stationery and branding and is very happy to be able to hand pick her projects and clients, allowing her final products to be much more interesting and personal. She finds inspiration from her designer husband David Block and her beautiful daughter, Anna Jae.

KEITH BOWMAN, THE DESIGN BUREAU OF AMERIKA
WWW.THEDESIGNBUREAUOFAMERIKA.COM

Keith Bowman has more than twenty years of experience in all aspects of graphic design. Four of those years were spent teaching advanced-level design courses at Montgomery County Community College outside Philadelphia, Pennsylvania. His unique ability to conceptualize and present solid design imagery has been the constant hallmark of his work throughout his career.

VICTOR BURTON, VICTOR BURTON DESIGN GRÁFICO LTDA

Victor Burton is director of Victor Burton Design Gráfico Ltda, in Rio de Janeiro, Brazil, which principally is involved in editorial and environmental design. He began his career working for the Franco Maria Ricci publishing house in Milan, Italy, where he created his first book covers. He has completed more than 2,500 book covers and 180 luxury book projects. He was twice awarded by the Bienal de Design Gráfico and won the National Book Chamber of Brazil Prize for best book cover eight times.

CASEY CAPLOWE
WWW.GOOD.IS

Casey Caplowe is the creative director and cofounder of *GOOD*, a magazine about the people, ideas, and institutions driving change in the world. *GOOD* was named one of the hottest magazine launches of 2006 by Media Industry Newsletter and Mr. Magazine. *GOOD* is expanding its coverage of the Web, video, live events, and feature and documentary films. Caplowe was instrumental in developing the editorial vision as well as the look and feel of the *GOOD* brand, and he helped create the Choose GOOD Campaign, which donates every $25 (US) subscription fee to a nonprofit organization of the subscriber's choice.

ART CHANTRY, ART CHANTRY DESIGN

Art Chantry began his life as a designer in the Seattle area, where he worked with musicians and record labels in developing a signature style for the grunge movement of the 1990s. He was art director of the alternative weekly, *The Rocket*, and also developed a body of work for Seattle independent record label, Sub Pop. He has recently relocated to St. Louis, where he continues to work as a freelancer. His monograph *Some People Can't Surf* (2001) is available from Chronicle Press.

MARGO CHASE, CHASE DESIGN GROUP
WWW.CHASEDESIGNGROUP.COM

Margo Chase founded the Chase Design Group twenty-three years ago. Noted early on for designing hundreds of logos and identities for clients such as Madonna, Cher, and Buffy the Vampire Slayer, the company is now equally well known for corporate identities, packaging and product design, motion graphics, advertising, and interior design. Widely recognized by many awards and accolades, Margo Chase was originally trained to be a veterinarian.

SETH CHEEKS, CREATETHE GROUP
WWW.CREATETHEGROUP.COM

Seth Cheeks, formerly of CheekyDSN, is the art director at Createthe Group, a design firm that strives to deliver innovative, forward-thinking, and emotional campaigns, communications platforms and commerce solutions in the wealth of emerging digital, mobile, and social media technologies. Some companies that Seth has worked with are MTV Networks, JWT, R/GA, The Chopping Block, Interscope, 3Sixteen, S.C. Johnson, Nokia and Nike.

ROBERTO DE VICQ DE CUMPTICH
WWW.DEVICQ.COM

Roberto de Vicq de Cumptich is from Rio de Janeiro, Brazil. He received his MFA from the Pratt Institute and, after ten years in branding, Web, and magazine design, he began working primarily with publishing houses in New York, first as creative director for Random House and then HarperCollins. He now has his own design studio where he develops an array of projects, from branding to typeface design. He has received numerous design awards, and his book, Bembo's Zoo, written for his daughter, was a finalist for the Newbery Award. He lectures and speaks frequently on design topics.

Mischen Clothing website design

MAYA DROZDZ, VISUALINGUAL
WWW.VISUALINGUAL.ORG

Maya Drozdz received her BA in philosophy and critical theory from Cornell University and her MFA in 2-D design from Cranbrook Academy of Art. Her interests center on graphic design theory, particularly its intersection with popular culture and the urban environment. Her professional experience includes identity, print, interaction, and environmental design, as well as teaching, lecturing, writing, and curating design exhibits worldwide. She is a partner at the all-media design consultancy VisuaLingual.

NICOLE DUDKA
WWW.CHICAGOTRIBUNE.COM

Nicole Dudka joined the Chicago Tribune in 2006 after working at the Hartford Courant, where her work was honored by the Society for News Design and Print magazine. A graduate of Ball State University, she has a fondness for white space and insists that everyone looks better in high contrast.

ROB DUNLAVEY
WWW.ROBD.COM

Rob Dunlavey's editorial illustrations have appeared in many magazines and newspapers, from the Wall Street Journal and the Los Angeles Times to Business Week and Better Homes & Gardens. He also created illustrations for children's museums and has collaborated with Motion Theory on television commercials for HP. Dunlavey attended art classes at the Art Institute of Chicago and Southern Illinois University and received a master's degree in sculpture from Claremont Graduate University.

AREM DUPLESSIS
WWW.NYTIMES.COM

Arem Duplessis is the art director of the *New York Times* Magazine. He has held design director and art director positions at various magazines including *Spin, GQ,* and *Blaze.* He has received numerous awards for his editorial design work and was nominated for a National Magazine Award in Design from the American Society of Magazine Editors in 2004. Duplessis has also judged and captained many design competitions.

ED FELLA

Ed Fella worked as a commercial designer for 30 years in Detroit before he went back to school at age 48 to get his M.F.A. at Cranbrook. He retired from Cal Arts after teaching there for 13 years. He still participates in the graduate classes and continues to pursue his "art practice." His work is shown widely, and his book of photographs, *Edward Fella: Letters on America* (2000), was published by Princeton Architectural Press. His latest book is the catalog for the show "Two Lines Align: Drawings and Graphic Design by Ed Fella and Geoff McFetridge."

JESSICA FLEISHMANN
WWW.STILL-ROOM.COM

After working as a chef and arts administrator, Jessica Fleischmann got an MFA in graphic design at California Institute of the Arts. She founded her own studio, still room, in the front room of her Echo Park home in 2006. Previously, she was design associate with Lorraine Wild and art director of Western Interiors and Design magazine.

VINCE FROST
WWW.FROSTDESIGN.COM.AU

Formerly an associate director at Pentagram's London office, Frost started his own design firm in 1994 and eventually moved it to Sydney, Australia. He has worked for a wide variety of clients, including the Sydney Opera House, Rizzoli Books, Tourism NT, Deutsche Bank, Mushroom Records, and various publications.

JASON GODFREY, GODFREY DESIGN
WWW.GODFREYDESIGN.CO.UK

Jason Godfrey started Godfrey Design in 2002 in London. He has designed books for publishers Laurence King, Dorling Kindersley, and Pavilion as well as artists' catalogs and other handmade books. He has also designed stamps for the Royal Mail and the literary magazine Beat. He also worked at Pentagram in London and Eric Baker Design Associates in New York.

CHRISTINE GODLEWSKI, GENIUS CREATIVE
WWW.GENIUS-CREATIVE.COM

Christine Godlewski (aka Genius Creative Inc.) has been living, breathing, and sleeping graphic design for the past fifteen years—eleven of which she's flown solo. In the span of her career, she has developed standout communication materials for Fortune 500 companies, nonprofits, and start-ups.

CARIN GOLDBERG, CARIN GOLDBERG DESIGN
WWW.CARINGOLDBERG.COM

Carin Goldberg studied at the Cooper Union School of Art. She began her career as a staff designer at CBS Television, CBS Records, and Atlantic Records before establishing her own firm, Carin Goldberg Design, in 1982. Goldberg has designed hundreds of book jackets for all the major American publishing houses, as well as dozens of album covers for leading record labels. In recent years, her image-making expertise has expanded to publication design and brand consulting for clients including AR and Martha Stewart Living Omnimedia. From 2003 to 2004, she was also creative director at Time Inc. Custom Publishing.

LIZZA GUTIERREZ, LIZZA'S ROOM
WWW.LIZZASROOM.COM

Lizza Guiterrez is the principal graphic designer of Lizza's Room, a design studio she established in the Philippines. Lizza has a master's degree in communication and packaging design from Pratt Insti¬tute, New York. A passionate student of color, texture, photography, and letterforms, Lizza takes a clean and thoughtful approach to design.

JOENG-KWON GYE

Joeng-kwon Gye worked on a campaign for the *New York Times* as an art director at Bozell New York. He has also served as a visual artist for the Frankfurt Book Fair, as well as the reopening event for the National Museum of Korea. Joeng-kwon has received the Adobe Design Achievement Award and has had exhibitions at the Art Institute of Chicago, Stuttgart Design Centre, and the Empire State Building.

LUKE HAYMAN
WWW.PENTAGRAM.COM

Luke Hayman studied graphic design at Central/St. Martin's School of Art in London. He has been design director of *New York* magazine, creative director of Travel + Leisure magazine, design director for I.D., and the creative director of Media Central and Brill Media Holdings. In addition, he was senior partner and associate creative director in the Brand Integration Group in the New York office of Ogilvy & Mather. Hayman's editorial design work has been given highest honors by every major design association in the United States and in England. He joined Pentagram's New York office as partner in December 2006.

STEVEN HELLER
WWW.HELLERBOOKS.COM

Steven Heller is a designer, educator, and writer. The author, coauthor, or editor of more than 100 books on design and popular culture, Heller was an art director at the *New York Times* for more than thirty years, where he also writes reviews and obituaries. He is the founder and co-chair of the MFA Designer as Author program at the School of Visual Arts, where he lectures on the history of graphic design. He is a contributing editor to *Print, Eye, Baseline,* and *I.D.* magazines, former editor at the AIGA *Journal of Graphic Design,* and current editor of AIGA *VOICE: Online Journal of Design.*

JENI HERBERGER, BIG FISH CREATIVE STAFFING/DESIGN MATTERS
WWW.GOBIGFISH.COM

As a nationally recognized speaker and corporate trainer, Jeni Herberger leverages twenty years of experience within the design industry to provide clients with practical strategies on "doing business better." Drawing from her own experiences as a business owner and her years of consulting, she works with company leaders to identify key issues and conducts onsite training sessions offering action plans that are grounded in strategy and focused on getting results.

ERIC HINES, HONEST BROS.
WWW.HONESTBROS.COM

Eric Hines is principal and creative director of Honest Bros and has worked with and brought success to Jackson Hole Mountain Resort, Special Olympics Colorado, Compaq Computers, Crown Castle, and Unocal. Eric has also taught at Metropolitan State College of Denver and currently teaches at Rocky Mountain College of Art and Design. His design work has been recognized in awards shows and publications such as *LogoLounge, Print Magazine,* SXSW, *Graphis,* Addy's, and the Art Director's Club of Houston. He received his BFA from Southwest Texas State University in 1999.

ARTHUR HOCHSTEIN
WWW.TIME.COM

Arthur Hochstein was the art director at *Time* magazine until 2009. After studying journalism at the University of Missouri, Hochstein held a number of editing and design jobs at small publications. He began at *Time* as a freelancer and worked in a variety of roles prior to being named art director in January 1994. His work has been honored by the Society of Publications Designers, the Art Directors Club of New York, and other organizations.

JD HOOGE, INSTRUMENT
WWW.WEAREINSTRUMENT.COM

JD Hooge led the collaborative studio of design and technology specialists known as Grid/plane and has since begun work with the design firm, Instrument. His past clients include XBOX, Google, Sony, MTV, Helio, Nike, Starbucks, Fortune Magazine, and Pulitzer Foundation for the Arts. Many publications and books have recognized JD's work. A graduate of the Milwaukee Institute of Art & Design, JD was named one of *Print* Magazine's "30 Under 30" New Visual Artists in 2005.

JOHN C JAY, WIEDEN+KENNEDY
WWW.WK.COM

John C Jay is a partner of Wieden+Kennedy, which has offices in New York, London, Amsterdam, Tokyo, and Portland, Oregon, and is also co-executive creative director for Wieden+Kennedy, Tokyo. Jay was chosen by *American Photographer* magazine as one of the "80 Most Influential People in Photography." He received the Gold Medal at the Leipzig Bookfair in 1998 for the book, *Soul of the Game.* He has received multiple awards including gold and silver medals from the NY Art Directors Club and The One Show in New York. Examples of Jay's work have also appeared in a variety of museum and gallery exhibitions including Museum of Modern Art, New York (film and video); Victoria & Albert, London; Cooper-Hewitt Museum, New York; the Pompidou Museum, Paris; The Field Museum, Chicago; and International Center of Photography, New York. Jay has served on the International Advisory Committee for the Wexner Center for the Arts, is a founding member of the Board of Directors of P.I.C.A. (Portland Institute of Contemporary Art), and a member of the Board for Camp Caldera, a nonprofit art and ecology center in Oregon.

ALICIA JOHNSON, THELAB
WWW.THELABNYC.COM

Alicia Johnson is a principal at thelab: a media arts company. We create and produce content in all media. We're a multi-disciplined bunch, with all manner of experience, from an assortment of industries, working in purpose-built teams to help our clients engage their audience.

TONWEN JONES
WWW.TONWENJONES.CO.UK

Tonwen Jones works in Brighton, UK, as a freelance designer and illustrator. Graduating from Central Saint Martins with a BA in design and illustration in 1999, she went on to work as a designer, continuing her illustration work in the evenings. She now works full-time as a freelance illustrator.

NICKI KALISH
WWW.NICKIKALISHDESIGN.COM

Nicki Kalish was art director of the dining section of the *New York Times* until 2011, where she had been a designer since 1974. Kalish graduated from the Connecticut College for Women and received a BFA and an MFA in graphic design from Yale University. Nicki is now owner and senior designer at Nicki Kalish Design.

ANITA KUNZ
WWW.ANITAKUNZ.COM

Anita Kunz has spent the last three decades making pictures for publishers in many countries. Predominately an editorial illustrator for the *New Yorker, Rolling Stone, Fortune, Time,* and many others, she also teaches, lectures, and has been involved with various advocacy organizations. Her paintings and sculptures have appeared in a number of solo shows in the United States and abroad, and she has won many awards. She was named one of the fifty most influential women in Canada by the National Post, Ontario, Canada.

KALLE LASN
WWW.ADBUSTERS.ORG

Kalle Lasn was born in Estonia during the middle of World War II. He and his family lived in a displaced persons' camp for five years before immigrating to Australia, where he received a B.S. in pure and applied mathematics. He worked in a variety of fields, including computer-simulated war games, market research, and documentary filmmaking. When mainstream media refused to run his spots about the disappearing old-growth forests of the Pacific Northwest, he launched Adbusters magazine, which was eventually followed by the Powershift Advertising Agency and social marketing campaigns such as Buy Nothing Day and TV Turnoff Week.

ADAM LARSON, ADAM+CO.
WWW.ADAMNCOMPANY.COM

Adam&Co. is an award-winning creative studio. We practice the art of design, specializing in branding, packaging, graphic design, and creative direction. Formed by Adam Larson in 2007, we work with a wide range of clients across many industries. We believe in the power of good design as a universal mode of communication, a functional artform, and an effective business tool. By collaborating with our clients, and a network of creative professionals, we create tailored design solutions and brand experiences that are equally as effective as they are creative.

JEREMY LESLIE
WWW.MAGCULTURE.COM

Jeremy Leslie was executive creative director at John Brown Publishing in London from 1999 to 2009. Prior to that, he ran his own studio, working for clients including *Blitz* magazine and *The Guardian*. Jeremy also spent three years as group art director at *Time Out*. He is a passionate advocate of editorial design, regularly contributing to the creative press and to design conferences on the subject. He is one of the three founders of the biannual independent magazine conference, Colophon—which launched in 2007 in Luxembourg—and has written two books on magazine design: *Issues* and *magCulture*. His blog can be read at www.magculture.com, where he is the creative director.

CALVIN LEE, MAYHEM STUDIOS
WWW.MAYHEMSTUDIOS.COM

Calvin Lee, creative director/principal of Mayhem Studios, runs a small award-winning design firm located in Los Angeles, California, developing identity and brand materials.

ADAM MACHACEK, WELCOMETO.AS
WWW.WELCOMETO.AS

Adam Machacek and Sebastien Bohner met while working as design interns at Studio Dumbar in The Hague, The Netherlands. They established their design firm, Welcometo.as in 2004 in Lausanne, Switzerland, and have worked on a variety of publications including magazines, exhibition catalogs, and theater programs. Machacek has an MA from the Academy of Arts in Prague and was the recipient of a design fellowship at Chronicle Books.

BRETT MACFADDEN
WWW.BRETTMACFADDEN.COM

Brett MacFadden first worked for Chronicle Books in San Francisco as an intern in 1999 and in 2002 joined the in-house team, acquiring a wife, many good friends, and no small number of book projects as designer and art director. In 2008, he opened his own design studio, Brett MacFadden Design, also in San Francisco. He holds an MFA from the Cranbrook Academy of Art.

M. MAVROMATIS, MM DESIGN STUDIO

In between her dashing performances at the Philadelphia Opera Company and cruising her classic Mustang down the main drag, the principal of MM Design Studio manages to provide high-level creative to a diverse set of clients for all things branding.

DEREK ARMSTRONG MCNEILL, GRILL CREATIVE
WWW.GRILLCREATIVE.COM

Derek Armstrong McNeill started creative work as an Air Force photo¬grapher, has since been formally educated in advertising and design, and has gone on to teach photography and design himself. He's become a jack-of-all-trades, working in ad concepts, on- and off-line design, as well as motion design compositing.

MILES MURRAY SORRELL FUEL
WWW.FUEL-DESIGN.COM

Miles Murray Sorrell FUEL has existed as a design group since 1991, when the principals were students at the Royal College of Art. Over the last twenty years, they have forged regular relationships with clients, including Marc Jacobs, Levi's, and MTV. Two books about Miles Murray Sorrell FUEL are available: *Pure FUEL* (1996) by Booth-Clibborn Editions and *FUEL 3000* (2002) by Laurence King. In 2005, they formed FUEL Publishing.

HIDEKI NAKAJIMA, NAKAJIMA DESIGN
WWW.NKJM-D.COM

Hideki Nakajima was born in Saitama, Japan. Educated in Tokyo, he established Nakajima Design Inc., in 1995. He has won numerous Japanese and international awards for his work. He was involved with Cut magazine as a photographer and art director. His two books, *Revival* and *Nakajima Design 1995–2000*, are available through Rockin' On.

LAURENCE NG
WWW.IDNWORLD.COM

Laurence Ng began his career in the graphic arts industry by providing color separations and color correcting services. He founded *IdN* magazine in 1992 and was a pioneer in using desktop publishing technologies in a commercially viable manner. Today, *IdN* is an "international publication for creative people, devoted to bringing designers from around the globe together to communicate with, learn from, and inspire one another."

ARJEN NOORDEMAN, ELASTICBRAND
WWW.ELASTICBRAND.NET

Arjen Noordeman was born and raised in The Netherlands and studied graphic design at the Hogeschool voor de Kunsten in Arnhem. He received his MFA in 2-D design from Cranbrook Academy of Art, where he met his wife, Christie Wright. After working in various arenas of design, Nooredman and Wright founded the New York–based multidisciplinary studio, Elasticbrand, in 2006.

MARCUS PIPER
WWW.MARCUSPIPER.COM

Marcus Piper studied product design and then brought this functional, 3-D approach to the printed page, focusing on the interaction between the user and the product. This approach is evident in his work for *Pol Oxygen* magazine and *Crafts* (the British Crafts Council Magazine), which incorporate tactility and handcrafted elements. Under his art direction, *Pol Oxygen* has been awarded five consecutive Golds for best magazine by the Folio awards and was named Magazine of the Year—the first Australian magazine to receive this honor—from the Society of Publication Designers. Currently he is joint creative director of one8one7 creative agency.

MARK RANDALL
WORLDSTUDIO, INC. AND WORLDSTUDIO FOUNDATION
WWW.WORLDSTUDIO.ORG
WWW.WORLDSTUDIOINC.COM

Together with David Sterling, Mark Randall founded both Worldstudio, Inc., a design company, and Worldstudio Foundation, a nonprofit organization designed to connect designers with a variety of political causes. The latter publishes an annual magazine called *Sphere*, which showcases its projects with a wide range of work by international designers.

MICHAEL RAY
WWW.ALL-STORY.COM

Michael Ray is the editor of *Zoetrope: All-Story*, a literary and art quarterly published by Francis Ford Coppola, as well as a screenwriter. Ray's film, The Princess of Nebraska, debuted at the 2007 Toronto Film Festival and is being distributed by Magnolia Pictures.

GRIM REAPER
WWW.MAGAZINEDEATHPOOL.COM

Grim Reaper was the hooded and scythe-bearing keeper of the blog *Magazine Death Pool* until 2010, which tracked the demise of "the golden age of magazines" and was dedicated to "those magazines that look like they may be joining that Great Trashbin in the Sky, polybagged onto the River Styx, with blow-in cards a one-way ticket to oblivion."

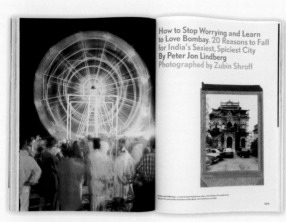

Travel & Leisure, Luke Hayman

MARTHA RICH
WWW.MARTHARICH.COM

Martha Rich lived the typical suburban life until, just short of a picket fence and 2.5 children, her average American life unraveled. To cope with divorce, fate led her to an illustration class taught by the Clayton brothers. They persuaded her to ditch the pantyhose, quit her human resources job, and join the world of art. She has since created illustrations for *Rolling Stone, Entertainment Weekly, The Village Voice, Jane*, and many others. She graduated from Art Center College of Design, where she also taught, and is currently based in Pasadena, obsessively painting underwear, wigs, lobsters, and Loretta Lynn. In 2006, a book of her works was published: *Freedom Wigs: Sketchbook Expressionism.*

EDEL RODRIGUEZ
WWW.ILOZ.COM/EDEL/

Edel Rodriguez was born in Havana, Cuba. He received a BFA in painting from Pratt Institute and an MFA from Hunter College. He utilizes a variety of materials to create work that ranges from conceptual to portraiture and landscape. In addition to editorial work for numerous publications, including the *New Yorker, Time, Rolling Stone, Texas Monthly, Playboy, National Geographic Traveler, the New York Times, Fortune, The Nation*, and *Vibe*, he has also illustrated three children's books and created a stamp for the U.S. Postal Service. His illustrations have been widely recognized and received many awards.

ROBERTA ROSENBERG, MGP DIRECT, INC.
WWW.MGPDIRECT.COM

Roberta Rosenberg, the "Copywriting Maven" and founder of MGP Direct, Inc. (www. mgpdirect.com) blogs at CopywritingMaven.com and is a contributing writer and Landing Page & Site Makeover Specialist for Copyblogger.com. Roberta has helped dozens of companies increase their website traffic, pop their search engine rankings, and get bigger, better click-through and conversion rates for their landing pages, PPC ads, email and related marketing programs.

JANDOS ROTHSTEIN
WWW.JANDOS.COM

Jandos Rothstein is an assistant professor at George Mason University and design director of Governing magazine. He has redesigned or helped launch more than twelve magazines and newspapers and writes regularly about design and social issues for a number of publications, including *Print* magazine, *The Design Journal, Voice: The AIGA Journal of Design*, and the *Washington City Paper*. He is the author of the magazine design blog www.designingmagazines.com and the book *Designing Magazines*.

JUDY ROZBICKI, LANTERN CREATIVE

Judy Rozbicki has been an artist and designer since childhood. Having played with pixels and crayons for most of her life, she founded Lantern Creative, focusing on photography and design. Judy gives a fresh perspective to her clients and strives continually to grow creatively through her works.

STEFAN SAGMEISTER, SAGMEISTER INC.
WWW.SAGMEISTER.COM

Stefan Sagmeister was born and trained in Austria. He worked for Leo Burnett in Hong Kong and now runs Sagmeister Inc., in New York City. His monograph, *Made You Look* (2000), is available from Booth-Clibborn Editions. In 2008, *Things I have learned in my life so far* was published by Abrams. He won a Grammy award in 2005 for his work on the design of the Talking Heads CD box set "Once in a Lifetime."

INA SALTZ
WWW.BODYTYPEBOOK.COM

Ina Saltz is an art director, designer, writer, photographer, and associate professor of art at the City College of New York in the Electronic Design and Multimedia Program. Her areas of expertise are typography and magazine design. She's also a regular columnist for *STEP Inside Design* and writes for other design magazines, including *Graphis* and *How*. For more than twenty years, she was an editorial design director at *Time, Worth, Golf*, and other publications. Ina also lectures at Stanford University's Publishing Course and has authored the books *Body Type: Intimate Messages Etched in Flesh* (2006), documenting typographic tattoos, *Typography Essentials: 100 Design Principles for Working with Type*, and *Body Type 2: More Typographical Tattoos* (2010).

SCOTT SANTORO, WORKSIGHT STUDIO
WWW.WORKSIGHT.COM

Scott and his partner, Emily, have been working together as Worksight for over twenty years. They were both adjunct instructors at the Pratt Institute; Scott continues to teach there and Emily has since been teaching graphic design at Queens College City University. Scott's experience in corporate culture includes early employment at Landor Associates where he developed visual identities for national brands and at Mobil Oil Corporation where he held the position of senior designer in charge of internal communications. Scott has also served for one year as treasurer (1998-1999), and two years (1999-2001) as vice president of the New York chapter of the AIGA. Emily holds a bachelor's degree in anthropology from Barnard College and applies this knowledge to the culture of graphic design. Worksight designs are included in publications by *Etapes Graphiques* (France), *Graphics International* (England), *ID* magazine, *PBC International, Plus Eighty One* (Japan), *Art and Design* magazine (Beijing), and *Print* magazine. They have won awards from the AIGA, ACD, NY Bookbinders Guild, and *Print* magazine.

DANIEL SCHUTZSMITH, MARK & PHIL
WWW.MARKANDPHIL.COM

Mark & Phil provides marketing and philanthropic strategy for non-profits, foundations, and socially responsible companies. We're built on the philosophy that all good causes deserve a chance to become great, and we're here to help them get there. Running a cause is hard enough without having to deal with the costly and time-consuming aspects of marketing and philanthropy. Mark & Phil acts as your organization's external marketing and philanthropy department. As a forward thinking company, we're committed to practicing what we preach. We believe that the future of our business should be focused on growing our triple-bottom-line, a no harm approach that will empower people, help the planet, and make a profit.

STEPHANIE SHARP, SHARP DESIGNS
WWW.SHARPDES.COM

Stephanie Sharp founded Sharp Designs in 1991. Sharp Designs' philosophy is to work with clients to express their brand with marketing pieces that inform and move the target audience while building traffic, sales, or the image of the client. As a graphic communications firm, Sharp Designs' focus is corporate identity, branding, and marketing communications.

TODD SIMMONS, WOLVERINE FARM PUBLISHING
WWW.WOLVERINEFARMPUBLISHING.ORG

Todd Simmons lives in Fort Collins, Colorado, where he runs Wolverine Farm Publishing, a nonprofit, volunteer bookstore, literary magazine, publishing house, and special events organization. He and his wife and son "are trying to find a run-down house that can easily be converted into a large book, one to read the rest of their lives." Todd is also working on a book about bicycles.

TERRY LEE STONE
WWW.TERRYLEESTONE.COM

Terry Lee Stone has worked with AdamsMorioka, Margo Chase, The Designory, and many others. Her clients have included Mercedes Benz, Adobe Systems, IBM, American Express, USC Law School, Sundance Film Festival, and BMW DesignWorksUSA. Terry has taught the business of design at CalArts, Art Center College of Design, and Otis College of Art and Design. She is author of *Managing the Design Process—Concept Development* (Rockport, 2010) and *Managing the Design Process—Implementing Design* (Rockport, 2010). In addition to books, Stone writes for *STEP* magazine, was a regular contributor to *Dynamic Graphics Magazine*, and often writes for the American Institute of Graphic Arts (AIGA). Stone has lead workshops, panel discussions and lectures for Dynamic Graphics Training, Credit Union National Association, AIGA, and The Art Directors Club in New York.

SCOTT STOWELL
WWW.NOTCLOSED.COM

Proprietor of the design studio Open, Scott Stowell was formerly art director at Benneton's Colors magazine in Rome, Italy, and a senior designer at M&Co. He is a BFA in graphic design from the Rhode Island School of Design and teaches at Yale University and the School of Visual Arts.

CHRISTINE TAFOYA, DELUXEMODERN
WWW.DELUXEMODERNDESIGN.COM

Deluxemodern is a graphic design company specializing in logos, branding, and business identity for photographers and other creative professionals, worldwide. Dear Miss Modern is the little sister company for those looking for a pre-made logos and marketing templates, cards, wedding invitations and announcements.

JASON TREAT
WWW.THEATLANTIC.COM

Jason Treat has been the art director for the Atlantic since December 2005. He previously served as the art director for Atlantic Media Company's creative services, designing in-house creative for the Atlantic, National Journal, Government Executive, Hotline, and other publications.

MICHELLE MCCARRICK TRUETT, 484 DESIGN
WWW.484DESIGN.COM

Michelle McCarrick Truett is an award winning designer and founder of 484 Design. Inc., a solo design practice specializing in identity work. A graduate of Rochester Institute of Technology, after many years of agency work, she opened her own firm in 2008 and found the perfect balance: working on great projects with clients all over the Northeast from her home office; snowboarding and hanging with her 10 year old son; and helping the community become stronger through volunteering and through the power of graphic design.

RUDY VANDERLANS AND ZUZANA LICKO, EMIGRE
WWW.EMIGRE.COM

Rudy VanderLans moved to California from the Netherlands in 1982 and studied photography at UC Berkeley, where he met the Czechoslovakian-born designer Zuzana Licko. They married in 1983. In 1984, they launched *Emigre* magazine. VanderLans and Licko were among the first designers to use the Macintosh computer as a tool. In addition to their quarterly magazine, *Emigre* creates and sells hundreds of digital typefaces. For twenty-one years and sixty-nine issues, *Emigre* fueled imaginations and inspired designers the world over.

Their company has been honored with numerous awards, including the 1994 Chrysler award for excellence in design and the 1998 Charles Nypels award for excellence in the field of typography. *Emigre* is also the recipient of the 1997 American Institute of Graphic Arts gold medal award and in 2000 they were nominated for the Cooper-Hewitt national design lifetime achievement award.

CHRIS VERMAAS, OFFICE OF CC

After traveling for many years around the world, Chin-Lien Chen from Taiwan and Chris H. Vermaas from The Netherlands founded their own design studio, Office of CC, in Amsterdam, where they specialize in identities, infographics, signage systems, and books. In addition, Office of CC has written many articles on design issues, and Vermaas has taught at several schools around the world. He is currently head of the graduate program of MaHKU's Editorial Design, lectures at the AKI-academy, and is a visiting professor at the University of Twente and the Plantin Institute in Antwerp. Chen and Vermass "have two kids, who do not have the intention of becoming designers."

TODD WATERBURY

Todd worked at Wieden+Kennedy from 1994 to 2011 as an art director to help develop and launch the advertising, packaging, and promotion for Coca-Cola's "OK Soda." Promoted to creative director on Coca-Cola, his responsibilities included global campaigns for Diet Coke, Brand Coke Olympics, and Barq's. His role expanded to oversee the brand advertising for Microsoft. Since then, Todd has been instrumental in helping win the PowerAde business with the "Very Real Power" campaign. Prior to joining Wieden+Kennedy, Todd worked as an art director and designer at Fallon McElligott/Duffy Group in Minneapolis on assignments for Giorgio Armani, Porsche, and Jim Beam Brands, followed by two years at Bloomingdale's. In addition to best-of-category medals from D&AD, The Art Directors Club, and *ID*, Todd's work has appeared in the international publications of *Eye*, *Archive*, and *Idea* as well as the *New York Times*' op ed column. His work is part of the permanent collections of the Victoria & Albert Museum in London, the San Francisco Museum of Modern Art, the Museum of Modern Art in New York, and his parents' family room in Macomb, Illinois.

JENNIFER WILKERSON, AURORA DESIGN
WWW.AURORADESIGNONLINE.COM

Jennifer Wilkerson started Aurora Design eighteen years ago, after the birth of her first child. She works from a large room on the first floor of her colonial home in Niskayuna, New York, creating thoughtful design solutions for clients such as Mohawk Paper, Union College, America Online, Glens Falls Hospital, the Sage Colleges and other organizations in higher education, manufacturing, nonprofit, and high technology industries.

ERIC WOLFE, ERIC WOLFE DESIGN, INC.
WWW.EWOLFE.NET

Eric Wolfe has been designing inter¬active experiences in the Seattle area for more than eighteen years. He has been working solo since 2006.

MICHAEL WORTHINGTON
WWW.COUNTERSPACE.NET

Michael Worthington has taught in the graphic design program at the California Institute of the Arts since 1995. He is the founder of Counterspace, a Los Angeles design studio specializing in editorial and identity projects for cultural clients.

AGNES ZEILSTRA
WWW.REDMAGAZINE.CO.UK

Agnes Zeilstra lives in Monnickendam, The Netherlands. She graduated from the Arnhem Academy in graphic design and worked as a graphic designer for a Dutch fashion brand in Amsterdam before joining the staff of Red, a woman's fashion magazine that is part of Hachette Filipacchi media. She is now art director at *Red* magazine.

Chapter One:

MANAGING THE BUSINESS

Nike Apparel print ads, designed by Todd Waterbury, Wieden+Kennedy, New York

1

TODD **WATERBURY**

FIND AN EMOTIONAL CONNECTION WITH YOUR AUDIENCE

Whereas some agencies spend a lot of time and money testing their advertising—addressing it with a scientific model of effectiveness—Waterbury stresses the importance of finding the emotional connection and inspiration in the audiences he speaks to. The scientific method quantifies data, which is only useful for analyzing events of the past. It does not predict the future, and it does not set trends. Because Wieden+Kennedy place a premium on the cultural relevancy of their campaigns, only a forward-looking model can power the organization.

When some clients look at the Wieden+Kennedy portfolio, they wonder if their product or service can match the "fun" and "exciting" nature of clients like Nike, ESPN, or Miller. "We have to remind them that the category wasn't so exciting before we came in. If you look at the sneaker category in 1971, it wasn't even a developed category. If you look at the cheap beer category before we got into it, I mean, who wants to advertise cheap beer?

That blue-collar thing was probably the most rejected idea you could think of," Todd Waterbury notes. By working with the client to communicate the potential of the product or service and to show and describe the creative strengths of the Wieden+Kennedy teams, Waterbury feels he can help companies take risks they might not otherwise want to take. "At the end of the day, the success of a project relies on people, not on companies," he says.

Waterbury and his teams seek out people within the corporate structures of the companies they work for, identifying those who make up what he calls the "microworlds" of the company culture. People who are changing the landscape or taking a risk are the people with whom Waterbury wants to work. If they end up moving from one job or industry to another, Waterbury follows them because he knows that they will be able to offer a potential openness and influence as they shift from place to place.

Seafloor International brochure, designed by Art Chantry

2

ART **CHANTRY**

DEMAND RESPECT, CREATIVE LICENSE, AND FAIR PAY

Art Chantry observes, "Graphic design is a weird art form; it is half business, half art. Most people who get into it do so because of the art. The successful ones get into it for the business. You may be a critical success doing art, but you are not going to get rich."

In making ethical choices about who to work for and what kind of jobs to take, Chantry decided that the system is designed to "make hypocrites out of all of us." In his early career, he was not particularly picky about who he worked for, recognizing the parallels between small and large businesses, even when one purported to be "independent" or "alternative." Chantry found working for corporations to be extremely difficult because he perceived that decisions were made out of fear and within an extremely complex hierarchy. Often the nebu-

lous "legal department" was called in to finalize choices about art—something Chantry finds antithetical to the process of making a good design. In addition, the process of actually getting paid by corporations was arduous and protracted.

At a certain point in the late '80s, Chantry decided to be more discriminating about his clients, and as he puts it, "not work for ass-holes anymore." Instead of a few big jobs, he did a lot of small jobs and was suddenly over-whelmed with work instead of having to search it out.

Budweiser advertising, designed by Art Chantry

Now when he assesses new clients, he uses what he calls the "bullshit meter," which is a measure of fakery and manipulation from the client's end. He is not willing to work in an environment where he is not respected, given creative license, or paid fairly for his work.

In Chantry's view, the graphic design business suffers from a delusion that it is somehow morally superior to the advertising industry because of its closer affiliation with "art." However, it is advertising's self-proclaimed mission to make money and exploit images for the purpose of selling products. Graphic design, as a colluding agent in this process, should come clean about its own culpability.

Chantry admits, "Sometimes I actually will do work for clients I don't like simply because I really believe in the project. I've turned down some huge-monied clients because I thought they sucked as institutions or as projects or even as personalities. However, I'm not suicidal—if they threw enough money at me, I'd certainly say yes. Then I'd turn around and use that money to help finance my work for clients I believe in. We're all whores, ya know."

Esolis launch materials, designed by Worldstudio Inc.

3

WORLDSTUDIO, INC.

EXPAND WITH YOUR CLIENTS

Worldstudio, Inc., did a project for the launch of a new skin care company called Esolis. In working with this client, they were able to use many of the skills they had already developed from working with other cosmetics clients. The nature of this job forced them to develop new skills and take on new challenges as their work with the client expanded.

Initially, Worldstudio developed the naming for the company and designed its market launch materials. This particular line of cosmetics was targeted toward Asian American women, and research told them that these women tend to do a lot of catalog and online shopping. Developing an attractive and useful website was a priority for the client, particularly one that showcased the technological aspect of the product that they were selling. Instead of the more familiar style of cosmetics advertisement, Worldstudio had to work to manipulate

a lot of information about the various products into an easily navigable and aesthetically clean form. The scientific basis of the Esolis product became the foundation for the website as well as for the catalog materials.

As the project grew and the product line increased, Worldstudio, Inc., was asked to handle all of the product and model photography for both the website and the catalog. Because Esolis was growing organically, the process and methods that the studio employed had to reflect and complement that growth. What started as a naming project soon developed into a much larger assignment, and the initial assignment soon expanded into a diverse range of projects and an ongoing relationship with the client.

"SUV" :30

"SUV" :30

VO: Leather seats, automatic transmission. Nowadays you'll hear people call this a truck. Well, a man knows a station wagon when he sees one. This car will only see off-road action if someone backs over a flower bed. If this vehicular masquerade represents the high life to which men are called, we should trade our trousers for skirts right now.

Miller High Life: "SUV," designed by Wieden+Kennedy

4

TODD **WATERBURY**

DEVELOP BRANDS THAT BOTH REFLECT AND INFLUENCE CULTURE

In contrast to the small studio of Worldstudio, Inc., Todd Waterbury directed a team of creative people at the New York office of Wieden+Kennedy. The work involved television commercials to print ads to identity work and packaging, as well as everything that serves to communicate what a brand stands for. The firm is the global agency for Nike and ESPN and has worked with with Avon to develop a new generation of products for teens. In 2003, Nike was awarded the prestigious Golden Lion award at Cannes for their comprehensive global advertising campaign—an award that in turn bestowed accolades on the work of Wieden+Kennedy.

For each of these clients, however, Waterbury had an overarching philosophy: the way that brands influence people's lives extends beyond traditional media, and people need to be able to embrace the brand at more intimate and respected levels than simply passively viewing a commercial on TV or in a magazine. This tall order involves a process that purveys to the audience an emotional connection to the brand and places it in the general suffusion of culture over a variety of human experiences.

SAVE FUEL

Save Fuel poster, designed by Miles Murray Sorrell FUEL

5

**MILES MURRAY
SORRELL FUEL**

HELP SAVE ELECTRICITY

Although somewhat obvious, Miles Murray Sorrell FUEL insists that one of its mantras of work is to always be open to new ideas. The "Save Miles Murray Sorrell FUEL" poster was designed in 1992 as part of a series for Virgin Records. It was one of Miles Murray Sorrell FUEL's first commissions as a group and was screen-printed by them at the Royal College of Art. Playing on the name of their group, they were able to convey a relatively uncontroversial ecological sentiment.

This sentiment may be important to the people involved at FUEL because they went to school together. The idea of collaborating under one light and gathering in the common room resonates with a sense of mutual purpose and interdependence.

Made You Look spreads, designed by Stefan Sagmeister

6

STEFAN **SAGMEISTER**

IF YOU ARE A DESIGNER, DESIGN;
IF YOU ARE A MANAGER, MANAGE

The flow of work through Sagmeister Studio is not complex. Initially, it comes in through Stefan Sagmeister. He works on it with his designer, Mattias Erstberger, and then it goes out through Sagmeister. Having only two designers in the office naturally limits the volume of work. At times, there are interns who Sagmeister judges to be particularly talented, and they work on jobs, too. Sagmeister takes on interns only if they are able to commit full-time to the studio—this generally means the person cannot have another job in addition to his or her work at the studio.

This pared-down office is a conscious choice for Sagmeister, whose previous work experiences reflected a very different model.

When Sagmeister worked for Leo Burnett in Hong Kong, he had a much larger group of handpicked designers. In that context, he was more of a manager, and from his perspective, managing a small design group is among the least interesting jobs there is. "If I would want to become a manager, I would much rather go to business school and work on Wall Street where you actually have some challenges," he comments.

Sagmeister serves as the art director for all of the work that comes through the studio. Keeping the chain of command simplified, particularly if you are the commander, makes for an efficient and focused work environment.

Eric Morecambe statue and grounds, designed by Why Not Associates

7

WHY NOT ASSOCIATES

ACCESSIBLE CAN BE SMART; SMART CAN BE FUNNY

Why Not Associates place a premium on sense of humor when approaching design problems. A fan of comedy himself, partner Andy Altmann was quite pleased when he was able to help with the Tern redevelopment project in Morecambe, near Lancaster. Rather than featuring a public servant in the classical sense, the redevelopment project proposed a statue of Eric Morecambe, the comedian who is closely associated with the town of Morecambe. By selecting a figure that melded with local culture and history, the designers were able to dispute the idea that only generals and princes could be the subject of statues, but that a man who made people laugh was also worthy of commemoration.

In collaboration with artist Gordon Young and sculptor Russell Coleman, Why Not Associates surrounded the statue of the comedian with quotes from some of his better-known sketches.

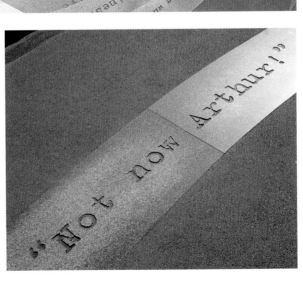

8

JOHN C **JAY**

HIRE INTERESTING, CREATIVE PEOPLE— AND LISTEN TO THEM

One of the most important parts of John C Jay's creative direction is establishing a vision for the office. Jay consistently asks: Who do you hire? How do you maintain the most interesting and skilled people in your company? He notes, "I want to bring in the most skilled, of course, but I also want the most interesting people who lead the most interesting lives—people who bring something into the office besides just focusing on a typeface."

If you go to the fourth floor of Wieden+Kennedy's office in Tokyo, you will find a studio full of DJ equipment-mixers and turntables so that employees can work on their music. This kind of accommodation was part of the Tokyo office when it was founded in 1998. Jay notes, "It all started with asking, what kind of people are interesting to have around you? The idea that an agency would need 'cool hunters' or researchers is just kind of proof that you don't know what is going on."

Wieden+Kennedy, Tokyo, has two DJs on staff, including one whose DJ career competes with his ad agency career. How does a company support these creative people? "We give them outlets. They are also on salary, of course. One wanted time off to go to the Barcelona Music Festival, for example, so he went. We support music people in our company in a variety of ways. And we ask them to produce events with us."

One such event was the Tokyo Designers Block, in which Wieden+Kennedy teamed up with a company called Sputnik and Kurisaki (who is known as the Japanese "dean of design"). Together, they created an exhibit that involved taking over a planetarium in the middle of Shibuya and turning it into a celebration of 1970s design in Japan, specifically the Osaka Expo. The VJs and DJs who worked for Wieden+Kennedy created an experience inside the dome in which images were projected inside the entire planetarium. These kinds of project are only possible with the right teams in-house to develop and drive them.

Another example of the unique approach to staff composition is an exclusive shoe design made for Wieden+Kennedy, Tokyo. The shoes were a limited edition of the Nike Air Force One. Designed by Hiroshi Fuijiwara, they were made by Nike in celebration of the opening of the new Wieden+Kennedy office in Tokyo. The pony skin sneaker was for staff only. The typography on back of the shoe, designed by the studio, spells "Tokyo." Inside the tongues are special Wieden+Kennedy Tokyo labels along with the special silver tips on the laces. These shoes were never for sale to the general public.

Pony skin shoes, designed by John C Jay, Wieden+Kennedy, Tokyo

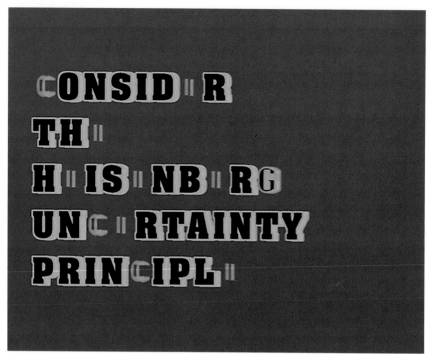

Sci-Fi Channel ID tags, designed by Miles Murray Sorrell FUEL

9

**MILES MURRAY
SORRELL FUEL**

ALWAYS KEEP THE VALVE IN THE OPEN POSITION

These words and images are taken from one of a series of animated identities that Miles Murray Sorrell FUEL produced for the Sci-Fi Channel. The Sci-Fi brief was flexible, but the main idea for the campaign was to produce something with a philosophical and scientific feel that challenged any audience preconception that the network solely caters to traditional science-fiction enthusiasts.

FUEL came up with the idea of a sinister voice, something between a warning and an advertisement. They chose the topics in the identities because either they are fundamental to science fiction or they have some relevance to the audience. They are intentionally phrased so that the viewer is left questioning the topic's validity.

Staying open to what ideas and images were related to the broader category of science fiction made it possible for FUEL to develop a creative and flexible campaign for a client who was trying to expand their market—and hence, the meaning—of their product. In a larger sense, this approach means considering intellectual and aesthetic ideas that may not be initially attractive or even useful. To do this, a designer must be not only a good researcher but an active cultural participant as well.

Chase Design Group studio space, designed by Margo Chase, Chase Design Group

10

MARGO **CHASE**

CULTIVATE A WORKPLACE WITH A SPECIFIC LOOK AND SOUND

In Margo Chase's office, she cultivates an air of excited calm. "I'm lucky, because Chase Design Group is a lively place filled with talented people and not a lot of ego issues. Conversation and open exchange of ideas flow freely. Even in the creative group, when a project is being executed by one designer it often gets kicked around, and the ideas get better. One of the things I look for when I hire designers is people who are open to that and not threatened by it."

What makes the studio unique? "Really loud music! We have an open plan in the creative department, and lots of conversations happen with everyone. We all have a great rapport, and we discuss all kinds of things, from politics to design, as a group. For some reason the business people upstairs prefer it quieter."

The design of the office serves the hierarchy of decision making at the Design Group. "There are three executives who make the important decisions: myself (as creative director), Chris Lowery (minister of the environment and production manager), and James Bradley (president). Sometimes we all agree, which makes things easy, but there's often a lot of conflict between us that we have to talk through. This leads to better decisions. James believes very strongly that a conflict-free business is the wrong goal. We embrace conflict as essential and a sign of life," adds Chase.

In addition to these decisions at the top, everyone in the office is encouraged to express his or her opinions about each project. Chase notes, "Even a bad or stupid-sounding idea may trigger something great. As creative director, I spend a lot of my time talking to designers about the work they are doing to make sure that they are really thinking things through and looking at their solutions from every angle."

11

KEEP DECISION MAKING SIMPLE AND NONHIERARCHICAL

Why Not Associates formed in part because the skills of three came in handier than the skills of one. Andy Altmann remembers, "The three of us were in college together, and we graduated in 1987, myself, David Ellis, and Howard Greenhalgh. [Greenhalgh] was asked to design a magazine, which he said he could do. He came up to the college and said, 'I've got to do a magazine. Can you help me?' Later, we thought up a name and set up a studio in Soho. Greenhalgh always wanted to do film things, so he eventually ended up doing pop videos. And we were doing graphics, so we were doing a mixture of things. Eventually he also set up Why Not Films to produce the pop videos, and we had two companies, Why Not Associates and Why Not Films."

Why Not Associates is not a business that works in any traditional, hierarchical system. When a job comes in, it is usually fronted by one of the partners. He goes to meet the client, decides who is free or who is best suited to that particular project, and then works with the client and sorts out some ideas. One of the partners takes the lead, and the rest of the office collaborates on it. Some other jobs might be done by only one person. All the

ideas get aired in the office, and everyone at Why Not gets a say in the project. "Is it any good? Does it make sense?" This process of sharing is a vital ingredient to the creative life of the office. "I couldn't work on my own," comments Altmann. "The client really wants just one point of contact, which makes it easier for them. Because we are so small, we know what is going on. I can just look over my Mac and see two other screens; I can see what is going on."

One example of this collaborative spirit guided by a singular vision is the graphics for the MTV Europe program, *The Fridge*. This show aired on Friday evenings from 2001 to 2003 and was meant to be watched while preparing for an evening on the town. Because the title of the show does not bear any particular relevance to the subject matter, when Why Not was selected to do the titling and opening sequence, there was not much direction in terms of the relationship between the word *fridge* and the idea of the show. Ellis came up with a diagrammatic style to treat the materials and worked within his office to see the project through to fruition.

The Fridge title sequence, designed by Why Not Associates

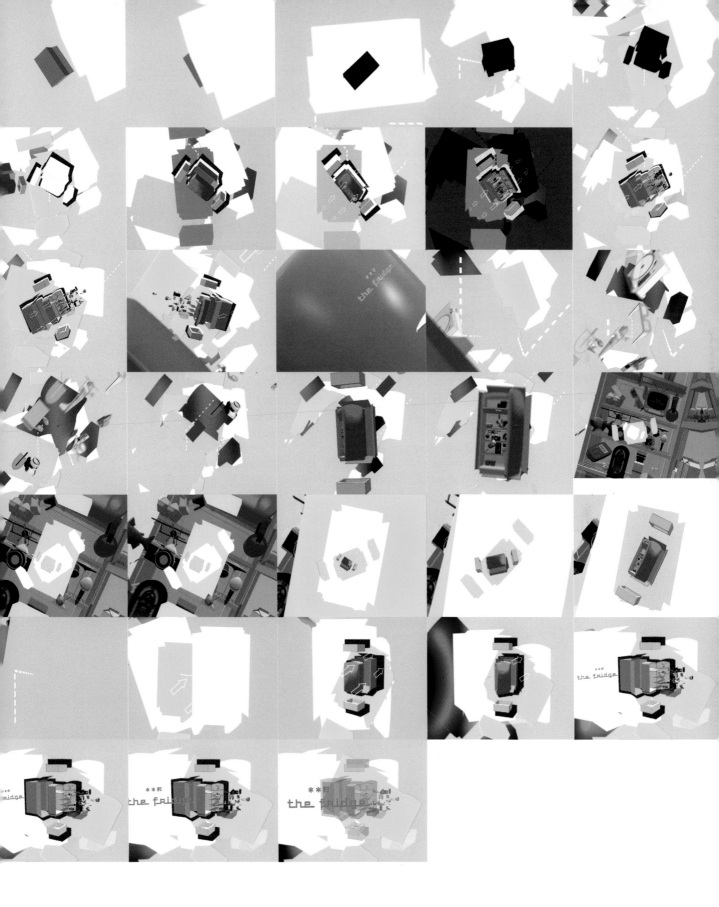

12

JOHN C **JAY**

CREATIVE DIRECTORS NEED TO STAY CREATIVE

John C Jay does an amazing job of balancing the mangagement of his award-winning creative team at Wieden+Kennedy, Tokyo, and running his own freelance studio, Studio J. At this studio he takes on jobs with high-profile clients such as Lucasfilm, for which he did the Star Wars, Episode One advertising campaign for Asia and Europe. He comments, "Wieden+Kennendy at this stage is a lot about creative mangement responsibilities, but at the heart of my existence I'm still an art director and designer. Certainly through my talented staff, I'm able to implement some of my thinking."

In addition to doing design work, Jay also writes and researches, developing his ideas for other media outside graphic design. The ideas he worked with in the Presto campaign for Nike in 2003 came from an article he wrote for the American magazine SOMA about the importance of the post-wild-style grafitti generation. "I wrote about how they were gathering in this tiny town in Tokyo called Naka Meguro, which has become a mecca for post-grafitti artists from all over the world, and how their art appears on lamp posts and walls and so forth, and how these people were completely different from the first grafitti artists.

This article became kind of like a launching pad for that Presto idea. The influences can come through my writing. Currently I am working on a basketball project as an art director. I do a number of diverse projects."

Star Wars, Episode One international ad campaign, designed by John C Jay, Studio J

EPISODE 1

one
choice

one
force

STAR WARS

Obi-Wan Kenobi, Jedi Knight, as portrayed in Episode I by Ewan McGregor

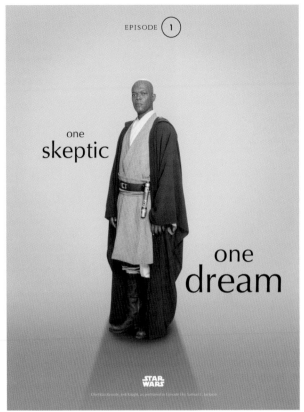

EPISODE 1

one
skeptic

one
dream

STAR WARS

Obi-Wan Kenobi, Jedi Knight, as portrayed in Episode I by Samuel L. Jackson

EPISODE 1

one
hero

one
destiny

STAR WARS

Anakin Skywalker, as portrayed in Episode I by Jake Lloyd

EPISODE 1

one
truth

one
hate

STAR WARS

Darth Maul, evil Sith Lord, as portrayed in Episode I

13

MARGO **CHASE**

LOOK FAR AND WIDE FOR YOUR SOURCES IN THE CREATIVE PROCESS

When developing the logo for pop star Madonna's "Drowned World" tour in 2001, Chase Design Group approached the work by gathering as much source information as possible. Doing the work to research and describe the aesthetic foundation of a particular design is essential to the way this company arrives at its final decisions.

Chase Design Group developed a custom icon and logo type to convey the unique and ethereal qualities of Madonna's show—described by Chase as "a multilayered musical and spiritual journey through diverse worlds"—as well as to address some of her personal interests. "Madonna is a student of the kabala, and she requested that we include references to that body of knowledge," comments Chase.

Chase's design references and incorporates both Arabic and Hebrew letterforms. In addition, the design references the mystical connections between religions and the idea of an intellectual as well as a physical journey. The design pictured was one of many logo designs that Chase proposed but not the one that Madonna ultimately chose. "This one was my favorite because it referred to more specific aspects of her show and because I had the chance to create the new letterforms."

Above and opposite: Madonna "Drowned World" tour logo, designed by Margo Chase, Chase Design Group

زمن الغوص
محار و لآلئ بحرية
و يم عجاج

14

ERIC **HINES**

JUST WHO DO YOU THINK YOU ARE?

"You can't expect clients to believe you can build their brand if you can't build your own. You have to create an overall identity for yourself and express it in your own marketing materials. It's not a bad idea to do this while you're in a salaried position so you can spend some money and do it right."

To gain access to business, you have to be seen as a business. Say it, repeat it, and say it again. Being a business does not mean that you have to give up the individuality, fervor, and entrepreneurial, indie spirit that drove you to go out on your own in the first place. Just put all those things into the expression of your logo, identity system, and creative brand. After all, what company is going to trust you in your creative expertise and guidance if you haven't displayed it in the work you've done for your very first client—yourself?

There are thousands of independent design businesses out there. Look around, check out the awards, find articles and books on self-promotion, and do some hard soul-searching to find out what kind of firm you want to be and what kind of clients you want to have. And then make a brand that speaks to your potential audience, not other designers you are hoping to impress with the latest tricks on your website. Clients aren't interested in tricks; they want results.

Here are some places to check out how other freelancers are setting themselves up and getting the right clients:

- www.thecreativegroup.com

- http://www.designmadison.com/self_promotion_guide.php

- www.creativepro.com

- Graphic design annuals

- *HOW* magazine's annual self-promotional issue

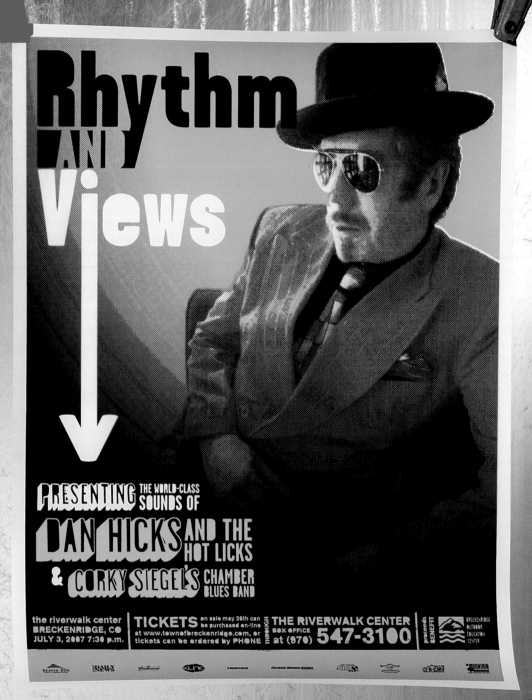

15

CALVIN **LEE**

"I'M NOT A BUSINESSMAN, I'M A BUSINESS, MAN!" – JAY-Z

"It's very important to learn the business side of running a business. Make sure you get the proper licenses and permits when starting a business to ensure you won't get penalized by the IRS or anybody else. Read up on and research which taxes apply to you, what tax breaks are available, what you can write off, etc."

Whether you're simply working for yourself, hiring the occasional subcontractor, or looking to expand with full-time employees, you have to take care of the government paperwork that's required as you go along, or you're going to be hit with substantial fines and taxes and other unpleasantness down the road, which can easily force you to close your doors. There are some benefits to working for yourself and having parts of your business and personal life overlap—that new client you're prospecting happens to be in the same town as your Grandma, so you might as well mix business and pleasure on the next trip—but if you don't keep the lines clear and the records straight, you're going to have some explaining to do to the government.

Some creative types love digging into the financial side of things. If you're one of them, go for it. If you're not, hire a good accountant immediately. A lawyer and a financial advisor aren't bad ideas either, even if you just schedule one or two visits to pick their brains and get some basic advice about what you need to be on top of.

Here are some business resources:

- Local chamber of commerce—Their main purpose is to help businesses.

- City hall—They'll tell you what paperwork you need to fill out and how you need to be registered.

- Business books—There are tons of books on starting a business; get one or two or three and read them.

Mayhem Studios website, designed by Calvin Lee, Mayhem Studios

Marchex demo video, designed by Eric Wolfe, Eric Wolfe Design, Inc.

16

STEPHANIE **SHARP**

WHAT IT'S WORTH TO YOU, AND TO THE REST OF US

"Do some research and think hard before you set your rates. Don't undervalue yourself or the rest of us by charging too little."

When you start out on your own, it's very tempting to try to get work by bidding low. You might think this is a good way to get the ball rolling and start new relationships. But this is a penny-wise and pound-foolish strategy. The low price might land you work, but then you've set a precedent that makes it hard to raise your rates in the future to a level that will keep you in business. In addition, by offering creative services well below the industry-accepted norm, you're reducing the perceived value of everyone's design product, industry wide.

Your previous employment probably gave you a pretty good sense of the hourly rates people with your level of experience get. And you probably also have a good idea of the larger value of the work you're creating. Put your rates somewhere in this range, keeping in mind that you may have less overhead and fewer resources than the big agency around the corner but that comparable creative output has comparable value to the client.

17

KEITH **BOWMAN**

GO FOR WHAT YOU KNOW . . .

"Determine what your strengths and weaknesses are as a designer and take on paying jobs that only play to your strengths. You can work on your weaknesses during downtime, on personal projects, or even on something done pro bono."

Don't use client's time and money to learn something new or wrestle with things you haven't tried before. If the majority of your work has been in print, your first website design should not be for a new client who expects every Flash gizmo and elaborate motion graphics. When starting out, you need to ensure that every piece of work you create is your best because that's what will keep the clients coming back and recommending you to other people.

Freejade Gallery "Superman vs. Darth Vader" exhibit posters, designed by Keith Bowman, The Design Bureau of Amerika

18

ERIC **WOLFE**

. . . AND THEN GO FOR WHAT YOU ACTUALLY LIKE

"Do some deep thinking up front and decide exactly what type of work you enjoy doing. Consider what you already can do, what you'd like to be able to do in the future and of course, what kind of earnings you can live with. Don't allow yourself to be pigeon-holed into work that you don't actually like just because you are competent at it and there seems to be a strong market for it."

Anyone's strength can become a weakness if that's all you do. We all need to mix it up or we—and our work—become stale and lackluster. Take a lesson from the fitness trainer: Cross-training keeps our physical, mental, and creative workouts interesting and effective. So, yes, play to your strengths and take work that you are confident you can deliver at the highest level possible. But also give some thought to deciding what type of work you'd enjoy doing down the road. And then do whatever it takes to get really good at that stuff, too, whether it's taking classes, producing projects on your own time, or finding someone you can work with a day or two a week so you can learn at the feet of a master while you build your own business. It's important not to get yourself pigeon-holed into one kind of work even if you're competent at it and there's a strong market for it; markets change, and you need to as well.

Here are a few ways to keep your skills and ideas fresh:

- Join the local AIGA chapter in your area. There isn't one? Well, start one.

- Invest in attending design conferences.

- Take a class to expand your design skills into a new area.

- Take a class to expand some other skills such as drawing, painting, or basket weaving. It's all about keeping the creative juices flowing.

- Visit museums, galleries, lectures, and concerts. Seeing other people's creative output will improve your own.

TOGETHER WITH THEIR FAMILIES

Stefanie Lynn Colella
AND
Cory Michael Walsh

REQUEST THE PLEASURE OF YOUR COMPANY
AT THEIR MARRIAGE

SATURDAY,
THE TWENTY-SEVENTH OF OCTOBER
TWO THOUSAND SEVEN
AT HALF AFTER FOUR O'CLOCK
IN THE AFTERNOON

CAIRNWOOD MANSION
BRYN ATHYN, PA

DINNER AND DANCING
TO FOLLOW

We wish to share our happiness
with you, our family and friends.

Please respond by September 27, 2007

___ SEAT(S) HAVE BEEN RESERVED
IN YOUR HONOUR

M _____

___ HAPPILY ACCEPTS   ___ REGRETFULLY DECLINES

Colella/Walsh wedding invitations and stationery, designed by Nicole Block, NicEvents

19

NICOLE **BLOCK**

BAD BAIT, BAD FISH

"Don't start out with a low price and expect good clients. Low pricing will only get you a lack of sustainable income, more difficult clients who don't appreciate you as a professional, and disrespect in the design community.

"If portfolio-building is the reason behind your low-price thinking, I would suggest doing work pro bono before you go out on your own. Working for free is easier than working for peanuts; the boundary on what your client can ask of you is drawn the minute they learn they're getting it for free.

"Budget clients, on the other hand, expect that since they are technically paying you, they can ask for whatever they want. There's no respect for a designer who can be gotten cheap. If you start to charge appropriate prices when you go out on your own, you will find that the higher your rate—within reason—the greater the respect for your services. Clients think, 'Well, they must know what they're doing if they charge this much.'"

20

BE HONEST WITH YOUR BOSS WHEN TAKING ON SIDE PROJECTS

DONOVAN N **BEERY**

"When I told my boss I was going to start freelancing for the parent company of the place I was working for, she said, 'That's not a problem. Why are you even telling me?' I replied, 'Because these situations can become a problem when people find out about it later, especially if I didn't tell anyone.' The point is to be sure to know the policies of the place you work for before you start freelancing. Some may not only allow freelancing, but might also let you use their equipment, send emails, and conduct freelance business during your lunch hour. But if they don't, then you shouldn't."

Many designers start their freelance careers while working as a staff person. Knowing the financial, personal, and creative risks inherent in leaping out into the void, you may be tempted to take on a project here and there and utilize the vast resources of your employer. After all, why make a trip to Kinko's when there's that great laser printer just down the hall? Well, if your employer catches you running out page after page of full, four-color printouts for some client who's not on their roster, you might find yourself out on your butt and behind the counter at Kinko's. Your boss, more than anyone, knows just how much time, energy, resources, and attention it takes to start your own freelance career—after all, he or she probably started that way themselves. While they might appreciate your need and desire to have creative outlets beyond the current client list and they may even think that letting you do the occasional freelance gig is a good way to keep you fresh and interested in that current client list, you have to always remember that until you leave the party, it's a good idea to dance with the one who brought you there.

Step Inside Design magazine, Vol. 22, No. 2, cover illustration, designed by Donovan N Beery, Eleven19 Communications, Inc.

STEP

INSIDE DESIGN

ANNUAL TREND REPORT

WHAT'S IN AND WHAT'S OUT IN 2006

+

DESIGN 100 ANNUAL
WINNERS REVEAL THE SECRETS BEHIND THEIR DESIGNS

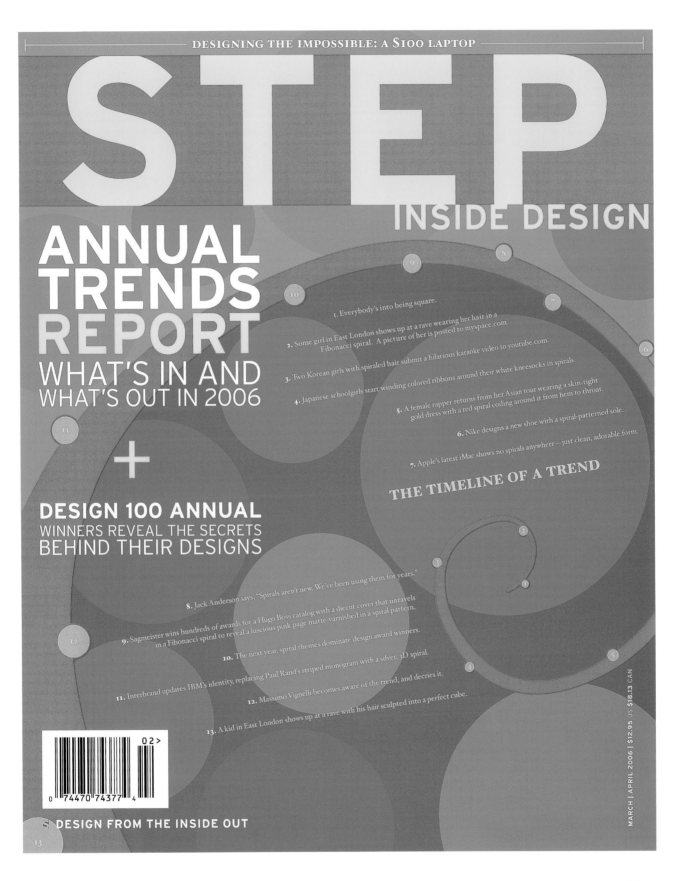

1. Everybody's into being square.

2. Some girl in East London shows up at a rave wearing her hair in a Fibonacci spiral. A picture of her is posted to myspace.com.

3. Two Korean girls with spiraled hair submit a hilarious karaoke video to youtube.com.

4. Japanese schoolgirls start winding colored ribbons around their white kneesocks in spirals.

5. A female rapper returns from her Asian tour wearing a skin-tight gold dress with a red spiral coiling around it from hem to throat.

6. Nike designs a new shoe with a spiral-patterned sole.

7. Apple's latest iMac shows no spirals anywhere—just clean, adorable form.

THE TIMELINE OF A TREND

8. Jack Anderson says, "Spirals aren't new. We've been using them for years."

9. Sagmeister wins hundreds of awards for a Hugo Boss catalog with a diecut cover that unravels in a Fibonacci spiral to reveal a luscious pink page matte-varnished in a spiral pattern.

10. The next year, spiral themes dominate design award winners.

11. Interbrand updates IBM's identity, replacing Paul Rand's striped monogram with a silver, 3D spiral.

12. Massimo Vignelli becomes aware of the trend, and decries it.

13. A kid in East London shows up at a rave with his hair sculpted into a perfect cube.

MARCH | APRIL 2006 | $12.95 US $18.13 CAN

S DESIGN FROM THE INSIDE OUT

21

STEVE **GORDON**, JR

KEEP YOUR CLIENTS HONEST

"Always remember the cliché, 'This isn't personal; it's business.' This isn't offered as an excuse to treat your clients poorly or let them rough you up. It's just that business, even creative business, is conducted more effectively if you keep the relationship very professional. While you may become friendly with your clients, they are not your childhood pals. And even though a friend may become a client, when it comes to the work, treat them like a client first and a pal only after the paperwork is done and the sign offs are completed."

What is meant by treating your clients like clients? Well, for example, make sure you have set clear expectations for the project, no matter how small. Get a contract with terms and work authorization written down and signed off before you start. Be clear about payment terms. Ask for a down payment up front to ensure the client is as invested in the project as you are and to ensure you'll have some money to cover your time if the project gets pulled down the road.

Of course, not every project will get the full administrative treatment. There's always one or two that we can't wait to get our hands on, no matter how fuzzy the terms. But let these be the very rare exceptions. Or get the paperwork complete after you've started. Being a stickler about crossing t's and dotting i's doesn't mean you have to be a finger-shaking schoolmarm. Just be candid and straightforward about your policy. After all is said and done, your clients will respect you more for your professional practices.

This especially goes for family and friends. Those closest to you can often be the greatest offenders of the professional parameters you're trying to set. Feeling loyalty or the need to extend or return favors encourages unprofessional practices. However, if your friends and family really care for you and are behind your success, then they should support everything you're trying to do to set yourself up as a real design professional.

Here are a few details you should get straight with your client—and down on paper—before you start any project:

- Overall budget for the project

- Billing expectations, as in hourly or project basis

- Payment schedule

- Delivery schedule, as in what phases have to be complete and to whom by when

- Final deliverable—Are you expected to show concepts only or deliver production-quality files?

- Subcontractors—Are you using them, or expected to use your client's? If so, how will they be paid, and by whom, and how much, and is there a markup?

Mr. Get It Ready Contracting logo and business cards, designed by Steve Gordon, Jr, RDQLUS

Randall McGaugh
owner/craftsman

402.301.7110
mrgetitready@yahoo.com

Professional service
Fair pricing
Free project quotes

MR. GET IT READY... GETS IT DONE!

PAINTING . DRYWALL . GENERAL MAINTENANCE... AND ANYTHING ELSE YOU CAN THINK UP!

22

CHRISTINE **GODLEWSKI**

GET A BUSINESS MENTOR

"If you are thinking about going freelance, you are probably already a qualified designer. But do you know how to run a business? Do bookkeeping? Set up billing? Pay your quarterly taxes? Find a business mentor who has already done this and can guide you."

You may be the best at designing killer collateral that creates sales, but what do you really know about running a business? Especially when you're going to be busy trying to get interesting clients and create challenging work? Your expertise in visual communications has no application to spreadsheets, tax preparation, and billing, among other critical business functions. Find a mentor by talking to other professionals, teachers, business organizations, chambers of commerce, etc. It doesn't have to be someone in the creative field. After all, you've got that covered already. Find someone who knows his way around all the paperwork that is critical to keeping a business running smoothly so you can stay focused on getting and doing the work you love.

Following are just a few areas where a competent business mentor can help you. And if you can't find someone willing to invest a few hours to explain these things to you for just the pleasure of your company and a few cups of coffee, then hire someone. This stuff is too important to leave to chance.

- Create a tracking method for projects so you can do effective estimating and know if you're making money.

- Set up long-term business and personal goals for growth and financial stability.

- Develop record keeping systems to ensure you understand where the dollars are coming from and going to.

- Make certain you're adequately insured and have proper legal instruments in place to protect yourself and your business.

- Find a plan for setting aside money to fund investments in equipment and/or employees to create future growth.

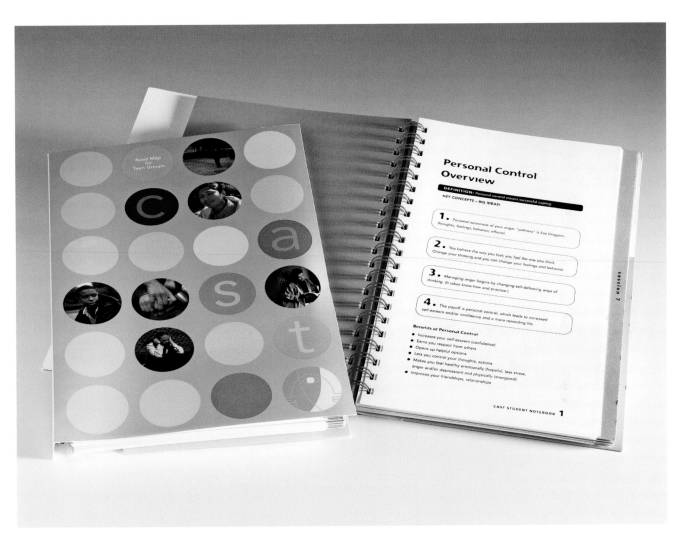

Coping and Support Training (CAST) teen program workbook, designed by Christine Godlewski, Genius Creative

Chapter Two:

TO FREELANCE OR NOT TO FREELANCE

23

STEVE **GORDON**, JR

KNOW THYSELF

"I know that this advice may seem a bit wide-open and perhaps even a little existential; but the point is to realize what kind of person you are and how that will affect your expectations, hopes, and preconceptions about being in business as an independent. I'm no rebel and I worked many years in-house and at studios, but the truth is, I knew early on in my career that I was going to eventually venture off to do my own thing. Being aware of this helped me get the most from my jobs and also curb behaviors that could have been mistakenly seen as an attitude problem or pinned me with a hard-to-work-with reputation. Instead, knowing my own long-term intentions allowed me to treat my early career stops as scholastic environments. I concentrated on learning everything I possibly could, keeping in mind that I always had the intention to take this postcollegiate, professional education with me in my own independent endeavor.

As you prepare to move out on your own, it is highly probable that you will also be simultaneously working for another company. It's important to consider how you want to manage your own plans with the responsibilities of your current job. Perhaps you can be up front about your long-term goals; perhaps you have to keep your budding business under the table. Whatever your situation, leaving in a huff is not the move to make. Once you go out on your own, you may need recommendations from your former employer, so be sure not to torch the bridges you crossed altogether."

Here are some points to remember:

- Don't put down your current employer to potential clients. It might feel good, even necessary, in the short term to vent frustrations and bash what you perceived as poor practices, but clients are not the people to do that with. Talk to your spouse, your pals, or your dog instead.

- Avoid actively pursuing clients currently on your employer's roster. It's one thing if they follow you of their own accord, but recruiting them results in bad creative and professional karma that could follow you right along with the client.

- It's generally not a good idea to admit to your boss that you're just biding your time at his or her studio. He or she will likely shorten your time-biding days.

- Don't pull a Jerry Maguire by making a big dramatic statement and storming out of the office. That only works in Hollywood; in real life, you may someday need or want help—or even a recommendation—from your previous employer.

BACK ROADS&BEACHES

Lorain County Visitors Bureau, OH, Back Roads and Beaches logo design by Nicole Block, NicEvents

24

NICOLE **BLOCK**

HOME COURT OR AWAY GAME?

"Many people's first expectation is that they'll work from home. Don't make the assumption that this will be the ideal situation for you. Some people are great at it and love to work in their own environment in their pajamas. Others need the social life of office spaces to stay happy and productive. And there are those that find that working from home tends to creep into their downtime, which includes time with family and personal activities, because they can't turn the professional world off. Maybe you're better suited to doing onsite freelance work; maybe you can share office space with other creatives just to have a social environment; or maybe you can set up your home office in a separate room and shut the door at the end of the workday. But be honest with yourself—it's not easy to be creative if you're in an environment that bums you out."

Pluses of home office:

- Short commute (although you lose the weather excuse)

- Best coffee around, just like you like it every time

- Tax deductions in abundance

- Work without brushing your teeth or combing your hair

- You can wear a tie if you'd like, but it will look really funny with boxers.

- Cheap rent, good landlord

Minuses of home office:

- Work without brushing your teeth or combing your hair

- Your kids/cat/spouse/neighbor/mailman interrupt you all the time.

- You find yourself working at 11:00 pm on Friday, or 2:00 am on Sunday, and perhaps not at 9:00 am on Tuesday.

- Loss of the collaborative environment can adversely affect your creative vibe.

Pluses of office space:

- You get up, get dressed, go to work— structure can help creativity.

- You have a place to invite clients and have meetings.

- By setting yourself up as a professional, you're more likely to act like one.

- By setting yourself up as a professional, your clients are more likely to see you as one.

Minuses of outside office:

- Rent can be expensive.

- Leases can be a drag, especially if you change your mind in a few months.

- It can get lonely without the cat/spouse/ neighbor interrupting you.

- Minimalism is good, but you'll need to invest in some furniture.

MR. AND MRS. ROBERT ELLMAN
REQUEST THE HONOUR OF YOUR PRESENCE
AT THE WEDDING OF THEIR DAUGHTER

Carrie Ellman
TO
Kenneth Larsen

AS THEY EXCHANGE MARRIAGE VOWS

SUNDAY, THE TWENTY-FOURTH OF JUNE
TWO THOUSAND AND SEVEN
QUARTER TO THREE IN THE AFTERNOON
ROUND HILL HOUSE
WASHINGTONVILLE, NEW YORK

RECEPTION TO FOLLOW   GARDEN PARTY BEST

YOU ARE ALSO INVITED
TO VIEW OUR WEBSITE,
www.kenandcarrie.weddingwindow.com
FOR INFORMATION RELATED
TO ALL THINGS WEDDING.

Ellman/Larsen wedding invitations and packaging, designed by Keith Bowman, The Design Bureau of Amerika

25

KEITH **BOWMAN**

DON'T QUIT YOUR DAY JOB. NO, REALLY . . .

"One of the best ways to start off as a free-lancer is to keep a full-time day job and take on freelance work that you can do on nights and weekends. Try to build up projects and clients until you have a flow of steady work and enough jobs to keep you busy for at least six months. It will take a lot of hard work and dedication to do this because you're basically working two full-time jobs, but the benefits will be well worth it in the end. The biggest benefit is that all the stress and long hours will help prepare you for going solo, managing clients, and dealing with dead-lines. And of course, already having a stable of clients and steady work coming in will make the transition to full-time freelancing go that much more easily."

Here are some places to look for your first free-lance projects:

- Any organization you're involved with, from church to your college alma mater, profes-sional associations and clubs, to restaurants, and other businesses you frequent

- Offer to do a project or two pro bono. It may lead to work with an interesting organization, interaction with professionals who serve on the nonprofit's board of directors, and if nothing else, it gives you the chance to build your reputation along with your portfolio.

- Freelance websites—There are tons of them listing thousands and thousands of gigs.

- Friends, family, neighbors—Tell everyone you know what you're looking for and ask them to spread the word. As the saying goes, if you don't ask, the answer is always no.

- Former employers are great resources, as long as you left on good terms. They frequently need help with overflow work and special projects.

26

JENI **HERBERGER**

TALK WORK LIKE AN INDIVIDUAL; TALK MONEY LIKE A BUSINESS

"Money is one of the most frequently over-looked factors in venturing out as a freelancer. It comes down to the naïve notion that by doing good work, the money will come in. Not true. You need to start with a budget for your life-style. Ask yourself, 'How much money do I need to live on for a year?' Add up all your expenses for housing, transportation, food, credit cards, and everything else you spend money on. Don't forget about taxes. Take this number and divide it by the hourly rate you plan to charge. This is how many hours you will need to bill in a year to pay your bills. Many of these hours will be spent on nonbillable activities such as administration, accounting, and looking for new work. Scary, huh? Just knowing this number will help you see the seriousness of collecting money from your clients, supplementing your income where need-ed, and understanding what a big responsibility you are taking on by working for yourself."

27

SETH **CHEEKS**

THE DAILY GRIND . . . AND GRIND . . . AND GRIND . . .

"You must know how to grind, grind, grind, as in work very hard and very smart. This may call for giving up weekends in the beginning and working more than you've ever worked for an employer. In addition to the time you spend on actual paying projects, one of the best ways to build your business is to whip up some creative projects of your own. Put them in your portfolio and show them to potential clients so they can see just what you're capable of."

Here are a few ways to take active breaks and keep the energy up and ideas flowing even after a lot of long hours:

- An easy, quick fix: caffeine

- A walk with the dog

- Talk to friends about what you do, even when they stare blankly.

- Not sure if you've heard of this new stuff called caffeine?

- Communicate with other trusted creatives.

- Dream

- This may even be a TV channel by now: caffeine.

- People-watch

- Engage in critiques and other creative mental exercises.

- Have I introduced you to my good friend, caffeine?

All-Hype Clothing poster illustration, designed by Seth Cheeks, CheekyDSN

28

CHRISTINE **GODLEWSKI**

LOOK THE PART

"Have a website and business card ready, even if your business isn't. These tools will produce instant credibility. Many times the first thing that a potential client will want to know is 'Do you have a business card? Is your website listed on it?' A client wants to know that you are as legitimate as they are. When you put a proper face on your efforts by acting like a professional, you start your business on the road to building a reputable, respected name. This is critical to finding more and more new business. Oh, and always have that business card on hand and give away two instead of one when you're asked. You always want to be ready to have a conversation lead back to your business."

Some essential tools for starting your business:

- Name/alias: A creative moniker is a nice touch; a silly one is just trying too hard and could easily be misunderstood.

- Logo and identity: The face of your new endeavor is critical as it's how you will be seen by the community.

- Business card, stationery, etc: Communication tools are important to supporting your new identity.

- Website: No longer a novelty, no longer optional, websites are as essential a part of setting up shop as printing business cards. If you don't have one, you don't seem serious about your work.

- Address: Hot tip—if you are working from home or an apartment, adding "suite" to your street address looks more professional and won't confuse your mail carrier.

- Portfolio: This becomes your body of work to show potential clients what you've done and therefore what you can do.

- Personal style: Stay fresh and look the part you want to play. As a design professional, your style is speaking for you, always!

FISCAL YEAR 2006 REVENUE

- Government 71%
- Private support 27%
- Student fees 2%

2%
27%
71%

FISCAL YEAR 2006 EXPENSES

- Student instruction 83%
- Management and general 14%
- Fundraising 3%

3%
14%
83%

EECS Annual Report 2005-2006

I decided to contribute to EECS because I am sold on the school's concept: serving the needs of the whole child. For our students, like students at any great public or private school, academic success means more than reading and writing. It means physical and mental health services, and exposure to art and culture, from Shakespeare to judo. EECS delivers on all fronts.

Melanie Madigan, MSW, LCSW, Board Member, EECS; Psychotherapist, Private Practice

Revenue and expense breakdowns are based on the EECS Fiscal Year 2006 audit. For complete Fiscal Year 2006 audited financial statements, please contact Erie Neighborhood House's development and communications office at 312.432.3293.

FOUNDING BOARD
2005 – 2006

Angeles Avila
Member, Parent Council
Erie Neighborhood House

Ricardo Estrada
Board President
Executive Direct[...]
Erie Neighborh[...]

Agustin Gom[...]
President
Wallin & G[...]

John R. H[...]
President [...]
Goose Is[...]

Mark H[...]
Board [...]
Senior [...]
McC[...]

Tro[...]
Bo[...]
D[...]
M[...]

Ruth Kane
Resource Development
Consultant

Melanie Madigan
Psychotherapist
Private Practice

Michael Milkie
[...]dent and COO

Sonia Rodriguez
Parent Representative

Alejandro Silva
Director
Corporate Currency
& Solutions Group
Merrill Lynch & Co.

Velia Soto
Teacher Representative

Annual Report 2005-2006

ERIE ELEMENTARY CHARTER SCHOOL
Chicago's next great school, fostering the habits of heart, mind and work

Erie Elementary Charter School annual report, designed by Christine Godlewski, Genius Creative

29

JUDY **ROZBICKI**

HAVE YOUR STUFF TOGETHER

"Be organized and stay on top of paperwork. Figure out a system that works for you and stick to it. From record keeping and invoicing to file saving methods—don't look at this administration stuff as the root of all evil. Instead, look at it as keeping you well armed for the road ahead. If you develop a system that works for you and attack the organizing duties in small blocks of time, you can reduce the weight of it all. Organization doesn't have to be a chore or a bore for that matter. Use funky labels, folders, stickies, or whatever it takes to keep it interesting and get the job done."

Here are a few tools that can help you stay organized:

- A great space to work: No matter where you choose to work—home or otherwise—the way your space is laid out will affect your ability to stay organized and therefore stay effective and creative.

- Filing methods: File folders, file cabinets, paper clips, and other essentials are easy to come by and can even be a stylish upgrade to your overall work space. Oh, and they help keep your vital papers in order, too.

- Project tracking: There are a few off-the-shelf software options available, but for the freelancer/indie creative, it's more cost-effective to come up with an intuitive method that makes sense to you and reflects the way you work. A method involving date, project number, and client name or alias is simple to develop and will help keep you and your projects from getting overwhelmed or out of control.

- Time tracking: Some kind of time cards or time tracking method is infinitely valuable and should not be viewed as a drag. After all, your time is directly connected to your income. Put priority on staying on top of where your daily minutes go. Yes, minutes! It all translates back to revenue.

- Budgeting: Budgeting and invoicing software simplifies the daunting task of managing your money. Look into products such as Intuit QuickBooks Pro, BusAcc X 2, Billable 1.1.2, or TaskTime 4.3.3.

HOWie Zine 10 "Robots" illustration and design, designed by Judy Rozbicki, Lantern Creative

30

JENI **HERBERGER**

REMEMBER THE BOY SCOUT MOTTO: BE PREPARED

"Hopefully, if you regularly spend four to eight hours per week developing your business, the tide won't roll out."

When you're busy working on projects and have a lot of deadlines to keep track of, it can seem strange or stupid to pull hours away from a client to work on business development and marketing. But doing so is critical because the work you do to promote yourself this week may not pay off for weeks, months, even years down the road. You have to always keep yourself in front of people and remind them that you're available. This doesn't mean making fifty cold calls a week. It means making sure staffing agencies have your current résumé on file, past employers know that you're available for project work, and business organizations and design groups are seeing you at their mixers and luncheons. Sure, send out an email blast a few times a year to show off new work and remind people that you're out there designing up a storm. But in the meantime, invest at least half a day each and every week on business development activities of some kind, any kind.

31

STEVE **GORDON, JR**

SAVE SOMETHING FOR A RAINY DAY

"No matter how good your work, how fair your prices, how much steady marketing you do, there are still going to be dry spells. So put some money away where you can't touch it. Most experts recommend you set aside enough to cover three months of expenses. Seems like too much? It's not when you consider how long it can take to get a new client or even develop a fresh project from an existing client. Only dip into this stash when you really need it, and the minute you get some cash rolling again, pay yourself back."

MISTLETOE

SUBSTITUTE SYSTEM
FOR EMERGENCY HOLIDAY SMOOCHIES

THAT'S JUST RDQLUS

{ MISTLETOE }

(I know it's just the word... inconsequential details!)

Step One:
*Place this card high overhead
in the vicinity of designated smoochee.*

Step Two:
*Invite person (or persons, you cheeky devil!) to
pucker-push with the following intro phrases:*

"Get in close for the real thing."

"Come get some."

or the proven classic,

"Awwwwwwww Yeah!"
(must be used in tandem with the "Awwwwwwww Yeah" look)

RDQLUS DESIGN QUANTUM

RDQLUS self-promotional holiday card, designed by Steve Gordon, Jr, RDQLUS

Create magazine "Agency Roll-Call" article layout, designed by Calvin Lee, Mayhem Studios

32

CALVIN **LEE**

FIND YOUR PLACE(MENT) IN THE WORLD

"Use a job placement agency to supplement your income until your freelancing really takes off.

Get yourself set up with a placement agency that specializes in finding work for creatives and design professionals. This can be done on a permanent, semipermanent, or purely supplemental basis. You can always turn down projects if you get too busy, but just imagine how sweet it will be to get a call from 'Designs 'R Us' on that dreary afternoon when the phone has been quiet for far too long."

There are lots of placement agencies in most major cities. In addition, there are a wide range of websites that specialize in freelance and contract work.

Here are a few agencies and sites to check out; a quick online search will uncover many, many more:

- Creativeplacement
- The Creative Group
- CNS
- Match Creative Talent
- Aquent
- Allfreelancework.com
- Sologig.com

33

STEVE **GORDON, JR**

SPEAK UP

"Network, network, network. There are so many reasons to get out there and meet people, many of which we've discussed throughout this book. But remember, when you're out there, you have to tell people what you do, what you're looking for, and that you're available for work. You have to be professional, you have to be polite, you can't go pressing business cards into every-one's hands, but you can always work what you do into a regular get-to-know-you conversation. You can always ask someone who they use for creative services as a way to inquire if they might need yours. Sure, everyone wants to pretend that they're too busy to take on new clients, but this is not the way to get new work or even more important, *better* work."

34

TERRY LEE **STONE**

GET READY FOR YOUR CLOSE-UP

"So, it used to be that you could be a recluse in doing design work; sitting in front of your computer with a coffee, an idea, and a closed door to block out the unwanted distractions. In fact, it may have even seemed cool to be a bit mysterious or have your persona and movements be a bit unknown. All that is different now."

Today, everyone has access. It's simple to find information on anyone you wish. It's quite easy for an unknown to become a well-known overnight because of the reach of technology and the thirst for more and more information. Instead of hiding from this, embrace it. Push your persona out into the stream of information being sought. Having a bio to tell a brief story about you and a headshot so that people can match the face with the name and the work is necessary, not a necessary evil.

Here are some pointers:

- Write two versions of your career biography: a one-sentence short version and a 250-word summation of who you are and what you've done.

- Create a résumé and update it frequently— save it as a PDF as this is perhaps the most universal document format so you can send it to anyone who asks and even those who haven't asked yet.

- Have a headshot or two done. Photoshop and color correct it as needed.

- Save your portrait in two versions: high-res for print, 300 dpi at 8 x 10 inches (20 x 25 cm) and low-res for Web, 72 dpi at 3 x 5 inches (8 x 13 cm). You never know when a publication opportunity will appear.

HOWie Zine 4 "Naked" illustration and design by
Steve Gordon, Jr, RDQLUS

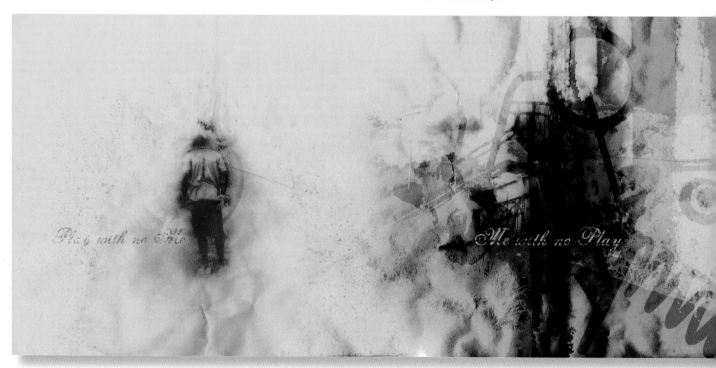

Paperback Cinema CD packaging design by Keith Bowman, The Design Bureau of Amerika

35

KEITH **BOWMAN**

FIND A HIGHER PURPOSE

"Take on pro bono work specifically for charitable organizations. Not only will it help build contacts, but it is good for the soul. Downtime is easier to deal with when you can at least work on projects that work for the betterment of community."

One of the reasons downtime is so stressful is because we seem to lack purpose and direction. You can easily regain focus—and do important, meaningful, creative work—by helping out a local organization. The food shelter needs a poster to tell the community their shelves are empty. The local pool and playground could use some flyers on upcoming programs. The neighborhood association would benefit from a newsletter on how to deter crime. You'll feel better doing not just something but something that makes a difference. And along the way, you also just might meet a few board members or community leaders who run businesses who could use your services and actually pay you for it.

36

STEVE **GORDON, JR**

SPRING CLEAN YOUR EMAIL, NO MATTER WHAT SEASON IT IS

"With all the emails coming in and out of your box, there's a very good chance that you have left something unanswered or dropped the communication ball with someone who could be a client. So sit down and go through all your messages. Delete things you don't need and organize things you do. Put attachments into folders. Rename messages so you know what information they contain. Update addresses.

Create mailing lists that you can organize into different categories at a single keystroke. Send out 'Hey, how are you?' notes to vendors, long-lost clients, and former classmates and no, don't answer that note from someone overseas asking you to cash a check for them, no matter how good the deal seems."

The Letter M brand development and website, designed by Steve Gordon, Jr, RDQLUS

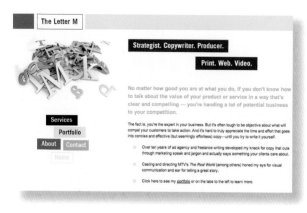

37

ERIC **HINES**

NOW, USE YOUR NEW AND IMROVED EMAIL FOR MARKETING

"Email campaigns are an inexpensive way to find new business on a budget."

Electronic media has made big-deal marketing accessible to small businesses and solo creatives like nothing else. Email lets you reach almost anyone, anywhere in the world. The cost of producing a promotional email is only the time you take to develop a message and design an aesthetic, which if you've branded yourself properly to begin with, shouldn't be much. And if someone isn't interested in what you have to say, they can delete your message with a keystroke, and no resources, such as paper and shipping, are wasted.

However, because there are so many emails bouncing around the web-o-sphere, it's important that if yours does get opened, it counts for something.

Make sure you keep the following things in mind as you're crafting your marketing message:

- Don't make something overdesigned so no one knows why they're getting this email. Keep your communication clear, direct, to the point. For the most part, you're talking to business people, not other designers.

- Make it easy to find you—a single click should get them to a response mechanism.

- Don't load it up with so many motion graphics and Flash animations that it will get kicked back or clog up someone's system.

- Don't make people do extra clicks to get to the meat of the message; if your intro is so long you're tempted to install a skip mechanism, you can bet plenty of people will skip the entire message.

- Spell check, grammar check, and address check. Mistakes like these may seem small to you, but a potential client may dismiss you out of hand for fear you'll make similar mistakes on their work.

Honest Bros. Concept Mechanic website

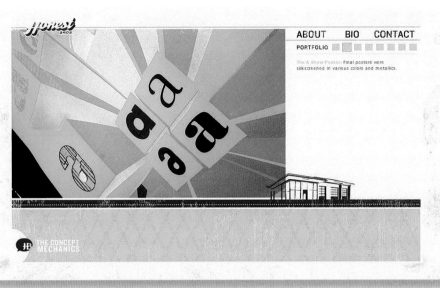

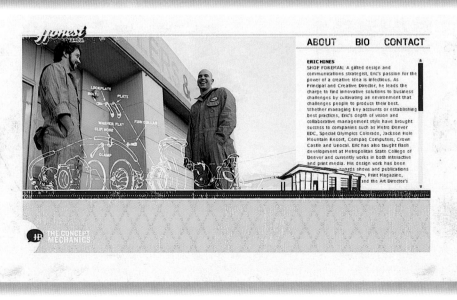

38 FIND A NEW DIRECTION IN A DIRECTORY

TONWEN **JONES**

"I send out lots of emails to potential new clients with samples of my work. [In the UK], a useful book to have is the *Writers' and Artists' Yearbook*. It comes out each year and has an extensive list of all the contact details for publishers, newspapers, etc. I use this book to ring companies up to get an email address for the art directors so I know my email and work are being sent to the right person."

There are plenty of other places to find people who might be interested in your work. Here are a few:

- Membership directories of all those design associations you've joined

- Yellow Pages—Yes, phone directories are still printed and produced and are often better than the online versions.

- Chambers of commerce and small business associations

- Listings of the boards of directors of prominent nonprofit and arts organizations such as the local symphony or ballet

The Guardian, December '07, "Binge Drinking and Exercise"
article illustration for the wellness section, designed by Tonwen Jones

39

PEOPLE WHO WANT TO BE DISCOVERED DON'T USUALLY HIDE

TERRY LEE **STONE**

"You don't need a publicist, but don't expect the media to come and find you. Reach out to publications that you read and respect and let them know when you've done something noteworthy. Make it personal, too—just as you would a cover letter, let your familiarity with that publication be known. (See, we all like to feel chosen.)"

Since journalists must pitch stories to their editors, you might consider pitching stories to the writers themselves. It doesn't mean you'll score a feature, but you will raise your profile with writers you like.

When you see a call for entries, enter. Getting your work selected by design magazine reviews and competitions offers great exposure and cachet. When you see a "contact us" link on a website . . . use it! It's there for a reason, so have something to say because they just might be listening.

about
logo
branding
print
web
illustration
packaging
room projects
photography

wedding essentials
espace, new york
timberland
seton hall university
seascapes
sharp, usa
longo
cebu x
vyteris
chubb
toto labrador
minolta, usa
hat life
deep blue
rob & nana
cmom
rustan's

1 2 3 4 5

lizza's room

cebu x is a furniture and furnishings show. it is held every year in the city of cebu in the philippines, which is known for world-class design and creativity. in 2004, lizza and photographer, lita puyat, were commissioned to work on the show's campaign theme and print materials.

Lizza's Room website design by Lizza Gutierrez

40

LIZZA **GUTIERREZ**

YOUR WEB PRESENCE IS NOT ONLY REQUESTED, IT'S REQUIRED

"When the lean times come, use it as an opportunity to update your online portfolio and website."

Of course you already have a website, right? I mean, that was set up before you even went out on your own, right? Because you already know and understand how critical having a good website is to your success, right? Well, chances are that if your site has been up for a week, it's already time for an overhaul. And there's no better time than downtime to take on this task.

Even if you're just updating work to make sure your latest and greatest is on screen and available for potential clients to review, spend some time cleaning up and improving your online presence. Even better, make sure your website is easy to navigate and has plenty of information about who you are, how you work, and the successes you've helped your clients achieve so it can do the same selling job that you'd do in person.

Loudonville Home for Adults brochure design by Jennifer WIlkerson, Aurora Design

41

JENNIFER **WILKERSON**

THERE IS NO SUCH THING AS TALKING TOO MUCH

"Tell everyone what you do for a living. It is a good way to fine-tune your two-minute description of your profession, and you never know where a good job is going to come from. For example, I've worked for many neighbors and friends."

Many people who might need graphic design services don't even know enough about what graphic designers do to ask for your help. By talking about your work, you enhance the industry, educate the public, practice your pitch, and may even get a fun project in the process.

42

DONOVAN N **BEERY**

THERE IS NO "FREE" IN FREELANCE

"There are some projects you're willing to do for free or even clients you're willing to work with for free or a highly reduced rate. I don't discourage doing pro bono work, as it can turn out to be the most rewarding work you do. But your clients should understand the value of what you're giving them, even if they're not paying you for it.

I follow the advice I got from Drew Davies of Oxide Design Co. on this issue. I put the full amount of the value of work on an invoice when the project is completed and simply add a 'design donation' amount that coincides with the reduced rate or full amount if it's a completely donated project. Hopefully, this helps the client realize what they've been given. After all, clients who value what you do are the best ones to work with."

As you do develop your business, there may be times when you want to do a project for free. You believe in the cause, it offers a great creative opportunity, you'll be able to do work in a new industry that interests you, or you think there may be more projects that actually pay down the road. However, just because something is free does not mean it has no value, and whoever is getting your services for no payment on their end should understand this. Which means it's up to you to understand it and communicate what your work is worth.

Torchwerks stationery and direct mailers, designed by Donovan N Beery, Eleven19 Communications, Inc.

43

KEITH **BOWMAN**

DON'T CHEAPEN YOURSELF BY GRABBING AT ANY PAYING PROJECT

"The ultimate goal of a freelancer is to have clients seek you out. Good design can only lead to better work. Even if it doesn't get you new clients right away, at least if you're doing your best work, you have the pride of knowing that you used your skills to the best of your ability, and you didn't compromise your principles.

Unfortunately, most jobs taken strictly for money instead of creative opportunity turn out to be bad experiences. Often the client is difficult and demands that I make design solutions that I know are wrong, and in the end, the stress and frustration never justify the financial gain. I feel it is better to walk away from a bad design job, no matter how much it pays. In the end, bad design will do nothing positive to further your skills.

Not everyone can do what we do, so it is our responsibility to do it right."

When you first start your freelance career, you may be tempted to scramble for every morsel of work you can scrounge up, no matter what it is. But try to remember why you went freelance to begin with. It wasn't just for the money. Most independent creatives chose the on-their-own route so they could perfect their craft, follow their ideals, and express their voice. Sure, ideals don't pay the bills, but following ideals creates the high level of skill and professionalism that creates a sought-after product that, in the end, does pay bills—without selling your soul in the process.

Tim McNally concert poster, designed by Keith Bowman, The Design Bureau of Amerika

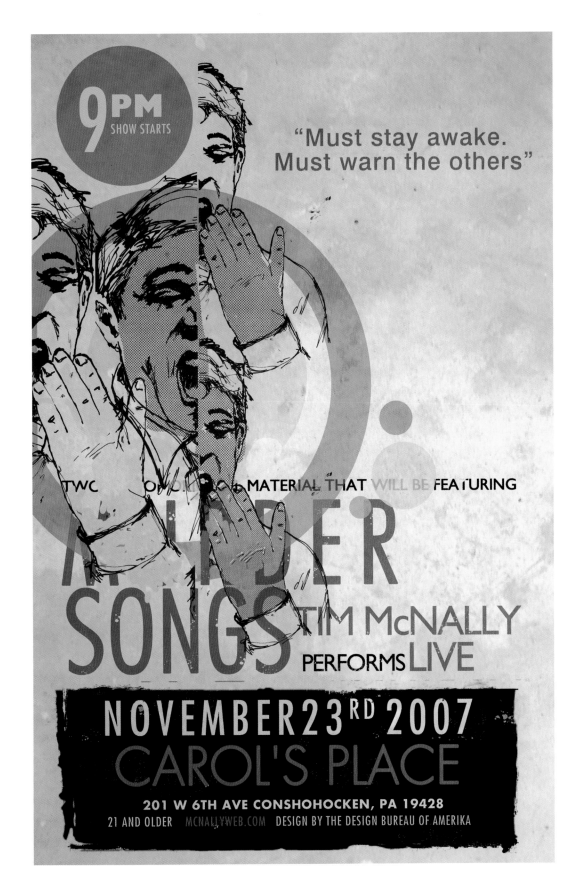

44

STEVE **GORDON, JR**

TURN DOWN THE VOLUME TO TURN UP THE PRICING

"It's just you now, so you won't be able to handle massive volumes of work. You can't take on everyone who knocks at your design door or every little project that comes along. The good news is that if you assign proper market value to your creative work, this will allow you to make the revenue you need and not nickel-and-dime yourself to the poorhouse or to freelance death.

If you lower the volume of the work that you are handling, you can pay more attention to the projects at hand and naturally, the quality of each project goes up. The better the quality of your work, the more you can charge, so you'll have to do fewer projects to make the same amount.

This approach also bolsters the industry at the grassroots level. There is usually plenty of work to go around in any city or town if there's not one shop greedily gobbling up everything in sight, offering bargain basement prices, and turning out low-quality work that drags the value of the entire design industry down."

Yale Park Collective logo design by Steve Gordon, Jr, RDQLUS

45

CHRISTINE **GODLEWSKI**

GO FOR THE VARIETY PACK

"For me, it's all about variety. Clients will come and go, so don't put all of your eggs in one basket. Try to have a variety of small projects, some medium-sized ones, and a big one, if you are lucky!"

It's tempting to hitch your wagon to one large client who may be willing to give you all their work. However, if this client then changes his or her mind, you're suddenly without any revenue. Not to mention, you'll have only one kind of project or work for only one industry in your portfolio. And let's not forget that you got into independence so you could be just that—independent, not tied to being a production house for a single company. So even if you find a large portion of your income coming from one source and that feels kind of comfortable, take the time to look around and diversify your clients. In the long run, your business and your creativity will thank you.

JWT/Microsoft "Options Are Good" card designs by
Christine Godlewski, Genius Creative

Lighthouse SPG capabilities brochure, designed by M. Mavromatis, MM Design Studio

46

M **MAVROMATIS**

STRETCH OUT THE TIMELINE

"I like to focus on larger jobs that have depth and breadth. Typically, larger projects also have longer timelines so I can immerse myself. This is very appealing to me as well."

Large jobs may also offer a plethora of tasks that provide you with some variety. You may have to create a document outlining your strategic approach, maybe some style boards to show the creative direction you're considering, or perhaps art direct a photo shoot or work with an illustrator. All these things present interesting creative opportunities and a chance for you to stretch into new areas and learn something. Just make sure that you are getting paid for all these activities and the client isn't expecting these services as part of the basic design fee.

47

TONWEN **JONES**

LET THEM KNOW WHAT'S ON THE MENU

Independent creatives often overlook the smaller details that come along with the process of doing the work. This is no different than burning money. Illustrations, photography, change orders, and even setting your thinking skills apart as a consultant to their staff are all ways to add revenue to your burgeoning business. You have a variety of things you are capable of, so why not give clients a taste?

"When designing, I often suggest adding some illustrations at an additional fee, which obviously bumps up the final figure.

I have a day rate for both illustration and design, so if the client's budget falls very short of this, I sometimes mention what I'd normally charge and they sometimes meet me half way and raise the budget slightly. Also, if they need a brief within a very tight timeframe, I say I'll prioritize their job but with the understanding of getting a better fee.

Change orders are important also.

Unless there is a set fee, I state that the job will include two sets of free amends [revisions] and then I will charge an hourly rate for every revision after that. This can often amount to quite a bit of extra money, especially if the client is disorganized and sends numerous emails with amends!"

Colagene Agency/*Chatelaine* magazine migraine illustration, designed by Tonwen Jones

48

ERIC **WOLFE**

WHERE DOES THE TIME GO?

"The biggest tip I can offer here is to keep very good track of every actual hour that you spend working on a project. Once the project is complete, compare actual time spent to your initial estimate or bid. It's not a bad idea to have a little postmortem meeting with yourself and actualize your hours. Did you overestimate? Underestimate? What went wrong with this project? What went right? What did you learn that you can use next time you have a project like this?

Also, always add some time to your initial estimate or bid to account for the unknowns. Unknowns could be anything from small revisions in copy to a completely new contact person on your client's side who requires a project briefing. Designers typically add 15–20 percent to whatever they think it is going to take to finish the job to help cover these unexpected surprises."

Microsoft Windows Live member letter, designed by Eric Wolfe, Eric Wolfe Design, Inc.

Windows Live Member Letter

here's what's cool with Windows Live

Running out of room?
Store up to 5GB of files on a virtual hard drive with Windows Live SkyDrive.

Get Started

Blog in 3D
Windows Live™ Writer makes it easy to insert and customize pictures, videos, Maps, tables and tags in your blog.

Find out how

noteworthy

Tune in to the Zune-A-Day Giveaway.
Rock on with Windows Live Hotmail® for mobile for your chance to win a Zune—every day until March 31.

Get it now! »

Everyone wants to be ready.
Whether you know someone getting ready for a blind date or a backyard barbeque, now you can send funny voice messages.

Get it now! »

you say

This month's poll
What is your favorite new Live Search game?.

Flexicon – Be the wordsmith
vote

Chicktionary – Unscramble the eggs
vote

Seekadoo – Find the answer
vote

Last month's poll results
How will you share your photos in the new year?

21% Windows Live Spaces
19% Printed Pictures
61% Email

fun stuff

Freebies
Lorem ipsum dolor amet, consectetuer adipiscing.

Get it now! »

Play Games
Lorem ipsum dolor amet, consectetuer adipiscing.

Get it now! »

Stay in Touch
Lorem ipsum dolor amet, consectetuer adipiscing.

Get it now! »

Be Ready - MSN
Lorem ipsum dolor amet, consectetuer adipiscing.

Get it now! »

email the editor

Got a question?
Just ask Lisa.

Q: How do I create a strong password?

A: Use a word that isn't a common word or name, or a close variation on a common word or name and make sure it contains seven to sixteen characters.

Your turn. Ask the Editor »

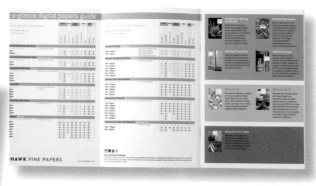

**Mohawk Fine Papers brochure designs by
Jennifer Wilkerson, Aurora Design**

49

JENNIFER **WILKERSON**

LOVE THEM OR LEAVE THEM

"I try to only work with people I like and respect.
That goes for vendors as well as clients."

Independent creatives can get pretty close to
their clients. After all, you may have to end a
call because the doorbell rings or a child falls
down while you're brainstorming a brochure.
Because the lines between personal and professional life can get a bit blurry when you're working for yourself, it's critical to surround yourself
with clients, vendors, and projects that fit your
life, values, preferences, and sensibilities, as
well as your professional aspirations. Don't forget that the opportunity to work on stuff—and
with people—you like is a big reason why you
went out on your own to begin with.

50

JENNIFER **WILKERSON**

PUT YOURSELF ON YOUR PAYROLL

"Treat your finances professionally. I have a strict cash-flow system I stick to, even if that means taking out loans when necessary. I take $X in a draw every month and take out loans to cover this, if required; X% of every check I receive gets put away for taxes; X% of every check goes to my retirement; X% of every check goes to pay off old credit card debt. This approach protects my family and keeps marital accord."

Not to mention, it just makes good financial sense. It's tempting to take that big payout check and go have a good time. You justify it by telling yourself that you've worked hard for so long. But if you don't show some profound financial discipline, you'll have nothing set aside for the dry spells, you'll owe money to vendors, yourself, and the government, and you'll be back looking for a day job.

Mohawk Fine Papers "Discover" sample brochure design by Jennifer Wilkerson, Aurora Design

Chapter Three:

WORKING WITH CLIENTS

Zumtobel annual report, designed by Stefan Sagmeister

51

STEFAN **SAGMEISTER**

VISIT THE CLIENT'S SITE—PHYSICAL AND VIRTUAL

In completing their first annual report, Sagmeister Studio discovered that the process differed from less conventional jobs such as music packaging. The client was Zumtobel, a European manufacturer. Sagmeister flew to the Zumtobel headquarters to immerse himself in their business. They gave him an extensive tour of their factory, showing him what they had done in the past and where they were in the present. Sagmeister returned to New York and worked out one very tight suggestion for the annual report based on what he learned about their business on his visit. They liked what they saw and adopted the design.

Sagmeister had sensed immediately that the client was unusual. He met with the CEO, who said that there was a 95 percent chance that the design, whatever it might be, would be adopted without reservation. This was a singular occasion for Sagmeister, who at first thought it was somewhat foolish of the CEO to reveal such information. "I could have just as easily taken advantage of it and come back with three half-penises on the cover. But as it happens in real life, if you get a lot of trust, you are very unlikely to misuse it," he comments.

Sagmeister believes this trust was established because of his face-to-face interaction with the CEO and the physical interaction with the space of the company. He knew for himself that he could not submit a design without being 100 percent happy with it. With this design, however, he was convinced of its appropriateness to the project at hand and knew that it fit the client's needs exactly. He notes, "The fact that we pushed it to that point had a lot to do with the trust we established because of a meeting."

Zumtobel annual report, designed by Stefan Sagmeister

Metropolitan Opera re-identification, designed by Worldstudio Inc.

THE
METROPOLITAN
OPERA

52

WORLDSTUDIO, INC.

RESEARCH CLIENT DECISION-MAKING SYSTEMS

Worldstudio, Inc., undertook a large identity project for the Metropolitan Opera, which involved navigating an extremely complex bureaucracy. The Metropolitan Opera hired Worldstudio because the new development director recognized that they needed to solve some important identity issues at the organization, which had a less-than-consistent identity. For example, new hires at the Metropolitan Opera had to design their own business cards. As a result, everybody had their own business cards, all with different logos, different wording, and different looks. The inconsistency made the development director's job difficult because the organization appeared to be so fragmented.

The development director went to the executive director and convinced him that they needed to hire a studio to get the identity materials in order. Each department of the Met is highly politicized, according to Mark Randall from Worldstudio, so they all—from publicity to promotions to design to scenics—were simply doing things the way they always had, and the Met was successful. Worldstudio, Inc., came to discover that this entrenchment would be the major challenge of the job.

Worldstudio decided the only way to get anything done was to get people on board with the idea of change and to give them some

ownership in the process. They interviewed all 13 department heads, talking to each person for over an hour. The department heads told Worldstudio what they thought the strengths of the Met were and what they wanted to communicate. The result was an "Objectives and Strategies" statement, which was circulated to and signed off by those same people. In this way, Worldstudio had a platform with the client on which to base the project.

The Worldstudio designers then worked with another group of six department heads and the general manager, meeting to discuss all the key points of the identity development. It was probably the most client-involved process the studio had ever done, and it took almost nine months to work through it.

Through the careful process of learning about the Metropolitan Opera, Worldstudio, Inc., was able to gain insight about a large, nonprofit client, which set them in a better position to pitch to such clients in the future. In addition, they learned about some of the pitfalls of working with an organization with so many departmental arms—as well as how to negotiate alliances and find support on many levels. They also learned that they should remain in the role of the designer and not to try to overhaul the system of an organization.

53

SPEND TIME WITH YOUR CLIENT TO BUILD CONSENSUS AND CREATE SHARED GOALS

JOHN C **JAY**

A good fit between the goals of a client and the goals of a designer or design firm can be created in many ways. In his office in Tokyo, John C Jay cites this extensive getting-to-know-you practice as essential for his business. "We spend a lot of time learning about the client. We visit each other, talk, and take time to understand the client's culture, giving them time to understand ours."

A primary concern for Jay is developing the consensus-building process, as well as developing the trust of his client. He has had an

additional hurdle of cross-cultural communication, an issue more and more designers face as international firms and corporations become the norm. Jay notes that the Japanese businesses with which he has worked are used to working with Japanese companies, presenting something of a stumbling block: "The big question [asked by Japanese companies] is 'How could you know us? How could pretend to know us?'"

Jay cites building trust as foremost in this cross-cultural communication. Primarily staffed with Japanese designers, Wieden+Kennedy, Tokyo, offers a blend, a hybrid of cultures. "We have the people who have the right DNA from a cultural standpoint, but they also have the right creative DNA. We just have to answer their questions and prove that we do understand them. That comes through a long series of discussions."

How and why would a Japanese company take a risk with a foreign company? Jay comments, "There are people who gravitate toward us, who already know something about us because of our work for Nike. As we began carving out a niche for ourselves and creating top Japanese brands, the walls came down. The proof is in our work and how successfully we can build projects piece by piece. If the question is, is it difficult to find people who share our passion for creativity, sure, it's hard. It's hard all over the world. But they are there; you just have to sort through the mess. Once you start sharing a business relationship, it is vitally important that a partnership is struck. Our goal is to earn their trust, and trust is not built through some presentation. Trust is built one meeting at a time, one campaign at a time, one project at a time. Hopefully there is an intuition up front, and hopefully we can prove them right, and hopefully our intuition about them is right."

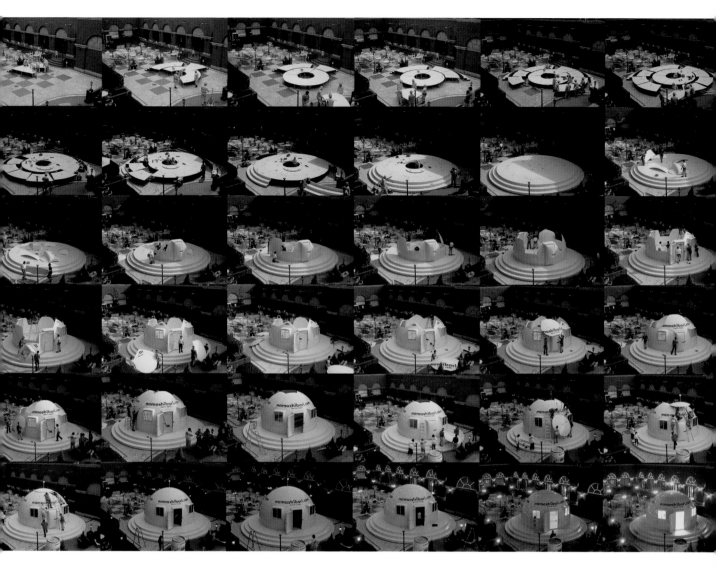

Opposite and above: Sapporo Beer Dome, designed by John C Jay, Wieden+Kennedy, Tokyo

54

**WHY NOT
ASSOCIATES**

EXPAND YOUR AUDIENCE BY DOING PUBLIC ART PROJECTS

The Cursing Stone and Reiver Pavement, which lists all the Reiver families from the area, is situated in the Tullie House Museum and Art Gallery in the northwestern English town of Carlisle. A collaboration with artist Gordon Young, the Cursing Stone is a 7.5-ton (6,804 kg) granite boulder inscribed with a 16th-century curse issued by the archbishop of Glasgow upon the Anglo-Scottish Reiver families who terrorized the borderlands at that time. The curse is long, detailed, and harsh. Young had been commissioned to create a piece of art for an underground walkway at the museum, and because he was from the bordertown where the curse was issued, he wanted to reproduce it somehow. His first inclination was to create a metal sphere, but he soon decided granite would be a more malleable medium.

In collaboration with Why Not, Young and the design team decided the curse should go around the sphere, which was a more difficult task than it initally appeared. Starting with a 9-ton (8,165 kg) boulder, Young eventually chipped and smoothed it down to a brilliant, smooth sheen. The text was applied as a mask and took three days to complete. It was then sand-blasted, leaving the curse on the stone.

Hundreds of people walk across the Reiver Pavement and look at the Cursing Stone each year. In addition, when it was initially completed, it garnered major media attention and various local calamities, such as the recurrence of foot and mouth disease, were blamed on the resurrection of the curse. Collaborating with a fine artist to make a type-based sculpture allowed Why Not to gain access to an otherwise inaccessible audience.

The Cursing Stone, designed by Why Not Associates

55

STEFAN **SAGMEISTER**

DON'T TALK ABOUT CD ART IN A CD ART MEETING

Stefan Sagmeister has developed an approach to music packaging that works. In general, he tries to talk to the band and to nobody else. This method is partially the result of a past trend in which when he found himself with three clients instead of one—the management, the label, and the band. Because that arrangement created problems for all three parties, Sagmeister tries to communicate with only one party, the most important one.

Sagmeister admits that he is lucky because the bands that come to him are interested in their packaging. Most of them have either rebelled against the label's in-house designers or the in-house designers are just too busy to take on the band's project. In early meetings, Sagmeister keeps the subject off the art itself, talking instead about the music, the lyrics— where they came from, how they were written, and why they were written—and what the band thinks about the album.

Next, Sagmeister gets rough cuts of the music to listen to as he designs. Finally, he comes back to the band with a recommendation, usually only one design that he develops to look like the final piece. "Meeting with the band is the most important part," Sagmeister says. "By talking about the ideas of the music, as opposed to the band's ideas about art, we are more likely to come up with a good solution."

OK Go CD Packaging, designed by Stefan Sagmeister

NATALIA, VALERIE, TASHA AND CHLOE PHOTOGRAPHED BY JUERGEN TELLER

MARC JACOBS

MARC JACOBS

Marc Jacobs print advertising, designed by Miles Murray Sorrell FUEL

56

**MILES MURRAY
SORRELL FUEL**

ALL WORK HAS ITS OWN UNIQUE CLIENT

Miles Murray Sorrell FUEL has worked with photographer Jürgen Teller for a number years, designing his books and exhibitions. This collaboration bore fruit when Teller was asked to shoot the campaign for the Marc Jacobs 2002 line. Although Miles Murray Sorrell FUEL discussed the ideas for the campaign with Teller, they did not direct him on his shoots. Their work for Jacobs includes advertising for clothes, shoes, bags, and perfume. The Marc Jacobs perfume campaign with Sofia Coppola won a Council of Fashion Designers of America Award.

Once Teller's photos were in, Miles Murray Sorrell FUEL worked with Teller to edit the photos. They then did the layouts and produced the artwork for the various ads. The idea that all work has its own client is particularly important for fashion design, where the look developed by the photographer and the graphic designer must be both unique and serve the clothing designer's work.

Every designer deserves work that is truly unique. Designers must continually reinvent themselves and maintain an understanding of the client and their needs. Only then can an appropriate solution be delivered.

57

TODO **WATERBURY**

LEARN THE LANGUAGE OF THE CLIENT

The designer must create consistent language and messaging for a campaign to be successful. The designer must listen, learn, and adapt the language he or she hears from the client. In this manner, the creative ideas of the designer can effectively move from the design table and into the boardroom.

Because Todd Waterbury and the creative teams at Wieden+Kennedy had a particularly intuitive way of working, they cannot work with just any client. Waterbury calls the initial meeting with the client the "chemistry" meeting. It is here that the representatives from the firm discuss their philosophy of creative work and show their portfolio of recent campaigns.

This is also when the clients describe their needs for the specific project, as well as overarching ideas about doing business and the client firm's core beliefs.

"Usually, once we show our work and talk about why we do what we do and how we believe in it, we can tell whether it is going to be a good fit," Waterbury notes. But there were also times when his team had worked with a client in an effort to develop a dynamic and creative relationship over time. In some instances this worked and in others it didn't. Companies who view business itself as a creative endeavor were generally more amenable to Wieden+Kennedy's approach than were companies who work within a strict paradigm of business practice.

Still, Waterbury notes that a dynamic and open environment can sometimes be the work of a single person within a corporate structure. "Even though the category or the industry may be seen by us, and by most people, as boring or dry, with the right people in the company who want to do something new, anything is possible. I genuinely believe that." In the initial meeting, Waterbury tries to keep an open mind to the opportunities that a company can offer his creative teams' and makes contact with the people within the client's company who he senses will be able to get things done.

Miller High Life: "Mayonnaise," designed by Todd Waterbury, Wieden+Kennedy, New York

"Mayonnaise" :15

VO: It's hard to respect the French when you have to bail 'em out of two big ones in one century.
But we have to hand it to 'em on mayonnaise. Nice job Pierre.

58

TODD **WATERBURY**

TEACH THE CLIENT YOUR LANGUAGE

Too often a creative person appeals to the client on the level of beauty, execution, or aesthetic cleverness, but he or she does not explain to the client how the idea will help them drive business.

The contrast between a small studio like Sagmeister's and a large advertising firm can shed light on the differences in approach that designers take to client interaction. In his work with Wieden+Kennedy, Todd Waterbury often worked for large clients with complex decision-making and communication hierarchies. In most cases, the marketing director, the CEO, the COO, and the communications person are different people. Waterbury notes that creative people rarely translate their needs and desires accurately from language that they have grown up with into language that is articulate and meaningful to the client. When presenting ideas, the creative person needs to communicate with the client in such a way that the person he or she is talking to has a high level of clarity and conviction about what the idea is. In addition, and perhaps more importantly, the client needs to be given tools to sell the idea with a similar level of clarity and conviction back in the company where they work.

Waterbury reminds us that in the corporate model, marketing departments are cost centers, as opposed to revenue centers, and the client views money spent on marketing as an expense, an investment that should yield returns. Every conversation with the client must involve language that incorporates this fundamental premise and uses it to create clear communication and conviction.

Waterbury worked on a branding campaign for ESPN that was meant to reignite a connection to sports in the lapsed fan. The objective of the campaign was to move the meaning of sports off the gridiron or the court and remind people that sports influence everything from music and fashion to the whole celebrity machine. Waterbury conjoined all these disparate entities in the question, "What would the world be like without sports?", always bringing it back to the client's product: "Can you go without . . . ESPN?" Although the tag line was not used in the commercials, it was essential in conducting meetings with the client to keep bringing them back to the core message of the spots. In this way, the client could understand the central premise of the campaign and could communicate it clearly.

ESPN Without Sports campaign, designed by Todd Waterbury, Wieden+Kennedy, New York

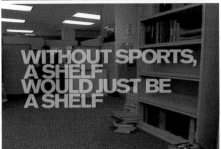

"Shelfball / Medical Condition" :30

VO 1:	Homer! Yes, Yes.
VO 2:	Nice, nice.
VO 3:	It only bounced twice.
VO 1:	No, no, I cleared it.
VO 2:	So what? It's a home run.
VO 3:	No, it's a double.
VO 1:	No, it didn't even hit the back of the shelf.
VO 3:	It bounces twice, it's a double.
VO 2:	What are you talking about?
VO 3:	I'm talking about rules—doesn't hit the back.
VO 1:	Those aren't the rules. You're talking about making up the rules.
VO 3:	No, I'm talking about... look, I play with shoes, you don't.
VO 1:	So what?
VO 3:	That's a rule.
VO 1:	I have a medical condition.
VO 2:	This is why no one wants to play with you.
VO 3:	Why? Because I'm right, and I'm better at it than you?
VO 1:	Take a nap.

"Coach" :60

VO 1:	We're still in it. Let's do it.
VO 2:	Look at the game. Watch who got the ball, watch who got the ball.
VO 3:	Now, that is mad-dog defense. That's a good defense. If they just work it a little, more like that.
VO 4:	Impossible.
VO 5:	Here we go.
VO 6:	Nice tip, nice tip. Way to crash the board.
VO 7:	Basketball 101, basketball 101.
VO 8:	They need to hurry up. What are they taking their time for?
VO 2:	Tackle somebody. Tackle somebody now!
VO 3:	That's bush league. That's all it is. Nothing but bush league.
VO 6:	Fourth quarter they always collapse.
VO 9:	Push it, Fisher.
VO 11:	Come on!
VO 12:	Terry's open, he's open, he's open!
VO 1:	Run, baby, run. Run.
VO 11:	Knock him down!
VO 4:	Don't foul.
VO 12:	Foul him!
VO 13:	Let it go!
VO 4:	What did I say?
VO 1:	Beautiful.
VO 2:	Make a play.
VO 3:	Hit him for God's sake.
VO 11:	Run it left. Run it left!
VO 2:	No, just him, somebody.
VO 3:	Take him on the boards.
VO 1:	Go, baby, go!
VO 3:	It's a disgrace, just a disgrace. They ought to be ashamed of themselves.

"Teammates" :60

VO 1:	May 13, 1947, we were playing in Crossly field.
VO 2:	The fans in Cincinnati were not very pro-black baseball player at that time.
VO 3:	Now, even though it's in the north, north of the Ohio River, it basically was a southern town in their thinking.
VO 2:	It was like going into a morass of discrimination, that's what it was...it was discrimination, segregation.
VO 3:	The fans were all over Jackie, giving him verbal abuse...and a...and some of them were very rank.
VO 1:	They were ruckus and were on Jackie's case, I mean, they were saying anything they could about Jackie, all the racial slurs they could conceive.
VO 2:	And Peewee Reese, a white baseball player with the Dodgers from Louisville, Kentucky, came over to second base.
VO 3:	And put his arm around him.
VO 1:	Put his arm around his shoulder.
VO 2:	And put his arm around Jackie Robinson, a black man with the Dodgers from Cairo, Georgia.

59

MARGO **CHASE**

SEEK OUT CREATIVE CLIENTS FOR SUCCESSFUL COLLABORATIONS

The Chase Design Group has been working with the Kama Sutra company for years. The company was founded and is owned by Joe Bolstad, who himself has a degree in design. "He's the only client I've ever had who graduated from Art Center," comments Margo Chase. "I think his degree in design is part of the reason we've been able to do such a good job with his products."

When Bolstad came to the Chase Design Group, the packaging for his products had been the same since 1965. The products were sold primarily in head shops and sex stores, but Bolstad wanted to grow the business and get his products into larger gift shops and department stores.

"The Kama Sutra name was our inspiration," says Chase. "We researched the original Indian artwork, paintings, and frescos and presented several different ideas for how to incorporate that feeling into their packaging. In the end, we created two different looks. The core product line, which includes Oil of Love, Pleasure Balm,

and Honey Dust, is wrapped in a green, ribbed paper with a gold metallic leaf pattern. Each flavor has a different bellyband design to distinguish it and tie it into the gift product line, which is decorated with illustrations based on the art of the original Kama Sutra."

Because of the redesign, Kama Sutra products can now be found in high-end gift stores all over the world, as well as at mainstream retailers like Long's Drug. Close collaboration with the company's owner elevated the dialog about developing designs to a very sophisticated level, creating an exciting and ultimately successful partnership.

Kama Sutra Packaging, designed by Margo Chase, Chase Design Group

60

WORKSIGHT

BUILD SMALL PROJECTS INTO ENGAGING, ONGOING WORK

A small project for Gilbert Paper ended up turning into a series on American subcultures for Worksight. "I found a culture at the paper company and that turned into other paper promos for other American subcultures, such as Coney Island, sturgeon spearing on Lake Winnebago, and a piece about Jackson Hole, Wyoming, called 'Branding the Great American West,'" says Scott Santoro of Worksight. Santoro asked the company if he could explore these subcultures in the context of a paper promotion, and they agreed. "Why do these cultures exist? What is so cool about them? Why would we want to tell their story? What do we find embedded in them that would be interesting to talk about? It all started from this one piece that we did on their hundred-year-old paper mill."

In developing a promotion for a paper company, the designer must show the capacity of the product and demonstrate its most salient characteristics. But this is virtually the only requirement, and paper companies often give creative license to designers when creating promotions. "They wanted me to make up my own assignment and turn it into a series," comments Santoro. "They wanted me to find tactile, textured stories that were interesting to me and then print them on their tactile, textured paper in the form of brochures that might interest other designers as well." By choosing to focus his work on subculture forms and figures such as cowboys, Santoro created projects that were definitely outside the mainstream yet were useful for the paper company to show off their product.

Gilbert Paper promotions, designed by Worksight

Queen Elizabeth II stamps, designed by Why Not Associates

61

WHY NOT ASSOCIATES

WORK FOR THE GOVERNMENT

"Working for the queen was probably the strangest job we've ever done," comments Andy Altmann of Why Not. In designing a series of postage stamps featuring the visage of Queen Elizabeth II, Why Not ran into many new and interesting issues about designing in a public context and for a public agency.

"The queen obviously has a lot attached to her. You want to do something your mother will like and, at the same time, you want to do something contemporary. You can't make it too kitsch, but you are trying to tell a story over five stamps. It isn't easy." One of three design groups that were asked to come up with ideas for a new stamp, Why Not was successful on their first bid. In addition, the process of working for the Royal Mail lacked the bureaucracy that attends even some small private firms who hire designers. They did have to run their final proposals by the queen, who gave her assent.

62

STEFAN **SAGMEISTER**

DEVELOP A CLEAR ETHIC OF CLIENT INTERACTION THAT WORKS FOR YOU

In determining how to approach a client, many designers try to understand the organization of the client structure and go from there. Before this even happens, Stefan Sagmeister asks a series of questions that helps him make decisions about which clients to work for. Although the answers to these questions are highly subjective, their general structure may be useful to other designers as they make choices about who to work for.

Sagmeister asks the following questions: How good is the product? How worthwhile are the client's activities? How much does he like the person who will be his daily contact? Do they have the money and the time to do the job properly? And is it challenging and exciting or something we have done before?

Every choice that a designer makes about his or her business is rooted in his or her own ethical code. Developing and sustaining such a code is essential to making good and consistent choices about work.

Made You Look, designed by Stefan Sagmiester

Little Company of Mary Hospital public health awareness brochure and
Children's Alliance 20th Anniversary invitation, designed by Christine Godlewski, Genius Creative

63

CHRISTINE **GODLEWSKI**

WHAT CAN I GET FOR THIS MUCH?

"I work with a lot of not-for-profit clients, so I've got this one down to a science. If you know there is a budget or suspect they don't have money to burn, do your best to get a firm dollar amount up front. There is no sense in wasting your time designing something they won't be able to afford producing."

Budgeting a project can be a bit of a you-go-first, no, you-go-first dance. The client wants you to tell them what the project is going to cost and you want to know how much they have to spend. One way to handle this is to explain that any project, from a simple letterhead to a corporate brochure, can cost as much or as little as can be imagined, and what you want to do is design the best and most creative piece possible within the natural constraints of their budget.

Tell your client you understand that a start-up or non-profit is going to have a different budget from a multinational corporation and you will do your best work if you have some idea of the parameters up front. Even a range or a not-to-exceed amount is helpful. Explain that you can use these guidelines to schedule time appropriately, to think of effects that are manageable, and to allocate resources between creative, production, and printing so everyone gets their fair piece of the pie and most important, the client gets the biggest bang for his or her buck.

64

DONOVAN N **BEERY**

WHEN IT COMES TO SAVING MONEY, THE PRINTER IS YOUR FRIEND

"Be creative with the printing of a project, wherever possible. I was designing wedding invitations for a client and the print budget was very minimal, but the last thing I wanted to cut was the creative parts. Printing the envelopes and inserts for the program myself (black and white on a laser printer) was one of the first cost-saving adjustments I made. Then I talked with another sole-proprietor and got some advice on which local printers did good work for the least cost. Talking directly with the printer is always advised, as they can tell you if certain paper or colors are used a lot in the shop (as these are normally cheaper), and you can get the exact sheet size that's most economical for that printer."

Krueger/Kracher wedding stationery and logo, designed by Donovan N Beery, Eleven19 Communications, Inc.

65

M **MAVROMATIS**

WHEN IT COMES TO SAVING MONEY, THE PRESS SHEET IS YOUR FRIEND

"Pushing your thinking in everything you do is a must. Getting the most out of the press sheet can help maximize the print costs in a budget."

As a one-person shop, you don't have the luxury of turning files over to a seasoned production manager. You have to be your own production manager. And this means thinking—while you're designing—about details such as understanding how your printer will set up your project on the final press sheet. Most designers don't realize how much paper is routinely wasted—and can therefore be saved—on a press sheet.

Fortunately, there's no reason to go it alone and waste long hours with complicated calculations and mock-ups. Simply talk to your printer. They'll be thrilled you brought them into the process early and happy to give you ideas about how to set up your project to save paper and still get all the white space you want and even the bleeds you need. However, it's definitely your job to approach the printer first. Even if they see opportunities for reducing wastage when you send your files, they will likely not have the time or inclination to go back to you and suggest changes. By that time, everyone's up against the clock and needs to get the job printed and to the client. So be proactive. You'll not only save time but also headaches, and you'll certainly learn something and become smarter along the way.

Waste not, want not—here are some tips for using press sheets wisely if you need to set up your own:

- If finishing the final piece yourself, use as much of the actual white-space as possible. This may be the only time you hear this as a designer! Careful positioning of artwork can maximize the sheet and give you more per page, so work the angles to fill the print area.

- When hand-finishing final pieces, common crop marks and bleed areas allow more space on the page for other artwork.

- If the printer is trimming and finishing the work for you, align the piece so that there is horizontal space between rows of artwork. This allows the printer to cut straight lines between the work for the batch cutter.

- Branding and identity work is great for gang runs because they utilize the same color palettes. Print business cards, notepads, and letterhead on the same sheet.

- Be creative with the final size of the work. Unique sizing may allow more print space, and the final products will likely stand out.

The Center for Emerging Visual Artists identity and brochure design, designed by M. Mavromatis, MM Design Studio

THE CENTER FOR
emerging visual artists™

MANY PERSPECTIVES. A SINGLE FOCUS.
Helping to build sustainable careers for emerging visual artists.

Annual Review 2003/2004

THE CENTER FOR
emerging visual artists™

Susan Cunningham
"Hands, 1931" 2.5" x 9.5"
Polaroid negative, 2002

Maggi Emberson
"Lottery" 19" x 25"
Acrylic, 2002

Jill Bell
"You're Not Trying To Get Better" 8" x 24" x 4"
Ceramic, 2001

THE CURATOR'S PERSPECTIVE

"I have been engaged in the work of The Center for several years as a member of the Board of Artistic Advisors, but I had never had the challenge and great pleasure of serving as one of its curators. By curating a show of current artists' work, I came to appreciate the very high quality and diversity of the work being done in the Career Development Program in a way I never had before. I was bowled over."

Leslie King-Hammond
Curator, Dean of Graduate Studies, Maryland Institute College
of Art and Member of The Center's Board of Artistic Advisors

Creating exhibition opportunities for artists and curators

Our artists have told us that it is a major motivation to have a challenging schedule of exhibitions. Last year, we gave them just that by finding opportunities for exhibitions in an expanded range of venues and geography with new curators. We mounted eight shows, from Baltimore to Princeton, in cultural, academic and corporate spaces — including the Delaware Center for the Contemporary Arts, Maryland Institute College of Art, Moore College of Art, Morgan Lewis & Bockius, the West Collection at SEI Corporation, and Educational Testing Service. And our Visiting Curator program provided motivation and opportunity for an emerging curator, as well.

For the future, we're beginning to develop a Community Exhibitions program in the Philadelphia area to bring art to public spaces such as hospitals and clinics — enhancing the experiences of visitors and expanding exposure for regional emerging visual artists — in and out of our Career Development Program. We're also searching for and selecting spaces that will allow us to move awareness of The Center's programs and artists to other important art-aware communities, such as New York, and cities in Europe and Asia.

66

KEITH **BOWMAN**

TAKE YOUR CLIENT'S HAND AND WALK WITH THEM

"I love working with smaller clients because many are aware that design is all about getting the message out and they realize that smaller budgets often require more creative solutions. However, a client may try to art direct or run the creative aspect of a project because they worry that the designer doesn't have a personal stake in the project and therefore won't arrive at the best design solution. This is especially true for clients on limited budgets who may be scared of the investment they are making.

Having an open discussion with your client about the limitations of a smaller budget is a good way to start the creative process. Show the client that you are passionate about his project. Do independent research and always give sound reasons for the creative decisions you make. If you not only show that you are passionate about the project but also bring some serious creative thinking to the table, it can often ease a client's worries, making them more receptive to your design concepts and less apt to meddle in or control a project.

For example, we created this one-color poster for a band that had little budget. The challenge was fun, and ultimately the black-and-white poster had more impact than a full-color illustration."

Also, try to remember that this walk goes in both directions. The best way to make a client receptive to the work you're trying to do as a designer is to be aware of what they're trying to do as a business or nonprofit. Go to the effort of learning about their industry or cause, about their sales and goals. Their budget for design may seem small to you, but it may be a huge percentage of their overall resources. If you can show you understand where they want to go, they will be much more open about having you partner with them on the journey.

The Rooms concert poster design, designed by Keith Bowman, The Design Bureau of Amerika

"EXIT THE TIGER,
ENTER THE ROOMS"

THE ROOMS " LIVE AT THE NORTH STAR BAR "
APPEARING AT 9PM-FEB 21ST CO-STARRING THE LAST CALL
ILLUSTRATION AND POSTER DESIGN BY KEITH BOWMAN - THE DESIGN BUREAU OF AMERIKA TDBA-PL-002

Mischen Clothing website design by Seth Cheeks, CheekyDSN

67

SETH **CHEEKS**

GIVE YOUR CLIENTS DESIGN EDUCATION, NOT JUST DESIGN

"Educating your clients will help gain their trust. As you walk them through the budget, explain the options and why what you are proposing is the best solution for the budget they have.

From my experience, clients often come to me as a referral or because they've seen something I've done already and they think they really must have exactly that same thing. My first question is, 'Aside from the look, why do you want that? Tell me about you and your company first.' I like to get to know the client because I want the work I do to reflect them as much as possible, with my vision on it.

When clients refer to designs in my portfolio and say they want something similar for their project, I tell them, 'That's a $15,000 (£9,215) project, and your budget is $2,300 (£1,413). Let's take inspiration from that project, but tailor something for you that will fit your budget and needs.'"

The bottom line is that the more your client understands what you do, the more they'll trust what you do.

68

YOU'RE LOSING A LITTLE COLOR

"Learn to work with two colors for cheaper printing. Keep your eyes open for great two-color work, and save samples for reference."

DEREK **ARMSTRONG**
MCNEILL

It's simple math—more colors mean more cost to print. While everyone likes four-color process and the printed punch you can get from so many rich, deep, and intertwined colors, you can save your clients a lot of money in printing costs by designing in two colors. You needn't look at two-color printing as a limitation—think of it as presenting a creative challenge.

Here are a few tips to get you going:

- Look for inspiration in places other than glossy magazines. How about T-shirts, posters, and other lower-tech outlets for great design?

- Use colored paper instead of white and get a third color right away.

- Use screens and duotones to get a variety of effects with the colors you have.

- Always begin logos and identities as one- and two-color options to allow them to grow but also work well in limited output scenarios.

- Utilize Pantone colors that take on different qualities as you change their percentages. It's like getting ten colors for the price of one. For instance, Pantone Black 4 will take on brownish earthtones as the percentage is lowered.

Feathercomb logo design by Derek Armstrong McNeill, Grill Creative

69

JUDY **ROZBICKI**

PORTION CONTROL: GOOD FOR DIETS AND BUDGETS

"Always take a very hard, cold look at how much your clients really need. Do they really need 100,000 brochures in the first print run? If you normally include three initial concepts for your clients but you have a new client with a tight budget, suggest showing them only two concepts; if neither works, you can always set a new, additional budget to do a third. If you normally spend thirty hours working up a logo, consider reducing your time incrementally to meet the client's budget."

Clients often think they need more than they really do. They have the misconception that as long as they're printing something, they should do lots of them. Or that they need a lot of animations and motion graphics to get traffic on their website. It's part of your job as the creative professional to help them get only what they need, when they need it, to meet their particular goals and strategies. Tell them they can always add Flash to their site later, and that if they print high quantities, their materials will be out of date before they've opened up the tenth box of brochures. By helping them spend less in the beginning, you're helping them have more resources later that may come back to you in the form of a long-term relationship and ongoing creative fees.

Ten places where you can help your client cut costs:

- Ask how they plan to use printed materials so you print only what they really need.

- Consider on-demand, self-produced, digital printing of materials.

- Think about using quick digital print/copy shops. See it as a challenge.

- Suggest offering the brochure as a downloadable PDF from the website.

- Decide if a Flash animation will really help sales or brand strategy.

- Phase in the development of printed pieces—do the basics and small stuff first.

- Remember that for smaller companies, extensive websites are not always necessary. A well done page or two will get a lot of good communication coming their way.

- Use blogs and other free and editable means of communication as they are great ways to maintain a wide-reaching presence on the Web.

- Design identity systems and logos to work in one- and two-color print methods.

- Be willing to offer a candid yet professional opinion when something is seen as an unnecessary item or cost. More stuff is not always the way to go.

70

JENI **HERBERGER**

I LIKE WHERE YOUR HEAD IS, EVEN WHEN IT'S IN THE CLOUDS

"Few designers do this, but I suggest that at the outset of a project, you ask your client to shoot for the moon. Ask them what they'd do if money were no object. This information should go into your initial design brief, and you should bid off of these specs. This allows the client to voice what they want but will give you a leg up on reigning them back in and setting more realistic expectations when you put that into the bid pricing and they see how much their dream design would cost. It also sets you up for dialog with the client as an expert in your field. This gives you a place to begin strategizing with your client on how to get the most from the budget they do have and helps you assist them in defining needs and choosing priorities."

71

LIZZA **GUTIERREZ**

PART CREATIVE SOLUTION, PART SPY GADGET

"A designer may be able to come up with designs that provide several solutions to a client's needs at the same time. For example, if a client has a small budget but really needs to have a newsletter and a poster, a designer may then conceptualize a piece that acts as both a newsletter and a poster instead of designing two separate pieces."

I was commissioned by Filinvest Development Corporation to design a set of brochures for Seascapes Resort Town, a beach community and resort located in the island of Mactan, Cebu, the Philippines. Each brochure showcased a product offered by the realty development, namely the beach club, the lots, and the villas and casitas. Designed to market a leisure and tourist destination, every brochure incorporated a marketing teaser or mailer which came in the form of a detachable postcard. The design and placement of the postcard was executed in such a way that the flow of the brochure's content would be consistent and seamless whether the postcard was detached from the main brochure or not. This design integrated two collaterals into one marketing piece, which saved the client money in terms of their production and distribution costs."

Appropriate, simple solutions like this will win the accolades of any client who has to work with a tight budget."

Other two-for-one design ideas:

- Promotional mailer that includes a punch-out business card

- Direct-mail piece that folds out into a poster

- Branded reusable "gift" items that have a subtle marketing message and contact information on them

- Any uniquely designed items that have longer usage and shelf life than simple paper-printed materials

Seascapes Resort Town, Filinvest Development Corporation, designed by Lizza Gutierrez, Lizza's Room

72

STEVE **GORDON**, JR

YOUR PART MAY BE PARTNERSHIP

"There are many smaller or start-up businesses that have a great product or service but no ideas and no budget for marketing. This may be your opportunity to become a venture capitalist with your investment coming not as cold, hard cash, but in creative capital. If you believe in the client, suggest taking a percentage of future sales or profits instead of up-front payment. In other words, offer to become a business partner.

This is a more common and acceptable alternative than you might realize. Your client now has direct access to marketing acumen and design skills. You now have access to a future payoff that could be much more than would have been made in fees. Yes, you may have to eat some costs and time in the beginning, but you may get a much bigger and more satisfying meal down the road."

Urban Times magazine, Kansas City; "Women of the Core" two-part article, illustration, designed by Steve Gordon, Jr, RDQLUS

73

JENI **HERBERGER**

GET IT IN WRITING

"Don't forget that the smaller client with the smaller budget is many times the most difficult to get paid from. Be sure you get a deposit up front, are insistent on change orders, and hold strictly to your payment terms. Don't do this to be harsh but to be a professional. A better educated client is simply better next go round."

Here are a few things to get clear on—and put down in writing—before you start to design:

- How many concepts are you going to present?

- How many rounds of changes are you going to accept?

- What are the payment terms?

- What is the timetable?

- What are the exact deliverables—final printed product or digital files, for example?

Chapter Four:

WORKING WITH EDITORS,
ILLUSTRATORS, VENDORS,
AND INFORMATION

Red magazine, designed by Agnes Zeilstra, captures the lifestyle of the busy European woman juggling family, fashion, career, and friends.

74

JEREMY **LESLIE**

INA **SALTZ**

THE EDITOR IS YOUR FRIEND AND YOUR PARTNER

In publication design, notes Jeremy Leslie, "Essentially you have an editor and an art director on equal footing. A good editor has to have an understanding of design even if they don't design, and a senior designer has to have a good understanding of words. The best magazines come from the best teams." Like most great partnerships, the one between editor and designer should be based on building personal and intellectual rapport—you may be fortunate and stumble upon an ideal situation, but it's more likely that you'll need to create it. "You're never going to have a great budget, great editor, great staff, and great subject matter all in one," Ina Saltz points out. "But if you have a great relationship with your editor, then it's a good job no matter what any of the other factors are. Because it's all about the power of the merging of visuals and content, there has to be a partnership and a trust and mutual reliance and respect. And to that end, the art director has to appreciate the power of the written word and the editor has to have good visual instincts." When all those elements come together, you get not only a magazine of excellence but a gratifying personal experience as well. "Working with great editors is like a drug," laughs Saltz. "It's very addictive and very satisfying."

Red magazine, designed by Agnes Zeilstra

75

ARTHUR **HOCHSTEIN**

THINK LIKE AN EDITOR

The best way to understand an editor and get more out of them is to try and think like one. As Arthur Hochstein notes, "Editors tend to see designers as a rare, sensitive species, like tropical plants or African violets. But if you can talk the language of editors, they'll bring you into the process more." Exactly how does a designer learn to enter the editorial mind? "You have to think about how something translates to a reader, rather than just how it looks," Hochstein advises. "You have to see design as a visual narrative, not just a decorative process. This is a huge distinction because some designers just think about the arrangement of things, but we have a story to tell."

Peggy Saman

'Ik ben steeds meer van *de makkelijke*'

Meer en meer vrouwen komen erop terug. Zes ballen in de lucht houden hoeft niet meer voor hen. Maar hoe pak je dat aan, want je wilt toch werken, veel aandacht aan je gezin besteden, uitgaan en sporten? Simpel, omarm de attitude of gratitude.

Vrienden van mij die geen kinderen kunnen krijgen, gaan twee broertjes uit Oekraïne adopteren. Mijn vriendin vroeg laatst: 'Heb je nog een advies voor me, voor als ik straks ineens twee kinderen heb?' Nu is mijn vriendin een van de meest praktische en georganiseerde vrouwen die ik ken. Ze heeft haar leven perfect op orde. Ze vergeet geen enkele verjaardag, zegt tegen iedereen op het juiste moment precies de juiste dingen, ziet er altijd gewoon uit, sport vijf keer per week, kookt zeven dagen per week gezond, weet alles in huis te vinden, en verspilt ook nog eens geen geld.

'Dat het allemaal niet perfect hoeft te gaan straks,' zei ik. 'Het geeft niet als je huis een chaos is, als je 's avonds een pizza in de oven doet. Het geeft niet als je kinderen raar gekleed gaan. Een kind is veel gelukkiger met een ontspannen moeder, dan met eentje die de hele tijd bezig is haar ambitieuze programma uit te voeren.'

Later dacht ik: dat is precies het tegenovergestelde van wat ik zelf doe. Ik ben altijd bezig mijn programma uit te voeren. Als ik op zaterdagochtend wakker word, heb ik al een hele lijst in mijn hoofd met dingen die er moeten gebeuren. Boodschappen doen, cadeautjes kopen voor verjaardagen, kinderen naar de kapper, kinderen nieuwe schoenen, boeken terugbrengen naar de bibliotheek, zwemles, borrel bij de buren. En dan is zondag voor familiebezoek, klussen in huis, afspraken met vrienden, werk. Laatst zei mijn vriend: 'Er is nooit ruimte voor iets spontaans.' Ik was het hartgrondig met hem eens. Alleen: wat te schrappen?

Live life to the max
Wat cultuursociologen opmerken is dat er een generatie van 'maximaliseerders' is ontstaan: mensen die zo veel mogelijk uit hun leven en tijd willen halen. Kinderen, een uitdagende baan, interessante reizen, een boeiend cultureel leven, een omvangrijk sociaal netwerk; ze willen alles. Misschien komt het doordat er voor vrouwen tegenwoordig nog maar zo weinig beperkingen zijn om het leven in te richten zoals ze zelf willen; bijna alles kunnen we zelf bepalen. Dat geldt ze->

De genoegnemers
'Perfectionisme is niet mijn struikelblok, ik probeer bewust geen superwoman te zijn. Maar het kost me wel moeite om alle dingen die ik wil doen een plek te geven naast elkaar. Ik heb er bewust voor gekozen om me op drie gebieden te concentreren: werk, gezin en spiritualiteit. Mijn werk is altijd belangrijk voor me geweest en er moet ook brood op de plank komen. Daarnaast wil ik graag een goede moeder zijn. En mijn man en ik maken onderdeel uit van een meditatiegroep die wekelijks met de kinderen bijeenkomt. Dat vind ik even genoeg.
Ik dacht: ik zal halfhalf gaan doen, maar dat vind ik niet leuk. Ik ga niet meer tot diep in de nacht uit, sport past even niet meer in mijn leven, ik heb mijn naaicursus niet vervolgd, en mijn danscursussen uitgesteld. Omdat ik mijn aandacht niet over al die vlakken hoef te verspreiden, heb ik meer diepgang dan ik vroeger had.'
Peggy Saman (34), loopbaancoach voor vrouwen

tekst: **Annemiek Leclaire** | fotografie: **Manon van der Zwaal**

76

INA **SALTZ**

CARIN **GOLDBERG**

VINCE **FROST**

GREAT PUBLICATIONS ARE NOT DEMOCRACIES

The very best publications start with the very strongest of ideas. This perspective usually emanates from the office of the founder or editor. "A magazine has to have a strong editorial voice," says Ina Saltz. "It's not a democratic process. The mission needs to be strongly defined, and everyone on staff needs to contribute to that mission and that voice." Because there are so many, sometimes competing, elements that need to go into a magazine—advertising, templates, editorial, features, illustration, photography, and more—it's important for designers to eschew anything that might dilute this core vision. "The best scenario for any project is to cut out the middlemen and decision making by committee," notes Carin Goldberg. "Get to the person whose vision is on par with yours. A magazine is like making a baby, and it's always best for the family to be like-minded and collaborative."

As a designer, working with editors in this way should be exhilarating and edifying. "The experience of working with editors has taught me so much about design and about communicating," says Vince Frost, who feels that he learns the most when he's pushed the most. "I love it when an editor comes to you and says, 'I want three stories on this page,' and you just want to put one big picture there. Yes, he's making my life difficult, but actually that's fun. He knows something I don't. He knows there's a reason for connecting these three stories, so I say, 'Let's make it work.' It's exciting."

"Stoner caught the best moments in a surfer's life."
—Art Brewer

Matt Warshaw is the former editor of *Surfer* magazine and has been writing about surfing since 1984. He is the author of *Surf Movie Tonite!* (Chronicle Books) and *The Encyclopedia of Surfing*. He lives in San Francisco.

Jeff Divine is the photo editor of *Surfer's Journal* and held the same position at *Surfer* magazine for more than twenty years. He lives in San Clemente, California.

Published in association with **surfer magazine**

Jacket design by Brett MacFadden

Manufactured in China

www.chroniclebooks.com

Photo/Stoner collects the work of one of surfing's most legendary photographers. In the book, images are grouped in a way that brings attention to the elegance of the design as well as the artfulness of the photographs.

77 CONSULT WITH THE SALES AND MARKETING STAFF

BRETT **MACFADDEN**

Sales and marketing staff are important resources who can bring critical perspective to the design process. "Sometimes sales and marketing people bring really concrete information that's great to have," Brett MacFadden notes, such as facts and statistics on sales, demographics, buying patterns, and more. He offers an example: "I had a New Age book on tips for living longer. We had designed it with a steel blue palette that we thought was cool and relaxing. Sales and marketing looked at it and said the cover needed to be red. The author was a Chinese doctor, so the cover needed to be Chinese red. Designers would avoid this solution because it seems obvious or trite, but when people are out there buying, they don't analyze things the way we do; they go for what seems right, and sales people are great at seeing the clear direction. There are times that we fight back; we feel it's not the right direction, or we think there's an untapped market because sales often sees the existing, not potential, market. In this case, the Chinese red was the right direction, as the book did extremely well." While the obvious solution may not always seem the right approach to an aesthetically astute designer, designers need to recognize that their taste does not always reflect that of the buying public, and that the buying public keeps them in business.

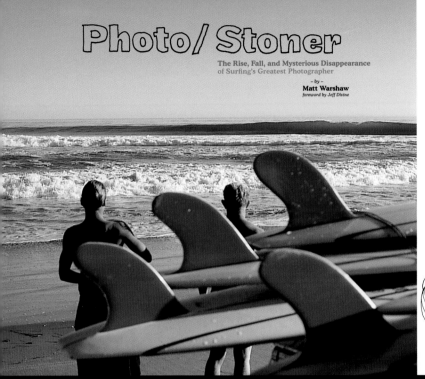

Photo/Stoner

The Rise, Fall, and Mysterious Disappearance
of Surfing's Greatest Photographer

– by –
Matt Warshaw
foreword by *Jeff Divine*

In 1965, Ron Stoner was the best surf photographer in the business. He captured the balmy beaches, bikini-clad girls, and achingly beautiful waves of Southern California in the full Technicolor they deserved.

When Stoner set up his Century 1000mm lens beachside to shoot, all the hot locals would paddle out to show off their moves. Stoner turned these local guys into heroes in the pages of *Surfer* magazine: Bill Andrews and Dickie Moon shot from the cliff at Black's Beach; style master Bill Hamilton cutting back at Swami's; Mike Hynson trimming out at Hollister Ranch.

Then, at the zenith of his career, Stoner stumbled off this sunny stage into drug use and mental illness. He was barely working by 1970. By 1977 he was declared missing. In 1991 he was declared dead. His photos disappeared into the *Surfer* archives, where they gathered dust for decades until surf historian Matt Warshaw and photo editor Jeff Divine tracked down all the negatives they could find and handpicked the best of the lot—many of which haven't been seen since the '60s.

In *Photo/Stoner*, Stoner's strange, dark story is recounted alongside his best and rarest images—photographs that capture an innocent Southern California where there were always plenty of waves, offshore winds, and time to surf. In word and in image, *Photo/Stoner* is a poignant ode to a lost era, and a lost man.

PHOTO / STONER

The Rise, Fall, and Mysterious Disappearance
of Surfing's Greatest Photographer

by
Matt Warshaw
foreword by *Jeff Divine*

CHRONICLE BOOKS
San Francisco

78

CREATE OPPORTUNITIES FOR COLLABORATION AND "CHANCE CREATION"

MICHAEL **RAY**

MARTHA **RICH**

Publications are group efforts, and the more a designer can contribute to creating an environment that enhances teamwork, the better the publication will be. When famed movie director Francis Ford Coppola started *Zoetrope*, according to Michael Ray, "He wanted to mimic the collaborative aspects of filmmaking. The cinematographer, director, actors, producers—all of these people are contributing to one thing. He likes the idea of chance creation." In *Zoetrope*, using artists who are not necessarily graphic designers to develop each issue independent of every other certainly ups the opportunity for unexpected bursts of creativity. "We select the stories and send them off to an artist, preferably someone who has never designed a publication before," says Ray. "Sometimes the artist reacts to the text, sometimes not. When he or she returns the design, it's necessarily out of our control."

For more conventional magazines, designers have the opportunity to create chance collaboration by working with illustrators. As Los Angeles illustrator Martha Rich says, "The more freedom I have, the better. If you have an art director who is nitpicking, it squashes your creativity." She encourages art directors and designers to remember that they're working with an illustrator's ideas, not just their product. "When you hire an illustrator, you're hiring them for their mind," she says. "The best thing for me is to work as a team where they know my strengths and they're using my mind in tandem with their minds to get a great result."

Unidentified surfers. (Opposite) Lower Carson, Rincon—
a *Surfer* cover shot from mid-1967. Stoner's photo was actually
shot in the late morning and is green-blue; *Surfer* publisher
John Severson "sandwiched" the photo of Carson with his
own image of a setting sun.

(Pages 98–99) Rinck's Beach. (Pages 100–101) Most of
Stoner's color slides are about forty years old, and those that
were stored improperly are now faded or discolored—
but eye-catching in their own right.

Photo/Stoner, designed by Brett MacFadden

Stoner's ad work: a 1962 photo for Jacobs Surfboards. (opposite) outtakes from Sherry Haley's Leopard Spots boutique ads.

Photo/Stoner, designed by Brett MacFadden

79

DAVID **ALBERTSON**

WHEN WORKING ON A LAUNCH, DON'T FORGET ABOUT THE AUDIENCE OF INVESTORS

"Prototype work typically focuses on the proof of concept," explains David Albertson. "And that often means you need to convince people with money that it's worth investing in this idea, getting the machine going, getting this brand off the ground. You need to convince people to make a long-term commitment to this venture." Design is central to helping investors see not just what a new publication is, but what it could be. "The prototypical work is very gestural," according to Albertson, "and you work hard on making sure the tone and overall sense has

jelled, and that it's hitting a sweet spot people can recognize. You're trying to pretend that it exists, that it's all ready and is a foregone conclusion, so they can see it's real and has legs to it." As challenging as this phase is, the even more difficult work is next to come. "Once you get into a launch, then it becomes, 'How do you fit everything in here and fulfill that gestural promise?' You're trying to match the reality to the dream, and your job becomes a lot harder."

80

DAVID **ALBERTSON**

ENGAGE WITH THE "THIRD DIMENSION"

Publications, even more so than other graphic design projects, involve bringing together different people, agendas, deadlines, and objectives, some of which may be working at cross-purposes. While graphic designers may know plenty about how to make things look good on a page, a publication designer has to juggle a lot more than fonts and pretty pictures. "A lot of graphic designers learn all about combining type and imagery, about using positive and negative space," notes David Albertson, "but I think that they learn less about—and it's harder to learn about—engaging in this third dimension, which is bringing together all of the components and layers and deadlines."

The "third dimension" involves artfully and gracefully keeping the publication world's equivalent of chainsaws, tennis balls, and flaming torches in the design air at one time. Albertson explains: "It's when you have a large photo and a headline and a sidebar and small photos and captions and a slug and a writer and an illustration or diagram and they're all coming from different places. You may have a creative idea about how to package the thing that you're trying to achieve, but you then have to do the job of making the page well organized and inviting, on deadline. You get squished between a writer who blew their deadline, the photographer who's late, the prepress people who need files, the pressmen waiting to go." Ultimately, it is precisely the multidimensionality of this challenge that makes the final accomplishment of the printed piece such a sweet satisfaction once it's complete.

LUXURIOUS CHOCOLATE · TENDER SHORT RIBS · SUBLIME FRENCH TOAST

CHOW
FOOD. DRINK. FUN.

Special Holiday Survival Issue

Step-by-Step Turkey Feast

Best New Year's Party Ever (the food, the bubbly, the music!)

PLUS

How to:
• Cheat with takeout
• Get better airplane food
• Bring the right wine
• Make the best eggnog
• Eat lucky

74 cool gifts

Great illegal cheese

12 must-haves for instant entertaining

PREMIERE ISSUE
Holiday 2004

Left and opposite: *Chow*, designed by Albertson Design, is "an alternative food magazine for an info-hungry audience, serving up recipes, restaurants, fast food, and travel in a bold and colorful way with a dash of attitude," according to Albertson.

81

JESSICA **FLEISCHMANN**

ARJEN **NOORDEMAN**

LOOK FOR THE VALUES OF THE CONTENT PROVIDERS

When casting about for a design approach, many publication designers express their respect and admiration for the creative work they're showcasing by amplifying the original artist's vision. "I try to look at the values of the content providers," Jessica Fleischmann explains. "I try to determine if they are interested in creating a private or a public space and then ask myself how this page and structure can serve as an intimate space or be more outward looking. So there is a reflection of, or a conversation with, the work being represented in the design. I aim to support and dialog with rather than comment on the vision."

This respect for the raw material at hand is especially important when dealing with the work of other artists. Arjen Noordeman designed many art books and catalogs while design director at a modern art museum. "When I was at Mass MoCA," he notes, "the work was about the craft of design and referencing the art itself in the design. Sometimes it worked, but sometimes artists didn't appreciate the graphic design, and they just wanted their work to show; they don't want design to interfere with their work. It's like photographers hate graphic designers who put text over their images." The solution in these, and many other cases, is not to defer to content but to enhance it. "We started to realize that we should not reference the artwork in our design but just create a structure that puts the art on a pedestal."

Summer Drinks

sip summer sweetly

Iced tea and lemonade, those brilliant summer staples, get a kick from a mix master

You know, of course, that there's no tea in Long Island Iced Tea. Vodka, yes. Tequila, rum, gin, triple sec—yes. But wouldn't it be lovely to have a cool summer iced tea that also packed a bit of kick? We asked a great bartender, Nick Mautone, author of *Raising the Bar: Better Drinks, Better Entertaining* (Artisan), to concoct some refreshing summer drinks using the real things. Iced tea and lemonade. He came up with some beauties.

Dark, Rich, and Beautiful

What is top quality and relatively inexpensive—and induces euphoria, energy, lust, and joy? Here's our guide to great chocolate, the gift no one ever returns

BY MATT PALMQUIST PHOTO BY ASTERISM

What's New

Like Scotch, olive oil, and wine before it, chocolate is appearing now not as a blend (the way it's been since the Industrial Revolution) but as a varietal, the product of a single variety of bean. You'll see one of three main cacao species: criollo (delicate but widely considered the most delicious), forastero (a hardy crop that dominates world production), and trinitario (a blend of the two).

Why varietals? Differences and nuances in flavors are easier to detect—though harder to describe, which gives way to language familiar to wine lovers, with "high notes" and "bouquets" and "hints of" unlikely flavors (like raspberries or rum. In general, chocolate is judged by how it smells, snaps (breaks), tastes, finishes (the duration of chocolate taste on the tongue), and melts in your mouth.

"Single origin" Chocolate is made from beans from one place, like Madagascar (light, no bitter aftertaste), Ecuador (spicy, less acid), Colombia (fruity), Venezuela (robust, bitter, complex). Be warned, however: there are no standards on the use of place-names in chocolate. An unscrupulous maker can get away with saying anything.

Racy New Bonbons

Confections, to purists, aren't chocolate. Confections are candy, but good confections create mind-bending experiences on their own: the first cool, subtle melt on your tongue; the snap of the chocolate; the explosion of flavor, which can be astonishing now that confectioners are inventing in ingredients such as Gorgonzola, saffron, cardamom, lemon grass, and chipotle.

How It's Made

After hand picking, roasting, and shelling the beans and crushing the nibs into chocolate liquor, the liquor is pressed, leaving a liquid cocoa butter) and a solid (cocoa powder). For dark chocolate, the liquor is combined with extra cocoa butter (which keeps it solid) and sugar. The paste is then conched—kneaded to smooth out the texture and flavor. The Swiss and Germans knead the chocolate longer than the Americans and English, which makes their products smoother (though not necessarily better). Tempering—warming and cooling to emulsify the fat and to make it shiny—is frequently done by the chocolatier.

The Bliss Molecule

Chocolate contains hundreds of chemicals, and so many of them induce pleasure that it's amazing the FDA hasn't tried to regulate it. Caffeine, theobromine, and phenylethylamine are all stimulants that energize. Tryptophan and serotonin produce euphoric effects. And anandamide (a.k.a. the "bliss molecule") acts a little like marijuana's THC—though it is present in such small quantities you'd likely keel over from the nausea of overindulgence before you'd feel even remotely high.

The Aztecs thought chocolate was an aphrodisiac. Nobody's been able to prove that's true, but the mix of energy and euphoria is a pretty strong combination. Maybe the most surprising component of chocolate are its antioxidants—the molecules that combat the free radicals that damage cells. The U.S. Department of Agriculture measures the antioxidant capacity of dark chocolate as more than five times that of blueberries.

A magazine about serious topics, the *Journal of Aesthetics and Protest*, designed by Jessica Fleischmann, works both aesthetics and protest into type treatments by taking a simple font and using it in a totally unexpected way.

82 GET THE RIGHT PERSON FOR THE JOB

NICKI **KALISH**

ANITA **KUNZ**

When working with photographers and illustrators, it's important to embrace their personal skills and style without trying to force a different aesthetic on them. "I think the most important thing is to use the right person for the job," says Nicki Kalish. "I try to match the assignment to the person. Who lives on Cape Cod, or has a certain kind of sensibility, or understands that something has to be cooked a certain way, or that something else has to be funny? I want to start off with the right person." Toronto illustrator Anita Kunz points out that a little bit of legwork will lead an art director to the right illustrator. "If they look through my work, they'll know what they're going to get," she says. But she also feels that responsibility for making the right match lies as much with the illustrator as the art director. "It's all about respect," she says. "I know I'm good at some things and not so good at other things." She's also knows there are times when the best option is to turn an assignment down or pass

it on to someone else. "Sometimes I don't think I'm right for the job, but I can think of one or two artists who would be better for the assignment," she says.

Then there are those stories that call for an illustrator with a very specific set of artistic skills and life experiences. "There was a cover about people who drink too much in restaurants," recalls Kalish. "It was kind of funny because it was about when people go out to very expensive restaurants; they're out to celebrate and they often behave in ways restaurateurs find very trying. We were trying to figure out how to do that cover, and we had an idea of photographing a maître d' at a restaurant with a fountain in the center. But if you saw that image, you wouldn't know it was about people drinking too much; you might think it was about the restaurant or the maître d'. I really thought it needed to be an illustration, and I wanted to call an artist who likes to drink so they would get it," Kalish says, laughing.

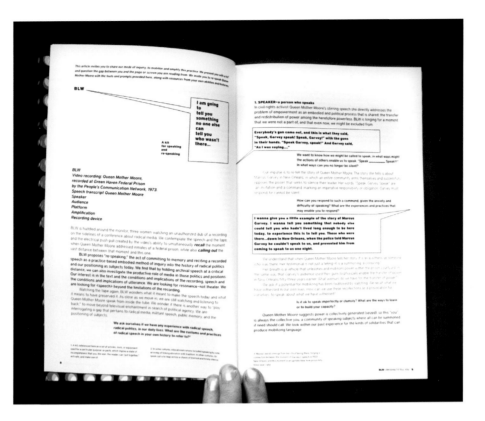

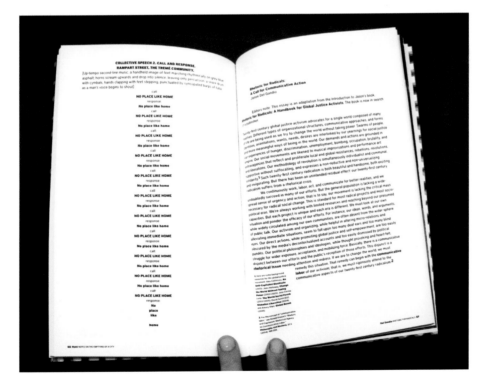

The *Journal of Aesthetics and Protest*, designed by Jessica Fleischmann

83

NICKI **KALISH**

JESSICA
FLEISCHMANN

BE CAUTIOUS WITH ADJECTIVES

One of the challenges when working with illustrators, photographers, artists, curators, and editors is trying to describe an image or approach that exists only as a fuzzy concept. Even the most specific word or phrase can be easily misunderstood or evoke contradictory images. "I think communicating is really important," says Nicki Kalish. "But I've learned that two people can use the same words and have very different pictures in their minds. So it helps to be very explicit if you want something done in a particular way."

Jessica Fleischmann suggests asking for visual references to back up a verbal description. "I ask them for other works or pieces that they think are relevant. And then I ask them what they like or don't like about it," she advises.

"It's good to know their aesthetic preferences, not because I'm going to mimic them but because it helps me know exactly what they mean. When we use subjective terms, they can sometimes be misinterpreted, so seeing a reference helps me qualify and quantify those subjective words. For example, they may say that they like something interpretive, but then they show me something clean and modern. Or if they say they like bold typography, well, there's such a range in that description." Plus, getting a very clear idea of where your collaborators stand helps the designer know how far they can move the project. "It helps me know what level of graphic sophistication they have," Fleischmann notes, "so I know how far I can push it."

84

NICKI **KALISH**

KEEP IT INTERESTING FOR YOURSELF

Many publications deal with the same topics over and over. There's the fall issue on foliage or fashion. There's the election roundup or the annual college rankings. As a designer, to keep it interesting for the readers, you have to keep it interesting for yourself. "This is why I try to have variety," says Nicki Kalish, thinking about a previous effort to design a cover about what to do with the year's end-of-season crop of tomatoes, among other repeat subjects. "I talk a lot with editors and photographers so I don't keep getting the same images over and over. It's especially helpful to have an editor who is visual so when you say something like you want to look at a bag of chips from inside, they understand—or simply have faith because what you've done in the past has worked."

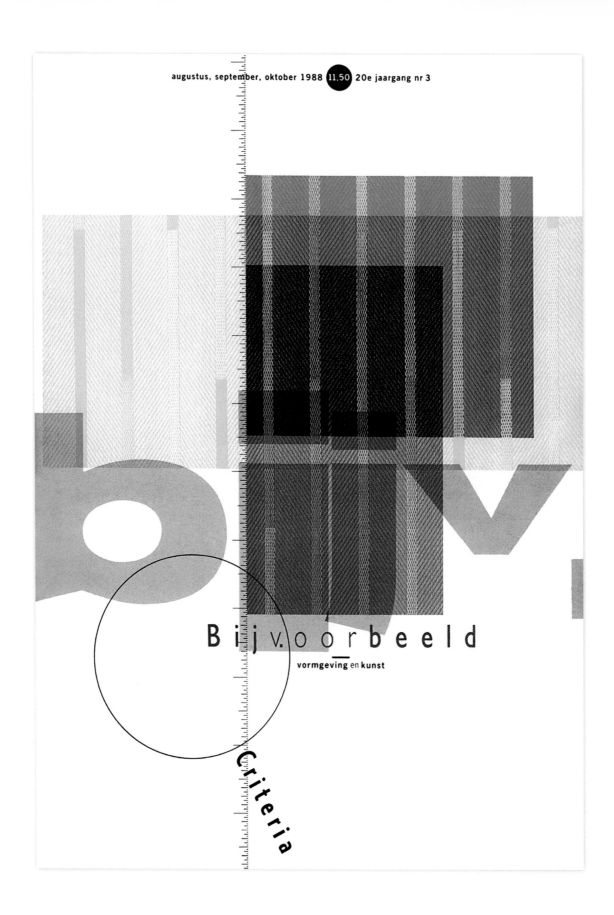

augustus, september, oktober 1988 11,50 20e jaargang nr 3

Bijv.oorbeeld
vormgeving en kunst

Criteria

85

ARJEN **NOORDEMAN**

CREATE YOUR OWN BUILDING BLOCKS

While all this emphasis on deferring to provided content and simplifying type and letting illustrators go can lead designers to despair that their job is simply to provide an artful soapbox for other people's creative output, there are many ways they can make their presence on the page known. "I try to create all my own building blocks," says Arjen Noordeman. "So instead of making wild compositions or intense color juxtapositions that get in the way, I would create my own patterns, fonts, and other graphical devices. Through these things, I would create a design that would not overpower the message, but my voice is being heard because I'm creating the building blocks."

86

ROBERTO **DE VICQ**

BE SEDUCTIVE

While there are standard, intellectual, objective ways to evaluate the success of a design—is it balanced, does it communicate clearly, does it provide clues to the reader for navigating the piece?—design is an artistic as well as commercial enterprise and as such, has the power to reach for so much more than mere competency. Design can and should use the tools of its trade to entice and entrance everyone along the continuum of concept to final printed piece.

"You still have to seduce the art director; seduce the editor; seduce the publisher, the author, and the sales force; and sometimes the agent," says New York city designer Roberto de Vicq about the craft of book design. If you have all these people clamoring for your work, the reading public will not be far behind.

Left: *Bijvoorbeeld*, a magazine on art and design, "shows all types of solutions and surprises based on the same grid," notes Vermaas. While the redesign "revived the magazine," he concedes that "many people were excited by the design, and some were upset by it."

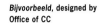

Bijvoorbeeld, designed by Office of CC

87

EDEL **RODRIGUEZ**

LEAVE SOMETHING OUT

There is power in empty spaces, in what is left unsaid, unknown, unsigned. "Sometimes editors don't trust the viewer or reader enough and they want to hand it to them really literally," says New York City illustrator Edel Rodriguez. "But I think readers want to be surprised and want to see some interesting visuals." Rodriguez entices his audience and creates the element of the unexpected by intentionally leaving a little to the imagination.

"I want the illustration to be a bit of a tease and get them to read the story. What's the purpose of telling the whole story with one image? You make the illustration lead into the story but not be the whole story. I try to leave something to be filled in by the reader."

Willie 92.5 radio logo design, designed by Eric Hines, Honest Bros.

88

ERIC **HINES**

"YEAH, I KNOW A GUY . . ."

"It's important to find a printer that has a good reputation and solid resources. The best way to figure out the best person to work with is to talk to other creatives. When you're sure the printer provides great service, then use them consistently."

No matter how great your design, if the printing doesn't bring it to life, all your creative brilliance is for naught. The best way to ensure the final product is as good as you imagined is to develop a professional partnership with a printer who cares about your work as much as you do. Not only will a good printer execute your vision properly but he or she can offer endless advice on how to get more for your client's money and make your ideas better with various onpress tricks and techniques. Quality printing is a fascinating blend of Old World craft and high-tech equipment, and good printers are skilled professionals. Treat them that way and your work will be better for it and your clients will thank you for it.

What makes a good printer good? Here are a few things you should look for in a printer:

• Constant communication—You're not just a project number to them.

• Attention to the details of your project—Looking out for issues and covering your back before there's a problem

• Making suggestions that will pass savings, ideas, or unique solutions down to your client

• A willingness to sit down with you before the project starts to offer some print techniques and ideas—Not just grabbing your print ready project and running with it.

• Do they bring you snacks and treats when they visit?

89

CALVIN **LEE**

WORKING WITH A PRINT REP

"There is really no special trick to working with a printer's representative. Just let your print vendor know what you want done. Most of the time, printers are happy to go over all the options with you. Some are great with suggestions and will try to save you money by going over opportunities such as work-and-turn, gang runs, and special finishes. They will also let you know about any problems with your files and work with you to resolve these problems."

While a print representative's job is technically just to collect the project parts and deliver the goods at the end of the process, the best ones will take their job to another level of service and go above and beyond the call of duty to partner with you in creating the best possible solutions. Many experienced print representatives are full of good information that they'd love to share with you. In fact, they're probably secretly hoping you'll ask questions and engage them in conversation about your project so they can show off. So let your print rep know up-front what you are looking for or what projects might be coming down the pike. This information can set the rep's wheels in motion and may uncover a whole host of interesting and unexpected solutions. And of course, if you treat them well and keep giving them work, you may earn yourself not just trust but an occasional discount, special deal, or referral.

Emtek Products, Inc. business stationery design, designed by Calvin Lee, Mayhem Studios

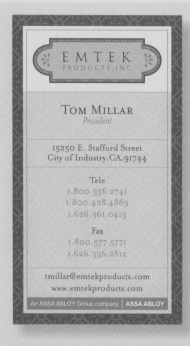

TOM MILLAR
President

15250 E. Stafford Street
City of Industry.CA.91744

Tele
1.800.356.2741
1.800.428.4889
1.626.961.0413

Fax
1.800.577.5771
1.626.336.2812

tmillar@emtekproducts.com
www.emtekproducts.com

An ASSA ABLOY Group company | **ASSA ABLOY**

15250 E. Stafford Street
City of Industry,CA 91744

15250 E. Stafford Street
City of Industry . CA . 91744

Tele:
1.800.356.2741 • 1.800.428.4889 • 1.626.961.0413

Fax:
1.800.577.5771 • 1.626.336.2812

www.emtekproducts.com

An ASSA ABLOY Group company | **ASSA ABLOY**

Joe D'Amico CD package design by Keith Bowman,
The Design Bureau of Amerika

90

KEITH **BOWMAN**

TRIAL AND, HOPEFULLY, VERY LITTLE ERROR

"Try out several printers, and don't just settle on the first printer you use. No one printer can supply every service you may need. Small shops may give better service and prices on small jobs but may be out of their league when it comes to bigger runs. Larger printers may have all the new gadgets and technologies but won't be able to print that two-color label cost effectively. It's worth your while to take the time to schedule tours of printers you're considering working with. Seeing what they've got, checking out the shop and equipment, and meeting and greeting staff can all be a huge benefit once you've got a real job in hand. And even if you think you know which printer is the best for a job, it's not a bad idea to get multiple quotes to compare and contrast not just the price but the service offered.

In time, you will find a printer that you feel comfortable with for the projects that most commonly come through your studio. Be loyal to that printer because there will come a time you will find yourself in a printing jam and the time you spent developing that relationship will pay off. I've also found that tipping printers with a couple of cases of their favorite beer is not a bad idea."

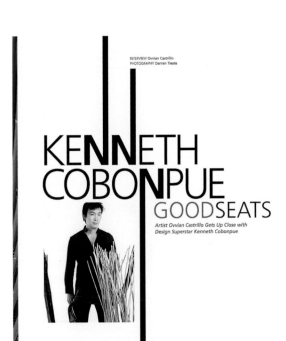

INTERVIEW Ovvian Castrillo
PHOTOGRAPHY Darren Tieste

KENNETH COBONPUE
GOODSEATS

Artist Ovvian Castrillo Gets Up Close with Design Superstar Kenneth Cobonpue

I take **KENNETH COBONPUE** from the pedestal he's been put on, and bring him close to where I can almost touch him. The man and his work are legendary—sometimes one preceding the other.

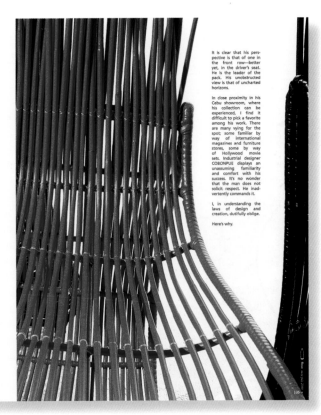

It is clear that his perspective is that of one in the front row—better yet, in the driver's seat. He is the leader of the pack. His unobstructed view is that of uncharted horizons.

In close proximity in his Cebu showroom, where his collection can be experienced, I find it difficult to pick a favorite among his work. There are many vying for the spot; some familiar by way of international magazines and furniture stores, some by way of Hollywood movie sets. Industrial designer COBONPUE displays an unassuming familiarity and comfort with his success. It's no wonder that the man does not solicit respect. He inadvertently commands it.

I, in understanding the laws of design and creation, dutifully oblige.

Here's why.

FLOW. While Cebu has always been on the map in terms of design and craftsmanship, yours has apparently become its most recognizable name. What does that mean to you and your work?

It's become a challenge for me to try to break out of the mold in which *Filipino Design* has put itself into in the world. On the global front, people know if it is *Filipino Design* by the use of natural materials and the high level of craftsmanship that is synonymous with it. I try not to use the same materials over and over again and I try to experiment in different things a lot. In doing so, I think I try to always redefine what *Filipino Design* is.

FLOW. I know you grew up in a manufacturing environment. Were you encouraged to take the design route? What early manifestations were there that 'this' was the way for you?

I've always loved playing with things as a child and I was never happy to take things out from a package. I've always had to do something to whatever it was. Early on, my mother had a furniture factory, which was literally in our backyard and I grew up with the carpenters, the workmen and craftsmen who would work all day. I would be playing with them, learning how to make things…

Design was a very natural thing for me to take up, especially since my mother was a very accomplished designer in her own right and I learned the value of design early on.

She was a designer first, and a manufacturer second.

FLOW. Coming from a privileged background and having obvious talent have contributed to your opportunities. Do you think having one and not the other would have brought you to where you are today?

It would have a brought me to where I am today, but probably not as fast.

I teach at UP (University of the Philippines) Visayas, UP Cebu…in the Industrial Design program and I meet a lot of kids who have talent but who probably don't have the resources to back it up. I know that if they worked hard, if they strive to make a difference, I am sure they will.

FLOW. In a large world like ours – where human beings are thinking simultaneously for universal needs, when do you think does one organically create something original?

People have at one time or another said that everything has been done, that everything has been designed. To a certain extent that is true. It is very difficult to define what 'originality' is. I've worked with a lot of designers both famous and unknown, and many years after (our encounters) they come up with designs that look similar to mine. I think it's very difficult to try to process its origins. I think design comes from your self, conscious and unconscious. It's very difficult to process, to recollect where that shape comes from or the idea comes from. I think the important thing is the intent.

I always say, "If someone must do something similar to mine, it should be better at least."

Flow magazine "Good Seats" article, page layout design, designed by Lizza Gutierrez, Lizza's Room

91

LIZZA **GUTIERREZ**

MEET, GREET, GET TO KNOW ONE ANOTHER

"Before a project goes on press, have a joint prepress meeting with client and vendor. During this meeting, discuss expectations and determine each party's responsibilities. Having a prepress meeting not only helps make the production run smoothly, it also enhances the symbiotic relationship between all parties."

Sometimes it seems that clients and printers are at opposite ends of the needs/wants spectrum. Clients want fast results that will flood their businesses with adoring customers. Vendors want plenty of money and time to produce the work. Each party sometimes forgets that they both want to create spectacular results, as great work serves both their businesses. This is where the designer comes in. You're not only designing that work but you can also help the two parties see how similar their goals really are. Showing your client where their work is being produced and all of the integral details that go into turning out the best possible end product educates them and helps them have more understanding of the process. The vendor gets the benefit of meeting the actual user of the printed materials and can respond directly to questions and explain why some client requests are, in fact, unreasonable.

92

STEVE **GORDON, JR**

DON'T BE PUT OFF BY ONLINE

"There is a common perception that online printers are not very reliable and their quality can't be very good. After all, you're printing remotely and have no say in the final output. While some of those points may be valid, consider these other points as well.

Online print vendors have become better in their offerings and quality of results. Better digital proofing means they are leaps and bounds ahead of where they were just a few years ago. Customer service has also improved, as many online print resources have grown into full-fledged creative solutions and are now staffed with a higher level of print professional.

Because these printers handle more volume—they gang-up your print runs with others and basically never turn off their machines—their turn-around time and prices are usually pretty good. As business has grown, so have their product offerings. It's now easy to find an online vendor that can get you anything from text-weight paper and pocket folders to digital media printing. Some will even blind-ship to clients, which means they make it look like the final product came directly from you.

While you may get some color shifting with online vendors—which drives us all a little nuts—let's be honest and realize that some clients will never notice. And if they're super tight on budgets, the trade off may make your clients very happy. If you set up your files according to prearranged templates, learn how to work the online proofing system, and build in time for the off chance that something may need to be run again, online printing can be an effective route for producing your creative."

Atomic Skis "Thug" artwork, designed by Derek Armstrong McNeill, Grill Creative

93

DEREK **ARMSTRONG MCNEILL**

THE GOLDEN RULE REALLY IS GOLDEN

"This one is so simple: Treat your vendors like you want your clients to treat you—like a peer, not a servant. Be good to your vendors and they'll remember you're a good guy when you really need them to help out in a pinch.

"Always remember that a professional vendor is always trying to give their clients the best possible products and services, just like you. And also remember that many of the complaints that you have about your clients, your vendors and reps have about you. Your clients ask you for tight turn-around time, they don't honor their deadlines, sometimes have bad attitudes, and always demand that you produce better quality for less money, and these are the same things you ask of your vendors. Remember that your vendors are part of your professional network and should be treated as professionals. Give what you want to get."

Here are a few of the primary pet peeves printers have about designers and how you can avoid adding to their aggravation:

- Add proper bleeds, crops, and other print production needs in the original files.

- Image resolution should be initially set and maintained according to final output needs.

- Resizing images above 25 percent of the original will cause rapid deterioration of image quality.

- Realize that specified papers and materials will often alter designs, colors, and final output.

- Do press checks to avoid final output surprises.

MY GARAGE HAS SPACE

My Garage Has Space logo design, designed by Christine Godlewski, Genius Creative

94

CHRISTINE **GODLEWSKI**

ONCE YOU FIND THE RIGHT RELATIONSHIP, STICK WITH IT

"Once you've found a few vendors you like working with, keep working with them. If they know that they are part of your team and will get regular work without always bidding things out, you will have a better relationship and better end products."

It's true in any relationship that the time-consuming part is in the initial getting-to-know-you phase. But it's worth putting the time in up front because it makes things function more smoothly down the road. There are some designers who think they need to keep vendors on their toes by always making them work for the work, always sending things out to bid, trying to get vendors to compete with one another. But this just creates bad blood. By offering a trusted vendor an ongoing flow of work, you develop a partnership that pays dividends down the road. Maybe they'll bump someone's project back to help you out in a bind. Maybe they'll pass on some savings on a certain paper stock. Maybe they'll just take a little extra care on your projects. No matter how great your creative is, when all is said and done, people want to work with the nice guy first and last and for as long as possible.

95

STEVE **GORDON, JR**

SAVE A TREE—PRINT ON SOMETHING ELSE

"When we think of printers, we usually also think of paper or maybe the occasional apparel item. But there are many vendors that specialize in printing and producing promotional marketing goods. While many see this type of vendor as producing nothing more than trinkets, their offerings have grown to include a surprising range. Sure there are the typical things such as pens, T-shirts, and key chains. But now you're just as likely to find custom-printed briefcases, sunglasses, banners, and even camping tents. You can print, embroider, etch, or apply vinyl to almost anything. Clients will appreciate your ability to think outside the box and provide a unique set of products featuring this logo."

VNDK8 Freestyle Equipment Co. "Kiss Me Deadly" apparel artwork, designed by Steve Gordon, Jr, RDQLUS

Chapter Five:

WORKING WITH OTHER CREATIVES

Jürgen Teller books, designed by
Miles Murray Sorrell FUEL

Märchenstüberl **JUERGEN TELLER**

96

**MILES MURRAY
SORRELL FUEL**

THE SECRET OF A SUCCESSFUL PARTNERSHIP IS TO NEVER COMPROMISE

The designers at FUEL have a strong working relationship. "Good ideas are formed without compromise," comments Damon Murray. "Equally good work is made easier if it is produced with like-minded creatives, such as the photographer Jürgen Teller. With him there is an element of trust and mutual respect. The best work is made by and for people who are not prepared to compromise."

Initially the team had asked Jürgen Teller to shoot a portrait of themselves in their studio for one of their magazines, *Grey*. The relationship grew when Teller asked FUEL to design an exhibition of his work at his house. FUEL then went on to design his show at the Photographers' Gallery in London and from that project other exhibitions across Europe and in New York. Throughout this period, FUEL also designed books and catalogs to accompany Teller's personal work.

For FUEL, never compromising means making choices early in the creative process, which assures that all participants are in agreement in terms of the parameters of the project. Although "like-minded" is a vague descriptor, when finding creative partners, FUEL insists they know it when they see it.

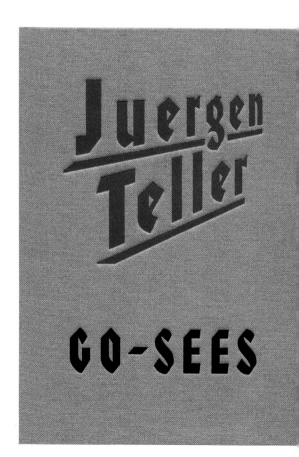

97

STEFAN **SAGMEISTER**

COLLABORATE WITH SOMEONE IN A DIFFERENT FIELD

Stefan Sagmeister co-directed a Lou Reed music video with Robert Peijo, a documentary filmmaker. Before working on this project, Sagmeister had no experience with moving pictures whatsoever. Because of his inexperience, he asked his friend for help—Peijo had much more experience with being on the set, directing a crew properly, and with postproduction. Sagmeister had worked directly with Reed before, designing the CD art for the 2001 release, *Ecstasy*, so he was comfortable with ensuring that the concepts that he suggested were clear with Lou and with the record label.

Sagmeister has gained new knowledge in the field of video design and production, an experience that will help him explore new technologies of the Internet, as well as open up imaginative processes that suggest new ways of doing design.

Lou Reed video, designed and directed by Stefan Sagmeister and Robert Peijo

98

COLLABORATE WITH SOMEONE WHOSE SKILLS COMPLEMENT YOUR OWN

ART **CHANTRY**

Jamie Sheehan's skills complement Art Chantry's in a dramatic way. Sheehan is adept at computer technology, whereas Chantry is self-admittedly not, instead taking a sociocultural approach to their usefulness. "Computers," says Chantry, "especially in their early days, were a process in erasing localized culture. And because culture is what I am interested in, it was a choice not to work with them. As it has developed it is now where underground subculture exists."

Chantry describes Sheehan as a "crack typographer" and himself as a "lettering artist," complementary and yet very different skills. Sheehan has had a lot of experience in copy writing and thinking up gimmicks, whereas Art's work is primarily the creation and promotion of a specific style.

Art Chantry's involvement in the do-it-yourself punk scene in the 1980s and '90s in the Pacific Northwest created the context for his distinctive style and the reach of his work. The graphic elements of such a scene are limited but distinct—record and CD packaging, event posters, and weekly newspaper design all fueled Chantry's success as a pioneering designer in this particular milieu.

St. Louis Film Fest poster, designed by Art Chantry and Jamie Sheehan

99

COLLABORATION DOES NOT DEPEND ON COMPROMISE BUT RATHER ON GOOD DECISIONS ABOUT WHOM YOU WORK WITH

RUDY **VANDERLANS**

ZUZANA **LICKO**

Although the content of *Emigre* magazine could not have existed without a number of creative contributors, editor Rudy VanderLans kept a close eye on the collaborative details. "The content of *Emigre* is determined by me," said VanderLans. "I invite people to contribute. They submit the work. Sometimes the work they submit is perfect, and we publish it nearly as is. Other times the contributors need input and feedback, and I give them my opinion."

VanderLans has worked with some of the best type and editorial designers in the world. In addition, by keeping his contributor list broad, he has established groundbreaking conversations between designers, visual artists, musicians, and writers. What makes it work? VanderLans explains, "The trick is to let people do what they enjoy doing and what they're good at, which is often the same thing. The success of any collaboration, I imagine, lies not so much in the willingness to compromise but in who you select to work with."

Emigre magazine, issue 24, posters, Supermarket book cover, designed by Rudy VanderLans and Zuzana Licko, Emigre

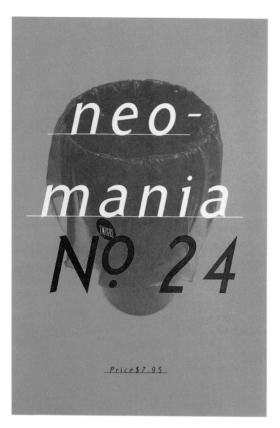

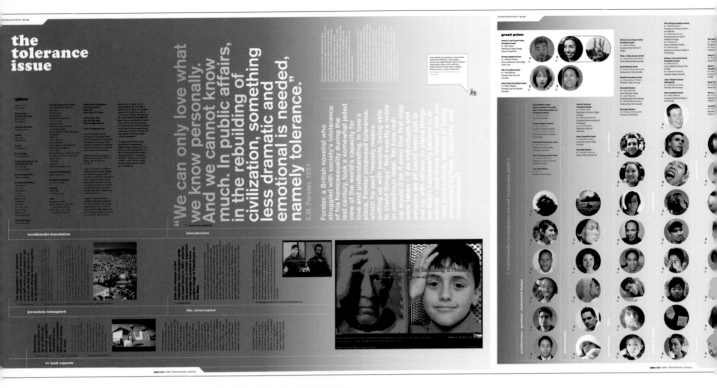

Sphere magazine, tolerance issue, designed by Mark Randall, Worldstudio Foundation

100

MARK **RANDALL**

FIND A MUTUALLY BENEFICIAL RELATIONSHIP

After the debacle of one issue of *Sphere* magazine (it was slated to come out on 9/11/01 and it featured some highly critical political images and rhetoric), Adobe showed interest in working on the following issue of *Sphere* that was slated to come out in February 2003. Adobe identifies strongly with what the magazine represents and wanted to participate in the process of its creation. Adobe was content to stay out of the editorial end but merged their interests with Worldstudio Foundation by supplying five Adobe Achievement Award winners.

These young designers, together with five Worldstudio Foundation Scholarship winners, were paired with graphic designers, including Michael Beruit at Pentagram and Karen Fong at Imaginary Forces. The teams created posters on the theme of tolerance, which formed the centerpiece of the magazine. The editorial content around these posters talked about how artists and designers deal broadly with the theme of tolerance in their work.

From a practical standpoint, it was the first time that Worldstudio, Inc. received money to actually design the magazine. Adobe underwrote the editorial costs and a large portion of the printing costs. Adobe benefitted from this partnership by reaching a highly qualified audience for their product, InDesign. A component of the project was that all the studios had to learn InDesign, and the entire publication has to be created using InDesign. It supported the ideals of the foundation, it got the message out to over 15,000 people, and it engaged the creative community in a pro-social project—posters about tolerance. In addition, this issue was distributed to schools and colleges as well as constituencies of the Southern Poverty Law Center.

worldstudio foundation

Born of the conviction that creativity holds enormous power for social change, Worldstudio Foundation nurtures a pro-active studio of tomorrow through its scholarship programs, mentorship initiatives and publications.

Putting its ideals into action, Worldstudio Foundation's college scholarship program is tailored specifically to increase diversity in the design/arts professions, and to encourage students to use their talents to give back to their communities. The Foundation's "Help Kids Create" mentoring program pairs at-risk teens with creative professionals to shape socially relevant public messages. Finally, the publication you are reading – *Sphere* – was designed to actively engage the creative community in the issues that challenge us today.

create! don't hate. tolerance poster project

The idea of publishing a variety of posters with a common cause

by the Editors

Initially came out of Worldstudio Foundation's ongoing "Create! Don't Hate: Campaign for Tolerance" mentoring initiative. The plan was to set up a mentorship program pairing design and illustration students with high-profile designers to develop the posters. The problem was finding the means to fund the project in a cash-strapped economy.

When Adobe expressed interest in partnering with Worldstudio to bring the next issue of Sphere to life, it occurred to the editors that the student posters might inspire an entire magazine devoted to tolerance.

For Adobe, which has an ongoing commitment to education and a long-standing involvement with the design community, the project presented an opportunity to give designers a voice. For Worldstudio, Adobe's partnership provided the means and the tools to launch the project. Both hoped the result would stimulate a lively discussion in the design community on an important issue, while reinforcing the point to young designers that design skills can have a role in helping social causes.

SUPPORT VARIETY

tarek atrissi & paul sahre

rikesh lal & rhonda rubinstein

dae hyuk sim & mark randall

paula azevedo & arch garland

michel baptiste & robert de michell

wanravee thavalit & brett wickens

ashana taylor & sean adams & noreen morioka

NIKESPHERE.COM   SWOOSH

Nike Apparel print advertising, designed by Todd Waterbury, Wieden+Kennedy, New York

101 ALLOW EACH CREATIVE TEAM TO DETERMINE ITS COLLABORATIVE APPROACH

TODD **WATERBURY**

Todd Waterbury, formerly of Wieden+Kennedy, worked with a writer as a creative partner for most of his Wieden+Kennedy projects. He found that the approach to collaboration in such a situation comes primarily from the creative team rather than being dictated by the project. He commented "Sometimes a writing partner who is completely opposite in viewpoint and style works because it creates conflict and forces commitment and clarity on what the solutions can be. This is based, though, on the approach that both work as individuals first and then come together to present, discuss, argue, rebuild, and so on."

At other times, however, the writer is the other side of the same conceptual coin and the collaboration is more of a deepening of sensibilities. This situation arises less frequently, but when it does occur, Waterbury finds that the results yield work that satisfies on a number of levels.

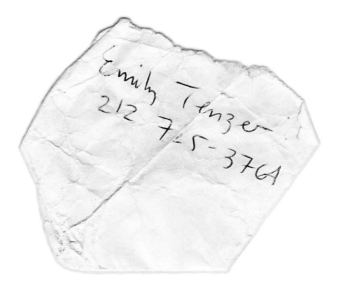

The number she gave, by Worksight Studio

102

WORKSIGHT STUDIO

TAKE A RISK IN CHOOSING COLLABORATIVE PARTNERS

Scott and Emily Santoro are co-principals of Worksight, which they founded. Scott had worked at Landor Associates, where he developed visual identities for national brands, and at Mobil Oil Corporation, where he held the position of senior designer in charge of internal communications. In 1986, he returned to school to earn a master's in graphic design.

"I was looking for office space in a typesetting shop where Emily was the office manager. I immediately began dating her and at the same time began forming my company. I asked her if she would like to help out with a project, which led to another, and eventually she wanted to leave her existing job and join me at Worksight. It was a big risk—there is probably some rule out there that states that one should never ask his/her date to help form a business together, but we knew that we were interested in each other."

Scott does the heavy lifting in design, and Emily manages the complex production of books and catalogs. Scott comments that Emily's training in a field outside of design makes her an ideal sounding board. "She brings another set of coordinates to the mix of graphic design and isn't tied down to any of the rules that we all learned. There's a kind of everyday smartness to her responses that affects all of the design work we create."

Although creating such a partnership involves taking a great risk, their collaboration and creative partnership push each other to new intellectual and creative endeavors, and their work is better because of their partnership.

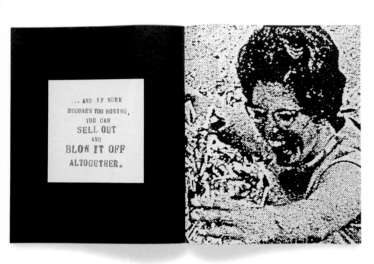

Appleton Paper Utopia promotions, designed by Art Chantry

103 PARTNER WITH COMPANIES WILLING TO TAKE RISKS

ART **CHANTRY**

The Appleton piece was part of a larger project for which Chantry had been hired. Appleton created an advisory design council, which was tasked with giving feedback to them on their new Utopia paper line. Part of the job was for each member of the design council to produce a piece as a part of a series. Each member was to interview a person of a certain societal niche—anyone from a prisoner to a CEO—and ask the person to define the word utopia.

The designers would then create a piece (within restricted specs) on Utopia papers presenting this personal vision. Sumata thought it would be funny to assign Chantry a CEO, so he chose Bruce Pavitt of the independent record label Sub Pop. Chantry notes, "This pointed out that 'CEO' can mean a lot of different things."

Tern proposal document, designed by Why Not Associates

104

**WHY NOT
ASSOCIATES**

PARTNER WITH CIVIC ORGANIZATIONS

Because Why Not has worked on so many public art projects, they have grown to understand the process of proposing and following through with projects that have very different audiences from their commercial work. The audiences for the public artwork are often in a different position than an audience for commercial work—they do not need to be convinced of anything, they do not need to be sold anything, and the information they are gaining by seeing a piece is often both highly involved in the form and not particularly essential.

On the other hand, partnering with civic organizations to produce public art requires that the concept of the audience remain broad. Although the pieces need not appeal to everyone, they generally should not offend, either.

In the pavement for the Tern project, for example, Why Not needed to come up with words related to birds. They chose to use quotations from a range of authors—not just Shakespeare and Milton. They chose to use vernacular language as well as literary language so that their work could be as comprehensible to as many people as possible.

Partnering with civic organizations to create public art puts the designer in touch with broader audiences than they would normally reach. The concerns of the public and their elected representatives must be respected and acknowledged in the process of design, which is something designers rarely have to consider in their work otherwise.

Lingerie Perdu, designed by Margo Chase, Chase Design Group

105 FORGE PARTNERSHIPS THAT BROADEN YOUR CULTURAL HORIZONS

CHASE DESIGN GROUP

Developing a lingerie store for a client in Jeddah, Saudi Arabia, tested the partnering abilities of the Chase Design Group, but it provided an effective outcome. When Chase Design Group was asked, before 9/11, to work with Ehab Mashat, they had before them the opportunity to create a context for the lingerie market that had never been known in the Middle East. Mashat's family had been selling lingerie in Saudi Arabia's bazaars for three generations, and Mashat had the radical vision of elevating lingerie from an under-the-counter commodity to the status of socially acceptable apparel.

Events of 9/11 resulted in strained relations between the United States and many Middle Eastern countries, but the partnership between Chase Design Group and Mashat remained strong. The first store was opened to great acclaim in 2001. The goal of the stores is to create a venue where Saudi women can get what they want: beautiful lingerie in a fashionable store that rivals designer boutiques abroad. Partnering with Los Angeles–based Chase Design Group proved a good match for this new company. Chase Design Group was involved in every aspect of the project, from choosing the name, creating the interior, specifying the fixtures, producing the signage, and designing the mannequins. Chase successfully created a branding strategy that adhered to the fundamentals of Islam and Saudi culture, while also meeting the modern business objectives of the client.

The largest problem was conceptual: how does one brand a lingerie store in a country where photos of sexy women cannot be used? Or where even any shape of a woman cannot be used? The Chase Design Group's solution is both effective and elegant. Starting with the development of a bilingual font and working with the tradition of sensual poetry in the Arabic tradition, calligraphic form played an enormous role in the solution to the Perdu brand identity. Suggestive texts and colors created a feeling of warm sensuality that became the core of the brand and identity while successfully avoiding the cultural restrictions. The client provided a challenging and exciting project for the Chase Design Group, and the designers provided just the right amount of Western marketing expertise and style to make the brand really stand out in Saudi Arabia.

The Hispanic sector is the fastest growing demographic in the U.S., a marketer's dream.
Hate crimes targeting Hispanics and Central and South American immigrants continue to rise.
Tolerance is more than economics.

Create! Don't Hate: Campaign for Tolerance, designed by Worldstudio Foundation

106 HELP OTHER PEOPLE COLLABORATE

**WORLDSTUDIO
FOUNDATION**

Part of the Worldstudio Foundation's mission is to help young designers find mentors as they move from their school years and into their professional lives. The idea of publishing a variety of posters with a common cause initially came out of the Worldstudio Foundation's ongoing "Create! Don't Hate: Campaign for Tolerance" mentoring initiative. The plan was to set up a mentoring program that paired design and illustration students with high-profile designers to develop the posters.

The mentoring aspect of the poster project was particularly successful. Essential design elements, such as information, experience, knowledge, and ideas, flowed back and forth, making the process valuable to both designers and students. Eleven teams took part, and the whole operation was funded in part by Adobe, who also provided the InDesign application for the creation of the pieces.

Although collaboration has always been a part of the way that the Worldstudio Foundation partners David Sterling and Mark Randall have worked, providing an opportunity for young people and more experienced designers to get together on a project with a high degree of social relevance was particularly rewarding.

INTOLERANCE DESTROYS THE FABRIC OF AMERICA

ALL QUOTES WERE FOUND ON INTERNET MESSAGE BOARDS OF MAINSTREAM SITES SUCH AS YAHOO, MSN.COM AND THE WASHINGTON POST

107

GOING SOLO DOESN'T MEAN YOU CAN'T BE PART OF A TEAM

JENI **HERBERGER**

"Isolation is not the most creative situation for an independent designer. If you look in the mirror and realize you haven't taken a shower in a few days and can't remember when you last missed the Ellen Degeneres show, it might be time to get out and work in a team environment for a while.

When working solo, you don't have the complexity of dealing with others, but you miss out on some of the collaborative coolness of being on a team."

Here are a few ideas about how you can inject some teamwork into your freelance work:

- Introduce yourself to specialty shops that might need design help from time to time, such as interactive-only studios or an agency that just landed a big client.

- Remember that larger agencies often need freelance help; build a relationship with a local firm and you may get not only steady work but steady opportunities to go into an office with better equipment and interesting designers.

- Bring in another freelancer on one of your projects. Even if you simply buy a few hours of their time to give you feedback on your design concepts, you might come up with some invaluable inspiration.

- Create a monthly lunch or dinner or other outside-the-office events for yourself and other independent creatives. Have a topic to discuss, bring in a speaker, or just hang out and talk shop.

108

JOENG-KWON **GYE**

BE CLEAR, BE CANDID, BE CAUTIOUS

"Collaborating with others is challenging and exciting, but it can also be stressful. Make sure you are clear about what you are supposed to do and what you can do and that everyone understands their roles and responsibilities. Don't get involved in other people's areas unless they ask you for your input. People can get edgy in the middle of projects. Your help or advice may be misunderstood as criticism. Maintain your artistic dignity but not at the expense of others. Remember, there is no I in team. The final product is the result of the group's effort."

Design Net magazine **cover artwork, designed by Koeng-kwon Gye**

Whether you're the one bringing in another creative person or you're joining up with an existing team, it's up to you to set clear parameters for what you're expecting and what you're delivering. Do you want only a few ideas and some honest feedback on some concepts you're working up? Are you expected to take on a job from start to finish because another firm is too busy? Are you supposed to be working hand-in-hand with the team on strategy and design but not get involved with the client directly? If you are meeting the client, how do you introduce yourself—as a freelancer, or part of the team? Spend a few minutes at the outset of the relationship to get these kinds of details of protocol clear, and you'll save yourself some potentially messy misunderstandings that can get in the way of the work further on down the road.

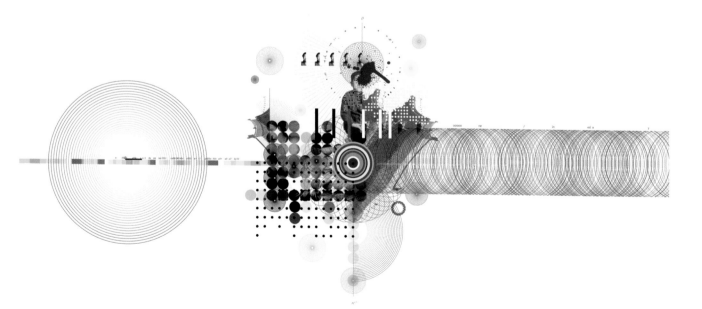

109

ERIC **HINES**

CREATIVES NEED OTHER CREATIVES, TOO

"Do work for artists in different areas of the creative fields and you may create a symbiotic relationship. Most of our work starting out came from an entire identity we did for a photographer. He and his rep landed six or seven jobs for us in the following months after the materials and site were done. We continue to do work for him and we continue to get referrals from him."

Working with other designers and creative professionals isn't always about working on the same project together. The creative may, in fact, be the client. And they can make really good clients, not only because they understand and are sympathetic to the process but also because their clients may become your clients. Few referrals carry more weight than those from one creative person about another creative person.

Texas Troubadours coffee-table book design and logo, designed by Eric Hines, Honest Bros.

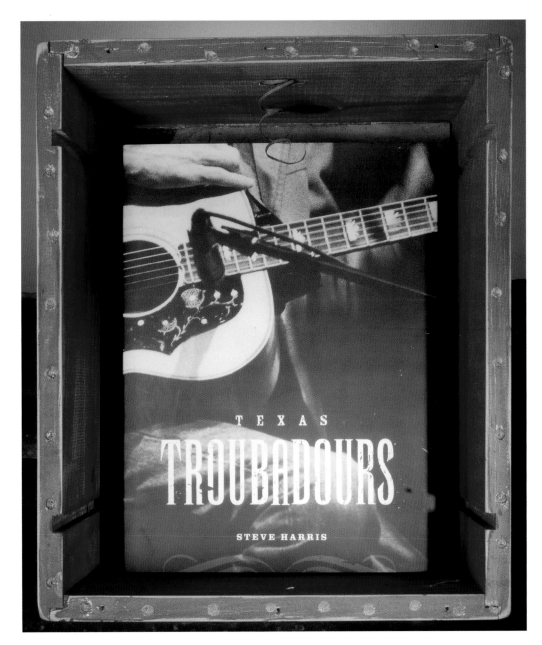

110

NICOLE **BLOCK**

YOUR LIMITATIONS CAN BECOME COLLABORATIONS

"Whether it's putting together the design for an event or working on an identity system that needs a website produced, it's inevitable that you can't always work on the entire project by yourself. Some things may be beyond your set of skills or the job is too large for you to handle on your own."

There's no reason to look at the fact that you can't do everything yourself as a liability. In fact, it's actually a great opportunity for you to provide your client with better work and better service while you work in some professional networking and creative collaboration along the way. The days of the "fully integrated marketing communications firm" that is a one-stop shop are going the way of handwritten letters. As new forms of media and technology are developed, the design and professional creative fields are splintering off into areas of increasing specialization. This is a good thing because, let's face it, design principles may be the same but the world of back-end flash animations and old-school letterpress printing are worlds apart, and yet you may find yourself with a client who wants and needs both. You don't need to do it all yourself, but as part of your service to your client—and your own creative edification—you should know who can do each of these things and who does them well.

Mr. and Mrs. James Bragg
invite you to the marriage of their daughter

DANIELLE BRAGG

to

GREGORY SHAWN

son of Mr. and Mrs. Harold Shawn

Prospect Park Picnic House
Saturday, June 7, 2008
5 o'clock in the evening

Reception to follow

RÉPONDEZ
S'IL VOUS PLAÎT

We look forward to your response
by May 7, 2008

name(s)

accepts

declines

Bragg/Shawn wedding invitation and stationery design, designed by Nicole Block, NicEvents

111

SETH **CHEEKS**

BRING SOMETHING EXTRA TO THE TABLE

"Playing a role in a creative team should always be about pressing yourself toward many roles. You should always try to do more than just what you've been tasked to do within the team. It's about growth and going the extra mile. If you push yourself further, then everyone else will push harder, and the product will be better—you'll also learn more than you can imagine."

If you're asked to participate on a creative team, you should always think about what else you can offer beyond what you've specifically been asked to contribute. Maybe you're being brought in for your skill with logo design—but what innovative strategic ideas can you offer about how that logo may be implemented in other materials? Or do you know someone with a particular skill that can help out? Possibly a strategist, writer, or photographer who can bring a fresh perspective? Do you have a hidden talent of your own that your teammates might not know about, such as illustration? Have you recently worked with a killer interactive company or printer that could help create just that unique effect the team is trying to develop? While working as part of a team, you certainly want to keep collaboration as the overarching goal and be sure you're not stepping into territories others have already claimed as their own; however, adding a little something extra to the mix not only encourages the whole group to achieve more, it can also help you distinguish yourself. Which, of course, encourages people to remember and call on you later as new, and often bigger and better, projects come down the pike.

112

ERIC **WOLFE**

REMEMBER, IT'S YOUR CLIENT

"When working with other creatives, be sure to set parameters for who does what. If it is your project, then you should remain the project lead and main client contact regardless of who is giving you additional help. Changing leads or contacts midstream can leave the client feeling insecure about your ability to complete the project successfully."

Setting parameters with the other creatives you bring into a project does not need to be a hostile or territorial effort. Keep in mind—and remind everyone else, if necessary—that it's all in the interest of developing a smooth operation that best serves your client's needs.

The lead on any project should be the person with the most direct contact and deepest relationship to the client. This principal creative should restrict or even in some cases prohibit contact between the client and the team of collaborators. You're not protecting the creatives from the client; you're protecting the client from the sometimes messy process of developing work for them. And you're keeping communication more streamlined by editing out the noise that can be confusing to staying focused on the project at hand. We've all seen how one off-hand remark from a client can stick in a designer's mind and derail a project (and vice versa). The principal creative person needs to be the gatekeeper between the client and the other designers, giving everyone the information they need to stay on strategy and on task.

Signature Townhomes website design, designed by Eric Wolfe, Eric Wolfe Design, Inc.

113

CHRISTINE **GODLEWSKI**

WELCOME TO THE CLUB

Christine Godlewski says, "I think collaboration is a huge part of the creative process. I find it's helpful to get together with a few designer friends and get their feedback on a project. Start a 'club' that meets once a week. Talk to a mentor about what you are working on. Involve some nondesign creatives, such as writers or photographers; they could be full of ideas that will enhance the project."

Let's face it—you can't have all the good ideas yourself. When you worked in a larger studio or agency, there were probably plenty of other designers around to look over your shoulder, check in on a project, or offer a tip or observation that accelerated the process and enhanced the design. Just because you're on your own doesn't mean you're all alone. You just have to set up some structures and systems that will allow you to regularly share information between fellow creative types.

Here are a few ideas to stay connected with fellow creatives:

- Organize weekly or monthly get-togethers over coffee, a meal, a beer, or a picnic.

- Regularly schedule Web teleconferencing creative brainstorming sessions.

- Join instant messaging and email groups.

- Design blogs—read a few or start your own.

- Invite yourself into other creative studios for a tour and then reciprocate.

Aviva Holistic Skin Spa brochure and direct mail, designed by Christine Godlewski, Genius Creative

114

STEVE **GORDON, JR**

BE A PART OF SOMETHING BIGGER THAN YOURSELF

"If you're going to work as part of a team from a larger agency or studio, you may feel a bit of anxiety. After all, this closely resembles the situation you left so you could work independently. Instead of letting your chest tighten in a claustrophobic memory of a former work environment, find a way to make your mark by focusing on doing one part, doing it well, and contributing significantly to the overall group effort."

Enjoy the fact that for a change of pace, you don't have the full project on your shoulders. With your smaller clients, you're the be-all and end-all; for these larger projects, you're a cog in a machine that's bigger than yourself. This is not a bad thing. It's a chance for you to find a niche role that lets a specific area of your talents shine. And it can become a means for you to develop a great reputation—and ongoing business—in one part of the design spectrum that you most enjoy. So cultivate your specialization and then go find teams that need your specific skill set.

Here are some ways you can get better, smarter, and more effective in your favorite design skill:

- Take an online course to brush up on your design skills or learn something new.

- Attend a conference such as the HOW Design Conference.

- Apprentice yourself to a master.

- Enroll in photography courses that reinforce and improve design skills such as composition and color balance.

Steve Gordon, Jr (RDQLUS), Adam Nielsen (Bi'Sto Design),
Donovan Beery (Eleven19 Communications), Nate Voss (Vossome),
Be a Design Group "Sound vs. Design" promotional poster collaboration

115

KEITH **BOWMAN**

TONWEN **JONES**

CREATE A COLLECTIVE

"Building a creative network is key to being able to take on a project instead of passing because you don't possess all the necessary skills needed for the job," notes Bowman.

"I am fortunate in that after graduating from my MA course, several of my classmates and I decided to rent a studio space together and one came up at the right time," says Jones. "Workhaus already had other freelance creatives on board, including furniture, Web, and product designers, so it was great to become part of a creative collective. I share my studio space with a packaging and graphic designer, so it's a good way of getting feedback on your work, especially when you hit a brick wall."

She adds, "We also have a system where we pass work over if we have too much work. Every now and then, we collaborate on projects if appropriate."

Sure, there will be times when you just need to bring in another designer, perhaps an illustrator, or someone with skills in animation to help out on a project. But instead of doing this only when you find yourself creatively cornered and desperate, how about setting up a standing collective of trusted and talented creative types who can call on each other anytime? No one has to give up their studios or clients, but everyone agrees to recommend and use one another's specific skill sets as needed. Kind of like a group of session musicians. You can even give yourself a name and introduce each other to clients.

"Trees You Are Unlikely to See" illustration, designed by Keith Bowman and Tonwen Jones

116

DEREK **ARMSTRONG**
MCNEILL

GO OUT AND GET SOME FEEDBACK

"I'm fortunate to live in a city with a great port-folio school (The School of Visual Concepts, Seattle, Washington), and I took three consecutive quarters of Teams/Advanced Ad Concepts classes. We were paired up with writers for projects, then were critiqued by local, successful professionals. The practice of working with another person and then presenting our work as a team was indispensable. If this kind of class isn't available to you, I'd try and re-create the opportunity artificially with friends, colleagues, or family. Show work to ten people—any people. Ask for feedback. Take notes. Was there a consistent thread of feedback? Integrate it. Get in the habit of exposing your work to others and hearing what they say all the time."

In case you haven't figured this out already, your clients are not always the best critics of your work. They often have too many other professional pressures and items on their own agendas to objectively look at what you're doing for them. They're wondering if their boss will like it, if it's going to come in under budget, and whether they'll have everything in time for the sales meeting. But for you to grow creatively and find the internal resources to come up with compelling new ideas, you need cold, hard critiques—consistently. And the only way you're going to get that is to ask for it. You may have to bribe a bit, offering pizza and a beer to help grease the opinion wheels, but the investment will be well worth it.

Carpenter Performing Arts Center "Schooled in Song" concert poster design, designed by Derek Armstrong McNeill, Grill Creative

Borderline indie rock band logo design, designed by Steve Gordon, Jr, RDQLUS

117

STEVE **GORDON, JR**

THE ANSWERS MIGHT BE RIGHT IN YOUR BACKYARD

"National design associations provide an invaluable service and represent our industry in important ways. But as they say, all politics are local, and many concerns of the freelance designer are as well. So, in addition to joining the big groups that impact your industry at large, look for smaller organizations that can offer local intelligence and business connections that may affect the day-to-day operations of your freelance operation."

Contact your local chamber of commerce. They can help you find organizations like these to join:

• Small business groups

• Business improvement districts that serve your area

• Local better business bureaus

• Young professional organizations

• Professional mentoring organizations

Inner City Teaching Corps logo design, **designed by Christine Godlewski, Genius Creative**

118

CHRISTINE **GODLEWSKI**

ACQUIRE VENDOR AND PRODUCT-SPECIFIC ASSOCIATIONS

"I've found paper-related events to be most beneficial, being primarily a print designer. These are usually intimate luncheons rather than large events. So there are opportunities to make a more personal connection. I usually walk away with a handful of business cards, having learned something about a new product, paper, or printing technique, and I usually get a neat parting gift. Getting to know my paper representatives has been a great networking tool as well as an educational one."

Look beyond the immediate design community for the associations and professional groups your vendors are a part of. They may offer smaller gatherings and specialty events that focus on a particular area of expertise or interest to you. Because their focus is narrower, you may get a deeper benefit in a more limited area that's especially beneficial to a one-person shop. You might have to dig around a bit to find the right organizations to get involved with, but the end result could be a treasure well worth the extra work.

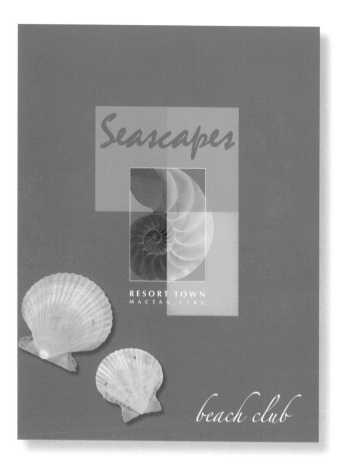

119

LIZZA **GUTIERREZ**

CAN'T FIND WHAT YOU WANT? START YOUR OWN

"When I lived and worked in the New York area, I was a member of AIGA. Being a member of AIGA exposed me to the numerous benefits of having a professional association. When I moved back to the Philippines in 2002, I then spearheaded the establishment of Liga Grafica, a group of professional graphic designers working in the Philippines, particularly in Manila."

There are many design organizations to join. However, there's also no reason not to start your own organization that reflects personal taste, style, interests, and location. How about web developers of the midwest with an interest in agriculture? Why not? Or what about multilingual expat designers of Asia? There's undoubtedly a need. Even if your organization serves only a handful of designers, if it serves them at all, it's worth the time and energy required to send out a few emails, get together a couple of times a year, share knowledge, gain some understanding, and most important, have a little fun.

Seascapes Resort Town, Filinvest Development Corporation brochure, designed by Lizza Gutierrez, Lizza's Room

Seascapes

RESORT TOWN
MACTAN, CEBU

villas & casitas

Chapter Six:

PROMOTING YOURSELF

MAK poster, designed by Stefan Sagmeister

120

LET THE WORK SPEAK FOR ITSELF

Stefan Sagmeister has never bothered to do any self-promotion, save a change-of-address-style postcard when he opened his shop in New York. "We basically don't do any self-initiated self-promotion. We haven't even done a Christmas card, ever. We have never sent out a press release, ever." Despite this fact, Sagmeister consistently has to turn clients away.

This admonition also belies the fact that Sagmeister does not actively create self-promotional materials to gain business; rather, he uses his design work to promote himself, creating posters for talks that he gives in New York and around the world, such as the one shown here for the Viennese museum, MAK. He considers these projects to be client work because he does not pay for the materials or

printing, yet he is able to render something new that is associated with both him and the talk he is giving. These posters actively add value to Sagmeister, whether the viewer associates them with the man or the studio.

In addition, Sagmeister participates in design shows but has never created work solely for this purpose. Sagmeister CD design work is prolific. He often asks the client for a hundred or so finished CDs to send to friends and clients—sort of a self-promotional gift. "We send them out to get work and also to friends at other labels. But we basically send out the CD and a letter, so that people in the street know what we just did. That's been working quite well for us. Because we try to design packaging for music we like, most of the CDs we package have good music."

121

CREATE PROMOTIONS THAT REFLECT THE GOALS OF YOUR COMPANY

MARK **RANDALL**

Worldstudio, Inc., keeps in touch with its clients by sending them thank-you cards and a fancy box of chocolates at the end of the year. In the note, they thank clients for their business and remind them that 10 percent of the proceeds from every job goes to the Worldstudio Foundation, their socially progressive, nonprofit organization. They highlight the Foundation's activities that year, giving clients a chance to recognize that they have helped without even realizing it. It is one of the only times that the clients of Worldstudio, Inc., hear about the activities of the Worldstudio Foundation. Otherwise, the partners keep the messaging about each entity as separate as possible. Randall says, "In the very beginning, we were really keen on merging Worldstudio, Inc., and Worldstudio Foundation by describing that we are a graphic design studio and a foundation and we care about our community and all of that. Not to be callous or mean about it, but basically, clients don't care. It's like, 'Oh yeah, that's nice, but what about my brochure?' Or 'I need a new logo,' or 'it's costing too much,' or 'I need that sooner.' They appreciate the fact that we do this, but it is not a deciding factor why people work with us."

The mission of the Worldstudio Foundation remains central to the principals of Worldstudio, Inc. In creating promotional materials for clients, it is important to them to make a strong statement about the identity of their firm, despite the fact that it may not have much impact on business development.

122

KEEP IN TOUCH WITH YOUR CLIENTS, PAST AND PRESENT

WHY NOT ASSOCIATES

Why Not's success has created the enviable situation in which they have never had to seek out work. Instead, their self-promotion has consisted of maintaining close client connections to keep the work coming in. Andy Altmann of Why Not explained what he did during one of their quietest times. "We checked with all the clients we have ever worked with in the past, and that's worked, so now we are busy again. It the past, we've been quite blasé about it, but it is a little different now. We are doing a lot of repeat work for existing clients, but that is not new work, exactly. A lot of going through the motions, but that is what keeps food on the table. The more interesting projects don't come along as frequently."

In 1992, Why Not Associates designed the catalog for a Nigel Coates exhibition of architectural drawings and ideas, which was shown at the Architectural Association in London. The subject of this project was the development of a mythical city, which was like a large body, living and breathing and interacting with its inhabitants. A few years later, Coates approached Why Not because he wanted to extend this idea to create what amounted to a guide book of this mythical city as a means of discussing the state of city planning.

Although the job stretched out for a number of years, the book was published in fall 2003. Working with an architect from the initial stages of an idea to the unique, book-form presentation has given Why Not a greater appreciation for the processes of architects, as well as a role in the organic development of a project—from a catalog to a book.

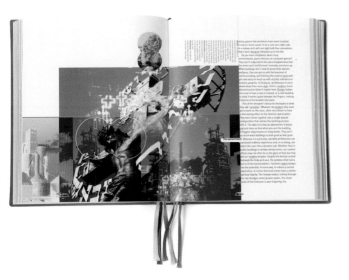

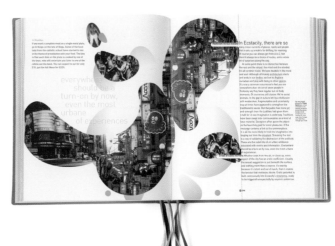

Ecstacity, Laurence King, 2003, designed by Why Not Associates

123

ART **CHANTRY**

LET SOMEONE PUBLISH YOUR WORK

Some designers, especially those who have been working for a number of years, have the opportunity to publish their collected work in a monograph. In 2001, Chronicle books published *Some People Can't Surf: The Graphic Design of Art Chantry*, an excellent introduction to Chantry's work written by Julie Lasky. "I've gotten a lot of mileage out of that book. It is a terrific piece of self-promotion, obviously. I think I can safely say that up until that book I didn't ever get any work out of self-promotion or magazine articles or anything like that. In fact, just the opposite is true. In the late '80s sometime, I was featured in *CA [Communication Arts]* and didn't work for nine months after that. Nothing. It did nothing."

Chantry notes, however, that in the design world, the monograph can also be the kiss of death for a career. Many of his colleagues advised him against doing it. He sees the monograph as a sort of stabilizer that demonstrates both the core and limits of a designer's capabilities. On the flip side, it can also create the perception that no one can afford to hire you anymore, that you are unavailable, or at

worst, dead. Thankfully, however, Chantry has proved this is not always the case. Chantry's other efforts at self-promotion come primarily from collaborations with clients who want to advertise their own capabilities using Chantry's work. This collaboration generally results in showpieces and collectable posters.

Because so much of Chantry's work has been on ephemeral objects, like posters and flyers, a book like *Some People Can't Surf* preserves a vital piece of the history of the graphic design of '80s and '90s punk culture, so much of which is repeated and copied in contemporary underground (and mainstream) music culture. For every piece in the book, Chantry insists that there are ten that he didn't include—so vast is the backlog of his work. "I have enough for probably five more volumes," he notes.

Publishing a monograph is not an option for every designer, but in the event that one has the opportunity to do so, it provides an important showpiece for prospective clients—however ambivalent the designer may feel about it.

Some People Can't Surf: The Graphic Design of Art Chantry, designed by Art Chantry

SOME PEOPLE CAN'T SURF

THE GRAPHIC DESIGN OF

ART CHANTRY

BY JULIE LASKY

INTRODUCTION BY KARRIE JACOBS

124

WIN AND KEEP CLIENTS WITH A MULTI-PRONGED APPROACH TO SELF-PROMOTION

MARGO **CHASE**

The Chase Design Group enters shows, such as those held by *Communication Arts*, *How*, and *Print*, and submits work to books as a way of self-promotion. In addition, they do occasional mailings that show their new work to specific types of clients. They also have an elaborate website on which they display a portfolio, a client list, and contact information.

Referral is a huge part of the Chase Design Group's business development, and it constitutes the means by which they get much of their new business. Maintaining a good account office is an essential part of this mechanism, almost as important as the work itself. Chase notes, "We are fortunate to have had ongoing work for many years with some clients. These are large and small corporations, as well as entertainment companies, where design plays a large role in their business. A lot depends on the type of client. If we do an identity for a company whose business does not involve design, they may not need us again for years, and by then, they may just want to try someone else. That part works in our favor also—people who have previously worked with others often call us to try something different."

The logo posters are a staple of the Chase Design Group's self-promotion, as well as an excellent catalog of their large and diverse client base. "The process of creating these has changed with technology," comments Chase. "The first poster we did was produced photomechanically because it was created before we had our first Macintosh. The second poster included a few logos that were done by hand, but all were scanned into the computer. The third poster was built in Illustrator. Even the hand-done, calligraphic parts of the logos were streamlined or scanned to create digital art for all the logos."

Chase observes that industry recognition keeps her firm visible among people who recommend design firms, and the business press keeps her firm visible among clients and prospects; she acknowledges the power of both. Publicity, such as being featured in books or winning awards, is also an effective tool. "We get most of our nonreferral business from people who have seen our work in magazines or books. We often get referred by people who have never worked with us, but they know our work and reputation." In addition, Chase often speaks at design trade shows, which she enjoys, and which serves to keep industry awareness of her firm high. For Chase Design Group, a combination of approaches creates a flexible and effective self-promotional plan that reaches many different markets and potential clients.

Logo poster, designed by Margo Chase, Chase Design Group

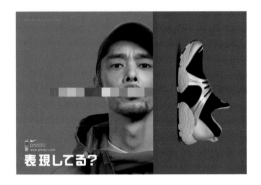

Presto 1: Emotions, Presto 2: Are you expressing, designed by John C Jay, Wieden+Kennedy, Tokyo

125

USE CULTURAL RELEVANCE TO CREATE ONGOING MOMENTUM

JOHN C **JAY**

In developing the multilayered audio and video pieces to advertise the first products in a Nike shoe line called "Presto," John C Jay, creative director and partner at Wieden+Kennedy, Tokyo, wanted to create a momentum beyond what their work is able to do for the current product launch. "The things we make are never for sale," he comments. These can include special CDs, DVDs, or LPs. "We use them for special promotions, although promotions wouldn't be quite the right word. We use these things to make sure that key influencers of sports and society are continuously inspired by Nike's view of the world and Nike's dedication to helping young talent. Through Nike, we are supporting young talent and giving them a place to express themselves."

In addition to giving the brand momentum, such campaigns accrue cultural capital for their creators. Presto advertisements tap into a social consciousness, as well as into a sports culture and a youth culture, establishing both Nike and Wieden+Kennedy as preeminent experts in these areas. The "Presto 1" campaign illustrates this concept well. The company's first pass at Presto involved the creation of an enhanced CD featuring five influential indie bands. "This campaign was in response to the whole 'indie' movement in youth culture– people playing indie sports, people leading an indie life, in the sense that they work toward a career that makes sense to them, not following the given path, the traditional path." For the print and outdoor advertising, Wieden+Kennedy asked musicians for an emotional response to the color of a given Presto shoe.

In their second Presto campaign with Nike, Wieden+Kennedy engaged top DJs by featuring them in the advertising with a color bar over their mouths and the copy "Are you expressing?" on a special series of vinyl LPs. By finding the niche for a product and communicating culturally appropriate messages about that product, Wieden+Kennedy not only demonstrate their skill in these conventional agency acts but they also associate their firm with cutting-edge culture.

Another project that Wieden+Kennedy produced for Nike, "Players Delight," was created to celebrate the twentieth anniversary of the emergence of hip hop and the release of "Rapper's Delight." "That campaign did not die. It lived on and on. One of the things we are trying to do is to break all these rules of the status quo about what advertising is. So often ad agencies, and clients in particular, just want to know what's next. There's no longevity of thought and brand extension." He says that each launch they do has "a very dynamic, different type of idea."

Worksight self-promotional cards, designed by Scott Santoro/Worksight

126

CREATE SELF-PROMOTIONAL MATERIALS THAT ARE DECEPTIVELY SIMPLE

WORKSIGHT

Worksight developed a series of postcards to illustrate the concept of "everyday design," which permeates their design philosophy. Scott Santoro explains, "They were experiments with the idea of the 'everyday' and functioned as promotional cards. They probably scared some people. Some people don't know what to make of them." Some of the photos are of trash or of scenes that do not immediately appeal in conventional aesthetic ways. Regardless of this fear, designers who come to Santoro's studio pick up the postcards as souvenirs of their visit. In addition, Santoro uses them to jot notes to clients—a highly decorated and conceptual form of stationery. "They are really just visual experiements based on my interest on the subject of the 'everyday' and how it relates to graphic design. However, they also function as promotional poscards for my studio. I suppose they might confuse people who don't know what to make of them, but that's OK."

The extension of this project is to make a bookmark. "We have a lot of publishing clients," says Santoro. "We think doing a bookmark would be an appropriate use of the idea for publishers. I'll get around to it one of these days."

Doing printed experiments can communicate aesthetics to potential clients as well as to colleagues in the business. They show a high degree of care for the small communication that happens on a daily basis, illustrating again the concept of the "everyday."

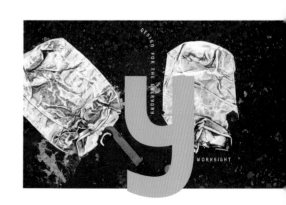

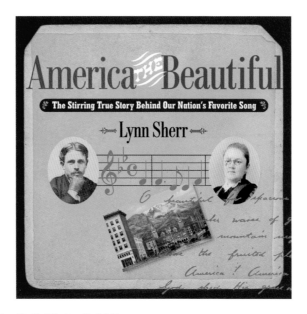

America the Beautiful cover, designed by Scott Santoro/Worksight

127

WORKSIGHT

DO AN EXTRA-GOOD JOB ON TINY PROJECTS

To solicit new business, Scott Santoro of Worksight does the conventional work of making calls and networking through existing channels. But Santoro finds that the best way to create new business for himself is to start small and count on a bigger payoff down the road. "I'll try to do an extra-good job on tiny projects in the hopes that a company will grow and use me again. Sometimes it works. With a new client I'll work especially hard to design something that's smart and efficient. I guess I'm trying to prove my designing capabilities to them."

A publisher called Publicaffairs hired Worksight to design its catalog and then a book. The publisher grew and asked Worksight to redesign the catalog, which Worksight continued to do every three months. It started as what Santoro calls a "quickie catalog design" four years ago and turned into solid business every three months.

Eventually, Publicaffairs asked Santoro to design a book called *America the Beautiful,* a book by Lynn Sherr on the history of Katherine Bates's turn-of-the-century poem turned song. Doing a complex project such as designing a book was certainly a step up from the previous catalog work. Scott has found that the strategy of starting small works for publishers in general. "If we get a book project, usually I'll try to work my butt off to get something designed really smartly or efficiently. I guess that is the hope of all designers."

Sometimes this strategy backfires, leaving the designer with a great portfolio piece but not much more in the way of new business. Worksight designed an identity and a website for a small start-up dot-com company. After the website was done, the company kept the logo but then asked the new president's son to redo the website. Even though this project ended up not leading to other projects, it was important for Santoro to do a good job on it. In the larger body of work of a designer, it is essential to pay attention to detail, even on the smallest projects, because this work can have a life beyond the client, to both fuel the imagination and provide portfolio material.

Revival, 57 Images from Cut Magazine, designed by Hideki Nakajima

128 DISTRIBUTE YOUR WORK THROUGH RESPECTED CHANNELS TO GAIN CLIENT CONFIDENCE

HIDEKI **NAKAJIMA**

Hideki Nakajima has published two books that feature most of his work. He finds them useful for establishing credibility with his prospective clients. The books also serve as his portfolio for exhibitions in which he is asked to participate. "Two books that collect my works are titled *Revival* and *Nakajima Design 1995-2000*. I also did the exhibition 'New Village/Code Exhibition' (2002). The magazine *IDEA* had a special feature on my work in 2000 as well."

Most of Nakajima's clients come to him over and over, so he has little need to self-promote. On the other hand, he also believes that award shows and competitions give his clients a sense of security, a validation by the design establishment that his work is recognized by his peers. For Nakajima, his reputation is built on his work and through the books and articles that feature his work. In developing a body of published work, Nakajima effectively creates a stand-in for what a conventional designer might use as a portfolio. His books are designed as books, created to stand alone as pieces of work in themselves.

Johnny Depp

Live, give, and don't take shit.

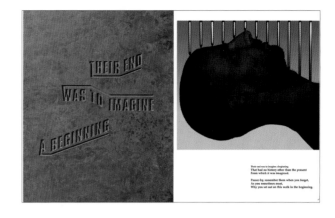

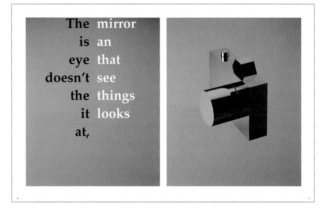

Fuel 3000 cover, spreads, designed by Miles Murray Sorrell FUEL

129 EVERYTHING YOU DO PROMOTES YOURSELF

**MILES MURRAY
SORRELL FUEL**

Miles Murray Sorrell FUEL began by publishing experimental magazines. "The publication of our own magazines and books is the foundation of our business. The books' broader distribution gained us a wider audience and subsequently helped to attract commissions," notes Damon Murray, one of Miles Murray Sorrell FUEL's partners. (The other partners are Peter Miles and Stephen Sorrell.)

The majority of Miles Murray Sorrell FUEL's work comes by way of referral, and they do not do any advertising or self-promotion per se. "The starting point for our personal work is not primarily to gain more commercial work. Often our personal work is too difficult to grasp in a commercial environment," explains Murray. Miles Murray Sorrell FUEL's client list of artists and other designers reflects the complex nature of their personal projects. This philosophy has created a situation where FUEL's client base is populated by artists as well, including photographer Jürgen Teller, Booth Clibborn Editions (who published both of their books), and fashion designer Marc Jacobs.

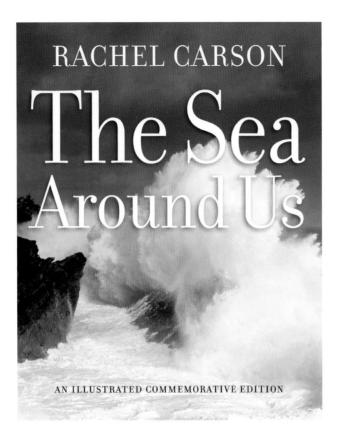

RACHEL CARSON

The Sea Around Us

AN ILLUSTRATED COMMEMORATIVE EDITION

The Sea Around Us cover, designed by Scott Santoro/Worksight

130 WALK AROUND A BOOK FAIR AND HAND OUT YOUR BOOK DESIGNS TO PUBLISHERS

WORKSIGHT

The combination of a lagging economy and some do-it-yourself pluck provided the circumstances for a novel business development tool: hitting the pavement. Scott Santoro of Worksight knew that he wanted more business with book publishers, so he decided to go ask them if they needed his services.

"I heard that there was a book-publishers' fair down at the Javits [Convention] Center. I thought, that would be a great place to bring laser prints of my book work. I'll walk around until I see books that I like. I'll walk right up to the people representing the company and tell them that I am a book designer and ask them if they could hand these off to the art director.

I handed out about 30 copies at a fair that had about 300 publishers. I ended up getting some nice work from it."

The strategy of direct self-promotion at a book fair was effective for them. One of the clients he gleaned through this jaunt through the convention center was Oxford University Press. They called him on the strength of the lasers that he handed out, and he was able to get an excellent project as a result. They were reprinting Rachel Carson's book, *The Sea Around Us*, which was first published in 1951. It was the 50-year anniversary of the first edition, one of the first environmentally oriented books written about the sea, and Oxford wanted a special treatment.

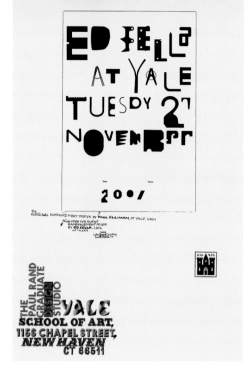

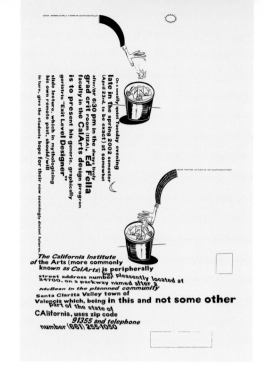

131

ED **FELLA**

CREATE AFTER-THE-FACT FLYERS

To complement his typographic experimentation, Ed Fella started experimenting with direct mail advertisements, or flyers. He began creating what he calls "after-the-fact" announcements, which function as a souvenir for the event they advertise. "I'll print it—a couple hundred copies, that's it. They become a kind of idea about art design and art practice. Those other ones that advertise, they function as real flyers—they print a couple thousand of them and mail them out. I would just get my 'cut,' fifty copies or so. The whole idea of what I'm doing now is to just print the designer's cut, not the announcement—just do an edition."

In the poster shown here, Fella combines sports lettering from Yale with odd kinds of old-fashioned lettering, creating a look of sports nostalgia mixed with thoughtful graphic design. The result is an eclectic mix that has nothing to do with the present. Fella notes, "I guess it's a kind of post-modernism. These pieces function autonomously. They don't function in the design world; they occasionally make it into the art world, into a gallery or a museum. The posters that I do are very specific to a very small audience. The Yale poster won't make any sense to anyone besides people who are involved with the Yale graphic design program. They will be the ones to get the nuances. Yet it works as a piece, an announcement. It's readable; it gives you the time and the place of the event."

All graphic design announces something: it is worthless after the event is over. Fella's philosophy drives him to create these seemingly obsolete pieces. "I make all these announcements for things that are already over. I pay for them myself. There are no editions; there is just the archive edition. In advertising you send out 200 posters and hope that twenty people come to the event. When you do it after the fact, you just make the twenty and give it to people who actually came to the event." Fella's experimental graphics give him an opportunity to create work associated with events but that do not advertise them ahead of time. They are graphic souvenirs and function to promote ideas rather than events, thus clearly reflecting the work and thought process of the designer.

Announcement Flyers, designed by Ed Fella

FELLA, andrew fella 02

PRESENT
IN AN ART DESIGNERIST TYPE SLIDE
PRESENTATION
AT YALE UNIVERSITY
8pm graphic design
TUESDAY 27 PROGRAM,
NOVEMBER th SCHOOL OF ART

132

ERIC **HINES**

IT'S DIFFICULT TO WORK AT THE PLAYGROUND

"Rather than try to develop relationships at industry gatherings, I've cultivated relationships with high-level creatives or marketing types I've worked with along the way. These relationships have usually led to referrals. And when someone has been nice enough to send a client to me, I make a point of sending them a thank-you gift or taking them to lunch."

Industry events are a great way to get out and about with colleagues, mingle a bit, learn something new, and meet people. But these events tend to be better for socializing than for business prospecting. That's why it's so important to make the effort to make contacts with people beyond the design world. After all, other designers want the same thing you do: new clients. A chamber of commerce mixer will put you in touch with business people who need brochures and websites; an AIGA event will give you a chance to talk shop, let your hair down, and enjoy a few drinks with other creative types. So while it's important to rub elbows with your cohorts, be sure to also look for opportunities to hand out business cards to people who might actually need your services.

Here are some great business networking opportunities:

- Chamber of commerce mixers

- Neighborhood association meetings

- Cultural events, lectures, and discussions

- Charity events and fund-raisers

Powerhouse Gym posters, designed by Eric Hines, Honest Bros.

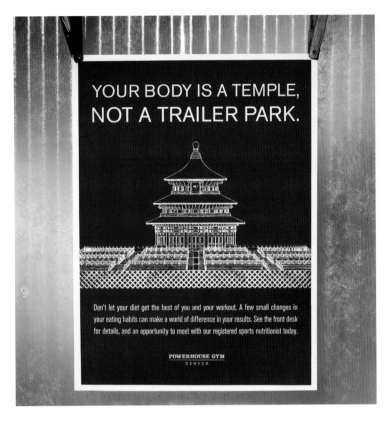

tulia™

sanctuary for your skin

133

M **MAVROMATIS**

GO AHEAD, BE DIRECT

"The majority of my work comes from direct-mail marketing. This approach has been successful for me because it triggers face-to-face meetings with potential clients. Once I get the initial meeting, I treat it as much as an opportunity for me to interview the client as for them to interview me. It's important for both of us to gauge if we'd be a good fit and have a productive working relationship."

A direct-mail marketing campaign can be used as a kind of portfolio review. Develop a mailing list of real people at organizations you'd like to work for (websites, annual reports, and basic online searches should give you plenty of contact information), create a schedule, and mail things out on a regular basis. Realistically, prospective clients will need to see several pieces from you before you'll even register on their radar. And don't expect them to just pick up the phone and call you. You have to be brave enough to do follow-up phone calls and ask for a face-to-face meeting.

Make sure your mailers don't showcase only the work you've done but are also inventive, arresting, interesting, and creative pieces themselves. In this day of faceless, high-tech communication, a well-conceived and executed piece of mail may actually stand out more than you expect. Which brings us to another important point: Make sure your mailer goes to a real person, with the right title, who is in a decision-making position, and actually still works at the organization you're targeting. Be sure to spell his or her name right. Make sure you know something about what the person or company does when you call. If you get a meeting, spend most of the time asking about the company's needs, not telling them how great and accomplished you are. Then follow-up with a personal note that tells them what you learned and how you think you might be able to help.

tulia™

Maria Mavromatis OWNER

PO Box 3674
Cherry Hill, NJ 08034-0567
P 609.987.6543
E maria@tuliaskincare.com
W tuliaskincare.com

sanctuary for your skin

tulia™

tulia™
sanctuary for your skin

To

PO Box 3674, Cherry Hill, NJ 08034-0567

PO Box 3674
Cherry Hill, NJ 08034-0567
P 609.987.6543
E info@tuliaskincare.com
W tuliaskincare.com

sanctuary for your skin

Tulia identity and stationery, designed by M. Mavromatis, MM Design Studio

Swing dancing brought
David and Michelle together.

To honor this, David and Michelle are sponsoring a beginner
swing-dancing workshop. No dance experience is required.

This is a FREE CLASS on Saturday, July 21st from 3pm – 6:30pm

It will be taught by Dance Manhattan, located at:
39 West 19th Street, 5th Floor • Mahattan, New York
212-807-0802

Even if you cannot attend the wedding, please join us for this class.
To RSVP, please email Michelle at msb323@aol.com or
call 212-928-0314

How about a picnic?

The day before the wedding, spend a
casual afternoon with Michelle, David,
family, and friends.
Saturday, August 11 from 1-4pm at the
Syosset/Woodbury Park.

RSVP to Michelle at msb323@aol.com or 212-928-0314

Directions: Take the Long Island Expressway
(495) to Exit 44N (Rt. 135 North) to Exit 14
East (Woodbury Rt. 25 East). At exit, turn
right onto Jericho Turnpike. The park will be
on the right at the second traffic light.

Michelle/David wedding invitations and stationery, designed by Nicole Block, NicEvents

134

NICOLE **BLOCK**

SUCCESSFUL BY ASSOCIATION

"If you have an idea that can be of use in some way to clients, then target events in that client's industry. These events are a great opportunity for them to meet you in person and hear from you why your work offerings can help them. For example, I'm doing an event this winter with a dress designer. We're inviting all our past clients, as well as publications and bloggers, expecting them to spread the word about what we do for this industry. I'll get to hang out with brides-to-be, show them my work, and get my name out there all at once."

There's a huge world of potential clients out there. One way to break it down is to look for opportunities that are a bit more focused on specific industries. For example, if you've done a concert poster for a recording artist, don't

just look for other poster gigs. Remember that this band is part of a larger record label that may need design work. There are concert photographers who may need promotional pieces and even T-shirt vendors who need to jazz up their offerings. This approach applies across industries and opportunities. Advertise your services at the local college where seniors will be looking for graduation announcements or at the local baby store where new moms will be looking for birth announcements.

If you've built trust with a particular client or client sector, then think like an octopus and spread your tentacles in different directions that are closely related to what you've already proven you're good at.

135

SETH **CHEEKS**

WELCOME BACK TO HIGH SCHOOL

"Many clients like to see that the creative people they're working with have received recognition by other entities. Credibility comes from having other recognizable clients, but it also comes in the form of awards. It's a good idea to enter design competitions. Many clients view these awards as a kind of honor roll that proves you know what you're doing. With this kind of recognition, you will be able to begin building a great network and attracting more clients."

It's just like high school—once the "cool" kids give you their stamp of approval, everyone else decides they can like you, too. How many times has the simple kiss of a pretty girl turned a frog into a prince? Winning some awards is like getting that coveted smooch. The other story line in this fairy tale is that everyone likes to feel that they've discovered the next hip thing. And that may be you. A client who thinks he or she has been smart enough to find you before you were recognized will be happy to brag about you (and by association, themselves) once you've gotten some awards. Once they tell their friends, these folks might become your clients.

Most design magazines have annual awards editions; look for them and submit to them. Here are some publication and other awards opportunities:

- The ADDYs—An annual local and national competition put on by American Advertising Federation

- The WEBBYs—Web and interactive design competition put on by American Advertising Federation

- AIGA Design Awards—Your local chapter's annual competition feeds the national competition

- Publications with design competitions— *Communication Arts, Dynamic Graphics, How, Print,* and *Step Inside Design*

Mixtape Monster logo, designed by Seth Cheeks, CheekyDSN

mixtapemonster

136

JENI **HERBERGER**

BUSINESS DEVELOPMENT IS AN ONGOING PROJECT

Jeni Herberger has been working with freelancers for years. "Those that keep me informed about their availability get the first phone call when a new project or job comes up.

"You have to remember that even when you have plenty of work, you still have to keep in touch with potential and existing clients, as well as staffing agencies. Otherwise, when today's project is done, there won't be another one ready for tomorrow. It's important to set aside time each week or even a few times a week to make calls, do some prospecting, and ping your clients so you stay top of mind with them."

137

CHRISTINE **GODLEWSKI**

KEEP IN TOUCH

"Most people stay with companies for just a couple of years, so keep in touch with friends and clients you have worked with in the past. Check in to let them know what you are up to. Even if they don't have a need for you presently, they might in six months or a year."

We all know we shouldn't burn bridges, but we often forget to maintain them as well. We have to keep our bridges solid, not only so we can cross them again but so other people can come over and find us.

It's not enough to make connections with people and hand out business cards. You need to collect business cards, too. And then send something to them on a regular basis. (Just not so regularly that you become annoying!)

Establish a quarterly email newsletter. Send out the occasional update about new work. Pop someone a note with a link to an article you read that has relevance to their business or follow-up a conversation you had with them. It's not just about spreading the good word about your work; it's about helping them be successful in their business enterprise, too.

Sometimes, after months or years of this kind of intermittent nudging, you may wonder if it's been worth all the effort. But then you get a call from someone who's kept your business card, noticed your notes, and finally has a budget and a project in mind. Sure, most of your contacts will ignore you, but once you get one, or two, or three projects—which lead to other projects—you'll see the multiplier effect of building and maintaining all those bridges.

Seattle's Union Gospel Mission annual report, designed by Christine Godlewski, Genius Creative

138

YOU DIDN'T KNOW YOUR DESIGN FIRM WAS A PERSONAL PUBLIC RELATIONS FIRM, TOO?

STEVE **GORDON**, JR

"Sure you want your clients talking about you, but you should also talk about yourself and your services to create positive word of mouth. While you need to be your own best fan, self-promotion of this sort does not mean you should be arrogant. There are professional ways to get your work noticed. An ongoing public relations effort should be part of your regular business activities.

Many designers new to the freelance game think the only way to get their name out there is by entering design competitions and hoping for that one-in-a-thousand shot at glory. But the competition can be stiff, fees can add up, and there are plenty of free and effective ways to get noticed."

Here are some ideas:

- Send email updates and work samples to editors at publications you admire. Editors are always looking for content. Maybe you'll get a small mention in a regular column or even better, you'll get included in a feature piece.

- Send holiday cards and direct-mail promo items to staffing firms, larger firms who might hire freelancers, and publications. It's just another way to say hello.

- Take note of who is writing articles you like in industry publications. Most are free-lancers themselves who are always looking for new ideas to pitch to editors and undis-covered designers to profile or quote. Send them samples of your work or even suggest angles for articles. And if a writer does contact you, be responsive. They're usually working on tight deadlines for little money and they don't have time to chase you—or your work—down.

- Design competitions are a great way to make media contacts. Don't enter all the competitions, though. Pick the ones that are right for your work. Writers and editors often look for new talent in design annuals.

- Offer to be a speaker at community events and business functions. Groups are always looking for someone to stand up before a monthly meeting to talk about their work and how it can impact the community at large, as well as business by business. You're supposedly an expert on visual com-munications, right? Offer to share your insights and expertise.

139

TERRY LEE **STONE**

PROMOTIONAL PREPARATION IS PARAMOUNT

There is a very good reason why the same designers get published over and over again. Certainly, the excellence of their work is part of it, and some employ PR firms and other promotional vehicles to broadcast their achievements. Having lots of money and an army of publicists is not required to get your work noticed, though. Most of all you should be media-ready—in other words, when the presses are ready to roll, not only do you have the goods to flaunt but also the know-how to package and deliver your message to the public. Don't be afraid to toot your own horn either. Having just recently filed several large feature articles on designers who were novices at dealing with the press, I am compelled to offer some suggestions to get all designers ready for their close-ups. Follow this advice and you'll be prepared when the opportunity arises—and happy with the coverage you get."

- Always archive images of your work promptly and completely.

- Get final project images together for every thing you do as soon as the project is done.

- Prepare one to three views/spreads/frames of each piece.

- Save images in two versions: high-res for print, 300 dpi at 8 × 10 inches (20.3 × 25.4 cm), or as large as possible low-res for Web, 72 dpi at 3 × 5 inches (7.6 × 12.7 cm).

- When you have a three-dimensional piece, photograph it. Save photos for both Web and print.

- Writer/editor/blogger Alissa Walker (www.gelatobaby.com) offers the following insight: "As a blogger, I need that low-res image and a link, either to the project on your website or a page that has images and more info—a place where people can buy it or see the piece in action. Your website alone is not good enough. I want to send my readers somewhere very specific to learn more and experience it."

Dan Sidor
PHOTOGRAPHY

140

ERIC **HINES**

GOOD WORK LEADS TO MORE WORK

"The best way to win new clients is by doing great work for your current clients. We've always found that if you wow them with the work you do, they'll tell their business associates about you and recommend your services. Then you get in the position of taking on the projects that you want, instead of taking on any project just because you need to."

The best endorsement you can ask for is from a current client. But the only way to get this recommendation is to make sure all your clients are delighted with your work. Even if a client turns out to be difficult or challenging, focus on making sure the end product is the highest quality you can produce and that you offer service with a smile. You can always turn down future work from this client. Just remember that every client talks to other potential clients, some of whom will be nicer and may have more interesting work and perhaps even bigger budgets for you.

It's also important to remember that your best client is your current client. It takes an awful lot of time—and time is money—to get up to speed with a new client. Make the people you're working with today happy, and they'll keep sending you work. And more work from the same client means you can spend more time designing and billing and less time prospecting and pounding the pavement.

Dan Sidor Photography logo and business cards, designed by Eric Hines, Honest Bros.

dor
Logan St.
Co 80210
nsidorphotography.com
.0714

Dan Sidor
1434 S. Logan St.
De   Co 80210
do
3

Dan Sidor
1434 S. Logan St.
Denver, Co 80210
dan@dansidorphotography.com
303.722.0714

Dan Sidor
1434 S. Logan St.
Denver, Co 80210
dan@dansidorphotography.com
303.722.0714

Chapter Seven:

STAYING CREATIVE

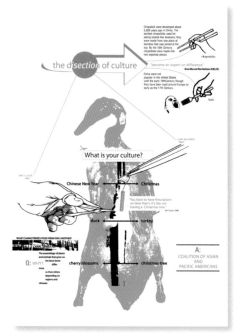

AIGA conference announcement poster, designed by Stefan Sagmeister

141

STEFAN **SAGMEISTER**

AVOID DESIGN CONFERENCES

Stefan Sagmeister jokes, "I think the last class I took was yoga. My last design-related class was when my former intern gave me Photoshop lessons."

Sagmeister admits that he usually goes to conferences if he is asked to speak at them and then takes the opportunity to visit other panels. But in general, he does not attend design conferences. "There are few conferences where I really have the feeling I have learned. It is more like a sense of education than a true education."

There are exceptions. Sagmeister notes that he has often attended the Technology, Entertainment, Design (TED) conference, which is about design, but he comments, "[It is] much more about science." The cross-disciplinary atmosphere of such a meeting of people has the effect of stimulating the imagination in methods and practices (not to mention images) far outside the purview of design. In January 2003, Sagmeister went to St. Mortiz to a conference where graphic designers were in the complete minority. "It was mostly product designers and educators, and I find that much more interesting. When there are people who do different things than I do, I learn from them."

142

WORKSIGHT

SUPPORT YOUNG DESIGNERS

Scott Santoro of Worksight was involved with the New York AIGA chapter, which kept him busy. "I served for two years as vice president, and I was really active. Since then, I started an AIGA student group at Pratt, which includes about fifty graduate and undergraduate students. We are able to attract good speakers, who also have a high-profile draw."

The students with whom Santoro works are interested in the wider industry of design, and this group gives them an opportunity to keep abreast of the variety of design-related events that happen all over New York City. Because the New York AIGA chapter is the largest in the country and Pratt has the largest number of graphic design students of any school in the country, providing a group for students seemed like a natural outgrowth of Santoro's work with the New York City chapter and his interest in teaching.

The students attend talks by figures such as Jean Widmer and Stefan Sagmeister and discuss what they've seen and heard. Involvement in the group can be a good foundation for the résumé for a student just out of school—being involved with a professional organization demonstrates interest in the field as a whole. In addition, involvement in the group gives students an opportunity to make contacts with people in the industry while they are still in school. "It was easy for me to start because I had so many contacts already," says Santoro. "I think it is a good thing to provide students with this opportunity."

143

ED **FELLA**

WHEN YOU RETIRE, DEAL WITH THE POSSIBILITIES, NOT THE NECESSITIES

Ed Fella describes himself as an "exit-level" designer. He has co-taught a general graduate-level graphic design seminar with first- and second-year students at California Institute of Arts (Cal Arts) in Valencia, California.

"The reason I do this is I'm retired. I'm not in the business anymore . . . I don't use a computer. I just make my own handmade pieces." Fella is also profoundly disinterested in business knowledge. He doesn't see the world of business today as any different than it was in the fifties, sixties, and seventies, when he was actively working. In addition, he doesn't know how to use a computer to do design—an essential element in the nuts-and-bolts education for design undergraduates today. "I don't really want to think about that anymore. It's part of the student's obligation to have to deal with professional practice, obviously. I have plenty of wisdom to impart, but I don't have so much knowledge anymore about the professional business and all the digital stuff. I enjoy my graduate seminar because there are other faculty involved with it. I can be kind of a grand old man of technical problems . . . I did teach full-time for about thirteen years after my career in professional work."

Staying engaged with the creativity of his older students and colleagues and maintaining his own studio on the Cal Arts campus keep Fella involved with a somewhat rarified corner of the design world, but that is OK with him. "In the grad program at Cal Arts, we deal in the possibilities, not the necessities. In undergraduate education you have to teach people how to be graphic designers. Graduate education is more experimental. By the time you come to graduate education you already are a graphic designer. In graduate education you deal with possibilities and experimental stuff."

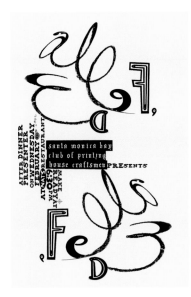

Announcement Flyers, designed by Ed Fella

144

ED **FELLA**

GO BACK TO SCHOOL, NO MATTER HOW OLD YOU ARE

Ed Fella worked in Detroit at a large design studio for the first half of his career. He had received what he calls a "Bauhaus" model of high school education—a rigorous trade education larded liberally with humanities topics— and when he got out of high school he went right to work. "In Detroit in those days you did work in large studios. It wasn't like now when designers are in small shops or individuals. We had studios with sixty people in them—that was how the profession was in those days. I did that work for a long time. I did it honestly and wasn't cynical about it. My father was an autoworker. I didn't have any problem helping to sell the cars."

"I finally went back to graduate school. I was 48 and said, 'Well, now I can become a full-time teacher and end the professional design career.' It was that Detroit idea of thirty and up, that Walter Ruther thought up—that you would work for thirty years and then you'd retire. You wouldn't be burnt out, and another person would take your place. I also could retire from professional design to teach, and I'd have time to do my personal work, which I've done since then. I'm famous now for my personal work, which is ironic—no one gives a shit about the thirty years of design work, the automotive industry, the heath care industry. These things are collectors' items now."

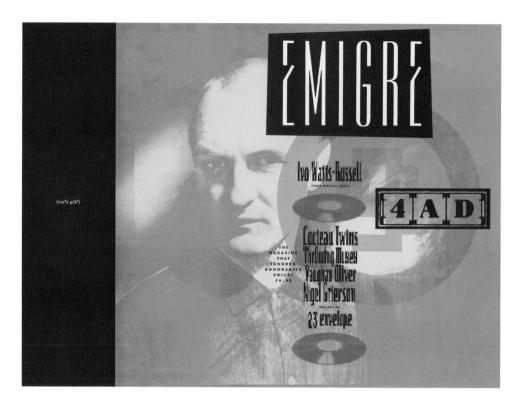

Emigre magazine cover: issue 4, designed by Rudy VanderLans and Zuzana Licko, Emigre

145

RUDY **VANDERLANS**

ZUZANA **LICKO**

START A MAGAZINE

Rudy VanderLans and Zuzana Licko created *Emigre* magazine, published between 1984 and 2005, because they were unhappy with their regular jobs. VanderLans describes the foundation of *Emigre* as "a tediously slow process that would make for some very boring reading when retold in detail. Let's just say we were very naive, and we worked very long days." In addition to working on the magazine, which in its first years was published sporadically, Licko edited fonts for Adobe and VanderLans did design work for other magazines. Their company was called Emigre Graphics, and their magazine was a forge for their emerging styles.

VanderLans and Licko were quick to adopt the Macintosh computer as a design tool when it was first introduced, a move that ultimately propelled the magazine to a higher level. By

being at the right place at the right time and applying her knowledge of font design to the new technology, Licko used the early bitmap design tools on the Macintosh to create some of the first digital fonts. Emperor, Oakland, and Emigre were designed for low-resolution printing and by the third issue became available for purchase. The sale of fonts created enough economic flexibility that the magazine was then published quarterly.

It takes a sustained effort as well as a persistent and keen business acumen to run a magazine. In terms of creative return, however, for VanderLans, the magazine format offered everything a designer could wish for: a chance to mix texts of all kinds, images, and headlines and deal with sequencing of pages. "And every time you're done with one issue, you start afresh with the next one."

Matteo Fine Linen identity and packaging, designed by Margo Chase, Chase Design Group

146

CHASE DESIGN GROUP

MAKE A LOW-BUDGET PROJECT LOOK EXPENSIVE

When Matteo's president, Matt Lenoci, first approached the Chase Design Group, Matteo had a logo and packaging scheme, but it was clearly in need of an update. The new logo is based on a classical roman serif font updated for a more modern feeling. Chase Design Group's solution for the packaging resolved two problems. The first problem was how to give the company a luxurious look without breaking its modest budget. The second was how to package the variety of sizes of product without requiring different-sized labels for each item. Chase Design Group created a single card-label printed on heavy rag stock, which is foil-stamped and embossed. These techniques would normally be prohibitively expensive, but Chase Design Group figured out a way to attach the same label to a variety of vinyl bag sizes using a grommet to hold the label to the center of the bag. This approach created a unique, high-end look for the products.

Chase Design Group also developed a series of postcard-sized info cards for each product that fit into a small custom binder of oversized fabric swatches, which allows the recipients to appreciate the full beauty of the fabrics. Expanding the concept of modern luxury across all of the company's materials established a cohesive brand that held up next to the competition and increased the integrity and appeal of the line for the consumer. As a result, selling Matteo to the end user became easier for the retailer.

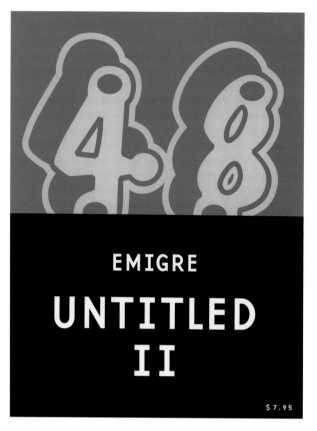

Emigre magazine covers: issue 48, issue 37, issue 47, issue 46, designed by Rudy VanderLans and Zuzana Licko, Emigre

147 READ IT ALL, FORGET IT ALL, AND DO YOUR OWN THING

RUDY **VANDERLANS**

ZUZANA **LICKO**

Because of their unique position as designers who made a magazine, advice from Rudy VanderLans and Zuzana Licko can be hard to categorize. "If you want to know how to set up a graphic design studio, you should probably talk to people like Milton Glaser or Pentagram," Vanderlans demurs. Citing their longevity, he supposes they must be doing something right.

Although Emigre does not follow the conventional model of a client-based studio, the insights VanderLans and Licko offered were nonetheless useful, particularly for people just getting started. In some sense, Emigre's work is the purest entrepreneurial model you can find—they create their own products and do their own sales and distribution. This style of business flies in the face of a conventional shop that depends on client work for its revenue and the direction of its work. Emigre essentially eschew dependence upon the client and the web of commercial acceptance. By having developed a catalog of fonts and having concentrated on the magazine, VanderLans and Licko kept themselves busy with the kind of work that challenges and satisfies them. They located a niche within the magazine market and filled it with what they wanted to see.

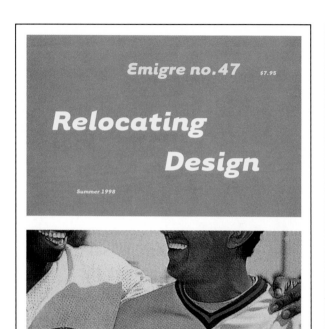

Emigre no.47 *$7.95*

Relocating

Design

Summer 1998

Emigre.No.Fortysix.Price:Seven.Ninetyfive
Fanzines and the Culture of DIY

Psychedelic Language poster, designed by Scott Santoro/Worksight

148 ACTIVELY PURSUE INTELLECTUAL SUBJECTS THAT RESONATE WITH YOU

WORKSIGHT

"I'm constantly getting involved with subjects that interest me, working months at a time, reading everything I can about it," says Scott Santoro of Worksight. This kind of intellectual curiosity drives him to research everything from psychedelia to Wittgenstein.

For a lecture about the art of the psychedelic poster, Santoro worked with a friend from Dartmouth College. "He wanted me to give a talk for a show about psychedelic poster art for which he was designing the graphics. I read everything I could find about the subject. I called every designer I knew who might know something about it. I talked to Kathy McCoy, who, it turned out, designed psychedelic posters when she was a college student, and

included her posters in the lecture. I spoke with people who were graphic designers during that time period. I also located a psychedelic typography catalog that was floating around New York, so I included that in the lecture. My friend asked me to do it from a graphic designer's point of view. The result was that a textile client of mine asked me if I had any lectures I would like to present for the Color Council in New York. It is so great to have someone ask you to give a talk like this because it forces you to learn and establish your own opinions and theories about a subject."

Santoro views this interest as ongoing; he has put the latest draft of his essay on the company website (www.worksight.com) to generate discussion and to spread the materials more widely.

Brooklyn Business Library brochure, designed by Scott Santoro/Worksight

149

WORKSIGHT

LEARN THE VERNACULAR OF A NEW FIELD

"I had just finished a piece for Gilbert paper, which was about the subculture of sturgeon spearing, and I brought it along to my meeting at the Brooklyn Business Library. The director there really liked it, and I knew I had the project just by her exuberance about it," Scott Santoro recalls when discussing an award-winning brochure he created for this small, specialized library.

The sturgeon-spearing piece was based on the subculture of people around Lake Winnebago who create small houses to drag out on to the ice each winter. Santoro hired a guide to bring him around the lake and spent some time watching the preparations, as well as the fishing itself. By learning about the traditions of this chilly pastime, he was able to accurately reflect the obsessions of the activity and speak its visual vernacular in the final piece.

In the environment of the library, where the subculture revolves around access to and mastery of information, Santoro went in with a similar, sociologically focused view. "I knew the people who ran the library were a very proud bunch. I spent three days with a copywriter and photographer doing interviews and finding vignettes of people who use the library." Libraries are often, ironically, lackluster about graphic design, especially considering the fact that books and the communication of information is the central task of such institutions. The brochure he created ended up winning numerous awards within the library system, so its effectiveness as a tool to speak to experts in the field was clear. In addition, it is a beautiful and intricate piece that works very hard despite its diminutive size. It also achieves the goal of introducing and orienting newcomers to the library in a hands-on manner. "I think it shows how much I like the library too," says Santoro. By incorporating language that was specific to the library and to library patrons, Santoro learned more about how business organizes information and how to better access that information in a visual manner.

150

CHASE DESIGN GROUP

CONTINUE YOUR OWN EDUCATION BY TEACHING

In addition to teaching Type 4 at Cal Arts, Los Angeles, designer Margo Chase also gave workshops from time to time. "I find it very satisfying," she notes. "It gives me a different perspective on the practice of design."

Dirty Words was a project that Chase did at a design conference in Nebraska called "Art Farm." About 40 local designers participated in workshops presented by several prominent visiting designers. The point was to escape the routine of the standard workday and get inspired.

Chase provided large pieces of white paper and pots of India ink. She asked the participants to search the grounds around the hotel and collect objects. They then had to use these objects to create letters and words. They could write by dipping the objects in ink, using them as stamps, or simply gluing them down. The participants raided trash cans, pulled weeds, and made ink stains on the carpet, all in the name of creative expression.

Dirty Words workshop, designed by Margo Chase, Chase Design Group

151

DEVELOP AND SUSTAIN AN ART PRACTICE THROUGHOUT YOUR LIFE

ED **FELLA**

Ed Fella occupies a unique position as a retired designer, functioning somewhere on the edges of the design world but not fully in it. "I've carved out this odd position where I'm still a graphic designer using graphic design but as an art practice. Graphic design has to have a subject, a deadline—all of that. With these pieces, I'm the subject—it's the opposite of graphic design, where the artist is never the subject. The designer is never the subject."

In 2000, Fella published *Letters from America*, a collection of his Polaroid photographs of lettering and surfaces. In addition to this, he has a backlog of work that he hopes to eventually get out into the public world. "I have a bunch of books sitting here, but I haven't really gotten around to them. I have one all on faces and landscapes. They are signs or windows or posters with faces and landscapes painted on them—Polaroid format. I have thousands of those. My wife has put them together and edited them, but we haven't gone to any publishers. I have about 80 sketchbooks with 100 drawings in each one. They are shown here and there, but they haven't been published. I like to make stuff; I don't really like to put it together. It is always such a pain in the ass just to send stuff to shows. I get plenty of calls, so I haven't gone out there and pushed." Although he supported himself doing conventional graphic design for many years, Ed Fella's personal work has been his most enjoyable, as well as his most successful and critically regarded.

Announcement Flyers, designed by Ed Fella

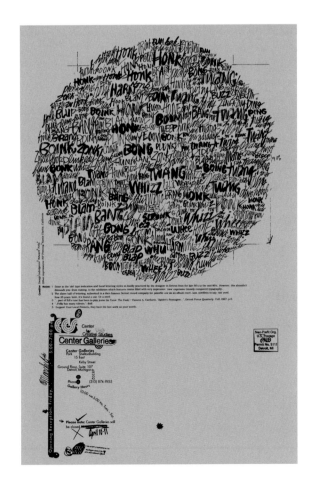

152

**MILES MURRAY
SORRELL FUEL**

NEVER STOP LEARNING, DON'T START TEACHING

The Miles Murray Sorrell FUEL team has never been drawn to teaching at art schools. Instead, they feel that they provide a good insight into their graphic sensibility as designers through their books. They continue to learn by producing work in ways that push the boundaries of their knowledge and keep their interest keen.

"We set up and photographed the adidas ad one morning in a local community sports hall. This ad was part of a European adidas campaign in which artists and designers were asked to come up with an image based around the line 'Forever Sport.' This campaign gave us the opportunity to generate an image for adidas that was not focused on a specific product or personality. We used the sculpture of our studio contents from our book (*FUEL 3000*, pp. 20 and 21) as a starting point. In the local community sports hall, we constructed a similar sculpture using the sporting equipment we found on the premises and added various adidas products."

By relating a commercial project to a more personal, noncommercial project, FUEL moves what might otherwise be a conventional shoe advertisement into a new realm, appropriating the products as elements in their own art, rather than allowing the product to dictate the content.

**adidas "Forever Sport" print advertising, designed by
Miles Murray Sorrell FUEL**

153 ENCOURAGE YOUNG PEOPLE TO MAKE ART

JOHN C **JAY**

John C Jay rarely participates in design conferences in Japan; rather, he concentrates his professional development on speaking with small groups or doing internal presentations for clients. In addition, he works with Illustration magazine to develop and encourage young talent. "I'm very involved with them in encouraging young artists . . . They did a call for entries for young artists in Japan. I wrote a brief, and the first thing they said to me was, 'Your client is Nike—why don't you do something like designing a new sneaker, a new Nike shoe?' I'm not here to train them for a career; I'm here to motivate them to think about the world in a way that perhaps they haven't before. One of the outlets is self-expression—to answer the question, why be an artist? And so I said in my brief, 'God—whichever one you believe in—has given us the ability to have emotions and to express those emotions. You have been blessed with another ability, which is a physical ability of some kind of artistic skill with which to express ideas. Express to me the most powerful emotion that you are feeling at the moment. Don't make it about trendiness and style. Don't worry

if it is a cool technique. Don't worry about whether it is something that your teacher or employer said you couldn't do. Don't worry if it is a thing that doesn't sell. Just forget all that and express the most powerful emotion in your body right now.'"

For the special competition, "expressing your emotions," the magazine received more than 500 entries. Jay spent hours looking through and judging them; he then made a presentation of the 15 that he chose, and they were featured in the magazine. Hiroyuki Yoda, whose work is featured here, was chosen by Jay as the first place winner. This contribution to the creative lives of the young artists of Japan is essential to the work Jay performs as a creative director. Through this project, he networks with a publication and lends his talents to their creative direction. He also stays in touch with Japan's nascent emerging talent.

Yoda illustrations, designed by John C Jay, Wieden+Kennedy, Tokyo

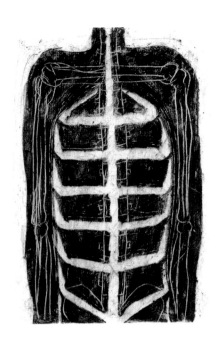

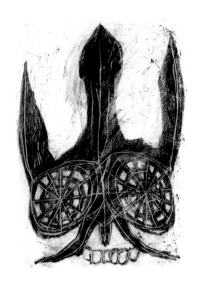

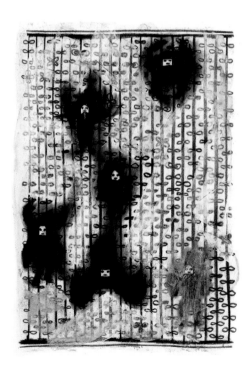

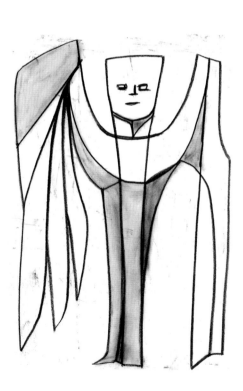

154

MARK **RANDALL**

TRAVEL AS MUCH AS POSSIBLE

The Worldstudio Foundation inspires co-founders Mark Randall and David Sterling by providing links to the outside world that are constructive and engaged, which help them to keep their perspectives fresh. Another thing they like to do is travel, and this interest connects with the interests of the Worldstudio Foundation, which, in part, concerns itself with cross-cultural understanding and the introduction of perspective into the work of designers and design students. When Randall travels around the world, he gets to see all kinds of voices that aren't seen in white, Euro-centric design offices. Part of the reason Worldstudio Foundation offers scholarships is to help art and design students who come from minority backgrounds get a leg up in their work and in the industry. These voices make a big difference when they are heard.

Randall prefers the spontaneity of travel as an educational experience to the comparatively staid environment of the design conference. Although such conferences are useful for meeting people, he remarks that in truth the last thing he wants to do is go to a conference about graphic design. He'd much rather go to a conference of physicists, or some other topic about which he knows little. He's been doing graphic design for over twenty-six years. "It's not that I know it all," he says. "I just want a little bit more diversity in my life—not to denigrate conferences, either. I went to the last AIGA conference because they invited me to speak, and I thought it was great. I thought they did a great job, and I saw a lot of really interesting speakers. It wasn't bad, but it is just not a personal interest of mine to go to conferences." Travel allows one to step into a completely unique environment and be bombarded with fresh ideas, sights, and sounds, which is invaluable in any discipline.

1998 *Sphere* magazine, designed by Mark Randall, Worldstudio Foundation

WHEN
SOMETHING
TERRIBLE
HAPPENS
PEOPLE
WAKE UP

Image from Worksight promotional card, designed by Scott Santoro/ Worksight

---

155

WORKSIGHT

LOOK AT THE EVERYDAY WORLD FOR INSPIRATION

The idea of staying grounded and connected to the world of the everyday continually infuses the work of Scott Santoro and Worksight. Through the use of the plumbing metaphor, Santoro infuses his work with a practicality and simplicity of language that belies some of the pretentious conceit that the profession of design sometimes exhibits. "My father directs the flow of water. I direct the flow of information. There's a basic similarity between what we both do for a living."

After taking a creative writing course, Santoro developed his observations into a short story about a backyard clothesline viewed from one of the irregularly shaped windows at the Whitney Museum of Art, part of which is excerpted here and can be read in its entirely on the Worksight website. ". . . I spoke his dialect from the land

of graphic design and knew exactly what he was getting at. Outside, in a neighbor's backyard, sat a poetic example of 'the everyday.' It effortlessly blended life and art, and was as deep as anyone wanted it to be.

"It's a bit of an oxymoron to bring up the philosopher, G. W. F. Hegel, when writing about 'the everyday.' His philosophy's better combined with rocket science. Yet Hegel's maxim should have been flashing above the window, 'The familiar is not necessarily the known.' Of course it would have ruined the refreshing unexpectedness of the moment. The clothesline seemed innocent of any intention other than reeling out a week's worth of freshly washed clothing. But, underneath that layer of utility, it begged the viewer for meaning to be assigned. As Z said, 'It wasn't trying to be anything.' It was nice that way; like a blank canvas—ready, waiting, and full of possibility.

"It's as if the clothesline was metaphorically available for anyone and everyone to pin meaning to it, each viewer as a potential author in a democratic kind of art. The location made sense in the back of the Whitney which touts itself as a museum of American art—clotheslines feel as American as apple pie."

Santoro's observations reflect his intense, daily engagement with the world of the everyday, and the fact that looking carefully at your surroundings can have a significant effect on your art. Letting in the seemingly unimportant and ephemeral can lead to inspiring observations and creative insights into the work of design.

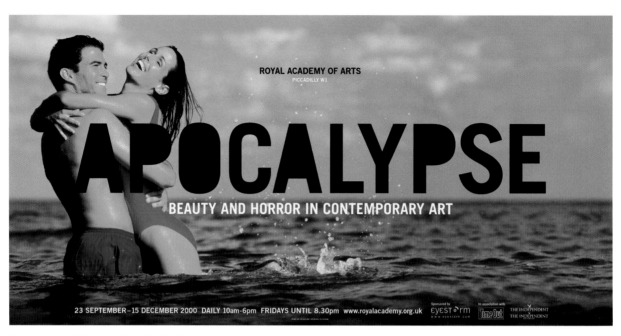

ROYAL ACADEMY OF ARTS
PICCADILLY W1

APOCALYPSE

BEAUTY AND HORROR IN CONTEMPORARY ART

23 SEPTEMBER–15 DECEMBER 2000 DAILY 10am-6pm FRIDAYS UNTIL 8.30pm www.royalacademy.org.uk

Sponsored by
eyest•rm
www.eyestorm.com

In association with
Time Out

THE INDEPENDENT
THE INDEPENDENT

Apocalypse poster "Swimmers", designed by Why Not Associates

156

**WHY NOT
ASSOCIATES**

WATCH VIDEOS OF COMEDIANS

To gain a sense of perspective and to get inspiration, Andy Altmann of Why Not Associates watches old English comedy videos. "Morecambe and Wise are probably my favorite. They were a comedy double-act, who modeled themselves originally on Abbott and Costello. They were very British, actually, in the end and became some of the most popular figures of their generation."

Part of his love for British comedy is bound to its surreal nature, which links it to art, such as Lewis Caroll's Alice in Wonderland, which makes the regular world look peculiar and the strange seem normal. Typographical experiments, as well as experiments with language and form, created new venues for early twentieth-century artists. "Some of these comedians can be quite surreal," Altmann notes. "They make you really look twice at things. This perspective is, in effect, what you want good design to do—make you think about normal things in a strange new way."

Spike Milligan is another comedian that Altmann considers to be not only a pioneering comedian but also very surreal in his approach. "The surrealist painters so often use humor to make their work effective. It makes sense that surrealism is such an important inspiration to me. Just juxtaposing a word and an image can have such immense power, especially when you least expect it."

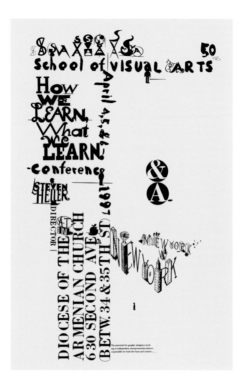

Announcement Flyers, designed by Ed Fella

157

ED **FELLA**

PRACTICE AND PREACH, DON'T THEORIZE AND TEACH

The work of a commercial graphic designer and the work of a graphic design teacher have very different demands. Nonetheless, these activities share certain elements, and Ed Fella, who has experienced both, has many insights on the subject. After working for over 30 years in Detroit in a large design shop, Fella returned to school at age 48, when he went to Cranbrook to get his master's degree. After graduating, he made his way to Southern California where he taught full-time at Cal Arts for thirteen years. He is now retired.

His aphorisms, such as "Rules are taught to be broken only exceptionally" and "Practice and preach, don't theorize and teach," serve as words to the wise as well as pithy summations of his sometimes eccentric approach to design. The precise work of a font designer, for example, is often disrupted in Fella's mostly hand-done lettering experiments.

His inimitable style clearly cannot be taught as such, but it can be "preached"—rather than displaying a series of rules to follow, Fella's work and teaching style emphasize courageous creativity. Deeply schooled in the theory of design, he eschews theorization per se in favor of a strong practice and also believes teachers teach best by doing rather than theorizing.

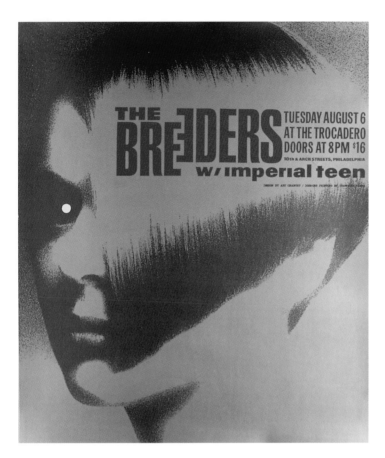

Posters for Trocadero club, AIGA, designed by Art Chantry

158

ART **CHANTRY**

CHANGE YOUR ENVIRONMENT

Although Art Chantry is from the Northwest, he moved to St. Louis in 2000. The change of scene provided a drastic change of perspective for Chantry. Often credited as the founder of the graphics style of some major Seattle music movements of the '80s and '90s, such as work for *The Rocket* newspaper, Sub Pop records, and Estrus records, Chantry had a history and identity in Seattle based primarily around subcultural movements. Consequently, when he moved to St. Louis and tried to get jobs outside of the world that he had formed (and that had formed him), it was tricky.

"I moved away from Seattle because I couldn't make a living there anymore," Chantry notes. The economic boom that gripped Seattle in the '90s brought with it both an inflated housing and studio market and a falsely healthy economy demanding design services. Chantry had previously been able to support himself by teaching and doing design work; in addition, he had a subsidized housing arrangement that he knew would not last. When the bottom fell out in the '90s, things had to change—he needed a change of scene, and he needed to be in an environment that provided more economic stability.

His partner, Jamie Sheehan, also a graphic designer, moved to St. Louis for work, so Chantry turned his back on his entire life and

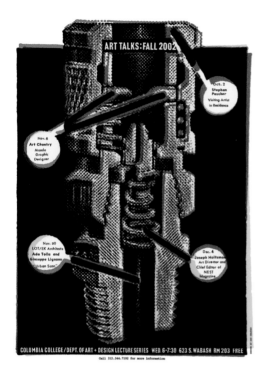

moved from the West to the "Gateway to the West." St. Louis could not be more different from Seattle in terms of culture, economic climate, and social makeup. Designers were paid what Chantry calls "New York rates," and many large corporations were based in St. Louis. All the designers he met worked for large agencies. He found the environment to be very conservative, and there was no alternative culture scene to speak of.

When the market bottomed out in St. Louis, it was like Seattle all over again for Chantry. There was one crucial difference: The weak real estate market in St. Louis had allowed him to purchase a house, which now serves as the home base from which he and Jamie do their freelance work. As a result of his work in Seattle, Chantry feels he is (for better or worse) pigeonholed into doing work for countercultural products and events such as film festivals, skate parks, and record companies—ironically, none of it originating in St. Louis.

Chantry changed his surroundings and as a result gained a new perspective from the different sights and environments to which he gained access. Although his client base did not change radically, his change of scene helped him get a fresh outlook toward his work.

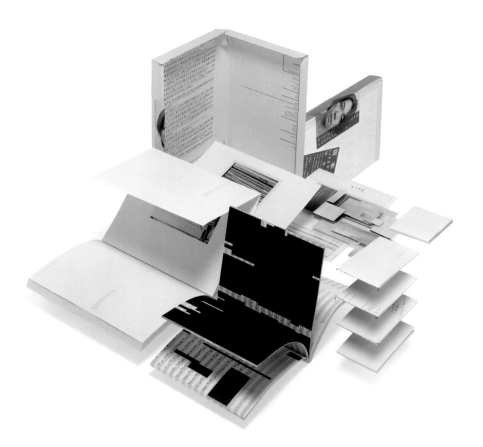

159

HIDEKI NAKAJIMA

HAVE CONVERSATIONS WITH GREAT TALENTS

Hideki Nakajima derives his primary inspiration from conversations with what he calls "great talents"—people both inside and outside the world of design, particularly musicians, fashion designers, and other artists. According to Nakajima, "The reason I do not go to the bookstore is I know that there is not 'new' creativeness in the strict meaning. It takes at least two or three months to publish a book from the beginning . . . It is nonsense to find 'new' creativeness in the bookstore. Real 'new' creativeness exists in the brains of great talents."

Nakajima took some photographs for an ongoing series of compositions for *Cut* magazine before he began designing the images utilizing surface, color, and typography. Realizing that he was not a photographer, he turned back to

graphic design. In an interview from 1999, he notes, "Through meeting various people such as Ryuichi Sakamoto, Andres Serrano, and Kyoji Takahashi, I realized that the world extends beyond my knowledge and that the outside world is full of extremely talented people. To compete with these people, I had to return to my field, graphic design."

Sometimes, however, great talents can be found at home. For Nakajima, his children are another source of inspiration. He cites "the birth and growth of my babies" as the singular most influential nondesign element that has affected his work. "Sometimes cute expressions I've never done before appear in my design. I used to prefer colorless and strict designs, but I tend to use colorful and soft ones today," he notes.

Ryuichi Sakamoto, Sampled Life, designed by Hideki Nakajima

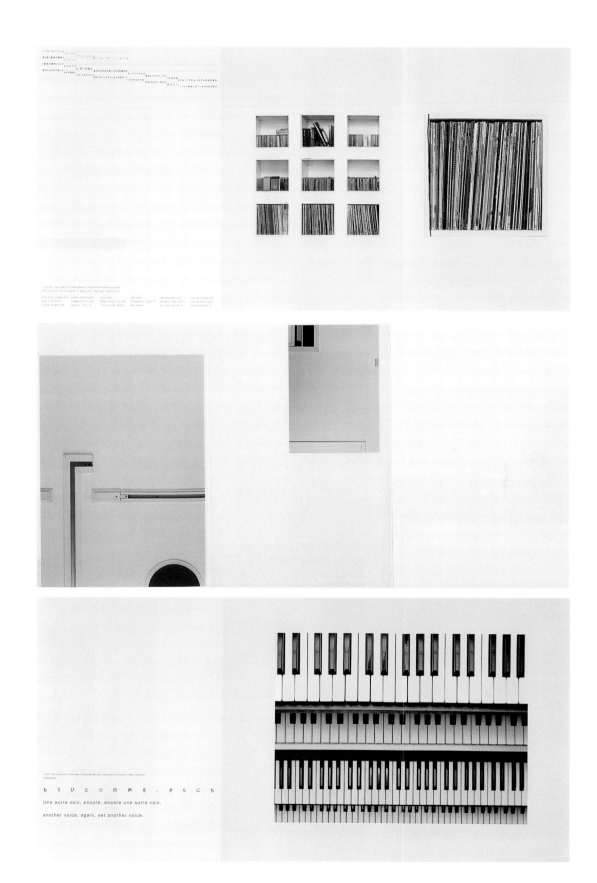

もうひとつの声を、さらにも

Une autre voix, encore, encore une autre voix.

another voice, again, yet another voice.

160 KEEP CREATIVITY ALIVE BY ANY MEANS

MILES MURRAY SORRELL FUEL

The books *Pure Fuel* and *Fuel 3000* inspired advertising agency creatives at Bartle Bogle Hegarty to commission Miles Murray Sorrell FUEL to create a print campaign for the European launch of Microsoft's new game console Xbox. Damon Murray notes, "We wanted a raw, spontaneous feel to the campaign. The images needed to look as real and natural as possible, and the snapshot quality of the pictures helped this. We took all the photographs for the campaign, art-directing ourselves. The design has a strong typographic element, similar to the FUEL books. The Xbox campaign responded to a brief, while at the same time, retained a feeling of our personal work."

Xbox print advertising, designed by Miles Murray Sorrell FUEL

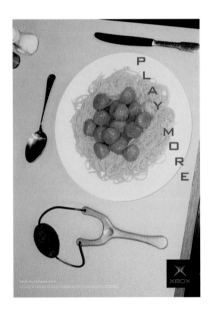

161

MARGO **CHASE**

READ A GOOD BOOK

Margo Chase derives a lot of creative inspiration from reading. "I really love to read, and I spend lots of free time doing it. I read both fiction and nonfiction, as well as that special category of reading that I call 'reading the pictures.' I do most of my reading in bed at night before I go to sleep. Really great writing can cause me to lose sleep and large chunks of my weekend until I've finished. My list of favorite books constantly changes based on what I've read most recently.

"I have rather catholic tastes when it comes to books, and as you might guess, they don't all have direct bearing on my work. A lot of my reading is just decompression and escape. A. S. Byatt's richly romantic writing falls into this category. So does Umberto Eco's Baudolino, which I'm currently reading. Germs, Guns, and Steel by Jared Diamond has had some effect on my thinking because it deals with the reasons why some societies are more successful than others. The author suggests that success is based on access to resources rather than on some innate superiority or intelligence. I think he would shudder if he thought I was applying his ideas to success in the design business, but some analogies seem inescapable.

"Chip Kidd's book has more obvious bearing because it's a witty book about design school. This Is Modern Art is a wonderfully sardonic and insightful overview of what's happening in modern art these days. Collings's comments and observations keep coming to mind in both positive and negative ways. I've quoted him to my design students more than once.

"As designers we are asked to solve all kinds of different problems, yet our own experiences are often too limited to provide us with the insights or understanding to do this well. I think the part of my brain that intuitively 'gets it' is the part that has unconsciously absorbed the ideas and concepts put forth in books.

"Reading is an extremely important part of my life, and I can't imagine what it's like for those who don't enjoy it. At the very least, it broadens my horizons and makes for interesting conversation at the dinner table!"

162

SET UP SHOP IN A FOREIGN COUNTRY DURING A RECESSION

JOHN C **JAY**

When Wieden+Kennedy first decided to open their shop, Japan was in the middle of a decade-long recession, and the Japanese economy was in shambles. Advertising expenditures around the world were down, and many observers considered opening a new Japanese office as a great risk. Jay notes, "From a business standpoint, if you read the *Wall Street Journal* or the business pages of the *New York Times*, one would think it would be economic suicide to come over here and open a new business, but we felt that anytime there is a long economic recession, cultural changes are bound to occur."

At times like this, unique business opportunities arise. Jay explains, "That was what we focused on; that's what we held as our faith. And of course, we were aiming to reach the youth culture that we knew was very powerful. But it isn't until the moment you truly get inside it yourself, really immerse yourself culturally, that you begin to understand how influential Japanese youth culture is to the rest of us in the creative world."

Wieden+Kennedy opened with only one client, but fortunately it was an enormous one: the Japanese arm of the company that grew up with the Portland office, Nike. Jay comments, "My goal was not to be a typical agency. Even within the Wieden world, we wanted to do something different. We wanted to come in and become firmly entrenched in the cultural landscape of Japan. We did not want to be an office that depended on Western clients for their leftovers, their small adaptation projects. We wanted to work with the best and the brightest of the leaders here in Japan, people who were looking for innovation, who were looking for change, and who were looking for the highest levels of strategic and creative execution. Getting our message across—you can only prove that point by doing work."

Taking the risk to open a new shop in Japan was based on Jay's confidence that he could find a staff that could partner with him and grow the company into a dynamic entity and into one of the leading ad firms in Japan. In addition, he saw the economic and cultural climate in Japan as ripe for change and for dramatic challenge to the status quo.

体力がある女

やせてない女

丈夫な女

食欲がある女

Nike Swim print advertising, designed by John C Jay, Wieden+Kennedy, Tokyo

163

TODD **WATERBURY**

WORK WITH VISUAL ARTISTS

For a number of years, Todd Waterbury of Wieden+Kennedy collaborated with visual artist Peter Wegner, whose work deals with the relationships between social conventions and formal artistic elements such as color.

The artist, who usually shows his work in galleries, wanted to work with Waterbury to express his ideas in a book. The artist's work tends to be very large pieces of plywood–8 feet x 10 feet (2.4 m x 3 m) at their largest. Rather than create a record of a particular show, Wegner wanted to explore and collaborate with another artist to see his vision in a different medium. Together, Waterbury and Wegner worked with the form of the book to translate the art into something more intimate. Although Waterbury had not designed a book before, he and Wegner share a similar aesthetic, as well as a love of ephemera. Their collaboration pushes the limits of the book form to create an experience that they hoped would be more memorable for the reader.

The process of collaboration was somewhat informal. Wegner had developed a body of work over a number of years. During that time, he would ask a few friends, including Waterbury, into his studio to discuss the work. This experience gave Waterbury insight into the process of the paintings, both how they were done and how the thinking behind them had developed.

The work that Waterbury does with Wegner is different from his work at Wieden+Kennedy because the collaborative nature of the project eliminates the idea of "creative" and "client." Because the relationship is not commercial in nature, Waterbury can try work that proceeds at a very different pace, with different aims. The ideas and sometimes complex execution provide an outlet for Waterbury to conceptualize the work of design outside of the commercial realm.

Peter Wegner, American Types, designed by Todd Waterbury, Wieden+Kennedy, New York

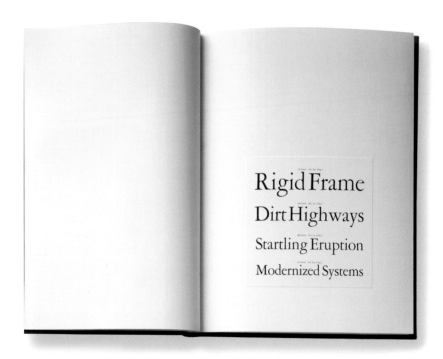

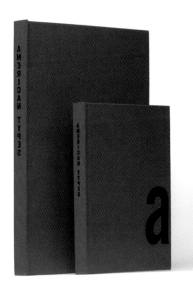

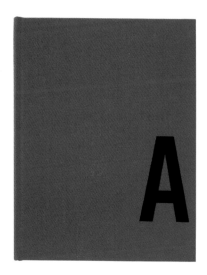

164

DEVELOP PERSONAL GROWTH AND PERSONAL TASTE; YOU ARE WHAT YOU EAT

MILES MURRAY SORRELL FUEL

Phaidon asked FUEL to design a 448-page art book after seeing *Fuel 3000* and the work they had done for White Cube. The books represents a major collection of work from 100 contemporary artists from around the world. It was a challenge for the firm to design a template for such an extensive collection of work that retained variety and interest while keeping a necessary order and consistency. It is the first book of this kind that FUEL has designed.

The double cover folds over with a magnetic fastening. The opportunity to work with art from some of the world's most renowned artists in the design of this book gave FUEL access to a steady diet of their peers: both nourishing and challenging.

Cream 3 cover and spreads, designed by Miles Murray Sorrell FUEL

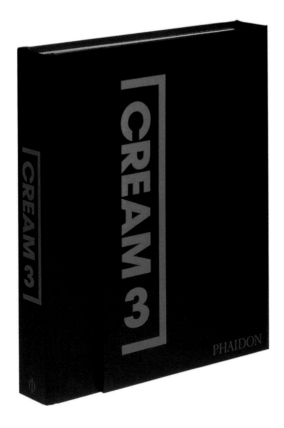

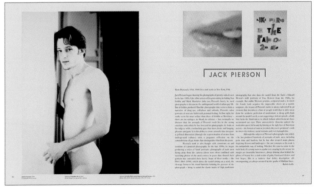

165

JOHN C **JAY**

TAKE RISKS WITH YOUR CAREER

John C Jay spent most of his career in New York City. He started in editorial design, gaining both experience in and reverence for both making magazines and collecting news. He worked with a variety of editors and writers, all the while learning how to tell important stories through visuals and words.

Then Jay moved into the field of fashion where, he observes, "many times words are not evident or necessary." He served as long-time creative director and then marketing director for Bloomingdale's in New York, back in the day when stores like that were important icons in the cultural (and not simply the retail) world. He cites his training in what he calls "cultural authenticity" to be the most important aspect of the editorial work that he brought into the fashion field. "Then, after 13 years, it seems to be in our nature to challenge our clients, to tell them they are not taking enough risks,

that they are not looking at the big picture. What happens is that creative people themselves become a victim of this, become too immersed in their tiny little businesses and lose sight of the bigger picture. Creative people tend to lose the ability to take risks."

In 1993, Jay left New York, not for his former haunts of Paris, Milan, or Berlin, but for Portland, Oregon. His move to Portland to work for ad giant Wieden+Kennedy was a risky one. He explains, "That was my first radical step in finding a way to not become too comfortable with myself, my career, and what I wanted to do creatively."

Looking for some way to shake up "my own status quo," in 1998, Jay moved across the Pacific Ocean to open the Tokyo office of Wieden+Kennedy. Tokyo offered Jay a unique opportunity to take the culture and values of Wieden+Kennedy to one of the most exciting cities in the world, a city that contains the most influential youth and pop culture. "I wanted to apply some of our thinking, be a sponge, soak it up, and see if we couldn't spread some of that learning through our network around the world."

Jay's approach to challenging himself permeates his work as well. The Presto 3 campaign was consciously created to avoid commercial conventions and to inspire physical movement viscerally through the movement of sound and visuals, without the image of an athlete or traditonal sport. Three types of "movement" were featured: the music of electronica, hip hop orchestra, and human beat box. The goal was to illustrate that the Presto concept had grown to another level.

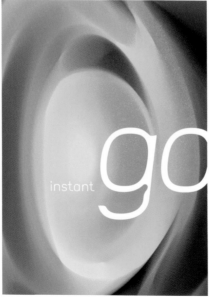

Presto 3: "Instant Go," designed by John C Jay, Wieden+Kennedy, Tokyo

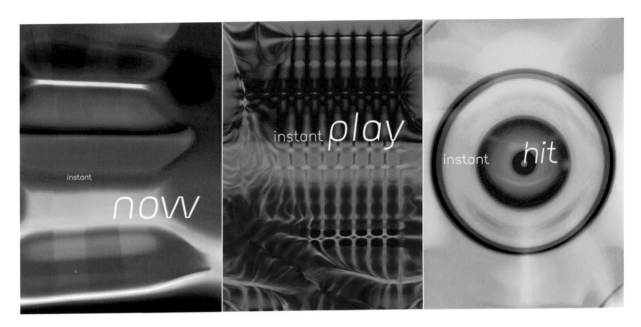

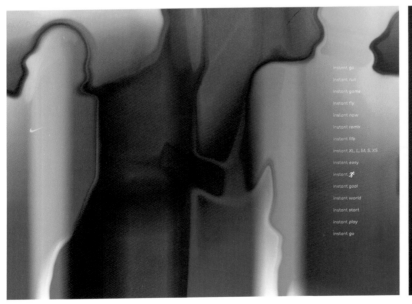

Presto 3: "Instant Go," designed by John C Jay, Wieden+Kennedy, Tokyo

166

DONOVAN N **BEERY**

DO IT FOR FUN

"Do projects that sound fun, whether you think you have time to do them or not. Some projects I had the most fun doing were pro bono. I did them at times where I was busy enough that I probably should have said no, but didn't.

"One of those fun projects was designing Halloween invites for a party a friend was throwing at a bar. This project gave me the opportunity to draw again, as well as the challenge of seeing if I could make 800 invites on a $100 (£61) printing budget.

It also doesn't hurt being able to say that the bar was supposed to go out of business three weeks after the party but did so well that night that they were still in business the next year.

"On this project, I wanted to print program covers, invites, thank-you cards, RSVP cards, and two small inserts to put with the program on the same print run, all two-over-two with full bleeds (total sheet size was 12" × 18" [30 × 46 cm]). The printer even allowed me to send the project with no crop marks (which allowed me to design the pieces ¼-inch [6 mm] larger), along with a PDF document showing where the cuts would be made afterwards."

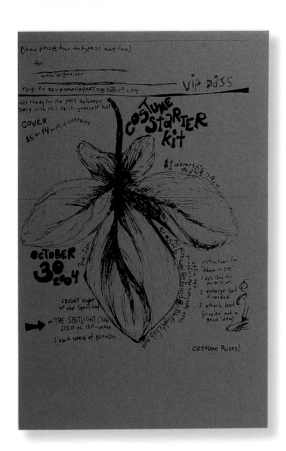

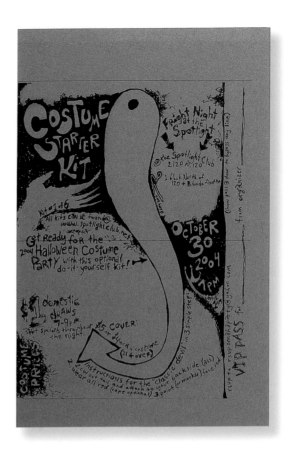

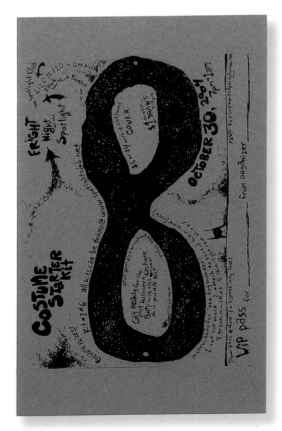

167

STEVE **GORDON, JR**

GET OUT IN THE GREENERY

"There is no designer more gifted, brilliant, and inspiring than Mother Nature. Look at the patterns of branches reaching into the sky. Check out the color combinations in the fall. Take note of how many shades of green there are in a single tree. Study the sleek lines in a pigeon or a falcon. As designers, we often find ourselves trying to force things, to manhandle type, color, and image into a pleasing composition. A mindful walk in the woods is a good reminder that the most stunning designs often happen naturally."

168

M **MAVROMATIS**

LOOK WITHIN

"Keeping motivated and fresh, like any other thing, starts from within. I use contemplation and questioning in such a way that it pushes my conceptual thinking and how I execute an idea. I chose design for a career that wouldn't be all consuming in my life. I think the diversity in my interests and activities impacts my design life in a positive way."

The Spotlight Club, "Fright Night at the Spotlight" Halloween costume starter kits, designed by Donovan N Beery, Eleven19 Communications, Inc.

AIGA Nebraska 365 show poster design, designed by Steve Gordon, Jr, RDQLUS

169

TAKE IMMEDIATE INSPIRATION FROM YOUR IMMEDIATE ENVIRONMENT

SETH **CHEEKS**

"Maybe I'll think of a funny line I heard someone say on the subway and that will spark a mental image, or I'll pass someone selling some old furniture and think 'whoa, that's a cool texture on that old table.' I'll pull out my point-and-shoot, snap a few pictures of the old wood, and boom—next thing you know, I'm in Adobe Illustrator, adding to my texture library."

170

LOOK FOR THE ROAD NOT TAKEN

JOENG-KWON **GYE**

"If you can, travel around without a destination.
If you can't travel, go out and take a walk until
an idea comes to you."

"Me Becomes Lotus, Lotus Becomes Me," designed by Joeng-kwon Gye

171

STEVE **GORDON, JR**

LEARN SOMETHING NEW

"It's tempting to sign up for yet another design class, or improve your Photoshop skills, or learn how to create a new typeface. But to really give your creativity a boost, go take a class in something that isn't design related. Take a creative writing class—you'll learn a lot about how to organize ideas and tell a story, skills that will help you present your work. Sign up for a small business course and figure out how to put all your accounts online—brushing up on accounting helps your brain and your business. How about drawing or painting? Pottery or knitting? Almost every town has a local arts center that offers several-week sessions of community classes in the evenings. Find yourself a creative outlet that has nothing to do with design and your designs—not to mention, your state of mind—will certainly improve."

VISIT
JACQUIE &
JASON'S
WEBSITE AT
YINANDTWANG.WEDDINGWINDOW.COM

❀ INFO ON THE WEDDING, DIRECTIONS, ETC.

STEPHEN CHI WING AND IDY SI LING LAI
INVITE YOU TO SHARE AND CELEBRATE
THE MARRIAGE OF THEIR DAUGHTER

JACQUELINE WING YUEN
TO
JASON LEE HEMBREY

SON OF MICHAEL LEE
AND DEBRA JENNINGS HEMBREY

SATURDAY, THE SIXTEENTH OF JUNE
TWO THOUSAND AND SEVEN
AT SIX IN THE EVENING

TRIBECA ROOFTOP
2 DESBROSSES STREET
NEW YORK CITY

RECEPTION TO IMMEDIATELY FOLLOW

172

NICOLE **BLOCK**

BE A TRENDSPOTTER AND SETTER

"I love to stay on top of what other creatives are doing in my field. It's important to keep up on trends, even if it's just to know what to avoid. I like to know what my clients will want, while also knowing what has been done to death. Looking at what other designers are coming up with keeps me sharp."

173

KEITH **BOWMAN**

MENTAL EXCERCISE KEEPS YOU FRESH AND FIT

"Look everywhere for inspiration. Find things that interest you and then try to understand why they interest you. The basic principles of design can be applied to almost everything.

Take music, for example. A good song relies upon, among other things, balance, unity, and emphasis. Find a song that you like and try to critique it based on the principles of design. Try to figure out what makes the music successful and really understand why you relate to the music. This will help you concentrate and think about the structure of how things work, which will ultimately help you in your design concepts."

Yuen/Hembrey wedding invitation design and illustration, designed by Nicole Block, NicEvents

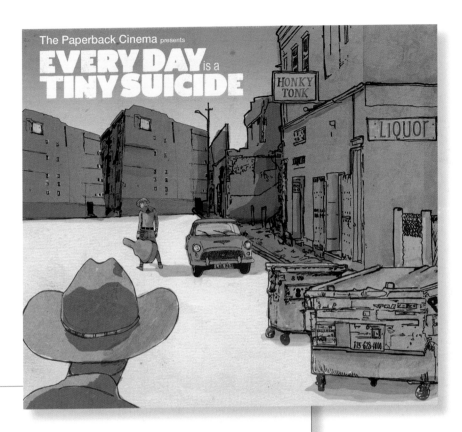

The Paperback Cinema presents

EVERY DAY is a TINY SUICIDE CD SINGLE
From the album, *When I Sober Up.*

Includes the bonus tracks
Whiskey Tears
The Sun will burn itself out
Wolves

Paperback Cinema CD package design, designed by
Keith Bowman, The Design Bureau of Amerika

174

CHRISTINE **GODLEWSKI**

STRUCTURE HELPS CREATIVITY

"Keeping a regular schedule keeps me motivated. If I keep business hours, I have free time in the evenings to look forward to doing other things I love."

Publicis/Nestlé, Nestlé Crunch media kit design, designed by
Christine Godlewski, Genius Creative

175

STEVE **GORDON, JR**

GET SOME CREATIVITY ON YOUR BACK

"Design a week's worth of T-shirts, get them printed, and wear them around. Not only will the creative exercise get your brain moving but you'll be excited every day by the idea of having something cool to wear, and you'll be marketing yourself every time you're out and about on the street. If they're really good and you get lots of compliments, put them up on CaféPress' website (www.cafepress.com) and you may find yourself with another revenue stream without any upfront costs."

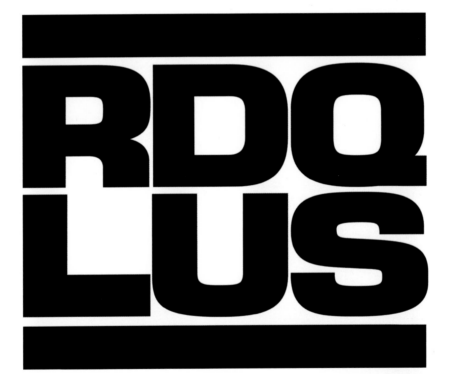

RDQLUS "Back in the Day" promotional T-shirt design, designed by Steve Gordon, Jr, RDQLUS

176

SETH CHEEKS

CREATE CREATIVE PRODUCTS THAT KEEP ON GIVING

"Learn how to make your work make you money while you're not working. Build and create ideas, concepts, and products that can exist for purchase or free download and will continually draw audiences to your work."

We are in the business of ideas—thinking up, concepting, producing, sharing, and ultimately selling our creative thoughts and expressions. If you think or create something that is a bit different and has a special twist, don't hold onto it—find a way to share it. You might not get paid much for some of the following ideas, but doing things like writing an article or creating a typeface help shape your creative output and get your name out there in a new way so people can discover you and your work.

Here are some ways you can expand your creative repertoire:

- Create a typeface.

- Design a character/icon set.

- Develop your own texture effects.

- Make your own set of Photoshop brushes.

- Offer tutorials on your design techniques.

- Start a blog.

- Write articles or books.

- Use your own photography or illustration in a project.

3Sixteen apparel website design, designed by Seth Cheeks, CheekyDSN

Chapter Eight:

DESIGNING PUBLICATIONS

According to Chris Vermaas the client for the secondhand-car journal, *AutoPrijswijzer*, told him, "'Leave the fashionable typographic tricks at home in your drawers.' He didn't want to win design awards; he didn't want to end up in the museum—these were his own words—he wanted to make a graphic tool that serves a need, reaches an audience, and generates a lot of money." All of which this publication did.

177

JEREMY **LESLIE**

STEVEN **HELLER**

INA **SALTZ**

READ THE CONTENT

The fundamental difference between publication design and other forms of graphic design is the primacy of content. Sure, if you're designing a brochure you have to understand the company you're working for, or if you're doing an album cover you should listen to the music. But most publications live, die, and are driven by words—lots of words—and a publication designer's audience is first and foremost a reader. So the designer must be as well.

Successful publication designers say familiarizing themselves with content is the most important activity they do. Jeremy Leslie, former creative director at John Brown Publishing in London and current creative director of the *MagCulture* blog, says, "The first thing is to read the stuff you're laying out. It sounds natural, but there are people who don't." Designer, educator, and writer Steven Heller echoes this exhortation. "There's a whole generation that's not

reading anymore, not just designers," he says. "But it's really simple: If you get a manuscript, you should read it. If you don't read the whole thing, you won't know what's going on, you won't get the nuances, and it will come back to bite you. There are times when you read something and it's boring, but even that is something you have to know if you're a designer."

And when reading, don't just look for word count or line length. "There are people who just flow in the words," says Leslie. "That's not design, that's filling up space." It's important to absorb, understand, and respect the work of the author. As Ina Saltz, an educator and designer, notes, "What differentiates editorial designers from others is that they care deeply about the content. Otherwise, they should go work someplace else where images drive things."

178

LUKE **HAYMAN**

INA **SALTZ**

STEVEN **HELLER**

KALLE **LASN**

JEREMY **LESLIE**

CONTENT INFORMS DESIGN; DESIGN YIELDS TO CONTENT

Experienced and effective publication designers try to enhance what's being communicated by the editorial mission of the magazine and what's being written in each specific article. Luke Hayman, partner at Pentagram and designer of such iconic magazines as *New York*, says it most simply: "Always defer to the content to drive the design." This doesn't mean that design is any less important to the overall finished piece but that design performs a slightly different function in publications than in, say, packaging. "Visuals are important," notes Ina Saltz, "but they are less important than the marriage of visuals and content. Being a magazine art director is all about enhancing the content and becoming a visual journalist."

Taking on this role is anything but a passive stance. In fact, the best designs come from using the content to inspire, inform, and improve design. "The thing that sparks my imagination is the content," says Saltz. Steven Heller agrees. "Let your mind make connections as you read," he suggests. "It's kind of a mystery where the inspiration will crop up. But you know when you look at a design that really works, that the designer really understood the concept and the content. And likewise, you can tell when they were just following the template." Jeremy Leslie suggests thinking of design as one member of a three-part team: "The big difference in magazine design is that you are working with content. You have the images and the words, and the designer is the third element on the page, who has to work with everything there. Even if the reader is not design-savvy, he should subconsciously know that the design has added something to the page and to the understanding of the content."

This is no small responsibility. Kalle Lasn, founder of *Adbusters* magazine, feels that designers need to recognize and then embrace the impact their work can have. "I think that designers are some of the most powerful people in the world, if only they'd wake up to that fact," he says. "They don't create the content, write the words, or come up with the concepts, but they are the people who take those concepts, words, ideas, and shape them, give a tone to them, create an aesthetic around them, and decide what's important. Designers set the mood and the tone of our culture."

Left and opposite: When Virgin Atlantic Airlines developed an on-board magazine, *Carlos*, they needed a publication that reflected the hipness of their brand. John Brown Publishing and creative director Jeremy Leslie developed a magazine that was full of style and substance, with features about celebrities appearing alongside reports from around the globe.

NICOLE
AN APPRECIATION
BY

KIDMAN

RYAN GILBEY

12

ILLUSTRATED
BY

WHEN SHE ARRIVED
IN HOLLYWOOD,
NICOLE KIDMAN WAS
JUST MRS TOM
CRUISE. NOW – AFTER
THE DIVORCE, THE
OSCAR AND ALL THE
RUMOURS – SHE'S
ABOUT TO STAR AS A
CLONED HOUSEWIFE
IN 'THE STEPFORD
WIVES', SHE'S THE
MOST POWERFUL
ACTRESS IN THE
INDUSTRY, AND SHE'S
THE FACE OF CHANEL.
SO JUST HOW DID SHE
PULL IT OFF?

JO RATCLIFFE

CITY
STORIES

Local news from our global correspondents

ILLUSTRATED BY
JONATHAN SCHOFIELD

06

JOHANNESBURG

STARS IN STRIPES – THE
SWANKA SHOWDOWN

As a chilly Highveld darkness settles over Johannesburg, a group of Zulu men congregate outside Jeppe Men's Hostel. Some sing traditional Zulu gospel songs in harmony. Others exchange conversation. They call themselves Swankas.

Every Saturday night, these poor, migrant workers come here to compete against each other for an unusual honour: that of best-dressed man. Dingaan Zulu is one of them. During the week, he wears dusty blue overalls and a hard hat when he works a jackhammer on Johannesburg's demolition sites. But on Saturdays he swanks, transforming himself into a dandyish city gentleman.

"Altogether I have about 13 suits, but there are only nine that I am entirely confident about," he says proudly. Tonight he is wearing a pin-striped, tailor-made suit. On his feet are shiny black and white brogues. Expertly knotted around his neck is a pink tie. With matching socks. It's an ensemble that he hopes will win him the weekly prize of R100 (about £7). It is not the money that keeps the Swankas coming here each week. Instead, they say they are after far greater riches: honour and pride.

Dingaan Zulu and his fellow Swankas move into the ramshackle hostel basement, which houses a makeshift catwalk. Audience members are trickling in, taking their seats to watch the weekly swank-off. **The men make sure to avoid the piles of rubbish and junk lying scattered across the hostel floor. They don't want to dirty their Italian leather shoes or soil the hems of their carefully chosen suits.** In the harsh, bright light of the hostel basement, these men resemble preening peacocks, shiny, colourful and proud. They are here to show off. "You need to make sure others see you looking good," Dingaan says, smoothing his tie.

"When we speak of Swankas we speak of those who dress well, who wear the latest suits and model

before the judges. These are gentlemen who are well dressed in the Western way and like to show off their attire," says one regular audience member. Judging a winner is serious business. To ensure impartiality and objectivity, organisers pluck a stranger from the dark Johannesburg streets. Once the rules are explained, he sits down with a pen and paper, and spends the rest of the night judging.

One after the other, Dingaan and his fellow competitors swank before the judge, who quickly learns to take this as seriously as the Swankas take it. No mirth allowed. Sartorial honour is at stake. The men perform elaborate modelling moves before him with presentation, style and detail all important. **They tip their trilbies. Smooth their silk ties. Twang their braces. Finger their buttons. Flick their cuffs. Twirl around on their walking sticks.** Flourish patterned silk handkerchiefs from finely stitched pockets. It is an astounding and mesmerising show.

Swanking has been going on nearly every Saturday in Johannesburg since the Fifties. It began when migrant workers, who mostly lived in single-sex hostels, returned home for their annual Christmas visit. They would parade in their best clothes to the villagers to measure their success, having practised and performed beforehand in the hostels. More than half a century later, the tradition still lives on in Johannesburg's migrant community.

Dingaan Zulu has been swanking for years now, spending much of his meagre income on clothes and accessories. He sends what is left back home to his family in rural Zululand. "The most expensive suit I've bought was R1500 (£109). On that day, when I left the store, tears came to my eyes. I thought, 'How

can I spend so much on something I can't even eat?'"

But he does not regret his fashion extravagances because he has often won the weekly competitions. Swanking makes him feel like a man amongst men – migrant men who, for one evening a week, can forget about the harsh realities of modern city life.
ROBYN CURNOW

LONDON

SLEAZE – STYLE BITES BACK

Sleazenation is dead. Long live *Sleaze*. From the years 1995 to 2003, *Sleazenation* was a feisty, independently-published style magazine that took a side-on look at popular culture while flying the flag for the cutting-edge music, style, asymmetric haircuts and electroclash bootlegs generated in

the clubs and bars of Shoreditch. That was until newly appointed editor Neil Boorman pulled the plug with a December 2003 issue bearing the letters RIP on an all-black cover. Rumours of its death proved exaggerated, however. A month later Boorman relaunched the magazine with a shortened name – just *Sleaze* – and a sharper attitude. The cover of the first issue showed a photo of Victoria Beckham in flames, reflecting Boorman's intention to abandon coverage of celebrity and "retail therapy" in favour of something angrier, edgier and paradoxically, more optimistic. "It's clear that we're heading towards a sterile monoculture but there's no point moaning on about it," he writes in his editorial. "We need to rebuild

Left and opposite: *Make*, as designed by Albertson Design, has become more than a magazine. By tapping into the growing D.I.Y. culture, the brand has grown from a quarterly publication to include books, products, events, and a comprehensive website.

179

DAVID **ALBERTSON**

ENJOY THE CONTENT

When comparing publication design to other forms of graphic design, David Albertson of San Francisco–based Albertson Design points to the profound impact working with interesting content makes. "Publications are deeper, richer pieces of communication, and in that sense, it's more fulfilling than, say, doing marketing communications materials," he explains. "The work derives from a personal vision as opposed to a business objective. Artistically it can be more rewarding because you're working with stories about people and current events, for instance. They're more rooted in the reality of what's actually going on, what's happening culturally, and it can be very rewarding to be involved with that kind of rich content." With the reward comes a responsibility to ensure the design lives up to the level of work that some

other creative, engaged, dedicated person created. "Good graphic design," Alberston says, "makes a publication something that you don't want to get rid of. It gives it a kind of staying power. You can see where somebody has put a lot of effort into design, and that makes you want to buy the magazine and keep it. And really good graphic design can elevate content—can make great content even greater—if it's done in an ingenious and creative way that makes everybody, including the publisher, editor, writer, designer, and photographer look really smart." Design should have a multiplier effect, making everything it touches more than it would be standing on its own.

180

AGNES **ZEILSTRA**

CASEY **CAPLOWE**

ACCEPT THAT DESIGN CAN ONLY DO SO MUCH

While design is powerful, magazines are—usually and primarily—meant to be read. And designers have little or no say over what's being written. When asked how she keeps the Dutch women's magazine *Red* interesting, designer Agnes Zeilstra says, "That question is more for the ones that write and especially for the fashion people." She limits her responsibility to what she, as a designer, can control. "For me, it's important that we're up to date."

Because publication designers defer to content, they also have to make the best of what's provided. As Casey Caplowe, a founding editor for *GOOD* magazine, points out, "Good design is not going to save bad content." But design can certainly make bad content more interesting to look at and the overall experience of paging through a magazine much more pleasurable. Focus on what design can do, and do it well.

181

NICOLE DUDKA

INTERN, INTERN, INTERN

Nicole Dudka, art director at the *Chicago Tribune*, has a simple piece of advice for aspiring publication designers: "Intern, intern, intern." And she adds, do it while you're young, unattached, and can check out newsrooms in different parts of the country, where the vibe—and the opportunities—will be different.

***Make* magazine, designed by Albertson Design**

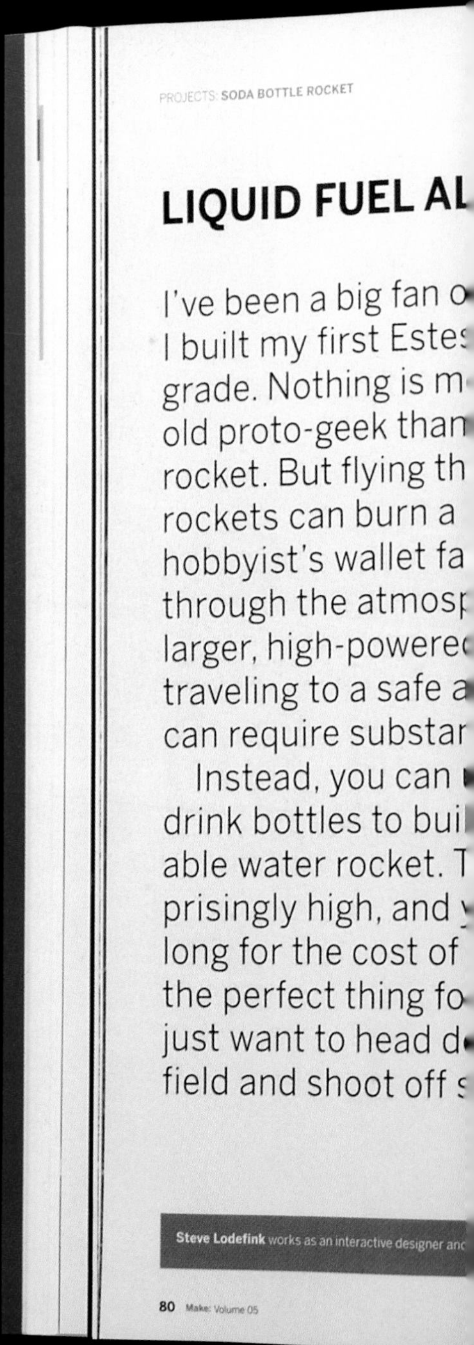

PROJECTS: **SODA BOTTLE ROCKET**

LIQUID FUEL AL

I've been a big fan o
I built my first Estes
grade. Nothing is m
old proto-geek than
rocket. But flying th
rockets can burn a
hobbyist's wallet fa
through the atmosp
larger, high-powered
traveling to a safe a
can require substar

Instead, you can
drink bottles to bui
able water rocket. T
prisingly high, and y
long for the cost of
the perfect thing fo
just want to head d
field and shoot off s

Steve Lodefink works as an interactive designer and

80 Make: Volume 05

NATIVE

l rocketry since
back in third
iting to a 9-year-
ing a homemade
e-shot solid-fuel
rough a young
an they burn
nd with today's
ts, locating and
able launch site
anning and effort.
ter carbonated
expensive, reus-
ll factor is sur-
 fly them all day
air and water. It's
 times when you
the local soccer
ockets!

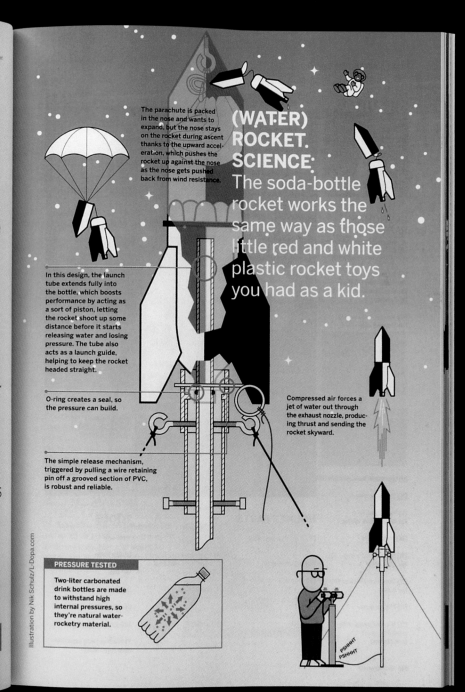

The parachute is packed in the nose and wants to expand, but the nose stays on the rocket during ascent thanks to the upward acceleration, which pushes the rocket up against the nose as the nose gets pushed back from wind resistance.

(WATER) ROCKET. SCIENCE.

The soda-bottle rocket works the same way as those little red and white plastic rocket toys you had as a kid.

In this design, the launch tube extends fully into the bottle, which boosts performance by acting as a sort of piston, letting the rocket shoot up some distance before it starts releasing water and losing pressure. The tube also acts as a launch guide, helping to keep the rocket headed straight.

O-ring creates a seal, so the pressure can build.

Compressed air forces a jet of water out through the exhaust nozzle, producing thrust and sending the rocket skyward.

The simple release mechanism, triggered by pulling a wire retaining pin off a grooved section of PVC, is robust and reliable.

PRESSURE TESTED

Two-liter carbonated drink bottles are made to withstand high internal pressures, so they're natural water-rocketry material.

PSHHHT
PSHHHT

Illustration by Nik Schulz/L-Dopa.com

182

VINCE **FROST**

JEREMY **LESLIE**

CARIN **GOLDBERG**

KALLE **LASN**

NICOLE **DUDKA**

LISTEN, LEARN, STUDY

"There's nothing worse than a young designer who thinks they know everything," says Australia-based designer Vince Frost. After designing for decades and working with dozens of fresh-out-of-school designers, "I'm always surprised at how little experience people have when they come out of college," he says. "But the most important thing is to be enthusiastic and want to learn and grow. The best designers are those that listen and learn." In publication design, the lessons are many. There are the basics of type families and grids and editorial wells. But there is also adopting the right state of mind. "We've set ourselves up as experts," Jeremy Leslie notes, "and you can't be an expert without questioning because that's how we learn. Children question everything. We have to behave like children."

Designer and educator Carin Goldberg says that one of the most useful things is to learn the history of publication design itself. "You have to study magazine design," she says. "A magazine's voice is the sum total of many parts, and it takes planning and organization. The process is less intuitive than other design media." She's suggesting an effort that should take designers far beyond the classroom. "Magazine design is one of the hardest things to teach because there are so many elements.

It's a complex project. You can't look at a magazine through a keyhole, one page at a time," she says. "You have to look at it as a complete thing that moves and undulates. I suggest to my students that they deconstruct and analyze the structure and voice of other successful magazines that work in order to understand how to organize a good one." She recommends, for example, the work of Alexey Brodovitch, Ruth Ansel, Bea Feitler, and Fabian Baron of *Harper's Bazaar* and other magazines; Cipe Pineles of *Seventeen*; Fred Woodward of *Rolling Stone*; M&Co. of *Colors* and *Interview*; and Robert Priest and John Korpics of *Esquire*.

For his part, Kalle Lasn emphasizes that it's just as important to look into the hearts as well as the portfolios of legendary designers. "When I look back on the history of design," he says, "it's filled with wild, passionate, crazy people who changed the aesthetic of their times and were involved in the big debates of their times." He's hopeful that the most recent generation of designers is ready and willing to do the same.

Above and opposite: Zembla, *designed by Frost Design, takes some standard magazine cover motifs, from the necessity of barcodes to the branding elements of titles and taglines, and combines them with type and image in inventive ways that will get noticed on a newsstand.*

183

MARCUS **PIPER**

ARJEN **NOORDEMAN**

IT'S NOT ABOUT YOU

"A magazine is for the reader, not the art director," notes Marcus Piper, who is the art director of *Pol Oxygen* magazine and also runs his own design studio in Sydney, Australia. "Graphic statements have their place and in that place make great pieces of work, but we are not designing magazines so people can see how incredibly creative we are." Publication designers consistently point out that whatever flexing of creative muscles they do is always in service to showing off the content. As Piper says, "Content is king. If the magazine were about me, it would be a different thing. Of course, there are some magazines you buy because of the person who designed it, but you may only buy it once. You have to be mature enough in your self to know when to be expressive and when to let the content do the work." Having said that, this focus on content is no excuse to shirk design duties. As Arjen Noordeman, partner at Elasticbrand in New York, notes, "It should never be about the designer. But you can add to the experience in a positive way."

184

CARIN **GOLDBERG**

CASEY **CAPLOWE**

AREM **DUPLESSIS**

SURROUND YOURSELF WITH THE BEST PEOPLE

The best way to learn the design restraint and humility necessary to publication design is through a process of soaking up, not showing off. As Carin Goldberg tells her students, "Seek out publications and creative directors who are the best in the business. No matter what the magazine is, what the subject matter is—it could be *Peanut Butter Today*—it's whom you're working with that's important. Work with the best and learn from them."

Beyond the team of editors and other designers, magazine art directors must also consider—and respect—the community of writers, illustrators, photographers, artists, and readers essential to a publication's success. As Casey Caplowe explains, "We really wanted to create a platform rather than a megaphone for ourselves. It's about creating spaces and then inviting really interesting people to play in those spaces. We want design to solve problems. We don't want to do design for design's sake."

This cooperative effort of magazine making leads to pretty deep gratifications, as noted by Arem Duplessis, art director for the *New York Times Magazine*. "The most satisfying thing for me is helping one of my designers get to a good place with their story. I love collaboration, and when everything is clicking, it's a wonderful thing."

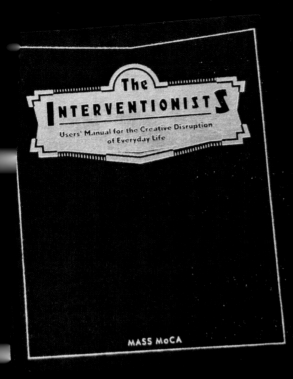

MASS MoCA

The Interventionists is a book featuring the work of forty artists. According to Noordeman, "A lot of these people were already nonconformists, so they appreciated that the graphic design was out there, with loud graphic elements and loud colors. They got a kick out of it because that's the way they made their art."

Project Description: Puett's oeuvre defies easy explanation because it combines entrepreneurial ventures with imaginative and historically informed installation. Inspired by the MASS MoCA site's origination as a textile mill, Arnold Print Works (1860–1942), Puett has embedded an unusual clothing business in the burnt-out rubble of an abandoned factory. Her project is not a facsimile or representation of a business, but, in fact, a real business called *That Word Which Means Smuggling Across Borders, Incorporated.* The company produces suits. During its hours of operation, a tailor will take orders and fit and sew suits for willing, and paying, customers. The suit itself is the operating metaphor in the project, as the artists reimagine the meaning of the suit and the history of this particularly charged attire. The suit's patterns are derived from insurance maps of the site during its use as Arnold Print Works.

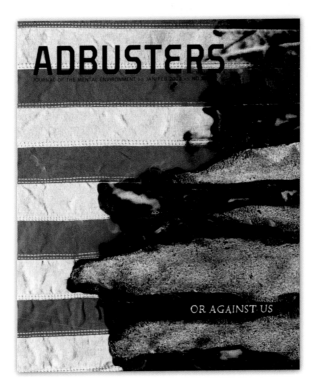

185

KALLE **LASN**

BE BRAVE, BOLD, PASSIONATE

"I think a magazine is supposed to engage in some kind of public discourse in an interesting way, a profound way, a provocative way," Kalle Lasn states. While he accepts that some mass-consumption publications are necessary, he laments that there are so few willing to take big risks. "The commercialization of magazines means that too many of them are playing a marketing game instead of giving their readers stuff that comes from their guts and is meant to provoke," he says. "The passion isn't there. Instead we have a passion to satisfy advertisers or a marketing idea. The soul of magazines has been lost. The whole idea of a designer as an author, a communicator, has been lost."

What's his answer? Designers need to reconnect to the primal source of their work. "Good design emanates from passion," he says, "from the very guts of the designer. The designer must take all their yearnings and passions and political views and anger and all the things that make up life and have it pouring into the design." However, even Lasn has a pragmatic side. "Of course the job of design is to learn how to channel all this emotion—to take the things that are closest to the designer and learn how to channel it. The important thing is not to turn design into a profession that is only serving the needs of clients. I realize you have to do this, but designers have taken it too far."

186

CARIN **GOLDBERG**

MARCUS **PIPER**

ADAM **MACHACEK**

BEGIN BY ASKING A LOT OF QUESTIONS

"There are all kinds of questions you always ask yourself no matter what you're designing," notes Carin Goldberg. "You have to look at what the publication is about, what the content is, who is the reader and where do they live, what is the mood, the agenda," she continues. "You have to think of the project holistically because you're solving several problems within one issue. Hierarchy and voice are priorities. Whether it's a book, or a magazine, or a poster, or book jacket, you always begin with the boilerplate questions and allow the answers to evolve as you begin to put pen to paper."

Every experienced editorial designer has his own set of questions, but they all reflect the effort of trying to understand what the publication is about. As Marcus Piper says, "I guess it's like knowing where the project is coming from and where it is going. The trick is to find the most appropriate and creative approach between those two points." In some cases,

these queries can and should lead to a certain level of subject immersion. Adam Machacek, cofounder of Welcometo.as in Switzerland, says, "The first thing is, of course, the research, when the topic is becoming part of your daily thinking." For example, he designed a book for an exhibit on rock music and its impact on the visual culture of the 1960s. He says, "We spent hours with the curator of the exhibition, touching, smelling, and selecting all the exhibits to be reproduced in the catalog. Being in his house, surrounded by his never-ending collection felt like being in a magic library." As they were designing, even the studio playlist changed to reflect the music of the exhibit and served to inspire the designers as they worked.

Opposite and above: After finding himself shut out by the mainstream media, Kalle Lasn launched *Adbusters* as a soapbox for the causes he believes in. The magazine design reinvents itself in every issue to reflect the challenging issues presented.

187

VINCE **FROST**

THINK ABOUT THE FUTURE

Publications provide a unique opportunity for a designer. In most graphic design projects, you design it, print it, and then it's over. A publication is more of a living, growing, evolving organism that blooms again and again in response to the environment in which it's created and the content that it presents. Therefore, it's important for the designer to be forward-looking. "In the beginning, especially on a start-up publication," says Vince Frost, "there may be no history. So we talk to the person about the future, not the past. They have goals, and we want to understand their long-term objectives and create solutions that are about the future, not where they are today." This clarifies another interesting point about publications: Instead of trying to achieve multiple, sometimes competing objectives in a single, one-time piece, an editorial designer can use several issues of a publication to fully realize the multifaceted vision of its editors and contributors.

Above and opposite: In *U&LC*, as designed by Carin Goldberg, type and image are not used in service to the design; they *are* the design.

188

INA **SALTZ**

ASK YOURSELF HOW YOU CAN MAKE A DIFFERENCE

This basic question is what Ina Saltz asks herself before approaching a publication design project, especially if it's a redesign. As with any project, the designer is there to solve problems, make improvements, and express a vision, within the constraints of time and budget. In determining how she can have the most positive impact, Saltz asks herself a series of defining questions: "Does the magazine already look great, or are they looking for something different? Is this something where I can make it ten times better or just take it up a notch? How much can I do, how much will I be allowed to do, how much will the budget allow me to do, what is the editorial mission of this product, and can I fulfill that mission in a better way?" While asking herself these questions, Saltz keeps in mind the fundamental nature of a publication: "A magazine is a product serving a need like any other product, but its purpose is to communicate, impart information, and inspire, so I ask myself how I can make that happen in a better way than it's happening now," she says.

189

START WITH SOMETHING SIMPLE

LUKE **HAYMAN**

AREM **DUPLESSIS**

Publications are complex projects with many disparate components to consider and integrate. So, especially when starting from scratch, sometimes the best way to ground the project is to start with the most basic component. "I try to start with something simple, first," Luke Hayman says, describing his process for designing a new magazine. "Mostly, I start with type, like for a column. I try to get the fonts working, get the basic grid and text font down first, and then build from there. I don't start with the features or the cover; I start with the nitty-gritty stuff first."

When the design is already established, some art directors, like Arem Duplessis, put pictures before fonts. "I start by conceptualizing ideas for the imagery," he says. "When the design process begins, the designers will create something specific to the content and imagery of their stories." These layouts are posted on a display wall so Duplessis can "check for an even flow." The rest of the design is filled in from there.

190

WORK QUICKLY

VINCE **FROST**

AREM **DUPLESSIS**

NICOLE **DUDKA**

"I enjoy doing things quickly," says Vince Frost. "Getting the energy up, being excited, just blitzing the project. The quicker you do it, the better it is for everyone. If you spend too much time analyzing it, it loses impact and passion." Sometimes working quickly is a necessity as well as a choice. Arem Duplessis points out, "We do not have the luxury of time working on a weekly. You have to be a quick thinker, and you have to know when to release the mouse." Nicole Dudka was drawn to newspapers specifically because of the speed in which she is forced to work. "I fell in love with

the deadlines," she says. "It's a faster turn-around, allows you to be creative really fast, forces you to think on your feet, and for better or worse, you start again the next week." Her technique for compressing her design process involves sketching at both ends of the spectrum. "I work in versions. I start by sketching a busy, mostly cluttered, energetic version and then go the opposite direction and come up with the most minimal version. Sometimes you find something in between, and sometimes people fall in love with the thing that only took two minutes. It's a process of elimination."

In the *Chicago Tribune*, Dudka illustrates articles on common topics by creating images other than "those things that immediately come to mind and every other publication would use."

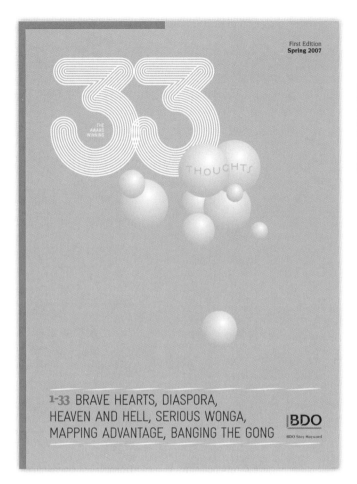

First Edition
Spring 2007

Left and opposite: *33 Thoughts* magazine was developed for an accounting firm willing to take some risks. "It's purely an experience for customers of that consultancy to show they're in touch with the concerns of that group," says Leslie. "They're also trying to position themselves as the outsider. So the magazine looks different from what you'd expect, but the content is very practical to its audience."

191

JEREMY **LESLIE**

CONSIDER THE CONTEXT OF THE CONTENT

As you get into actual page design and laying out specific pieces of writing, you must begin to consider not just what's being said, but how it's being said. "You need to understand not just the nature of the piece but also the angle of the piece," says Jeremy Leslie. "Is it a puff piece, a diss of a celebrity, a harrowing news piece, or an upbeat news piece? Once you figure that out, you have to look at the article in the context of the whole magazine as well as the history of the magazine." It's important that these considerations, which will not appear overtly to the reader, are implicit in the design. This gives a reader clues as to the nature of the magazine, the content of what they might be reading, and creates cohesion from one issue to another so readers can navigate and bond with the publication.

40 Paying attention?

How multimedia communications give us self-inflicted attention deficit disorder (ADD).

VOCAB FOR A WIRED ERA
Screen-sucking: wasting time stuck online when you could be working.
EMV or email voice: the ghostly phone voice that people assume when they are talking to you yet reading their email.
Gemmelsmerch: the ubiquitous force that distracts us from whatever we are doing.
Source: *CrazyBusy: Overstretched, Overbooked and About to Snap! Strategies for Coping in a World Gone ADD, by Dr Edward Hallowell*

It was only a matter of time before the frenzied pace of wired life began to draw serious attention from the medics. Constant demand via email, mobile and BlackBerry has long been seen as a cause of stress. But now psychiatrist Dr Edward Hallowell, a former practitioner at Harvard Business School, has come up with a still more worrying diagnosis. Society is suffering, he says, from an epidemic of self-inflicted ADD.

Sounds alarmist? Well, check out the symptoms: struggling to focus, restless, impatient, frustrated; juggling multiple projects but getting none done. "In general, feeling busy beyond belief, but not all that productive."

The upshot is that the multi-tasker can't take in the whole picture or think in depth - zapping instead from one superficial thought to another. The implications for business are clear: instead of concentrating on one task and doing it well, people end up doing two or more below their true ability. As for creativity, forget it. The problem has become so bad, says Hallowell, that it is even prompting people to report what they fear is early Alzheimer's. "But it's not that people's memories are deteriorating; it's just that they cannot absorb all the information being thrown at them."

Short of doctoring the water cooler with Ritalin, or imposing a multimedia blackout, what's to be done? The answer lies in self-discipline. "Business people are suckers for this idea that you have to work harder all the time. But to manage in this environment, you have to exercise restraint." Above all, keep this as your mantra: "The harder work is the thinking, not the collecting of information."

signs of the times

Given the new phase of volatility in the markets, we need every bit of help we can get second-guessing the future. Try the following alternative market indicators...

SKIRTS. Attention has always focused on hemlines - the longer they go, the worse the outlook. But don't disregard shape. Connoisseurs of past investment manias may well find themselves troubled by this year's Tulip styles. The concurrent revival of that 1980s standard, the Bubble, gives even more cause for concern.
SKIPS. The prevalence of builders' accoutrements - scaffolding, battered white vans and so on - has long been a favoured informal indicator of rosy times. Economist David Smith prefers the skip index: proliferating numbers on the streets are "normally the first cuckoo of economic spring".
LADY IN RED. During the 1990s boom, the Wall Street day traders learnt to pay close attention to business channel CNBC's anchorwoman, Maria 'Money Honey'
Bartiromo. Whole web sites were devoted simply to discussing the nuances of every change of hairdo - and when Money Honey wore red, it was taken as a sure 'buy' signal.
BOY RACERS. US economists have established a link between the number of speeding tickets traders clock up and the turnover in their portfolio - a useful way of gauging market volatility. Trades increased by an average of almost 10 per cent for each speeding ticket received.
SLAP AND TICKLE. Strong cosmetics sales are a warning that the all-important female consumer is tightening her belt. Lipstick is a cheap fix if you can't afford a new outfit.
HIP-HOP LYRICS. For an insight into future consumer trends, pay close attention to what da crew have to say about luxury brands. Market research outfit Brandstand has a Billboard Charts index that tots up the references in rap songs, such as Busta Rhymes and P Diddy's *Pass the Courvoisier*.
NORTHAMPTON. This seemingly uninspiring Midlands town apparently tracks the rise and fall of the national economy perfectly...
TOWER BRIDGE. The number of times the bridge is raised is no longer a useful indicator of UK import/export activity, just of the traffic in cocktail cruisers.

When Money Honey wore red, it was taken as a sure 'buy' signal

---

57

"Charm is the ability to solicit the answer 'yes' before the question has been posed."

Jean Cocteau

IN

Swearing (in moderation)

Hello

Using a mobile phone in company - though not, intriguingly, a BlackBerry

SPADE

Straight-talking

In and out: modern standards of behaviour, according to a survey recently compiled by the Aziz Corporation

58 Business manners

Taken together, they mark a decisive move away from 'the old standards of conviviality'. As one old-school business commentator observes: "Where once we were treated to 'Yours obediently', it's now a case of 'Up yours'."

But that kind of reaction is typical of the current dilemma surrounding manners, says Nigel Nicholson, professor of organisational psychology at London Business School. "The erosion of hierarchy and authority, and the growing pluralism of society have left people less clear about how to behave at work. We used to know where we stood a bit better. Now, everybody has different standards."

One advantage of what might be termed the new 'Gordon Ramsay style': it at least has the virtue of clarity. Excessive politeness can be damaging to business - causing confusion, preventing people from voicing opinions, and hindering change - as they are discovering in Japan, where language-use still hinges on status. Common words used between women and men, and peers and non-peers can vary widely. Typically, younger people use humble words about their own actions, and respectful ones for those of a senior. Such linguistic restraint makes it even more painful than it is in a western hierarchy to speak out against the opinions of a senior.

Talking rubbish

Drinking alcohol at lunch time

Ordering expensive items off the menu

OUT

192

BE WILLING TO BE SMART INSTEAD OF BEAUTIFUL

VINCE **FROST**

STEVEN **HELLER**

ARTHUR **HOCHSTEIN**

AREM **DUPLESSIS**

Great design almost always serves the project at hand rather than itself. This is especially critical for content-driven projects like publication design. The designer's role is to enhance the subject matter provided, make it more intriguing, engaging, and edifying for the reader, and to never upstage what's happening on the page. Designers should always be looking for the best means to visually communicate what's being written. "It's not about making it look cool or finding a cool font," says Vince Frost. "It's really about finding the best approach for that particular opportunity. You don't want to inflict your style on a project." Or as Steven Heller suggests, "Try not to impose your signature on something that shouldn't be signed."

This willingness to stay behind the scenes is perhaps nowhere as important as at a news magazine. Arthur Hochstein, art director at *Time*, says that brains must come before beauty. "We take a restrained approach," he explains. "Being part of the news process is as important as good design. You have to throw a lot of work out, you have to change things all the time, and you have to be someone who can roll with things. You have to understand that it's a collective pursuit, and design is one aspect, but it's not the final determining factor. Sometimes you want to be the smartest girl in the class instead of the best looking."

Arem Duplessis concurs. "You can't just design to make something beautiful. Read the stories and understand what the editorial mission is. You should know the magazine's demographics and who the core audience is before you even touch a sketch pad."

Above and opposite: & is a magazine from D&AD, a U.K.–based "educational charity that represents the global creative, design, and advertising communities" by "setting industry standards, educating and inspiring the next generation, and demonstrating the impact of creativity and innovation on enhancing business performance."

obsession n 1. an idea
or feeling that constantly
occupies the mind

Editor
Lakshmi Bhaskaran
lakshmi@dandad.co.uk

Design & Art Direction
Vince Frost &
Anthony Donovan
Frost Design, Sydney
www.frostdesign.com.au

Advertising
Katherine Howells
katherine@dandad.co.uk

'&', D&AD
9 Graphic Square,
Vauxhall Walk
London SE11 5EE
T: +44 (207) 840 1111
E: ampersand@dandad.co.uk
W: www.dandad.co.uk

Printed by Beacon Press
using purprint
environmental print
technology

'&' is printed on
100% Recycled Paper

Cover Photography
Ben Stockley

Welcome to this, the first issue of our new look members' magazine '&'. As longstanding members will recall, '&' has existed before in a number of different formats. In 2003, D&AD spent a year experimenting with its design, before taking respite to carry out a major review and consider the magazine's future. In an age fuelled by digital communication we even found ourselves asking the question, 'do we actually need a traditional magazine?' The answer was a resounding Yes and the feedback unequivocal; that our members value, not only the tactility of a traditional publication but also its content – from the latest D&AD news and views to industry-related features to profiles celebrating our most inspiring creatives. Our research also led us to the format you see before you as the most preferred by our members ● And so we are back, stronger than ever, with a new design, definitive format and updated content that we hope you will find as exciting and stimulating to read as we have to create. I am also absolutely delighted that the creative team who produced the last award-winning issue of '&', Lakshmi Bhaskaran as editor and Vince Frost as creative director, are back with us to take '&' forward as a permanent fixture here at D&AD ● D&AD members will receive four issues of the magazine a year from September 2006. And, as with all of our print material, '&' will adhere to D&AD's strict environmental policy, which we began to implement in mid-2005 ● We are re-launching '&' in the run up to Congress 2006 and will be using the magazine to keep you fully up to speed about this world-class event, as well as other activities here at D&AD ● This is your magazine and we would love to hear what you think. Get in touch by email to ampersand@dandad.co.uk
Michael Hockney Chief Executive, D&AD

welcome

ALAN FLETCHER

Alan Fletcher, the most highly regarded graphic designer of his generation, died in September. Quentin Newark offers a personal recollection of an iconic figure

Alan Fletcher is dead. Suddenly, the whole world of design is so much smaller. There seem to be no figures of his grandeur and depth waiting in the wings. He was the last of his kind. Fletcher immediately takes his place in the pantheon of greats, many of whom he knew: Herbert Bayer, Saul Steinberg, Willi Fleckhaus, Josef Müller-Brockmann, Paul Rand, and two of his personal friends and mentors, Saul Bass and Robert Brownjohn.

Alan was there at the birth of British graphic design. With his partners Colin Forbes and Bob Gill, and a handful of others, he created a marriage of dry grid European modernism and sassy Madison Avenue 'Big Idea' advertising that most recognise as the best form of graphic design: structured, cool typography supporting a clever, simply executed concept.

He also co-founded D&AD, in emulation of the New York Art Directors' Club. From its inception, Alan and his friends ensured that it exceeded its model. D&AD admitted both art directors and designers. And, as we have seen, this fundamental principle of inclusion has seen the value of D&AD's pursuit of excellence expand far beyond any disciplinary or geographic border.

Alan went on to co-found Pentagram, which became one of the most influential and highly regarded design studios in the world. It remains the only true inter-disciplinary practice of any scale, combining architecture, graphic design, product design and interiors. Anyone who visited in its heyday, when its founding partners were still at the helm, could see that it was part workplace and part club. You ate lunch there, read the papers, gazed at Theo Crosby's mask collection and sat with Alan in the evening when he held court over a jug of iced Vermouth. Alan was always open to conversation, with anyone. He could appear fierce - he sported a four-inch scar on his cheek - but he was actually very warm and at ease in company. He always accepted people, was always attentive, always frank. He had countless friends.

Alan often talked of design as 'sensual pleasure', and the feel of a project that was going well as 'drunkenness'. He did his best to construct his life so he could be 'drunk' as much as possible. The world, he said, would be a better place 'if everyone concentrated on having a good time ... they wouldn't be arguing, or cutting each other dead in the street, or shooting each other, or whatever. because that is contrary to having a good time. What is the alternative? Having a boring or unpleasant time? Design is a style of living.' He talked of the integration of his life and work as 'seamless', and he took this literally. At his home, a big sliding door could be pulled open to join his white studio to his living room.

After 20 years at Pentagram, Alan left to work freelance, quickly landing a plum job as art director of Phaidon Press. In a typical understatement, he said he found dealing with art as a subject matter was 'more stimulating than dog food'. He played no small part in making Phaidon the great art publisher it is. Five years ago, he won Novartis as a client and worked with a small team on the regeneration of a campus occupying a huge part of the city of Basle. I know this project made him very happy, since it so completely fulfilled his mantra of being 'involved with intelligent people on stimulating projects'. As well as a logo, he designed fountains, street signs, an aptary, and the 'wonderwall' a long, painted steel fence skirting the site, elaborately cut through with hundreds of silhouettes of nearly every item on earth: jet fighters, yachts, snails, knights, elephants and artichokes.

Alan's productivity in his last years was astonishing. He exhibited an unforgettable set of bizarre papier-mâché animals at the Royal Academy. His work expanded to include watercolours of flowers, drawings made while walking, collages involving sandpaper, sculptures made of pencils, and several dozen drawers of alphabets cut from the crude lettering on cardboard boxes. I once sat with him and looked through a pile of 300 drawings of people's shadows he had made over the course of a month. While none of this is strictly 'design', the images and ideas were often used as the centrepiece of a poster, a logo or the cover of a book.

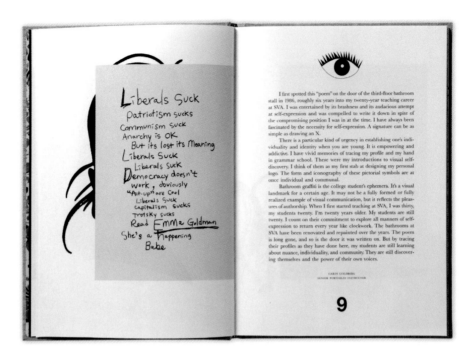

193

STEVEN **HELLER**

ARTHUR **HOCHSTEIN**

CARIN **GOLDBERG**

THINK OF DESIGN AS A COMPASS

"Great design," says Steven Heller, "creates an identity, a personality for a publication. And a personality helps because you know where you are. A magazine is a storehouse of very disparate stuff, but a good design will glue it together and give you a sense of place. It's like having a compass that tells you how to get where you're going." This is the primary role of publication designers: to create a way for readers to understand, access, and navigate the information being presented. Designers are notoriously interested in change, both creating it and following it, often simply for the sake of change. But in many cases, this inclination does nothing but cause confusion for the reader. "I try to distinguish between designer boredom and utility for the reader," Arthur Hochstein explains. "We might want to do something different just because we already did it last week, but in terms of what the reader is getting, this may be a problem."

Readers expect a certain comforting familiarity in a destination they return to weekly or monthly or even just a few times a year. Even if their expectation is to be surprised, they still don't want design to confound the habits they have formed when it comes to how they peruse their favorite publications. "There's a great deal of responsibility designing a magazine," Carin Goldberg notes. "A magazine is something that will hopefully be around for a long time. You want your readers to become loyal customers by meeting their expectations while continuing to surprise. For example, departments are the sections a reader looks forward to and anticipates. They give the magazine continuity and a foundation. A magazine must have a philosophy that cultivates followers. The designer has to approach this philosophy responsibly because it doesn't just happen once."

Above and opposite: Carin Goldberg designed and edited this book for the School of Visual Arts, *Senior Library 2004*, which discusses art, design, and education and also shows various artifacts from the process.

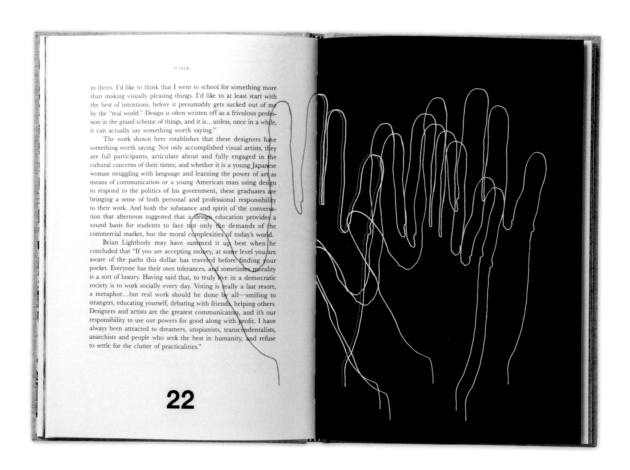

194

MAKE SURE YOUR MAGAZINE SPEAKS INTELLIGENTLY TO ITS AUDIENCE

JEREMY **LESLIE**

A magazine, unlike most other graphic design projects, is a kind of repeated, continuous conversation between audience and contributors. As with any conversation, it is respectful to keep in mind the background, interests, and opinions of those you are attempting to engage. "The first thing to consider is who the magazine is for," says Jeremy Leslie, "because there's nothing sadder than a magazine without readers." It is also vital to assume your readers are smart and paying attention. "People experience a magazine more than once," Leslie notes. "It's an ongoing relationship and you need to know that a fair amount of your readership will recall something that happened six months ago, and so you have to build a visual language that is both instantly recognizable and intelligent." After all, there are so many publications available that if readers don't like one, there's certainly another one close by on the newsstand that is bound to attract their interest. "Anyone can create a magazine and put it out there, but if no one buys it, it's a failed magazine no matter how great it looks or how well designed it is," he concludes.

World business
NOV/DEC 1996 • $3.95
THE GLOBAL PERSPECTIVE
ASIA/PACIFIC
Acer of Taiwan Has Reached The Top Ranks; Taiwan Itself Has Helped
EUROPE
There Are Ways To Do Business In Russia Without Going Mad. Really.
MANAGING
An Old Word You'll No Doubt Be Hearing Anew: Intrapreneurism
THUROW
Business Sometimes Ignores R&D, but Only at Its Peril
When Brand Is Grand
Nike sounds a clarion call; twenty-first century, look out!

195

KALLE **LASN**

CHALLENGE YOUR READERS

If you assume the inherent intelligence of your audience, then you know they're not only going to be insulted by pandering and patronizing in any form but they will probably enjoy the bracing effect of an occasional challenge. "If you start second-guessing your readership," says Kalle Lasn, "then you've lost your passion. If you think deeply about what readers really want, they don't necessarily want the same grid or familiarity; what they really want is to be surprised and delighted and to have an epiphany from you, something that knocks them for a loop. They want their comfort level broken rather than enhanced." After all, even someone simply looking for a bit of gossip while waiting in the doctor's office is still looking for the titillation of discovering something they didn't know. As Lasn says, "A really successful magazine is a surprise with every issue."

Above and opposite: *World Business* and *Worth* magazine covers, designed by Ina Saltz, are demonstrations of the balancing act a logo has to play with strong images and variety of typefaces in order to attract readers and potential readers.

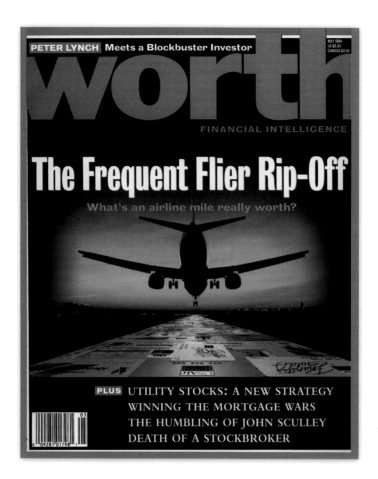

196

JEREMY **LESLIE**

VINCE **FROST**

CONSIDER THE BUSINESS SIDE

A commercial publisher is a business, and magazines are its product. So drumming up sales—both from readers buying the magazine and advertisers paying for pages—should be every much a part of the design equation as font styles and column inches. "You have to consider things such as how the publisher is going to go about creating a strategy for distribution and such," notes Jeremy Leslie. "These are not just considerations for the business team but for the designer as well, and if a brief comes out and it doesn't have that information, you must go and get it." By expanding your role beyond straightforward graphic design, you also have the added advantage of making yourself much more valuable to the client, whether that's your editor or a corporation. As Vince Frost says, "I take a very entrepreneurial approach and look at the whole business. There's so many ways we can help, such as creating better systems. To me, it's about giving design business advice."

197

ARJEN **NOORDEMAN**

EDIT YOURSELF

Designers seem naturally inclined to try new things. And sometimes, they try all of them at once. This approach may be extremely productive as part of initial explorations, but knowing what to take out is as important as knowing what to put in. "I like to be lavish and luxurious and add as many bells and whistles as possible," notes Arjen Noordeman, "But then I want to scale it back. That's often for the budget, but it's also good for the design. I have a tendency to want everything that's possible, but concepts often communicate more clearly when you bring it down to the essence, and when I'm forced to do that, I'm happier in the end."

Noordeman draws on his design education first and then on his design upbringing. "I come from the Dutch school of design," he explains, "where everything is very stark and minimal, where the teachers are always saying 'why is this here?' 'why is that there?' Dutch design whittles everything down to the bare essentials needed to get the message across. I was seduced by the Deconstructivism approach to design, and I went to Cranbrook to see this other kind of design. I really expanded my vocabulary there, which was great, but then I was struggling with restraints and wanting to pull out all the stops and discovering that it's not always good to do that, either. So I've taught myself to pull out all the stops at first and then edit, edit, edit down to the essence of the design."

Cyber-Neologoliferation

In the age of
the Internet, the Oxford
English Dictionary is coming
face to face with the boundlessness of the English language.
By James Gleick

When I got to John Simpson and his band of lexicographers in Oxford earlier this fall, they were working on the P's. *Pletzel, plish, pod person, point-and-shoot, polyamorous* — these words were all new, one way or another. They had been plowing through the P's for two years but were almost done (except that they'll never be done), and the Q's will be "just a twinkle of an eye," Simpson said. He prizes patience and the long view. A pale, soft-spoken man of middle height and profound intellect, he is chief editor of the Oxford English Dictionary and sees himself as a steward of tradition dating back a century and a half. "Basically it's the same work as they used to do in the 19th century," he said. "When I started in 1976, we were still working very much on these index cards, everything was done on these index cards." He picked up a stack of 6-inch-by-4-inch slips and riffled through them. A thou-

Typography by Sam Winston

54

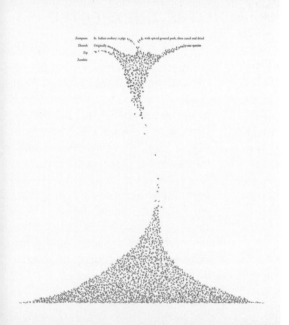

and radio transcripts. The corpus sends its home-built Web crawler out in search of text, raw material to show how the language is really used.

I'm too embarrassed to ask the lexicographers if they have a favorite word. They get that a lot. Peter Gilliver tells me his anyway: *ruffler*. A twiffler, in case you didn't know, is a plate intermediate in size between a dinner plate and a bread plate. "I love it because it fills a gap," Gilliver says. "I also love it because of its etymology. It comes from Dutch, like a lot of ceramics vocabulary. *Twijfelaar* means something intermediate in size, and it comes from *twijfelen*, which means to be unsure. It's a plate that can't make up its mind!"

Fiona McPherson gives me *mondegreen*. A mondegreen is a misheard lyric, as in, "Lead on, O kinky turtle." It is *named after* Lady Mondegreen. There was no Lady Mondegreen. The lines of a ballad, "They hae slain the Earl o' Murray/And laid him on the green" are misheard as "They hae slain the Earl of Murray and Lady Mondegreen."

"A lot of people are just really excited by that word because they think it's amazing that there is a word for that concept," McPherson says.

I have my own favorites among the newest entries in O.E.D.3. *Pixie dust* is, as any child knows, "an imaginary magical substance used by pixies." *Air kiss* is defined with careful anatomical instructions plus a note: "sometimes with the connotation that such a gesture implies insincerity or affectation." *Builder's bum* is reportedly Brit. and colloq., "with allusion to the perceived propensity of builders to expose inadvertently this part of the body."

It is clear that the English of the O.E.D. is no longer the purely written language, much less a formal or respectable English, the diction recommended by any authority. Gilliver, a longtime editor who also seems to be the O.E.D.'s resident historian, points out that the dictionary feels obliged to include words that many would regard simply as misspellings. No one is particularly proud of the new entry as of December 2003 for *nucular*, a word not associated with high standards of diction. "Bizarrely, I was amazed to find that the spelling n-u-c-u-l-a-r has decades of history," Gilliver says. "And that is not to be confused with the quite different word, *nucular*, meaning 'of or relating to a nucule.'" There is even a new entry for *miniscule*; it has citations going back more than 100 years.

Yet the very notion of correct and incorrect spelling seems under attack. In Shakespeare's day, there was no such thing; no right and wrong in spelling, no dictionaries to consult. The word *debt* could be spelled det, dett, dett, dette or dept, and no one would complain.

Then spelling crystallized, with the spread of printing. Now, with mass communication taking another leap forward, spelling may be diversifying again, spellcheckers notwithstanding. The O.E.D. so far does not recognize *straight-laced*, but the Oxford English Corpus finds it outnumbering *strait-laced*. Similarly for just desserts.

To explain why cyberspace is a challenge for the O.E.D. as well as a godsend, Gilliver turns to the phrase "sensitive ears."

"You know we are listening to the language," he says. "When you are listening to the language by collecting pieces of paper, that's fine, but now it's as if we can hear everything said anywhere. Members of some tiny English-speaking community anywhere in the world just happen to commit their communications to the Web: there it is. You thought some word was obsolete? Actually, no, it still survives in a very small community of people who happen to use the Web — we can hear about it."

In part, it's just a problem of too much information: a small number of

lexicographers with limited time. But it's also that the O.E.D. is coming face to face with the language's boundlessness.

The universe of human discourse always has backwaters. The language spoken in one valley was a little different from the language of the next valley and so on. There are more valleys now than ever, but they are not so isolated. They find one another in chat rooms and on blogs. When they coin a word, anyone may hear.

Neologisms can be formed by committee: *transistor*, Bell Laboratories, 1948. Or by wags: *booboisie*, H.L. Mencken, 1922. But most arise through spontaneous generation, organisms appearing in a petrie dish, like *blog* (c. 1999). If there is an ultimate limit to the sensitivity of lexicographers' ears, no one has yet found it. The rate of change in the language itself — particularly the process of neologism — has surely shifted into a higher gear now, but away from dictionaries, scholars of language have no clear way to measure the process. When they need quantification, they look to the dictionaries.

"An awful lot of neologisms are spur-of-the-moment creations, whether it's literary effect or it's conversational effect," says Naomi S. Baron, a linguist at American University, who studies these issues. "I could probably count on the fingers of a hand and a half the serious linguists who know anything about the Internet. That hand and a half of us are fascinated to watch how the Internet makes it possible not just for new words to be coined but for neologisms to spread like wildfire."

It's partly a matter of sheer intensity. Cyberspace is an engine driving change in the language. "I think of it as a saucepan under which the temperature has been turned up," Gilliver says. "Any word, because of the interconnectedness of the English-speaking world, can spring from the backwater. And they are still backwaters, but they have these instant connection to ordinary, everyday discourse." Like the printing press, the telegraph and the telephone before it, the Internet is transforming the language simply by transmitting information differently. And what makes cyberspace different from all previous information technologies is its intermixing of scales from the tiny to the smallest without prejudice, broadcasting to the millions, narrowcasting to groups, instant messaging one to one.

So someone can be an O.E.D. author now. And, by the way, many try. "What people love to do is send in words they've invented," Bernadette Paton says, guiding me through a windowless room used for storage of old word slips. *Will you put the word I have invented into one of your dictionaries?* is a question in the AskOxford.com FAQ. All the submissions go into the files, and until there is evidence for some general usage, that's where the wannabes remain.

Don't bother sending in *FAQ*. Don't bother sending in *wannabes*. They're not even particularly new. For that matter, don't bother sending in anything they find via Google. "Please note," the O.E.D.'s Web site warns solemnly, "it is generally safe to assume that examples found by searching the Web, using search engines such as Google, will have already been considered by O.E.D. editors." ■

> 'When you are
> listening to the language
> by collecting pieces of
> paper, that's fine, but now
> it's as if we can hear
> everything said anywhere,'
> says one editor.

In the *New York Times Magazine*, Arem Duplessis and his team show how free and flexible a designer can be, while still maintaining the integrity of the brand and bringing dimension to information, text, and images.

198

JEREMY **LESLIE**

BE WILLING TO ASK, "WHAT IF?"

Publications are a group endeavor. Hopefully, your team is made up of really smart people who've given plenty of thought to what they're trying to create and how it will live in the world. Unfortunately, designers are often brought in toward the end of the planning phase and asked to tactically execute on a strategy they may not have participated in developing. But it's never too late to step back and challenge assumptions. "Never take stuff for granted," says Jeremy Leslie. "It comes down to teamwork. If you're sitting around with a group of colleagues trying to work out how something should be, I would hope that at least one person at the table would say, 'what if?' What if that really isn't good enough; what if we dropped the intro and went straight here; what if we chopped it up into pieces . . .." If your team is intelligent, courageous, and interested in making an impact with their publication, they'll certainly value the questions and explorations, even if, in the end, they serve to reinforce the original approach.

199

NICKI **KALISH**

AGNES **ZEILSTRA**

BALANCE THE FAMILIAR WITH THE UNEXPECTED

Magazine and newspaper readers tend to come back to the same publication over and over again. As creatures of habit, they also tend to develop a personal method for navigating the content, perhaps skimming everything before digging in, maybe going directly to a favorite section, or methodically moving from front to back. Publication designers respect reader expectations by maintaining consistency in familiar places even as they carve out areas where they can play with the element of surprise. "You want people to know where to look for things," notes Nicki Kalish, former art director of the Dining Section of the *New York Times* and current owner/designer of Nicki Kalish Design. "There are always our regular columns, so there's continuity. The Minimalist and the restaurant review, for example, always fall on the same page." In Agnes Zeilstra's woman's magazine, *Red*, they regularly feature "articles about real people and famous people—and there's always one fashion production about clothes."

This consistency does not mean that publication designers lack issues to wrestle with. "We just changed a font and that made the magazine look fresh again. But it's also very important to be consistent," says Zeilstra. For Kalish, "The design challenge comes with the cover stories. There are usually three of them, and they all jump to their own space on the interior pages. Those need to be reinvented every week. There's consistency from week to week with the regular columns falling in the same place, so there's a certain amount of the new and a certain amount of the familiar. I strive to make each cover as distinct as possible from the last one, so there is variety."

Because the *New York Times Magazine* does not have to compete on the newsstand, its designers have more freedom, especially with covers.

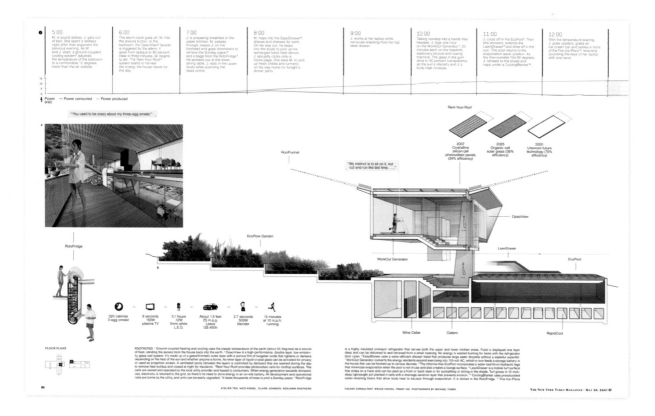

200

MAXIMIZE THE OPPORTUNITIES THAT PRINT MAKES POSSIBLE

LAURENCE **NG**

IdN, international designer's network magazine, is a showcase for design from all over the world. Each issue has a theme, planned as much as six months in advance, to which designers contribute, creating a publication that is chockablock with powerful images and artwork. Publisher Laurence Ng explains how his team uses the power of the printing press to make all this design shine individually and the magazine work as a whole: "Our job is to make the artwork more presentable and more visually impactful," he says. "Most of it has a lot of visual impact already, but because there are so many different articles and we don't want them to crash, we have to package them individually. So, we use different page layouts, printing techniques and even, in some cases, different paper, to make them look different." This means magazines are printed in at least six colors, with sometimes up to six different papers, a few different varnishes, and even different-size sheets in a single issue.

One of the ways *IdN* keeps everything from becoming too crazy is by using a grid for individual articles but no overall grid for the magazine as a whole. While Ng readily admits that this process—which requires them to do all prepress work in-house and sometimes work with several different printers in several different countries on a single issue—is a "nightmare," the results are spectacular. "A lot of designers out there still want to feel and touch. On the website, you don't feel the paper, the print quality, so we still want to produce quality magazines," he says.

Above and opposite: *IdN* magazine, produced in Asia, features the best in graphic design from around the world. The extreme visual impact of the content is showcased in pages that push printing capabilities by using multiple varnishes, extra colors, several kinds of paper, and even different sheet sizes in a single issue.

201

ENJOY THE END OF THE PROJECT AS MUCH AS THE START OF IT

JASON **GODFREY**

JEREMY **LESLIE**

Magazine work is cyclical. Whether it's a weekly or a monthly or quarterly, there is a rhythm of creating a structure, filling the structure, sending it off, and starting over again. Jason Godfrey, of Godfrey Design in England, fondly recalls his time working for Conde Nast in New York. "You design for a month, you get it out of the studio, and then you start again. I quite enjoyed it," he says. "And I think it's peculiar to the publication design process where every month you start with a completely clean slate. Other projects can tend to drag on, but with a magazine, you work for a month and then start over. You work toward the day you get it off to production, and there's this palpable sense of relief. And then you start on a new one."

Of course, that relief may be moderated by some degree of frustration over what you were not able to accomplish in the deadline allowed. "I think that picking up a magazine and checking it out is always a thrilling and nauseating experience," says Jeremy Leslie. "You put a lot of yourself into this thing, and it's exciting to see how some of it comes off, but also it never really fully works." Fortunately, there's always the next issue waiting for your attention, giving you the opportunity to improve on your own work. "I love working with magazines because they're still developing and moving on," Leslie explains. "There's a really gentle, pleasant cycle to seeing it come out, and it's never perfect, and you're always stretching for perfection."

Casting off thE shacklEs of socialist rEalism

text by Eva Ruthina

拋開社會寫實主義的桎梏

俄羅斯 - 建構主義發源地。但說到設計創作，在將近 100 年前，不幸地被到板教條給牽制住了。1920 年代，當時的前衛藝術家如 Lissitsky，Malevich，以及攝影師 Rodchenko 發明了現代印刷藝術的基本原則 - 圓、三角和四角的樂趣性，留白的重要性，照片的龐大奇效果，和戲劇性的透視效果。但是，他們明智的遺見，很快就被 1930 年代蘇聯的宣傳攻擊和社會寫實主義的陰影給淹沒了。

過去這 80 年來，俄羅斯可說是毫無「設計」可言。「設計」這個字只意味工業設計，由於蘇聯時期所製造的產品皆其貌不揚又呆板，甚至還有負面的意涵。對蘇聯的職業設計師來說，使用這些日常機械工具，可真不是什麼賞心悅目的事。而人們卻還得天天生活在沮喪糟糕的建築、大量製造的家具，和沒有美感的室內裝潢之中。

這樣的蘇維埃聯邦在 15 年前已經瓦解了，但可怕的後果仍是到處可見。儘管莫斯科改變迅速，但靠再找到一家老式的咖啡館和商店，因為所有地面上的物件都被重新設計過和改造。但在嶄新的購物廣場和流行的風潮中，建來維著養工廠和蕭氣的典型五層公寓。

這種對比令人沮喪，尤其對那些適應了新生活、而不願意認同過去的當代設計師們而言。只要開車稍微離開莫斯科，他們會覺得自己正經歷著過往的創傷。這樣令人灰心的文化傳承，是俄羅斯現代生活的背景。然而，每年的新觀念又一層一層往上加，希望盡快地將 20 世紀的恐懼淡忘。

1998 年的經濟危機，重大地改變了這個國家的視覺文化。新世代的設計師顛覆了新規則，一步一步改變著週遭的世界。所有東西，從電視台的識別，到社酒的標籤，都變得典雅致又簡約。俄羅斯人複製荷蘭最頂的印刷設計，並快速學到如何再製二流的西方編排。設計公司出產的作品平均水準快速遽提高，但少有真正有趣的作品現身。

這篇文章報導的俄羅斯藝術家皆很獨特，各有其強烈的個人風格。有時他們隱藏自己俄羅斯的根源、有時又將俄羅斯民族的特色表露無遺，無論創作的方式是向主流的國際風格靠攏，或是回潮到民族根源的認同，他們的作品總是極為幽默，又不曲高和寡，令人耳目一新。

IdN magazine, published by Laurence Ng

202

ACCEPT THE INFLUENCE OF THE WEB

JEREMY **LESLIE**

ARTHUR **HOCHSTEIN**

MARCUS **PIPER**

With almost every publication now appearing online as well as in print, the designer must consider both media, often simultaneously. And because consumers are getting so much information from the Internet, it is inevitable that the habits and devices used in interactive design are bleeding onto the printed page. "The Web has had a very specific effect on page design," says Jeremy Leslie. "It's accelerated a process that was happening anyway, with the bite size chunk of information getting smaller and smaller. You have to have pictures and pull quotes and sells and as many devices as possible." This is the result of the changing nature of our culture. "All magazines looked like the *New Yorker* seventy years ago," he says, "but now, a new magazine couldn't hope to have a successful launch looking like that. It's just a matter of degree, of how much you're going to cede ground to this process."

The Web has not only influenced how print looks, it's also changed the kind of information people gather from different resources. For example, people are increasingly going to the Web for quick hits of fast-breaking and changing news. This has forced news magazines especially to rethink the kind of information they present in order to stay relevant and compete on their own ground. "For a while," Arthur Hochstein notes, "print was trying to emulate the Internet, and now there's a backlash, which is smart because print is print and electronics is electronics and each should do what it does well." In the case of *Time*, this includes focusing less on breaking news and more on analysis and opinion, using columnists and features to help readers interpret and understand the information they've been gathering all week from their desktop.

By working together, the two media actually support and reinforce one another. "The Web is not an enemy," says Hochstein. "We encourage our reporters to contribute to both our online and print versions. They're increasingly seen as one entity, but the magazine doesn't need to and shouldn't need to keep up with the Internet. News magazines have been on everyone's hit list for twenty years, but the more likely scenario is simply a retrenching, a redefinition." Marcus Piper agrees: "The Internet has changed the way people interact with things, their attention spans, and how they receive information. People want snippets, and they need to be grabbed and told to read something. Creatively, the dominance of the Internet as a source of information is a great thing because magazines are forced to be better. Things like tactility are now key for publication designers. It's an opportunity to make magazines work harder and be better, and that is exciting."

The open feel of page layout and type choices in *Western Interiors and Design* magazine are as crisp and clear as the light and landscape where the images were taken.

contents

July/August 2004.
special art issue

features

letters to the editor:
5410 Wilshire Blvd.,
Suite 200 West
Los Angeles, CA 90036
editorial@westernid.com

for subscriptions call:
1.800.477.5988 in US
1.850.682.7644 in Canada
and all other countries

visit our web site:
www.westernid.com

JULY/AUGUST 2004

WesternInteriors
AND DESIGN

special art issue!

winner
Best New Consumer Magazine
2004 Maggie Award

photography by Hester + Hardaway / text by Laura Mauk

DONALD JUDD'S MARFA

THE LANDSCAPES OF WEST TEXAS INFORMED THE SEMINAL AMERICAN ARTIST'S INVESTIGATIONS OF SPACE AND COLOR. SINCE HIS DEATH, THE COMPLEX OF BUILDINGS HE BOUGHT IN MARFA HAS BECOME AN INTERNATIONAL MECCA FOR THE CONTEMPORARY ART WORLD, WHICH IS STILL COMING TO TERMS WITH HIS POTENT LEGACY.

Donald Judd (1928-1994) left New York for Marfa, Texas, in 1977 to develop large-scale art in the desert landscape. His untitled fifteen works in concrete (left), 1980-84, are permanently installed at The Chinati Foundation, a military base he converted into a contemporary art museum. top: Judd's downtown Marfa ranch office. above: The artist outfitted the Block (or La Mansana de Chinati), his compound/live-living space, with a Gustav Stickley table and chairs and his 1963 "harp piece."

121

203

EMBRACE THE DIFFERENCES BETWEEN PRINT AND THE WEB

ARTHUR **HOCHSTEIN**

CASEY **CAPLOWE**

JASON **GODFREY**

By focusing on the strengths—and pleasures—of print, publications can and will remain relevant. After all, while legions of people indulge in the guilty pleasure of checking the latest Hollywood gossip online before the boss gets in, it's the print version of *People* magazine that gets stuffed into the beach bag. Arthur Hochstein thinks of print as "more of a niche experience but also a more satisfying experience, like the 'slow foods' movement. You have to focus on what you do well, like presenting photography and having discursive stories that are more pleasurable than utilitarian." Casey Caplowe agrees. "Certainly you consider how things will work online when you're designing the magazine, so there's that interplay. But

it's important to make a good magazine first. You have opportunities to do things in print that you can't do online, such as big pictures and illustrative headlines. The interplay of text and images is way more interesting in print than online." After all, there's something deeply gratifying about the experience of turning pages. As Jason Godfrey notes, "I don't see the Internet as a replacement for books. Books are the most interactive stuff that we have, actually."

The open feel of page layout and type choices in *Western Interiors and Design* magazine are as crisp and clear as the light and landscape where the images were taken.

204

VINCE **FROST**

HURRY UP

"If you're into making books, hurry up before there are no more books being published," says Vince Frost. "I think there's going to be a migration to people producing things online." Frost sees printing books as an outdated mode of communication. "It's quite an antiquated thing to produce a book," he says. "Publishers are buying digital companies and things are changing." Certainly, with the advent of digital book readers, self-publishing, on-demand publishing, and authors serializing their books online, there are changing opportunities for people who want to be read, beyond the more standard channels of traditional book publishing.

"It's going to be far more fluid than it is now," Frost predicts. "It's very exciting." He also points out that the digital world can certainly help address some of our pressing global concerns. "There are serious environmental issues here," he notes. "We're using up all the world's resources, and now the digital world is taking off."

Spin magazine, art directed by Arem Duplessis, combines photographs that reveal character and type that tells a story before you even read the words. The ambience on the printed page captures the essential vibe of the subject matter at hand.

Who The F*ck

Is Ryan Adams?

He's a former punk brat, an alt-country cult hero, a hopeless romantic, a clichéd celebrity, and a self-conscious nice guy who can't commit.

Will one of rock's most talented songwriters ever make a classic album?

Depends on which Ryan you talk to

By Marc Spitz

Photographs by Collier Schorr

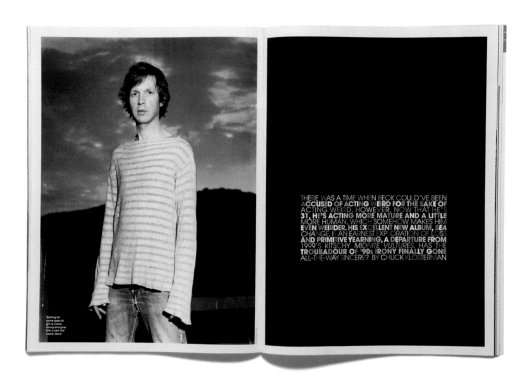

Waiting for some special girl to come along and give him a new first name. Beck

THERE WAS A TIME WHEN BECK COULD'VE BEEN ACCUSED OF ACTING WEIRD FOR THE SAKE OF ACTING WEIRD. HOWEVER, NOW THAT HE'S 31, HE'S ACTING MORE MATURE AND A LITTLE MORE HUMAN, WHICH SOMEHOW MAKES HIM EVEN WEIRDER. HIS EXCELLENT NEW ALBUM, SEA CHANGE, AN EARNEST EXPLORATION OF LOSS AND PRIMITIVE YEARNING, A DEPARTURE FROM 1999'S KITSCHY MIDNITE VULTURES, HAS THE TROUBADOUR OF '90s IRONY FINALLY GONE ALL-THE-WAY SINCERE? BY CHUCK KLOSTERMAN

Spin magazine, art directed by Arem Duplessis

205

KALLE **LASN**

CASEY **CAPLOWE**

JEREMY **LESLIE**

TODD **SIMMONS**

WHEN IN DOUBT, MAKE YOUR OWN

When clients, deadlines, and conventions begin to chafe, or there's no apparent place to speak with an alternative voice, there's nothing quite like starting your own publication for the like-minded. *Adbusters* was the concrete result of just this dilemma. Formerly a documentary filmmaker, Kalle Lasn got involved in Pacific Northwest political issues and set out to use his film skills to make and air television spots. "I was interested in getting people together and airing these spots to get some provocative stuff on the television," he recalls. "But none of these stations would give me any airtime." Instead of being stymied by the available media, he simply made his own, starting first with a 'zine, which became a newsletter, which became a magazine, which now has a circulation of 120,000 worldwide. "I got into it because of a passion for what I was doing, and I learned my lessons along the way," he says.

The advent of *GOOD* magazine followed a similar trajectory from film to page. "The founder, Ben Goldhirsh, wanted to be involved in creating media that mattered and could reach a lot of people," notes Casey Caplowe. He started a film company with a mission to make films "around socially relevant topics that would put people in seats but have a socially redeeming value." Then he and his cohorts realized they were not alone. "We started to realize that there was this burgeoning movement of people who wanted to live well and do good in a new way that's not just pure idealism but sees the system as part of the solution." *GOOD* magazine became their means of collecting and providing communication opportunities to and for this group of similarly inclined people: "a publication that would celebrate, inspire, and catalyze this movement."

Even if your aspirations are less grand or socially redeeming, creating your own publication is a great means to meet people, share ideas, and learn how to use financial and production limitations to inventive and fruitful design ends. "When I was in university," Jeremy Leslie recalls, "we published our own music fan 'zines. They were just black-and-white copies with staples, which was the correct aesthetic of the time, but that wasn't through choice; it was the only aesthetic available to us." The advent of cheap computers, printers, and the Internet has made much more possible. "What is available now with digital technology," he notes, "is that it's relatively cheap and easy to produce a few thousand copies of your own magazine—subject to your and your friends' skills and abilities. The only way I could sell my magazine was go to concerts and stand out there and try to get someone to buy it. Now I can print 5,000 copies of something, and if it's all right, I know I can sell 500 in London, 500 in Paris, 500 in Berlin, New York, Tokyo, Sydney, etc., through the Internet. The logistics are far easier, and so there are a lot of really good independent magazines out there; there are plenty of poor ones as well, but that's not the point. There's an audience out there that is hungry to buy international magazines that are cool." This means there's no reason for any creative, inventive, and enterprising publication designer to limit him or herself to conventions of commercial magazines, alone. If you want to see your designs hit the page, create the page as well as the design. As Jason Godfrey notes, "Self-publishing will not dumb down design. If anything, it allows people to do what they want and create quite personal things, and I think that's a good thing."

Chapter Nine:

THE ELEMENTS OF A PAGE

206 EMBRACE THE STRUCTURE

ARTHUR **HOCHSTEIN**

INA **SALTZ**

JANDOS **ROTHSTEIN**

NICOLE **DUDKA**

CASEY **CAPLOWE**

"Each magazine is a continuum of adherence to the template and what hits it every week," says Arthur Hochstein. "It doesn't exist in the perfect world of the designer; it has to exist in the real world." This real world, when it comes to publications, includes the framework of style sheets, font families, front of book, back of book, grids, regular columns, mastheads, specific sections, and more. "Some people hate structure and want chaos all the time," Ina Saltz points out, suggesting these people would perhaps not make the best publication designers. "I like some sense of orderly progression," she continues. "I need to know that there's a cycle that is repetitive and dependable; it's not all up for grabs every single time; you're not reinventing the wheel every month." For Saltz, as for many publication designers, structure enhances rather than limits her creativity. "I think of creativity as flowing water," she explains. "For me, if I have a narrow pipe, it goes faster and further; if it's a wide pipe, it just trickles."

Jandos Rothstein, magazine design director, educator, and book and blog writer, also sees the grid as a way to enhance creativity. He compares publication design to jazz: There are only so many rhythms in music, but you can bring in instruments in whatever way you want, he points out. "What the grid does for you as a designer is give you the structure in which you build pages. It helps with the mechanics of putting it out every month, is a timesaving tool, gives you something to work against and work with. Sure, there are magazines that have been built on no grids, but those magazines had one designer doing everything, so there was a continuity and visual vocabulary because it all came from one person. With a grid, you have regularity and rhythm, but you still have quite a bit of freedom." Nicole Dudka also finds plenty of room to move within the grid. "One of the things that I always say is that it's a canvas, not a page. Try not to focus too much on the grid and the structure and the restrictions, but let the artful part drive your design. Once you have a good concept, photo, or illustration, you can let the restrictions and grid fall into place around it."

Great magazines usually create an architecture at the outset—or in redesign—that provides flexibility. At *GOOD* magazine, "We have very consistent sections, but some of these sections are very freeform," explains Casey Caplowe. For example, different artists create several loosely thematic spreads for the "Graphic Statement" that comes before the table of contents in each issue; different designers are given the opportunity to create interpretations and representations of statistical information in the "Transparency" section; the "Op Ed" portion features a different illustrator each month. "All these sections are opportunities where we've created frameworks and then invite people to participate and interpret them each time," Caplowe says. "We don't have a firm, dogmatic idea of what *Good* is. It's an exploration. There's a foundation that's ours, but a lot of the details are other people's."

The structure Pentagram partner Luke Hayman created for the redesign of *Time* magazine is flexible enough to accommodate a variety of editorial content and images so readers have the comfort of knowing they are in the specific world of *Time*, even as they encounter striking artwork, familiar columnists, and the occasional surprise.

The Truth About Talibanistan

Islamic militants have turned the borderlands between Pakistan and Afghanistan into a new base for al-Qaeda. An inside look at the next battleground of the war on terrorism

BY ARYN BAKER

KABUL, AFGHANISTAN

THE RESIDENTS OF DARA ADAM Khel, a gunsmiths' village 30 miles south of Peshawar, Pakistan, awoke one morning last month to find their streets littered with pamphlets demanding that they observe Islamic law. Women were instructed to wear all-enveloping burqas and men to grow their beards. Music and television were banned. Then the jihadists really got serious. These days, dawn is often accompanied by the wailing of women as another beheaded corpse is found by the side of the road, a note pinned to the chest claiming that the victim was a spy for either the Americans or the Pakistani government. Beheadings are recorded and sold on DVD in the area's bazaars. "It's the knife that terrifies me," says Hafizullah, 40, a local arms smith. "Before they kill you, they sharpen the knife in front of you. They are worse than butchers."

Stories like these are being repeated across the tribal region of Pakistan, a rugged no-man's-land that forms the country's border with Afghanistan—and that is rapidly becoming home base for a new generation of potential terrorists. Fueled by zealotry and hardened by war, young religious extremists have overrun scores of towns and villages in the border areas, with the intention of imposing their strict interpretation of Islam on a population unable to fight back. Like the Taliban in the late 1990s in Afghanistan, the jihadists are believed to be providing leaders of al-Qaeda with the protection they need to regroup and train new operatives. U.S. intelligence officials think that Osama bin Laden and his deputy, Ayman al-Zawahiri, may have found refuge in these environs. And though 49,000 U.S. and NATO troops are stationed just across the border in Afghanistan, they aren't authorized to operate on the Pakistani side. Remote, tribal and deeply conservative, the border region is less a part of either country than a world unto itself, a lawless frontier so beyond the control of the West and its allies that it has earned a name of its own: Talibanistan.

Tribal turmoil *Waziri chiefs like these two chiefs resist outside authority but have seen their villages taken over by the Taliban*

28

Photographs for TIME by Balazs Gardi

207

FORGET THE STRUCTURE

INA **SALTZ**

TODD **SIMMONS**

KALLE **LASN**

There are many other publications where consistency of structure is not only less necessary but actually impedes the editorial mission. Magazines less interested in the mass-market—literary, youth market, rabblerousing, niche, and others—have developed audiences that expect and embrace change. Ina Saltz points to, for example, the Transworld family of skateboarding, snowboarding, BMX, motocross, and surf magazines, which maintain their edgy vibe by constantly changing their look—even their logos—to keep themselves up to date and relevant with their hyped-up, adrenaline-fueled, youth-market readers.

The all-volunteer literary magazine, *Matter*, foregoes not only structure but also more fundamental navigational devices, such as a table of contents. Todd Simmons, the magazine's publisher, explains, "We want to start with the work rather than the table of contents or an editor's note. We try to make it hard to navigate because this makes it more direct and immediate. We want the reader to start on the cover and go straight through as if every part were as important as every other." For the crew at *Matter*, standard procedures are something to be challenged. "We try to question and investigate for ourselves what value common

practice has and how it adds or subtracts from the experience," Simmons says. "Until you do without something, what do you really know about it? Or until you make it your own, how do you know it completely? We want to make sure we're not doing something for the sake of doing it because there's so much busy-ness in the world already."

Adbusters is another magazine where repetitive structure is outright rejected as overly constricting to both the magazine and its readers. "The trap that a lot of art directors have fallen into is they think their job is to just somehow follow a formula," Kalle Lasn says. "Every now and again they redesign, but then there is a new formula, and the job of the designer becomes rote and boring and just filling in the grid." *Adbusters* seeks to shake up the world by shaking up each issue. "Every magazine should be as close as possible to a one-off. You should design it from the bottom up because if you start with a grid, you're lost before you start. The formula that I have is to have a single, powerful narrative, one seamless story line that flows from front cover to back cover in one passionate, existential blast." A formula which, while not for regular readers of supermarket tabloids, is central to Lasn's mission of creating meaningful debate on important social issues of our times.

The literary magazine *Matter* arranges each issue, very loosely—around a theme. The magazine also does away with traditional front material or makes things like the table of contents "virtually useless or so hard to decipher that most people flip past them immediately," says publisher and editor Todd Simmons.

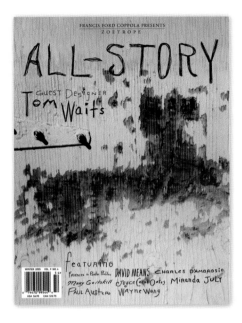

Zoetrope: All-Story engages a different artist—usually from various nonpublication media—to design each issue of the publication. This issue was designed by musician, Tom Waits.

208

MICHAEL **RAY**

ENHANCE THE IMMEDIACY OF THE MEDIA

"What's great about magazines," says Michael Ray, editor at *Zoetrope: All-Story*, "is that because they are disposable, they can be continually reinvented." *Zoetrope* maximizes this opportunity to be a moving target by asking a different person, usually a non-graphic designer who is an artist in some other medium, to design each issue. Musician Tom Waits, photographer Marilyn Minter, and actor Tim Roth are just a few of the magazine's guest designers, who may or may not connect their ideas to the literary content or call on the staff designer for assistance. "The independence versus interdependence between magazine staff and artist varies from issue to issue," says Ray. "There's this really interesting potential when we sit down together. As far as we're concerned, the farther from magazine design that this artist's principal pursuit is, the better. The more unexpected, the better."

However, even this stretching of boundaries does have its limitations. "There's always some sort of negotiation," Ray concedes, clicking off the necessary compromises between art and practicality. "On a basic level, we want to make sure the text is readable; we don't want to challenge our readers unnecessarily. We want to be respectful of the writers as well, so we present their work in a format that can be consumed as easily as possible. We need to have a barcode. It's nice to have the logo at the top so it can be seen on the newsstand." Beyond these concerns, there are the actual stories themselves. "In each issue, we publish six to eight stories or one-act plays," Ray explains. "But otherwise, the magazine is a surprise." And *Zoetrope* recognizes that this element of surprise will inevitably limit its readership. "This is not an impulse buy in the checkout line of a supermarket," says Ray. "We have an entrenched readership who knows what to look for. And they like finding something new in our approach every time."

Left and below: *Zoetrope: All-Story*
designed by performer, Will Oldham

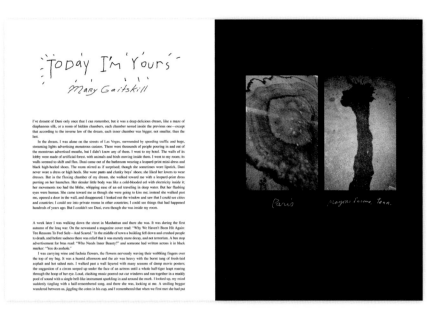

Zoetrope: All-Story designed by musician, Tom Waits

209

LET THE MATERIAL CREATE THE STRUCTURE

LUKE **HAYMAN**

ADAM **MACHACEK**

More mainstream publications naturally adhere to a more formal and recognizable architecture. "There is a real pattern that most magazines follow, with a clear logic," Luke Hayman points out. "There is a table of contents, with the editor's note and masthead and letters section up front, with lots of small stories that don't develop into longer pieces, then longer stories, then features in the middle or the end." This inherent structure gives a designer not only the raw material to develop the design but also a way through the material. "It's a logical pacing," Hayman notes.

Even when the publication does not have a well-established structure, a designer should let the form of the final piece develop organically from the material provided. Adam Machacek says, "I think the rules come out themselves with each project, during the process. In most cases, the client comes with two piles: texts and images. Sometimes, these are very well organized and edited, and then it's easier to foresee the structure of the book." However, as a young, two-person shop, Machacek and his partner don't generally get clients as buttoned-up or well established as those that tend to appear on the doorstep of Hayman's Pentagram office. "Mostly, it's all just mixed up," says Machacek, "And so together, with the author, we are editing, planning, and building it up like a house."

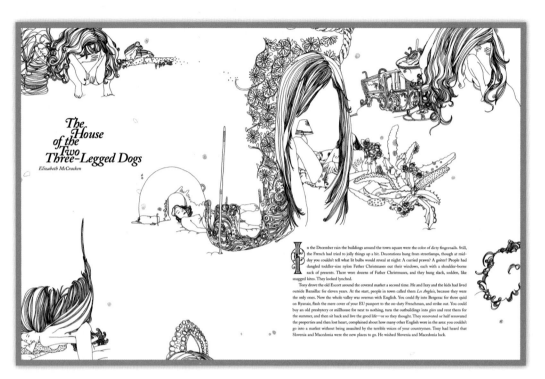

Zoetrope: All-Story designed by performer, Will Oldham

210 DEVELOP A STRUCTURE THAT IS SIMULTANEOUSLY LINEAR AND NONLINEAR

ARJEN **NOORDEMAN**

DAVID **ALBERTSON**

"The main thing that's different about book design versus other kinds of design," says Arjen Noordeman, "is that you have to think about the story developing. It's an experience that has a timeline like a movie." While this is especially true of narrative books, where readers generally start with the cover and dutifully turn the pages one by one, people may enter the "story" of an art book or magazine at different points, looking at pictures and reading articles here and there. "You have to build up the experience," says Noordeman, "but also create an overarching structure that can work nonlinearly."

The structure needs to be solid so readers feel firmly in the grip of the editorial viewpoint and yet flexible enough that they can express their own browsing and reading eccentricities. "Really good graphic design points the reader in the right direction so they're looking at the right thing at the right time," says David Albertson. "It's about structuring the magazine experience so it's functionally enjoyable. Sometimes you see a publication where every page pretty much looks the same; the photography looks the same; it doesn't look like anyone was working hard to bring it to you. A publication like that could be successful, but it makes me sad," he notes.

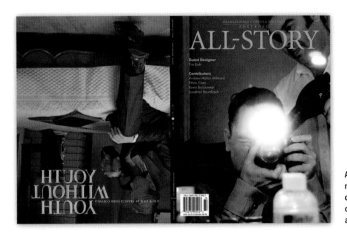

A special edition for fall 2007 featured a mid-magazine flip, with half of the magazine dedicated to the usual short stories and the other half to a movie by magazine founder and director Francis Ford Coppola.

211 DESIGN A SYSTEM THAT ENGAGES PEOPLE, OVER AND OVER AGAIN

CHRIS **VERMAAS**

JESSICA **FLEISCHMANN**

SCOTT **STOWELL**

To create a magazine that provides functional reader benefits and keeps readers coming back designers need to put even more attention on the basics. "Think about choice of typefaces, point sizes, structures within the layout, imagery, paper stocks, use of space, and so on to express the editorial elements; they all have to work together," says Chris Vermaas, partner with Chin-Lien Chen in the Office of CC in the Netherlands. "You can see a successful publication design as well-functioning machinery that directs the already embedded knowledge of your audience about how to read and use a magazine."

Jessica Fleischmann, of the Los Angeles design studio still room, finds herself focusing on two critical implements: "Structure and typography are super weighted in publications," she observes. "I believe in getting out of the way of the work and for design to support the content, so I have to have strong conceptual and functional reasons for choosing typefaces and developing structure. In addition to image selection and pacing, my voice, as a designer, is going to show mainly through type and structure." Part of why structure is so important and yet needs to remain flexible is that you don't always know what's going to happen within the confines you've created. "You're

working with something over a number of pages, so you have to make sure that it's really going to function and it's going to make the argument or statement that you want to convey over all those pages, knowing that the content is shifting."

These shifts happen not just over the hundred or so pages of a single magazine but over many iterations. "A striking difference between publication design and other fields of graphic design is that in publication design, the stage, the medium, and the platform are set up to be in use for years," says Vermaas. "They must offer enough flexibility to generate every issue as a separate entity. The challenge is in creating this diversity within unity." For Scott Stowell, of the New York design studio Open, this challenge is his favorite part of publication design. "What I love about magazines," says Stowell, "is that it's creating a system within each magazine, but at the same time, the system has to work over time. Each issue has to be new but the same." For Stowell, playfulness is critical to engagement. "The constraints of an assignment are like setting up the rules of a game," he says. "So if you set them up well, you can play a game that's very fun but different every time."

Morf is a magazine on the history and theory of design, directed and distributed to Dutch design students to "enhance their knowledge on the history and theory in their field. To stress the seriousness of this mission, we kept the design plain, yet gave the publication a face that could be recognized," according to Vermaas and his partner Chin-Lien Chen.

212

LET YOUR DESIGN BE THE NINTH THING

MICHAEL **RAY**

At *Zoetrope*, guest designers are given an exceptional amount of leeway. Because the magazine uses a different (usually) non-designer to create each issue, the usual boundaries, rules, and conventions are not necessarily broken as they simply don't apply. Each issue is a one-off, an opportunity to explore some creative obsession or preoccupation that will, intentionally, never come again. "Fundamentally, when I say that the design supports the text, what I hope is just that it doesn't interfere with the text," says Michael Ray. "But fundamental to our mission is to give the guest designers as much freedom as possible. We're giving them the magazine and saying, do whatever you want to do. If you want to mimic the stories in mood or narrative, go ahead, but if you don't want to, you don't have to."

What this creates in each issue is a tableau of multiple visual and literary voices moving to their own internal rhythms, which may or may not have much to do with one another but are individually coherent, artistic, well crafted, and expressive. According to Ray, "Some artists read the stories and some don't. Some don't want to be influenced. They feel like the most obvious thing to do is create a visual manifestation of the writing. These guys are looking at designing an issue once and maybe never again, so they want to take more risks and do something unexpected. I've heard it repeatedly from artists that the magazine has eight stories and they want their design to be a ninth thing."

213

JEREMY **LESLIE**

KALLE **LASN**

CHALLENGE THE GIVENS

Design is, by nature, the merging of creative impulses with pragmatic considerations. There's always an audience, a budget, schedules, sales goals, and the limits of producing something in the particular time space continuum of planet Earth. It is from these demands and realities that rules are born. Unfortunately, because so many magazines are facing not only these same considerations but also trying to grab a piece of the same consumer pie, they end up with similar solutions. "Magazines have all begun to really look the same in terms of how they present themselves," Jeremy Leslie remarks. "There are a lot of techniques and wise words about how front covers should appear, how to make it sell, how the newsstand is a very particular environment, and how to be successful there. Various people can give you those five, ten, or fifteen rules, but what I enjoy doing is challenging those rules."

However, there's no point in creating difficulties just for the sake of being a contrarian. Every challenge must have a purpose in mind, a goal in sight, a means to an end. Leslie offers this advice: "I always look at a brief for what we can challenge, where we can make a difference, how we can make it stand out from the competition, not by being different for the sake of being different, but by looking for what will work for the magazine and best represent the client," he says.

Kalle Lasn, as would be expected, expands his idea of rule-breaking all the way to the most basic underpinnings of what publications are doing in the larger world. "Throughout the history of magazines," he fulminates, "it's always been the case that there are commercial publications, and I don't care if eight out of ten of them are that way, but I lament that 99.9 percent are that way, and 99.9 percent of the designers are going along with it." He longs for a day when designers are doing more than catering to commercial interests. "I lament that there's not one of ten that go against the grain. I lament the fact that our culture has become so commercialized, so homogenized, that there's no dissenting voices speaking back. This speaks of a culture that's a dinosaur." The answer, he believes, is in challenging the status quo by asking bigger questions and demanding more interesting answers. "Our culture has lost its soul and its passions, and the designers have, too. To hell with the rules," he concludes. "The real movers and shakers are rule breakers."

214

IF YOU'RE GOING TO BREAK THE RULES, KNOW WHAT THEY ARE

MARCUS **PIPER**

INA **SALTZ**

MICHAEL **RAY**

CHRIS **VERMAAS**

As in life, so it is with magazines: Sometimes the best way to bring attention to a limitation is to step beyond it. "Breaking the rules is the way to add pace to a publication," says Marcus Piper. "By breaking the rules, you can stop the reader in their tracks, get their attention, and remind them they are inside your publication, engaging with it." However, randomly ignoring all conventions and expectations leads simply to chaos that benefits neither the reader nor the publication or publisher. As Ina Saltz says, "Rules can be broken in divinely successful ways, but it takes someone who knows what they are doing to break the rules well."

The smartest effects of rule-breaking come when the intention is somehow contained within the act itself. "Regarding the conventions of magazine design," says Michael Ray, "it's most interesting to break them if you first know what those conventions are and why you're breaking them." It helps if your readers know about them as well. "For every new graphic problem, we believe in defining a new set of rules," Chris Vermaas says. "We present the users with the basic structure, the rhythm, the size, the known, the hierarchy, and so forth. Once the graphic parameters are set, it becomes possible to show your audience when the 'rules' are being broken. Using an italic, a shifted baseline, a double word space, starts to stand out, starts to get its meaning, and will not be seen as a mistake."

integration became an urgent concern. Since it was also clear that most people did not have the necessary mental baggage to found such integration on a rational conception of the functioning of machines, it had to be on an irrational conception. Thus the machine became eroticized—a living organism.

A side effect of this development is that a truly functional streamline, for things that really have to go against the wind, has never materialized. The air resistance of current cars is hardly lower than that of those before 1930. Modern car bodies, then, are not really

streamlined—they are *tumescent*. This explains why cars, mixers, and vacuum cleaners rarely have flat or singly curved surfaces: the characteristic shape is the slightly swollen surface. It is a physiological form that reminds one of the puffing up of a taut membrane by pressure from within. Our technical design reflects a disgust of pure geometric shapes. Like machines, after all, geometric shapes are rational forms, constructs of the mind, abstractions, nonexistent in nature. Apparently most people have far more affinity with the incomprehensible than with the abstract. [TB]

184-185 Turn on the Light: postscript

AUTHOR	DUTCH TEXT
Marjan Unger	page 102

Chin-Lien Chen observes that students of graphic design in the Netherlands, as opposed to those in the US, hardly read theory, but that their final work still betrays visual force and professionalism. Chen thus raises the larger issue of how students of design should deal with theory.

It turns out that the correlation between theoretical skills (asking students to read and write a lot) and design skills is largely speculative. Of course it is important to be articulate, also for designers, but there is also the risk that schools will merely produce theory-minded designers who quickly end up in teaching positions or other jobs that keep them from doing what they were trained to do.

As art history instructor I always hated it when my colleagues complained about their students' limited knowledge. How much did they themselves know when finishing their formal education? My own knowledge was fragmented at best, and only later on it developed into something more substantial. Indeed, knowledge of art and design history is the kind of knowledge that has to grow on you. We all have our individual frame of reference, and it is important to demonstrate to students how we built our knowledge by drawing causal relationships between the various historical practices, artists and periods, as well as by simply telling stories about what we know. I must add that I have also had many colleagues who did so. Therefore I feel that instructors at Dutch design schools can perfectly explain future designers how to tackle theoretical concerns.

As for students, at any moment you are free to start exploring and deepening your knowledge of art and design, and how it specifically applies to your own work and interests. [TB]

185-188 On Pottery

AUTHOR	DUTCH TEXT / IMAGES
B. Majorick	page 107
ABOUT THE AUTHOR	
B. Majorick is an alias of sculptor/typographer J.J. Beljon [1922-2002].	

ORIGINALLY PUBLISHED IN	YEAR
"Ontwerpen en verwerpen. Industriële vormgeving als noodzaak", Em. Querido, Amsterdam	1959

VIEW IMAGES IN COLOR
www.morf.nl

[► P 2 6 8]

145-163 Taste and Fashion [Chapter XVIII]

AUTHOR
James Laver
ABOUT THE AUTHOR
James Laver [1899-1975], British art critic and fashion historian.

FIRST PUBLISHED IN	YEAR
Taste and Fashion. From the French Revolution to the Present Day, George G. Harrap & Co., London	1937

INTRODUCTION

In the concluding chapter of his book *Taste and Fashion* James Laver captures the fashion cycle in a straightforward timeline, which has become known as 'Laver's Law'. As the driving force behind this cycle he saw the evolution of taste, which in turn is determined by economic and social factors. In the second part of this text he argues that the continuous changes in taste are not only reflected in dress, but also influence our appreciation of interior design and architecture.

We have now pursued for a hundred and fifty years the complex story of the evolution of European dress. We have sketched its main outline and pursued the subject through some tempting bypaths, and we have seen many seeming trifles take on an unexpected significance in the light of historical perspective. Only the superficial will consider such a subject a waste of time, for although the history of feminine elegance and the history of culture are not precisely the same thing, their courses are curiously

Morf, designed by Office of CC

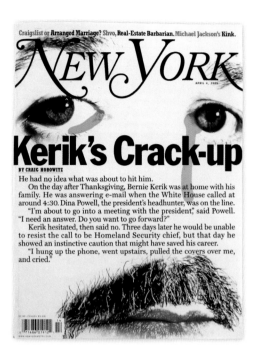

215

SIMPLIFY TYPE

LUKE **HAYMAN**

INA **SALTZ**

AREM **DUPLESSIS**

Because the primary role of type in a publication is to convey information and provide guidance throughout the activity of reading, most publication designers recommend using just a few fonts, in a systematic way. "Usually," says Luke Hayman, "the rule of thumb is to simplify. Two families of fonts are typically what I go for." Ina Saltz agrees and amplifies. "In general, you want to work within two to three type families max: one for body copy, a sans serif for contrasting other elements, such as bylines, captions, and so on, and maybe a display type for large headlines that would have a little more refinement." But she hastens to point out, there is no reason to let this limit also be a constraint. "If you choose well," she explains, "within each family, you will have a broad array of weights, slopes, width. Some type families have up to fifty members, but those families are designed to work well together. The choice of which of those three families will work together is a complex thing, and many factors need to be considered, such as type classification, the designer's taste, and again, the needs of the magazine."

At the *New York Times Magazine*, "We design with only two typefaces," says Arem Duplessis, "Stymie and Cheltenhem, both of which have been redrawn for the magazine." Again, this apparent limitation proves no brake to creativity. "This helps elevate the level of invention," he notes, "while keeping the magazine familiar and cohesive. Even with such a limited arsenal of fonts, it's always a real challenge packaging such diverse subject matter. Let's see, Next Gen Robots and a story about workplace discrimination?" In publication design, there are enough complications for a designer to contend with without adding the unnecessary confusion of competing fonts.

Above and opposite: *New York* magazine, as redesigned by Luke Hayman, kept some iconic elements, such as the magazine title, while bringing in a variety of other type treatments to delineate special sections like the back-of-the-book events listings.

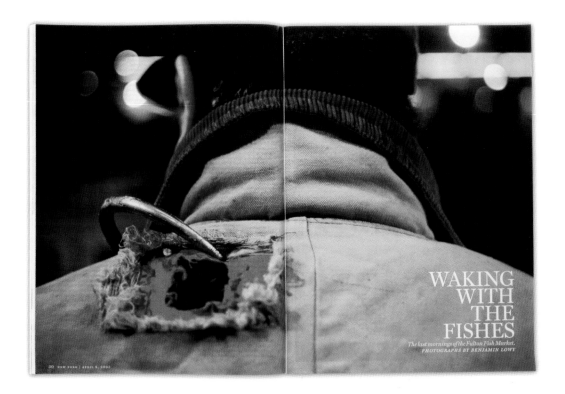

The magazine cover reads:

GALLUP
MANAGEMENT JOURNAL

SUMMER 2001 • DATA-DRIVEN MANAGEMENT INTELLIGENCE • WWW.GALLUPJOURNAL.COM

COVER STORY
THE **LOYAL CUSTOMER**
THE CARE AND FEEDING OF YOUR MOST VALUABLE BUSINESS ASSET

PLUS The HUMAN SIDE of BRAND• LEADERSHIP'S many MOLDS• ZERO in on SOLUTIONS to CUSTOMER COMPLAINTS• HOW a SO-SO ECONOMY AFFECTS a PRESIDENTIAL ELECTION• WHO'S HAPPIER on the JOB: MEN or WOMEN? PROOF THAT TRAINING PAYS OFF• 60-PLUS YEARS of DATA on RELIGIOUS FERVOR

216

LUKE **HAYMAN**

CARIN **GOLDBERG**

USE LOTS OF TYPEFACES

While Luke Hayman says "Typically I look to simplify," he concedes that there are exceptions—such as the multi-award-winning *New York* magazine. "It had a lot more tangents and nuance and subject material," he explains. "And there were historical references to the early days of the magazine, as well as a font we used only for the listings. It was unusual."

These special cases can certainly work, as long as they have a reason for being and are handled with insight and intelligence. As Carin Goldberg explains, "Generally speaking, you go with the rules of thumb that call for one setting for text and then creating a hierarchy of typographic choices for heads, bylines, etc. But that's just the template you start with, and from there, you can expand and move in any direction. You could use 150 typefaces, of course, if the content calls for that. These rules of thumb simply provide a baseline for developing voice and tone. These rules and choices create the engine that will propel the magazine." As with any complex construction, start with a strong foundation and build upward and outward from there.

Above and opposite: The clarity of the type treatments in *Gallup* magazine, as designed by Carin Goldberg, are not only fresh and easy to grasp but are also a demonstration of the magazine's values.

217 USE TYPE AS A BRANDING ELEMENT

INA **SALTZ**

CARIN **GOLDBERG**

Publications use type at many levels, but they all work together to create a navigational system that helps readers understand and find their way through the content to determine what they want to read. A headline offers a certain kind of information that is distinctly different from what's in a caption; reading the masthead or calendar listings is a different experience from reading a piece of investigative journalism. While type's primary role is to be read, it can and should do double and triple duty as an identity and branding element, as well. "Type is there to communicate, to establish the personality of the magazine, and to advance the mission of the magazine," Ina

Saltz explains. "Type also has a personality, and it communicates style and content. So the choice of typeface is extremely important to the identity of the magazine, and it functions to separate and distinguish the magazine from its competition." Like delving into any graphic design endeavor, getting the tool of type to live up to this important challenge requires extra work from the designer. "When designers, art directors, and editors have a high level of courage and vision," says Carin Goldberg, "the typography can and should be an integral component in conjunction with the photography and illustration, and that's when things get exciting."

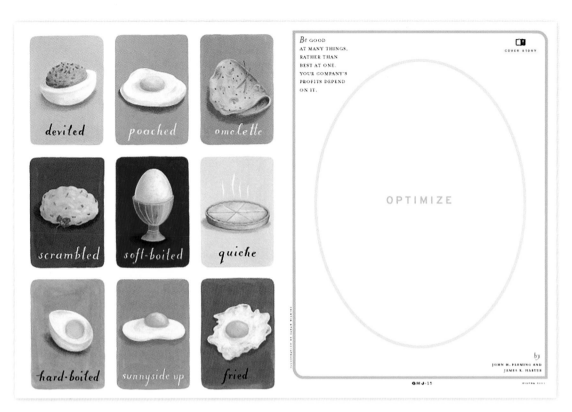

Gallup magazine, designed by Carin Goldberg

218

ARJEN **NOORDEMAN**

MAKE TYPE ENTERTAINING

"Beyond legibility, the first thing that comes to mind when I think about type is entertainment," says Arjen Noordeman, describing a quality not normally associated with fonts but clearly present in his numerous hand-drawn type explorations. "I want to evoke an emotion or story," he says, "so before you realize what it is, it transports you to a certain mood or atmosphere." Sometimes experiments do go wrong, and when it comes to type, the results can be illegible or suggest confusing aesthetic directions. "Sometimes, it backfires, I have to admit," says Noordeman. "But it's often better to just take a stand and please 40 percent of the people instead of trying to please everyone and ending up pleasing no one. The alternative is playing it safe or just boring people. There's a place for that," he says, "but it's not my place."

The catalog for this theater company, designed by Welcometo.as, includes a fold-out poster that interacts with the program, creating a changing kaleidoscope of different images and messages, along with information about events. See how it unfolds on the following pages.

219

ADAM **MACHACEK**

LUKE **HAYMAN**

AGNES **ZEILSTRA**

LET THE IMAGES DO SOME OF THE WORK FOR YOU

"Great images make a big part of the job done," says Adam Machacek. "If we are lucky and have great images to work with, our design becomes far less visible." And it also allows him to put his attention toward the other aspects of graphic design. "Instead, we focus more on the rhythm and context in which the images are shown. We focus more on papers, typeface, and production details." Images can, and in many cases should, set the tone for these other design exercises. When redesigning *New York* magazine, Luke Hayman notes that the magazine "wanted to become smarter, with more attitude and assuming a greater intelligence of the audience." While the design needed to express this shift, "a lot came through with the photography," says Hayman, "which was quite sophisticated and arty."

Of course, great images are not guaranteed. "Sometimes I work with photos I don't like," says Agnes Zeilstra. "But I have to see it as a challenge to make a beautiful page." In some cases, this requires manipulating the materials provided to make them more interesting or greater than the sum of their parts. "When we receive mixed images, such as bad photocopies and low-resolution screenshots together with serious pictures, then we have no mercy, and we start to cut, draw, Photoshop, destroy, and distort wherever we can—of course, within the concept or rules that we've developed for each publication," says Machacek.

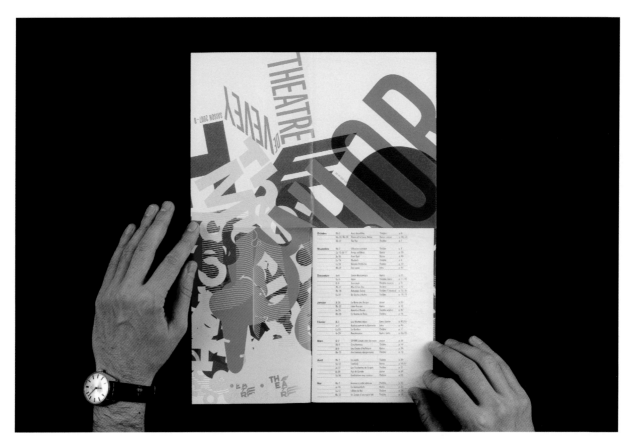

Above and opposite: theater catalog, designed by Welcometo.as

220 KEEP IN MIND WHERE THE MAGAZINE WILL LIVE IN THE WORLD

LUKE **HAYMAN**

MICHAEL **RAY**

Magazines get to their audiences in two principal ways: through the mail or off the newsstand. This creates logistical issues that a designer must be aware of. As Luke Hayman suggests, "You have to ask yourself, 'Where will this magazine live in the world?'" In some cases, Hayman says, he's worked up two covers for a publication, one with a large area for the address label and another that addresses the unique demands of the newsstand. "It's very much a part of design to consider how it will work on the newsstand. You look at it from a distance and adjust the scale. You want impact, so you may have to make it less elegant—hopefully you can do both at the same time. I have done something that's larger, more aggressive for newsstands. When

I've worked on magazines that are 95 percent subscription, it's a different need because you know it's not competing next to *Us* magazine."

Zoetrope is mostly subscription-based, so it is less concerned about how it will get attention or even be recognizable on the newsstand. "We encourage people to reinvent the title," says Michael Ray, recalling one designer who split the masthead and had a barcode on the front and back. "Some people didn't recognize it. And it created major headaches for our newsstand distributors," he concedes. "But it's our mission to be as open to these artists' ideas as possible and manifest them in as many ways as we can."

221

MICHAEL **RAY**

RESPECT PRACTICAL LOGISTICS

While *Zoetrope* may not concede very much territory to the demanding environment of the newsstand, the magazine does have to take into consideration certain practical logistics, just like any other. "We started as a tabloid," says Michael Ray. "Out of Francis Ford Coppola's nostalgia for the broadsheets from the 1930s." (Director Coppola is the founder of *Zoetrope*.) Unfortunately, reality got in the way of this particular vision. "The problem was that because it's a small magazine and we're shipping it out, magazines were arriving to subscribers shredded. Newsstands didn't want to carry them; they didn't know how to stock anything that broke conventional dimensions."

Even though the sizing had been integral to the original goals, respect for both the contributors and the readers forced a change in execution. "We liked the idea of a magazine that was the product of so much effort drawing on the talents of so many artists and yet was ultimately fragile and temporary. While we liked that idea, we also wanted the magazine to succeed and find readers, and we wanted to be fair to those subscribers who, issue after issue, received shredded magazines." So *Zoetrope* was reinvented in a more conventional format, complete with traditional binding and semigloss or newsprint paper, according to each artist's preference. The content remains the same, and readers don't have to tape pages back together to read them.

222

INA **SALTZ**

MAKE SURE THE IMAGE AND WORDS WORK TOGETHER

The most frequent mistake that Ina Saltz sees is images and words working against, rather than for, each other. "The biggest and most common mistake," she says, "is when the words and image do not send the same message. Sometimes words don't apply to the image or the other way around. They shoot

each other in the foot instead of enhancing and amplifying each other." This mistake is especially egregious on magazine covers, which are supposed to instantly telegraph a strong and cohesive message that grabs attention and entices people to pick up, open, and buy the magazine.

223

INA **SALTZ**

LUKE **HAYMAN**

PAY ATTENTION TO WHERE THE ADVERTISING IS

Most publications, unlike other graphic design projects, include advertising. This puts the designer in the unique position of incorporating what someone else, usually with a completely different agenda, has created. To maintain editorial as well as design integrity, the designer therefore has to be on the lookout for perceived conflicts of interest between advertising and editorial. "The readers' perceptions influence everything," Ina Saltz explains, "and there will often be jarring or confusing adjacencies from advertising to editorial. The conflict might involve any number of factors, from too-similar type treatments or images, to confusion because of the way elements are arranged, to conflicting or confusing subjects and backgrounds. Wherever the reader may experience a disconnect or a miscommunication," she says, "a good designer will create clear separation. Someone needs to oversee the advertising and editorial adjacencies."

Luke Hayman offers a couple of pragmatic ways to handle these "concussions" when they occur. "There's a stage of magazine design where you get to see ads next to the editorial," he says. "If it looks as though there's an editorial conflict or the pages visually merge, then you have to have a discussion with the ad manager and publisher to ask if ads can be moved. Other times, I've just created a clear boundary so the pages that face ads have, for example, a rule going down the gutter, so editorial doesn't bleed into the gutter and never actually touches an ad." These and many other fixes are available to the designer; the important thing is to make sure that the fixing gets done wherever it's needed.

224

INA **SALTZ**

LUKE **HAYMAN**

CREATE A FEATURE WELL

"Within the framework of the magazine, there should always be an editorial well," says Ina Saltz, "which is a series of spreads, uninterrupted by advertising, where the editorial voice can be most clearly heard. This gives the readers a chance to bond with the magazine and creates reader loyalty, which is what is deeply desired." Luke Hayman points out that the well also serves "the requirements of advertising, which likes to be up front. But the goal is always to have a section, hopefully of features, that can be uninterrupted by advertising. Not every magazine has this, but it's better if they do." Better, not only for the reader, but for the designer, as this well is the one place where their page designs can stand on their own, without the visual noise and clutter of advertising.

Travel & Leisure, as designed by Luke Hayman, lets powerful images and simple type tell the story of the stunning locations and elegant travel destinations that readers expect to see in its pages.

One, designed by Albertson Design, was a national consumer magazine that sought to "bring the growing national obsession with design to a general audience."

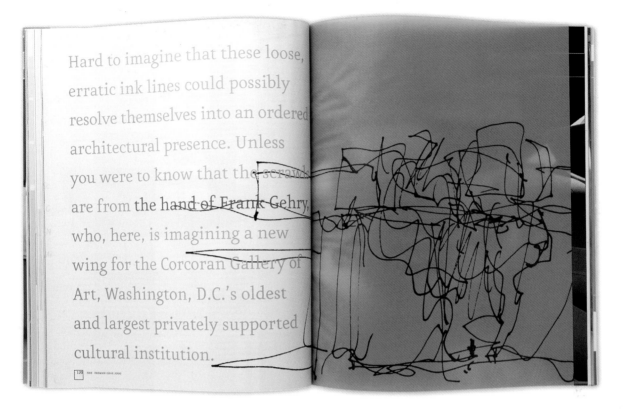

Hard to imagine that these loose, erratic ink lines could possibly resolve themselves into an ordered architectural presence. Unless you were to know that the scrawls are from the hand of Frank Gehry, who, here, is imagining a new wing for the Corcoran Gallery of Art, Washington, D.C.'s oldest and largest privately supported cultural institution.

225

LUKE **HAYMAN**

SPEAK SOFTLY

In addition to sharing the same space between two covers, editorial content must also compete with advertising for the reader's attention. Advertising is rarely subtle and often covers similar topics as the articles. This can dilute the editorial mission and create confusion for readers who may be unsure of how to comprehend what they're looking at. Luke Hayman provides an example and a solution from one of the magazines he's worked on: "In *Travel & Leisure*, the editorial has stiff competition from the advertising, which is everywhere, is strongly designed, and has the same kind of imagery. So it's important to make editorial look like editorial and stand apart from the advertising. Sometimes, by stripping out color and making the editorial quieter, it stands out more."

Big in New York City   Number 7

Bold images and confident type in black and white ensure that each spread of *Big* magazine, designed by Frost Design, makes a singular statement without distracting design back flips.

226

INA **SALTZ**

MAKE IT A PHYSICAL OBJECT

In the end, a magazine is something that will be picked up, held in hand, flipped through, brought to the sofa, beach, chair, or bed. Especially in this day of computer-generated everything, the quality of the physical experience of paging through the finished piece is critical to the success of any publication. "I am a firm proponent of setting up a wall where every page of the magazine is put up so everyone on staff can see them, even if they are reduced in size," says Ina Saltz. "This allows the magazine's pacing and flow to be visualized. Designers and editors typically work on one story or layout at a time. When you can see the flow of the pages from one story to the next, it is a good way to spot mistakes that might not otherwise be evident, such as too-similar headlines or type treatments in contiguous stories. It's also a good idea to have a binder with sleeves where pages are slipped in so everyone can see the facing adjacencies. This gives you the added advantage of allowing you to page through the magazine as a reader would." Whether it's a wall, table, floor, or binder, all publications must get out of the computer and into the hand before design is finalized. It's as much a designer's job to consider what readers will do as what they will see.

227

AREM **DUPLESSIS**

STEVEN **HELLER**

JEREMY **LESLIE**

AVOID OVERUSING DESIGN DEVICES

"I tend to lean toward the 'less is more' approach, which especially helps with a title like the *New York Times Magazine*," says Arem Duplessis. The point is that design should not be distracting. "I like the little tweaks that bend the design to force thought. But please, nothing over the top," he continues. "One twist and that's it; no layers. The idea should be concrete and confident." Steven Heller similarly cautions designers against mindlessly doing design gymnastics. "It's things like using asterisks too much, hairlines too much, having multiple typefaces on pull quotes." he says. "It's the things that are seen over and over and just become thoughtless. It becomes this thing that people did, and someone thinks it looks cool, so it gets done ad nauseam. You have to have some restraint."

What's the way to maintain this restraint? Question each thing you put on the page. "My big belief is that everything on the page has to be there for a reason," says Jeremy Leslie. "Everything has to have a purpose and not be there just for decoration." He goes on to recommend ruthless self-editing. "There are a host of little additions and tricks and visual elements that get added to the page because something else doesn't work or because the design wasn't right in the first place," he says. "For example, if you place the caption in the right place, you don't need an arrow because it will be obvious what picture the caption is talking about. A lot of these additions are just lazy shorthand, and if the page was designed with more consideration and care, you wouldn't have had to add those tricks in."

228

VINCE **FROST**

LUKE **HAYMAN**

WHEN REDESIGNING, START WITH A DISCUSSION

"If it's a redesign," says Vince Frost, "we want to work with the editor and publisher to understand what's wrong, to really try to understand all the problems and what their day-to-day work life is like so we can improve things not just visually but by putting systems in place. We can help them not just with the design but with the way they work." In addition to uncovering problems from the past, when redesigning a magazine, it's important to understand the agenda for the future.

"It starts with discussions with the editor and their vision for the magazine and what that is," says Luke Hayman. "It's trying to find the reasons they want to change, what works and what doesn't work, feeling around the project and trying to get a sense of what they're trying to achieve, the tone, the functional issues, and the structure."

In most cases, the process will be evolutionary, rather than revolutionary. After all, if the editors want a radical change, they could, and probably should, simply start a new magazine. "Magazines tend to evolve," says Hayman. "They try to remain contemporary so they don't feel as if they're aging with a generation. Editorially, they're not saying they're becoming a new magazine. I think that when magazines say they want to attract a new or broader audience, essentially what you're trying to do is make it more contemporary to serve that purpose."

229

ARTHUR **HOCHSTEIN**

BRING IN AN OUTSIDE VOICE

When *Time* magazine wanted to embark on a redesign, they called Luke Hayman at Pentagram. "The reality is that an outside designer can come in, and they're empowered to make more change than a staff art director," says Arthur Hochstein. "When you hire someone from outside and are paying good money for them, you're supposed to do what you're told." Not to mention, the outsider generally has a long record of successful publication design. "The editors can count on the designer's history of doing good work, solving problems, and having a vision," Hochstein points out. "And that allows editors to relax a little."

This process does not absolve the in-house designer from responsibility. It's his job to shepherd the new design system through internal processes and ensure that the design integrity is maintained, even as it evolves to accommodate changing needs. "I'm finding myself being a guardian of what's been done," says Hochstein. "In the first few issues, you're planting the seed, and then over the course of time, you try to remold it to make it work better and serve the editorial needs a little better. I see my role as being an advocate of the work that's been done." If the in-house art director does not perform this role, then the magazine design tends to drift, become diluted or confused, and soon enough, and you're back to needing a design overhaul to regain clarity.

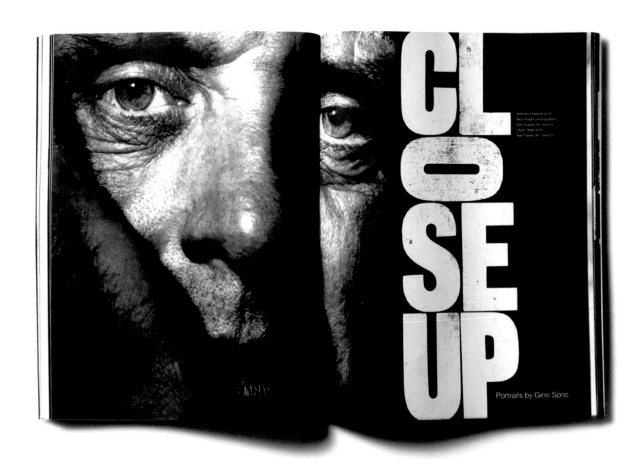

CLOSE UP

Portraits by Gino Sprio

Big magazine, designed by Frost Design

230

VINCE FROST

LUKE HAYMAN

BE RESPECTFUL OF THE IN-HOUSE TEAM

Not all in-house art directors see the value of bringing in outside designers for a fresh perspective. "When the editor or publisher decides to go externally, it pisses off the people working on it," notes Vince Frost. "They have egos and pride and the idea of someone else doing the redesign is difficult because they're doing the day-to-day work and they have habits and systems in place to make their lives easier. They get upset because the redesign means that they're going to have to learn new systems." Understanding this situation is the key to working productively within it. "It's always quite a difficult process, and when you come from the outside, it really shakes things up," says Frost.

So, an outsider needs to be a diplomat as well as a designer, and the job becomes managing the people as well as the publication. "For *Time* magazine," says Hayman, "we worked closely and collaborated with the staff so they had ownership, too. We weren't forcing anything on them." And accept that in spite of your best efforts, the design you create may not last more than a few issues. "I don't think you can ever really guarantee that a design will be taken forward," says Hayman. "The more your design serves the needs of the publication and the staff working on that publication, the more likely it is that they will embrace it, protect it, and carry it into the future."

231

NICKI KALISH

MAKE THE MOST OF THE FORMAT YOU HAVE

While the functional requirements of printers, the post office, budgets, and reader expectations mean most magazines end up being similar sizes and even utilize similar paper stock, the special sections of newspapers present different challenges and opportunities. "One of the biggest problems with newspapers is paper," notes Nicki Kalish. "Because everything prints terribly on newsprint."

However, the sheer size of a newspaper makes other, more interesting things possible, even on newsprint. "You can do things on a much larger scale in a newspaper that you can't do in a magazine," she says. "So you can do something big and grand, where you're more limited by size in a magazine." For Kalish, special sections have a hybrid quality to them. "I try to design my covers as if they were magazines," Kalish says. "They don't have a real newspaper look and fall into a slot of their own. The scale is very different and falls in between a spread and a poster. I think that when the covers are successful, they could be blown up as a poster." Seeing one's work, whatever the original form, pinned up on a wall as a poster is the ultimate compliment.

Big magazine, designed by Frost Design

232

CREATE MULTIPLE ENTRY POINTS

SCOTT **STOWELL**

As much as reading a publication is generally defined as a linear experience, rarely does someone pick up a magazine, open to page one, and methodically follow the prescribed route to the back of the book. Blame it on the effect of the Internet, information overload, or our growing impatience and shortening attention spans, but the fact is that people skim, jump around, and flip through pages. Designers must work with this reality, without overwhelming the page with directive starbursts and bold type. "You get the sense from a lot of magazines that there's a kind of desperation," says Scott Stowell. "There are these screaming headlines, and you get this feeling that it's amped up so far that it's saying, 'please read us before we go out of business.' It's off-putting because I don't want to be sold once I've already bought the magazine." The way to avoid this used-car salesman approach is to make every spread interesting and engaging on its own terms and within the larger context of the publication. "The idea," according to Stowell, "is to offer a lot of entry points for people, so you can pick it up anywhere and start reading. It's like creating a smorgasbord."

The most unassuming of shapes and objects can become fertile fodder for magazine layouts as shown in these *ID Design Sourcebook* spreads, art directed by Luke Hayman; a spill of liquid and a cluster of capacitors become beautiful images when paired with a graphic and type that enhances without competing.

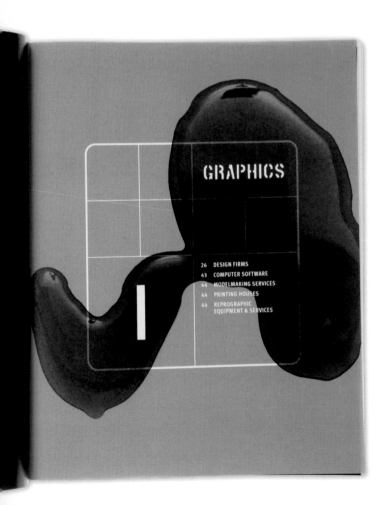

GRAPHICS

26 DESIGN FIRMS
43 COMPUTER SOFTWARE
44 MODELMAKING SERVICES
44 PRINTING HOUSES
44 REPROGRAPHIC
   EQUIPMENT & SERVICES

233

LOOK BEYOND PUBLICATIONS FOR INSPIRATION

AREM **DUPLESSIS**

CHRIS **VERMAAS**

NICOLE **DUDKA**

One of the ways to avoid copying other designs, and therefore design mistakes, is to look for ideas and thought-starters beyond the printed page. "I think the most common mistake in editorial design," Arem Duplessis says, "is looking only to other magazines for inspiration. There are so many magnificent things in the world. Magazines, as beautiful as they can be, are not the be-all-and-end-all."

"Our inspirations come from many areas of interest: the books we've read, the places we've visited, the ordinary objects and events of our daily life, our own cultural backgrounds, and the education we've received," says Chris Vermaas. Nicole Dudka finds ideas simply by walking in the world. "Always keep your eyes open," she says. "I find inspiration in a lot of stuff around me—music, a poster design, a sign, a CD cover, a greeting card. They all can spark an idea or teach you something aesthetically." A digital camera along with a willingness to see things with a fresh eye can also provide just the refresher a designer needs when faced with yet another blank page. "It's easy to get in a rut with the daily grind of deadlines and such," Dudka notes. "But if you can find inspiration in the things around you, it will keep the creativity flowing. I got a digital camera and it changed my life," she says. "I took pictures of different things I could use for reference or that could be used as a basis for an illustration. It might be random stuff, like textures, outdoor venues, little flyers for a simple event." Inspiration is all around—you just have to open your eyes to it.

234

ARJEN **NOORDEMAN**

MICHAEL **WORTHINGTON**

ADAM **MACHACEK**

USE SPECIAL EFFECTS

When designing a book or publication, there are many techniques—beyond manipulating type and images—to make it unique. "You can design a book in a number of ways," says Arjen Noordeman. "You can pick paper and focus on visual design, or you can make it a more tactile experience. Could it be a box or incorporate metal, wood, or plastic? Could it be injection molded? There are so many things you can do, and often, if you can express a concept with a material, it enhances the narrative of the material without being overly direct."

Remember and work with the tactility and dimensionality of a publication. "It's important to consider the materiality of the book," says Michael Worthington, a partner at the Los Angeles design studio, Counterspace. "How do you experience it as an object? How does it open, what kind of paper is it printed on? What size is it? Sometimes," he continues, "these are things that are much harder to learn because before you experience them, you have to imagine them. Even if you print out the pages, you don't experience the materiality."

Ecstasy, designed by Counterspace, uses a few special techniques that exactly capture the mood of the content in this book about a museum show of artwork that explored altered states.

Adam Machacek has utilized a variety of special techniques that not only enhance the story a particular piece is telling but ask the reader to become more physically involved with the publication in hand. For example, he and his partner made a book jacket that can be unfolded into a poster, included a set of promotional stickers inside the front cover of a catalog, and made a map that folds out of the cover of a booklet. "From the feedback we've had, these little details made people remember the publication and have fun with it," says Machacek. "And we had fun creating them as well."

However, these techniques are used "only when we think it's appropriate to the project." And this is perhaps the most important point—when overused, design effects become overwhelming or irrelevant. "Special techniques are about setting a mood and a tone," says Worthington. "In the worst case, they can become gimmicks with no relationship to the content. In the best case, they make the book an object where the content and technique gel together so you don't notice the special effect; it's just the right effect for that book. When you have a design idea, it should communicate to the audience even when you're not there to explain it."

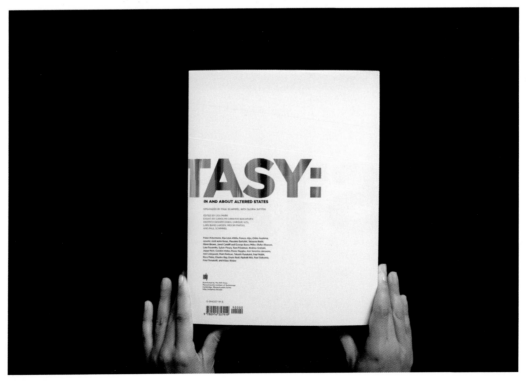

Ecstacy, designed by Counterspace

235

VINCE **FROST**

DON'T STOP AT DESIGN

Your responsibility as a designer does not end when you turn over the digital files. Once you've created the virtual product, you want to make sure the real one will measure up. "Be totally on top of the process or things fall apart quickly," says Vince Frost. "You can design a great book, and then the publisher decides to use some crappy paper or reduce production values." Of course, a designer may not have a say or be able to influence every aspect of how the final piece is made, but you should try to exert quality control wherever possible. Speak up, ask questions, and get involved to ensure the complete integrity of the final piece you worked so hard to design so beautifully.

236

BRETT **MACFADDEN**

ADAM **MACHACEK**

WORK WITH A GOOD PRINTER

You've used up hours, consumed caffeine, and spilled sweat selecting images, making the most of the grid, selecting typefaces, and getting the captions just right—don't put all that hard work in the hands of a low-cost printer. (Unless you're looking for some kind of grunge effect.) Brett MacFadden, senior designer at Chronicle Books, puts it succinctly: "Sub-par printing is bothersome." Even more, working with a good printer can create opportunities you didn't consider. "It's important to work with a good printer, even if it costs a little more," says Adam Machacek. "A good printer gives you advice, and a bad printer or binder may spoil all the time you invested."

237

INA **SALTZ**

GO AHEAD, TAKE CREDIT

Publications offer designers something few other graphic design projects can—the opportunity to sign your own work. "When you're an editorial designer, your name is on the magazine," points out Ina Saltz. "That's so satisfying to me. You're credited for your work in a very visible way. Your parents may still not understand what you do, but they can see your name there."

Chapter Ten:

DESIGNING BOOKS

The sophisticated balance of illustration, pattern, and type, in this book, designed by Victor Burton, makes for an elegant object that is a delight to hold, flip through, and make one's own.

238 BE A LOVER OF BOOKS

JASON **GODFREY**

VICTOR **BURTON**

Book design places a unique set of demands on a graphic designer, asking simultaneously for a deep level of engagement as well as a surprising degree of restraint, along with substantive technical skills. On top of this, book design tends to be less lucrative than some other forms of graphic design work. So why do designers choose this media? It's for love of the objects themselves. "I've always loved books and collected books and thought they were fantastic things," says Jason Godfrey of Godfrey Design in England. "I think that it's the same with anything; you have to have that interest and passion before jumping into these areas."

After all, interest and passion, especially when directed to making something as beautiful and satisfying as a book, are certainly excellent raw ingredients for a satisfying career. Victor Burton of Victor Burton Design Gráfico in Brazil, describes how his lifelong love affair with what lies between two covers led him to design: "Technically I am not a designer. In truth, I consider design an instrument to create what I most love—books," he says. "My grandfather, a Frenchman from Lyon, was a bibliophile, and his library was the object of my fascination and desire since my childhood." This visceral attraction led him to a trainee position at Franco Maria Ricci Publishing House in Milan, Italy, where he was able to turn his obsession into a profession. His design career since then has focused almost entirely on making books that are beautiful enough to inspire the next generation of would-be book designers.

O Rio de Janeiro, designed by Victor Burton

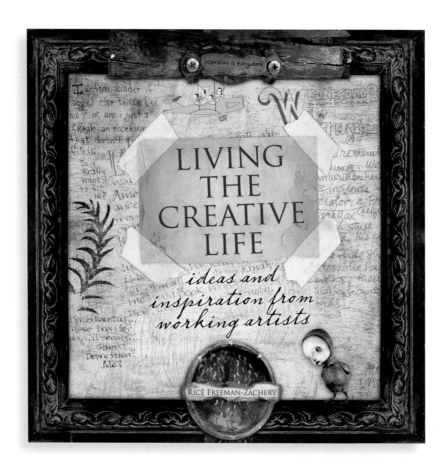

239 ONLY DO A BOOK IF YOU REALLY LIKE THE SUBJECT MATTER

BRETT **MACFADDEN**

VINCE **FROST**

It is no accident that designers use the language of human relationships to describe the process of making a book. While some design projects come and go so quickly they leave no memories behind, books require a different kind of commitment. "Most of my projects are based on things that I have an affinity for," says Brett MacFadden. "Any book is many months of work, and so you want them to be things that are dear to you." Books are designed over many months of image and text manipulations—affection for the content will ensure the book continues to hold interest from the beginning to the faraway end of the project.

Like any relationship, that with a book demands some sacrifice as the price for creative satisfaction. "Why go out with someone if you don't like them?" Vince Frost asks. "Books take a long time to produce and are a phenomenal amount of work. And books don't pay a lot of money. But I still love doing them." At the end of the day, simple affection for the things themselves continues to feed the creative spirit of book designers.

Living the Creative Life, designed by Maya Drozdz, demonstrates in design the content provided by the contributors, who are working artists in a variety of mostly mixed-media, including collage, assemblage, textiles, beads, and more.

240

BRETT **MACFADDEN**

MAYA **DROZDZ**

UNDERSTAND THE WHOLE PACKAGE

A book is a product. Like any other, it goes through the full cycle of development, from concepting, to design, through marketing, and then onto life in the crowded and competitive world of a bookstore shelf. To be effective, a designer needs to understand this entire continuum. "We start with a series of meetings," explains Brett MacFadden. "The first is the creative, and that's often before we've even had an accepted bid for the book. We've brought a book to the board, and now we go to the author or agent and make an offer." Nitty-gritty concerns are some of the first things that need to be nailed down. "We have to begin by talking about what the book is going to cost to produce," he says. "We discuss page count, trim size, whether this subject matter inspires certain effects or treatments. Then, once we have a sense of our hard costs, we can calculate the offer."

In all of these considerations, working with the group, gathering information from other departments, and juggling different agendas is critical. "Getting a book off the ground involves talking to a lot of people internally," says Maya Drozdz, partner at VisuaLingual. "The acquisitions editor, the assignment editor, the editorial director, the creative director of the imprint, reps from sales and marketing. It's not only getting to the essence of that book but also the context of how the book will be marketed and sold, what's going on in this category, the challenges of the context of the book once it's out in the world." While a designer may be itching to get out of the conference room and back to his desk to begin designing, all of these meetings provide important information that will influence the form and look of the book itself and ensure its eventual success on the shelf.

CONTENTS

4

Living the Creative Life, designed by Maya Drozdz

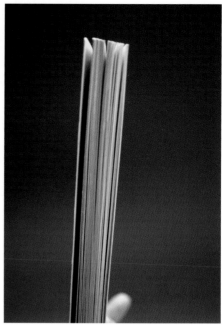

241

JESSICA
FLEISCHMANN

MICHAEL
WORTHINGTON

START WITH A CONVERSATION

While it is not always possible, many book designers, especially those who work on art or museum books, begin their concepting process by discussing the project with the person whose work they are representing. "I start, as much as possible, by having a conversation with the artist, curator, or editor," says Jessica Fleischmann. Michael Worthington begins in similar fashion. "We have a certain process when we work with artists," he explains. "We have a dialog about the way they work."

In both cases, the designers are looking for the artistic sensibility of the work at hand so they can find the best way to graphically represent it. "We tend to sit down and talk with the artist to find out what the show is about and what

might be a sympathetic graphic environment to showcase those ideas rather than having some preconceived idea of 'This is cool,'" says Worthington, whose approach should not be seen as a means of limiting designer freedom. It is, in fact, an opportunity for creative minds to work together to come up with something greater than the sum of its parts. "We don't go in with a house style," says Worthington. "We try to make the discussion open and interesting. The artists' work becomes the central point of the discussion, and the project becomes a collaboration."

Democracy When utilizes the deceptively simple technique of different-colored papers to visually communicate the diversity of the voices expressed within its covers.

Democracy When, designed by Jessica Fleischmann

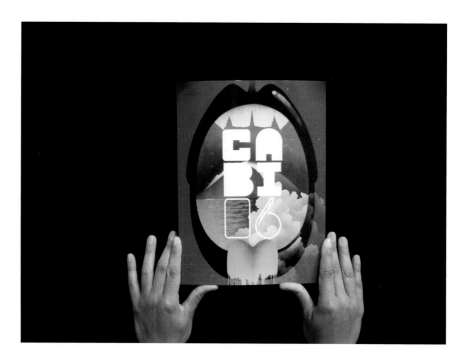

242

CARIN **GOLDBERG**

MAYA **DROZDZ**

VICTOR **BURTON**

VISUALLY EXPRESS THE AUTHOR

Book designers feel a powerful obligation not simply to the nature of the content provided but to the writer who created it. It's all about one artist understanding another. "We are on the same page, literally and figuratively," says Carin Goldberg. "You and the author become a team, and the goal is to get the voice and spirit of your teammate. There must be a respect for the writer's intent and vision. My responsibility is to have a visual response or reaction to their vision, their art."

To create this "visual response," Maya Drozdz calls upon the tools of marketing as well as the conventions of design. "I try to understand, in my head, what I call the author's brand," she says. "When it works, it's because the author has an aesthetic that's evident, and I can find ways to complement that aesthetic through art directing the photography and all the design decisions I make throughout the book. Ideally, the aesthetic of the author and designer should come together."

It's important to note that this coming together tends to run mostly in one direction. Because the writer isn't going to change his work to meet the creative desires of a designer, it is incumbent on the designer to bend his own aesthetic will to that of the author. "I don't collaborate with an author," says Goldberg. "The collaboration is by reading the work responsibly." Especially in cases where the author is not only no longer living but also a legend. As Victor Burton says, by way of example, "Above all, I believe that in order to successfully create a cover for an Ezra Pound book, I need to speak graphically about Ezra Pound."

The book that accompanied the 2006 California Biennial at the Orange County Museum of Art features photosensitive ink on the cover, a nod to one of the many effects that southern California sunshine can have on art.

CaBi 06, designed by Counterspace

Becoming Animal, a book accompanying a show at the Massachusetts Museum of Contemporary Art, Mass MoCA, featured a hand-drawn typeface manipulated to reflect animal parts. Early versions had to be dialed back a bit to increase legibility.

243

ROBERTO **DE VICQ**

BRETT **MACFADDEN**

FIND THE GRAPHIC STANCE

How, it would be fair to ask, can a designer cram so many different agendas and opportunities from so many different departments onto the small canvas of a book jacket? "It's a little like packaging an animal," says Roberto de Vicq. "The publisher says it is a leopard and the marketing person says we are selling rabbits . . . so you have to package the leopard looking like a rabbit." He likens the process to the story of a bunch of mice feeling different parts of an elephant and trying together to determine what kind of animal they have in front of them. "Even when you do the jacket, you can only show the ears of the rabbit. You see only part of it. Even the concept of the rabbit is very general. It's a very difficult combination."

Brett MacFadden tries to solve this conundrum by looking for the "graphic stance of that particular book. Some are fun or jokey, and those have to feel appropriate to the subject, have to feel light, but also have to reach a certain price point. Some may require something more sparkly or jazzy about them." For MacFadden, distribution strategy provides a welcome angle to consider his design approach. "Because a lot of Chronicle books go into gift stores or museums, that allows us to represent these projects as packages rather than just reading material." This is yet another example of how careful consideration of the many issues that need design resolution can sometimes suggest solutions and help focus the design effort.

Becoming Animal, designed by Arjen Noordeman

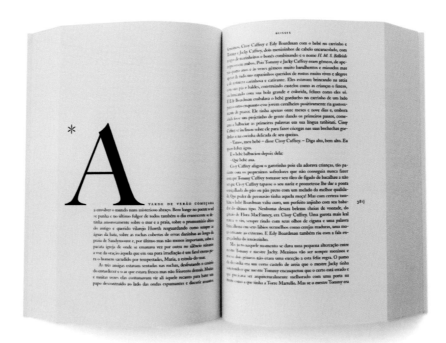

244

MAYA **DROZDZ**

MICHAEL
WORTHINGTON

BEGIN DESIGN WITH THE COVER

Books are different than other publications because so much is riding on the cover. Sure, magazines need compelling covers to get someone to open the magazine, but once inside, there are many opportunities to use the tricks of the design trade to engage the reader. With books, the interiors are frequently much more muted and may be text alone. This means the cover has to do everything, without overdoing anything. "The cover is the face for the book, and it's also the single image that has to encapsulate the whole book," says Maya Drozdz. Because the making and buying cycle of books takes place over many months, the cover also frequently has to sell the book often before there even is a book. "Conceptualizing a cover direction is the first thing that's needed to start marketing the book and preselling it," says Drozdz. "It determines the direction and all the decisions made inside the book."

Designers are often asked to design a cover without much information about what's going to be in between the covers. Sometimes content changes enough from conception to completion that the cover has to change as well. "If you're making a book for a commercial publisher," Michael Worthington explains, "in most cases, the cover gets designed before the book is completed because they want to put it in a catalog or take it to a book fair. However, we always find that if we do a cover first, we do so with the caveat that we'll probably change it. We often find that if we design a cover first, and then we work on the inside of the book for six months and we know what that looks like, then we need to redesign the cover." In these instances, the long lead time gives the book designer an opportunity for a welcome do-over so he can ensure the promise of the cover is delivered when someone opens the book.

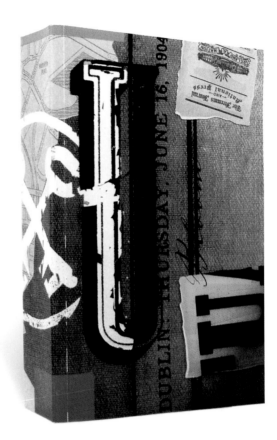

Opposite and above: As designed by Victor Burton, one of literature's most famous classics, *Ulisses*, gets an update, including a jacket printed on vellum and a cover that "once purchased, would have a life of its own, without any commercial information, a purely aesthetic object."

Icons of Northern California Modernism   by Pierluigi Serraino

NorCalMod

245

CARIN **GOLDBERG**

ROBERTO **DE VICQ**

READ IT TO GET IT

While some books require design when they are merely twinkling concepts in an editorial eye, plenty are fully written before they get into the hands of designers. Understandably, time pressures make it impossible for busy book designers to read every word in every book they work on, but it's still important to get an adequate sense of the story. When Carin Goldberg was in the thick of the book design phase of her career, she was creating "100 book jackets a year, minimum," a load that changed the way she worked. "The experience of doing that in such a concentrated way affects the way I responded to the problem solving," she says. For her, this meant reading enough, but not too much. "The times I have

read an entire book, cover to cover, have not been the most fruitful. I've either liked it too much, or not enough, or became too invested, and that leads to subjectivity," she notes. "As soon as I intuitively know it, I put the book down." Roberto De Vicq follows a similar procedure. "I read until I have a jacket," he says. "I read until I think I get it." Of course, there are times when he has to hit the book just a bit harder. "I come up with a jacket, and if they don't like it, I keep reading."

Reflecting the linear, spare aesthetic of its subject, *NorCalMod*, designed by Brett McFadden, uses design techniques to enhance the subject matter while allowing the designer to make his presence felt.

Introduction

My suggestion, which has the earmarks of a paradox, is that in order to look to the future with confidence it will be necessary to look to the past with understanding. In other words, I would like to re-examine that obscure concept, TRADITION. The paradox is of course superficial, for our idea of architecture itself is consciously and unconsciously formed from an experience of its past, and it will be difficult to decide where it is to go if we do not know where it has been.

James S. Ackerman
California Monthly, 1954

246

CARIN **GOLDBERG**

DON'T BE A CRITIC

How you read is as important as how much you read. "It's important to not become a critic," says Carin Goldberg, "but to look at the book analytically, to look at what the writer had in mind and try and understand what he or she was trying to do as an artist, an academic, a historian." This is a fine balancing act because even though book designers need to think critically about what the writer is doing, they can't critique the book itself or the writer's level of artistic achievement. A designer must focus simply on expressing the vision the author already created, whether you like that vision or not. "You can't become critical. You have to remain objective," Goldberg explains. "It's an analytical, deconstructive way of looking at another person's creativity. You read the book the way you'd look at anything—architecture, art, a play. You analyze it formally and conceptually and then try to interpret it visually."

She focuses on the design job she has to do and just that job. "I'm not in the business of telling the reader the beginning, middle, and end, or who the main character is, or what she looks like," she explains. "Not only is that going to be too obvious or blatant, but it's irresponsible. As I'm reading, I switch on my visual process. I am reading with the pencil in my hand. I will look for clues, a voice, a temperament, and I will immediately make associations in my head on how I'll approach it visually, how I will take their art and translate it into visual art. My aesthetic will often be evident, but it's not about me."

NorCalMod, designed by Brett MacFadden

247

VICTOR **BURTON**

LET DESIGN TELL A STORY

A book tells a narrative story; design must tell a visual story. "To design a book," says Victor Burton, "is to tell a story and allow the reader to receive this pleasure. Also, I always remember that the basic function of our job is to fascinate and to bring in the reader to a particular book, which in turn needs to stand out from a sea of stories that overcrowd bookstores today." He explains how he achieves this singular quality in the books he designs. "What is important in creating a book is a visual, referential background that will allow the understanding of a period, place, and atmosphere." In other words, give browsers enough of a visual story on the cover that they can't wait to open the pages of the book and read the rest of it.

248

MAYA **DROZDZ**

DESIGN A BLAD

BLAD stands for "book layout art document," and it's another necessary tool to ensuring a book's design and commercial success. "On a technical level, after the cover has been designed and approved, I design a BLAD," says Maya Drozdz. "It's a promotional piece to presell the book. Typically it's eight pages and gives you a front cover, table of contents, and sample of the content that will be inside the book." The BLAD is not used to sell the book to the public; it is a marketing tool to present the book to the legions of booksellers who are trying to decide what will appear on their shelves in the coming season. Drozdz notes that a BLAD also performs a very useful service for the designer. "The good thing about a BLAD is that it forces you to start making inte-

rior design decisions without having to contend with a book of 100 pages. It's like a practice run." The BLAD also gives the designer the opportunity to begin negotiating with the various elements that can occur in a complex book; by the time he has all the material for the complete book, the designer already has some experience with the component parts. "Once the manuscript is completely finished," Drozdz explains, "I get an annotated list of all the various instances of all the different kinds of elements inside the book. The editor will annotate sidebars that are shortest or longest or the captions that are longest and shortest. I get a map of sorts, so I can think about what I want to develop and what limitations the design has to accommodate."

4

And I said to myself: "This is going nowhere." I was not comfortable. Some stuff is terrible, and they want to publish anyway simply because you had developed a Mickey Mouse reputation. It just bothered me, and I shut it down, I disappeared. I don't want any of this stuff.

Beverley (David) Thorne
Interview by the author, November 10, 2002

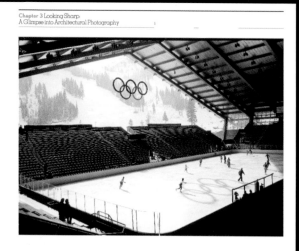

02
Olympic Arena,
Squaw Valley
William Corlett, architect
Beverley Partridge,
photographer, 1959

The selection of Squaw Valley for the Eighth Winter Olympic Games in 1960 generated state-of-the-art facilities for this well-known ski resort in the High Sierra. The Blyth Arena—built for Charles R. Blyth, then California Olympic Commission Chairman—was designed to shelter 8,500 spectators sitting on three sides with the fourth one open to the southern exposure. A hallmark of the scheme was the clear three-hundred-foot structural span covering the eighty-five-by-one-hundred-and-ninety-foot ice hockey rink. Sixteen tapered steel masts supported the roof which was made of hollow cellular steel decking connected with steel bridge cables. The Olympic Arena received a 1960 A.I.A. national award. In 1984, the Olympic Arena collapsed due to compound in the waterproofing.

NorCalMod, designed by Brett MacFadden

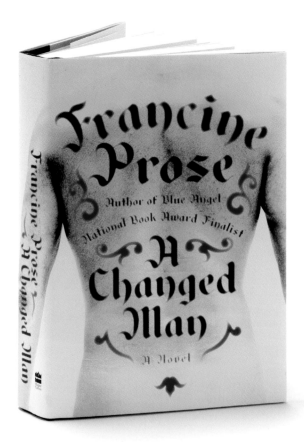

In these book covers, Roberto de Vicq combines illustration with type to create a singular, arresting image that "seduces" the casual browser as well as the well-read fan.

249

JASON **GODFREY**

COUNT THE WORDS

Books are about words; book designers make those words pleasing to read. "The most important thing you have to work with is how much text there is going to be and working out how many words you're going to have per page," says Jason Godfrey. "A lot of books work around one spread per item, but I prefer the ones with running text, where you have to work out how many words per page, which tells you how dense it will be." The word count and the text density then give you a basis for creating the structure of the book. "Working from there and using the context of the book, you decide how you want to set up a grid, how many columns you'll have," he explains. Of course, within this system, the designer should also create opportunities for their creativity to show. "There's always this underlying thing," says Godfrey, "this ideal book you have in your mind, and you're trying to twist the structure in some kind of fashion to give it a bit of interest, to figure out when it's best to play your cards."

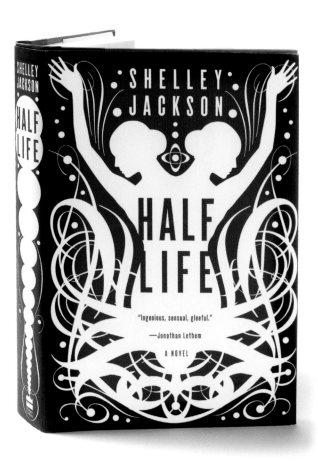

250

MAYA **DROZDZ**

FIND OUT IF IT WILL BE TRANSLATED

If a book will be translated, this will affect design in a variety of ways that must be considered and accounted for. "One of the logistical challenges we face is that in almost every case, we want our books to be easily translated and reprinted," says Maya Drozdz. "So if a title has any potential for translation, we have to face plate changes, which means type has to be black or gray. Plus, different languages take up different amounts of space, so this has certain effects," she explains. "Like we can't reverse out type and we have to consider if something becomes longer or shorter and how that affects what's on the page. I can't just use typography willy-nilly or hand-draw letters or customize them in all the ways I'd like to because I have to consider production challenges." Looking down the long and some-times dark production road in this way allows a designer to work up solutions before prob-lems occur that could force a later—and more costly and disruptive—redesign.

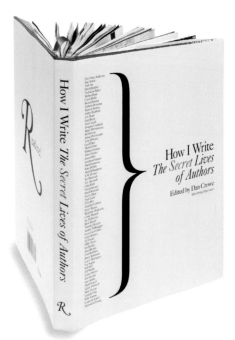

How I Write, designed by Frost Design, takes the simple form of an iconic punctuation mark and turns it into an elegant design device by using it as both artwork and type tool.

251

JASON **GODFREY**

RESPECT THE GIVENS

Books, like other publications, generally follow a certain format, meeting reader expectation for a logical progression of information and the conventions of standard navigation. Whereas magazines may offer more leeway to confound these structures, books are usually more conservative in their adherence to form. "With books, there's a more formal process," says Jason Godfrey. "Books have the front matter and the chapters, and often, as a designer, you come to it after things have been worked out to a certain extent. And book work has a lot more things that are quite standard or necessary for each book, such as pagination and running heads and things like that. There are component parts that have to be in there. There is a different set of rules that you have to pay attention to."

Of course, this doesn't mean that a designer shouldn't try to do interesting things, where possible and where the unexpected might serve design requirements. "Some publishers have their own styles in terms of what they expect and in terms of what needs to be on there," says Godfrey. "And then there are some things you argue out." He describes a book he was designing that included a series of numbered items. "I was trying to make a case that we didn't need pagination, that the index at the back would refer to the item numbers, and the table of contents would tell the chapter contents, and therefore pagination was not necessary. I thought it was superfluous. But this is one of these bridges some people can't cross with books; people can't conceive of a book without page numbers."

While Godfrey didn't win this particular design argument, he doesn't let these kinds of constraints limit his creativity. "I like the conventions," he says. "I like that the design has this kind of history behind it. It's healthy in a way; it's evolved in this way because I think that it helps the reader. There's no harm in every now and again breaking from that, but I don't feel constrained because it's always quite interesting how you spend care and effort doing pagination and running heads. It can be an important part of the design."

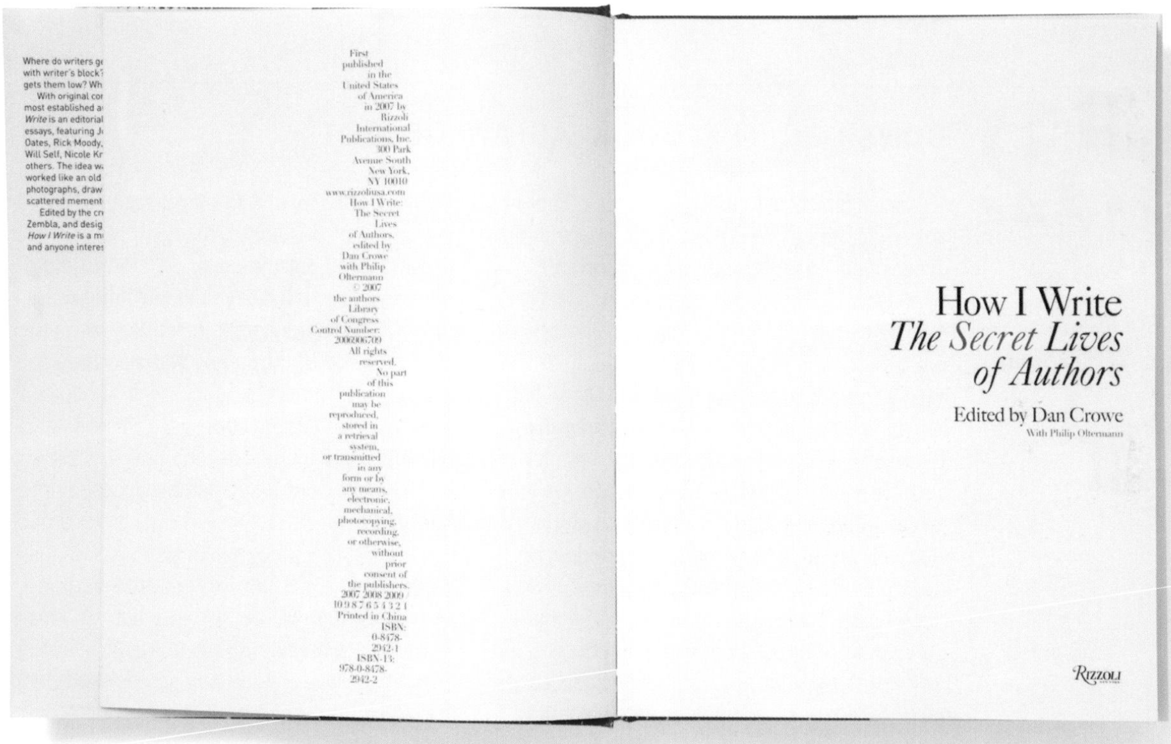

Where do writers ge
with writer's block?
gets them low? Wh
With original co
most established a
Write is an editorial
essays, featuring J
Oates, Rick Moody,
Will Self, Nicole Kr
others. The idea w
worked like an old
photographs, draw
scattered mement
Edited by the cr
Zembla, and desig
How I Write is a m
and anyone interes

First
published
in the
United States
of America
in 2007 by
Rizzoli
International
Publications, Inc.
300 Park
Avenue South
New York,
NY 10010
www.rizzoliusa.com
How I Write:
The Secret
Lives
of Authors,
edited by
Dan Crowe
with Philip
Oltermann
© 2007
the authors
Library
of Congress
Control Number:
2006936719
2007 2008 2009
10 9 8 7 6 5 4 3 2 1
Printed in China
ISBN:
0-8478-
2942-1
ISBN-13:
978-0-8478-
2942-2

How I Write
The Secret Lives of Authors

Edited by Dan Crowe

With Philip Oltermann

RIZZOLI

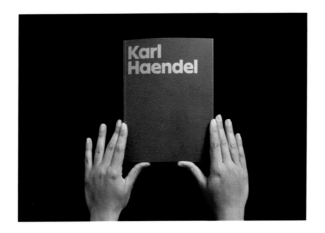

252

JASON **GODFREY**

VINCE **FROST**

BRETT **MACFADDEN**

CONSIDER THE BOOK AS AN OBJECT

The sheer physicality of the book as object has a dramatic effect on design. "Books are three-dimensional objects, and that's important," says Jason Godfrey. "As opposed to identity and things, you're dealing with quite an interactive object, with page turning and such. You have to be conscious about what's happening behind you and in front of you as you're doing it," he explains. And in this age of computerized everything, designers have to work a little harder to engage with the dimensionality of the book they're working on. "I started working two years before Macs came along," says Vince Frost. "I was familiar with typesetting. I continue to print out books at 100 percent and lay them out on the floor or the walls so we get the book out of the computer and make it a physical object as soon as possible."

Designers ignore this step of getting the book out of the computer at their own peril. "The scale of the computer and its ability to zoom in on details affects how the book actually looks," notes Brett MacFadden. "I was working on a 7 x 7-inch (17.8 x 17.8 cm) book, and on screen, the presence of the type seemed too big. But then, when I printed it out, it seemed too delicate. It's always useful to just vary your options," he suggests. "Try to make strong gestures in a variety of ways, try to scale things up, or make type more diminutive than you think will work, and then just print it out. It is important to look at it as a physical object."

Godfrey goes even one step further when working on cover designs. "When you're making a presentation, put the cover on a bit of foam or something to make it a three-dimensional object," he suggests. "It looks very different than on a flat bit of paper. You also have to look at how the cover reacts with the spine. Especially on bigger books, the spine can become quite important, and how it interacts with the front can be an important aspect of how you treat it."

Book designers never forget that a book is something that will be held in a human hand. "A book is a medium that's physical," says Frost. "I believe a book has an aura and people are drawn to it because it has this energy that comes out of it. You have to create an identity that's radiating out of the thing."

Karl Haendel's work involves a range of different scales, sizes, and interpretations, often of the same piece. "He's interested in the idea that there's no authoritative image of the work," says Michael Worthington. "We tried to find a way to demonstrate that in the book by using a bunch of different strategies, such as having things wrap over the edges, making some captions way too big, and using odd scale relationships."

253

DON'T FORGET THE FUNDAMENTALS

JASON **GODFREY**

Describing a book project where he was expecting to have stunning photography, only to find the pictures were "quite ordinary," Jason Godfrey reacquainted himself with the pleasures and satisfactions of old-fashioned design work. "Sometimes it's nice to create a standard, straight book that is anonymous in design and well put together," he observes. "You may have this idea of an idealized book, and you try to lay out things to give it a bit of fun, but sometimes it's good to do a straightforward and honest-looking book that doesn't scream out that you're the designer of this book." This is not to say that a simple design is any easier than a complicated one—in fact, as Godfrey notes, it's quite the opposite. "People forget that it's not as easy as it looks to work in all the standard things you have to have for a book. It's quite hard work to get that type of look. You have to go through lots of galleys with different kinds of leading so it looks right. It can be hard to just say I'm going to do a fundamentally good book instead of always trying to push the envelope, but the danger is that in five or ten years that book may look dated, whereas a good book will have quite a long shelf life."

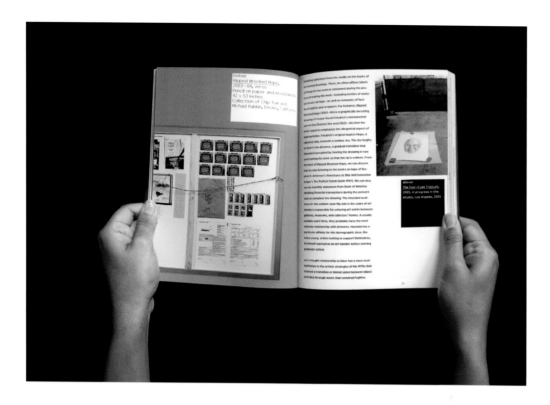

Karl Haendel, designed by Counterspace

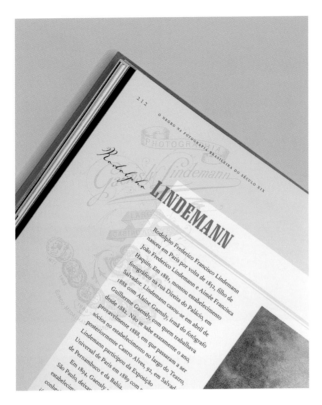

The book *O Negro* "tells, through nineteenth-century photography, part of the dramatic history of black people in Brazil," says Victor Burton. "The typographic eclecticism evokes nineteenth-century aesthetics by placing Egypcia Shadow, with its abrupt, almost violent strokes, as a principal actor. I also used gold to evoke the metallic materials used in developing photographs at that time."

254

MICHAEL **WORTHINGTON**

BRETT **MACFADDEN**

CREATE A SECONDARY NARRATIVE STREAM

Just because book designers work hard to let the content shine does not mean that they make design subservient or invisible. It's a matter of design and content working with one another. "We're creating a sympathetic graphic environment," says Michael Worthington. "You can't mess with or totally overshadow the artwork, so the design has to be a little more subtle, and that tends to involve strategies that might be considered as a secondary narrative stream."

Even the strongest visual content does not let designers off the hook. "In a philosophical sense, I've never been on board with the idea that the designer should stand back and let the art take center stage," says Brett MacFadden. "To me, that's shrinking from the greater challenge, which is trying to make design an active partner. I've always tried to create a typographic or visual language that rides along with the art."

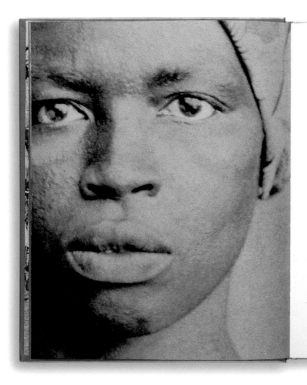

George
Ermakoff

G.Ermakoff CASA EDITORIAL   Rio de Janeiro 2004

O NEGRO NA FOTOGRAFIA BRASILEIRA DO SÉCULO XIX

SONHO DE LIBERDADE

Capítulo 2

POR TER A ESCRAVIDÃO PERDURADO quase quatro séculos, abrangido uma população de alguns milhões de cativos e estado presente em todas as províncias do Império, todo comentário sobre o dia-a-dia dessas pessoas é muito relativo, em razão da diversidade de opiniões deixadas por contemporâneos do regime, tanto escravocratas quanto abolicionistas. Alguns estudiosos posteriores ao regime escravista, embora tenham tido a oportunidade de examinar detidamente a documentação disponível, emitiram conceitos e opiniões que, em nenhum dos casos, podem ser consideradas verdades absolutas.

Em seu memorável *Casa-grande e senzala*, Gilberto Freyre polemizou, ao afirmar:

Da energia africana ao seu serviço cedo aprenderam muitos dos grandes proprietários que, abusada ou esticada, rendia menos que bem conservada; daí passaram a explorar o escravo no objetivo do maior rendimento mas sem prejuízo da sua normalidade de eficiência. A eficiência estava no interesse do senhor conservar no negro — seu capital, sua máquina de trabalho — alguma coisa de si mesmo. De onde a alimentação farta e reparadora que Peckolt observou dispensarem os senhores aos escravos no Brasil.

A alimentação do negro nos engenhos brasileiros podia não ser nenhum primor de culinária, mas faltar nunca faltava. E sua abundância em milho, toucinho e feijão recomenda-o como regime apropriado ao duro esforço exigido do escravo agrícola.

O escravo negro no Brasil parece-nos ter sido, com todas as deficiências do seu regime alimentar, o elemento melhor nutrido de nossa sociedade patriarcal [...]. De modo que de antigo ordem econômica persistia a pior parte do ponto de vista do bem-estar geral e das classes trabalhadoras — desfavto em 35 o patriarcalismo que até então emperou o escravo-alimentou-os com certa largueza, socorreu-lhes na velhice e na doença, proporcionou-lhes aos filhos oportunidades de acesso social. O escravo foi substituído pelo pária de usina; a senzala pelo mocambo, o senhor de engenho pelo usineiro ou pelo capitalista ausente. Muitas casas-grandes ficaram vazias, os capitalitas latifundiários rodando de automóvel pelas cidades, morando em chalés suíços e palacetes normandos, indo à Paris se divertir com as franceses de aluguel.

As afirmativas de Gilberto Freyre podem se aplicar a alguns casos, mas não podem ser generalizadas para todas as regiões do país, nem mesmo no Nordeste e talvez sequer nos engenhos da Província de Pernambuco.

Os negros se submeteram ao trabalho escravo e ao rigor do cativeiro pressionados pelos castigos corporais, mas nunca perderam o ideal de liberdade. Consumeiramente, esse ideal os levava à fuga, em busca de uma existência menos sofrida. As tentativas de fuga eram muito perigosas para os escravos porque, quando recapturados pelo "capitão do mato", o castigo vinha em dobro e não raro era fatal.

Um exemplo da busca da liberdade coletiva foi a formação dos quilombos, comunidades de negros fugidos que buscavam a vida em comum em segurança. Para eles, a segurança sempre foi muito relativa, pois eram alvos constantes das milícias armadas dos escravistas, que não lhes davam sossego. A força da união dos quilombolas, entretanto, permitia a defesa de seus domínios, e assim o fizeram muitas vezes com êxito, à diferença das ações individuais, invariavelmente mais arriscadas.

A primeira concentração de escravos fugidos de que se tem notícia ocorreu entre Alagoas e Pernambuco e ficou conhecida como quilombo dos Palmares. Provavelmente, formou-se na passagem do século XVI para o século XVII, pois entre 1602 e 1608 já havia sido atacado por ordem do governador Diogo Botelho, que incumbira Bartolomeu Bezerra de formar uma expedição para aniquilá-lo.

Os escravos oriundos das fazendas pernambucanas se aplicar ao aproveitaram da desorganização causada pela invasão holandesa para fugir em grande quantidade, incrementando a população dos quilombos.

Čornošice is a town in the central Bohemian region of the Czech Republic, just southwest of Prague. This publication, designed by Welcometo.as, combines a fold-out map bound with a booklet that gives historical and travel information, coded so everything is easy to find. The back of the map features a picturesque image of the village.

255

MAYA **DROZDZ**

MICHAEL **WORTHINGTON**

BRETT **MACFADDEN**

FIND A WAY IN TO THE MATERIAL

Sometimes the best way to balance content and design is to allow design to flow from the content itself. "A book is so complex and composed of so many parts that even something like meeting the author and liking him or her helps me find an 'in,'" says Maya Drozdz. Other opportunities come from the work instead of the words inside the book. For example, when designing an art book, Michael Worthington tries to pick up themes from the show itself. Drozdz tries to create connections between the material provided and her personal experiences. "I try and look out in the world for the common ground between the book and what's inspired me," she says. Brett MacFadden looks for "graphic cues," which may come from things he finds in the photographs that appear in a book. "I look for bits of typography or colors in the photos," he says. "A lot of times, I'm hunting for where the graphic design is within the imagery." He also looks within the tone established by the writer. "I look at the style of writing. If it's more academic and has footnotes and is scholarly, a lot of the design is logistical, in a sense. Other books are jaunty, so their design should also be open and fun. There's a tone you can interpret really quickly."

256   LOOK FOR INSPIRATION FROM HISTORY

CARIN **GOLDBERG**

BRETT **MACFADDEN**

Another way into the design and material of a book is to research the historical period the content reflects. "Years ago, I designed a non-fiction, historically referenced book titled *Soviet Power*," says Carin Goldberg. "It would be kind of dopey to not look at the posters of the period." However, this is not a recommendation to poach historical references indiscriminately. "I'm not trying to re-create or pillage history; I'm responding to it," she emphasizes. "This is where you find accurate visual connections and references. You have to go to the source but also create a unique interpretation."

Brett MacFadden uses historical research to "look for things that will inspire a direction. I'll start by looking at stuff from that era—magazines, ads—trying to get a sense of the graphic tics of the time." Like Goldberg, he espouses using references in moderation. "A lot of times, it's not super strong gestures," MacFadden says. "It's a balance of the two eras—the time of the content and of the current offering. Even if I tried to ape an era perfectly, it would inevitably come off inexact. It's more like pulling some gestures of that era, some typographic fashions of that era, but otherwise, making sure the layout and use of imagery and printing feels current."

257

USE TYPOGRAPHY AS YOUR PRINCIPAL INSTRUMENT

VICTOR **BURTON**

MICHAEL **WORTHINGTON**

ROBERTO **DE VICQ**

"Typography is my principal instrument," says Victor Burton. "It is the only one that is specific to our profession alongside the architecture of the white page. A good project or book cover does not exist without good typography. And the best image can be destroyed by wrong typography." Roberto De Vicq concurs. "Type is the only thing that is particular to graphic designers; you don't borrow it from the other arts."

So what makes good typography in a book? According to Michael Worthington, it's a combination of art and practicality, old and new.

"We try to walk a fine line between things that are expressive and connotative of the theme of the show or the artist's work," he says. "And then the other side is purely about functionality: how well a typeface is drawn, how well it functions on the page. We try to do both things. One of the ways we do this is to use a combination of typefaces and unusual things that you haven't seen together before. Some of it is about discovering new typefaces and rediscovering old typefaces that have been overlooked. We'll try to work something that's traditional and known with something designed just this year."

258

ANYTHING BUT HELVETICA

MICHAEL **WORTHINGTON**

For Michael Worthington, as for many designers, books present a welcome opportunity to deeply consider the possibilities presented by a primarily typographical-based design solution. They're not about to waste this chance on any old typeface. "As a typographer, I get bored looking at the same typefaces," says Worthington.

"When I see yet another book in Helvetica, it's just not that interesting to me. I know what it does; I know when it works well and when it doesn't. It's been examined pretty thoroughly." With all the fonts available, setting another book in Helvetica suggests, perhaps, nothing so much as design laziness and inattention.

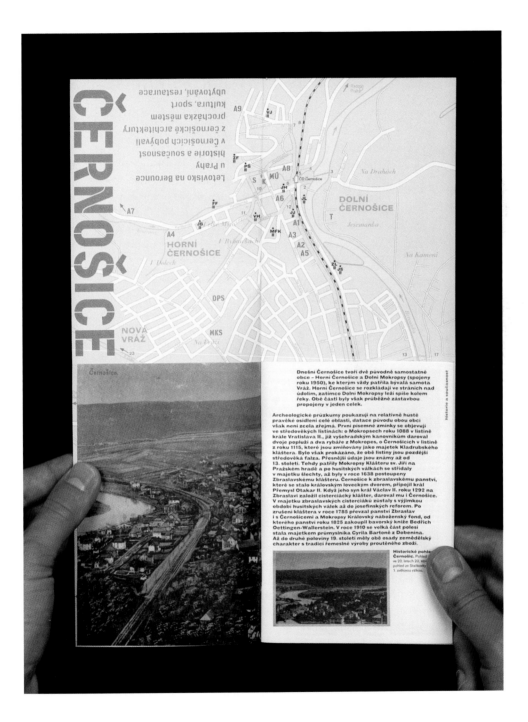

Černošice, designed by Welcometo.as

259

CARIN **GOLDBERG**

MAKE SOMETHING YOURSELF

Because almost everything is done on computers these days, especially in the design world, many designers seem to have forgotten the pleasures and satisfactions of low-tech solutions. "The budgets for book jackets were never very high, so very rarely did I have the option to hire a photographer or an illustrator," says Carin Goldberg. "So I made a lot of things out of what was at my fingertips." Not that this was a problem. "This is what I enjoy anyway. Half of my book jacket career was done without a computer, so a lot was done with a photocopier, cutting and pasting. I had a different way of approaching the work back

then. Making things with my hands was more interesting than art directing." While she concedes that working on a computer helped her work in many ways for the good, she also feels, "My work got more mechanical and colder when I started working on a computer because of my limitations and knowledge of the applications." Personally making a completely customized piece of artwork for a book cover—whether out of necessity or preference—is also a way to enhance the dimensionality of the object while adding a welcome hint of humanity to the end result.

Černošice, designed by Welcometo.as

260

ROBERTO **DE VICQ**

USE YOUR **"DRAWER OF WONDERS"**

When describing how he finally found a book-cover-excuse to use an image he'd been admiring for years, Roberto de Vicq referred to his "drawer of wonders." "It's something Chip Kidd said," de Vicq recalls. "It means all those things you hold onto forever, waiting for the opportunity to use them." In other words, whether they get thrown into a drawer, bin, folder, or on your desktop, don't discard those pieces of inspiration, found images, or favorite ephemera—you never know when you'll find the perfect opportunity to use one of them.

In a book of thesis projects for an art school in Holland, "most of the artists tend to dislike graphic design and don't want design to interfere with their work," notes Arjen Noordeman. "We wanted to honor the wishes of the artists to have their work on a white page but also wanted to impress people with our design. We solved this by inviting people to send us their sources of inspiration, which we made into a collage that wraps around the group, but within the book, all their work was displayed as if within a gallery."

HKA, designed by Arjen Noordemann

For a book on the craft and design innovations that took place in California during the boom years between the mid 1950s and mid 1970s, MacFadden took color cues from some of the highlighted products and interspersed the bold palate with the reprieve of black and white.

261

MICHAEL **WORTHINGTON**

BRETT **MACFADDEN**

PAY ATTENTION TO PACING

While a designer cannot completely control how a reader works his or her way through a book—especially an image-filled book on art, photography, or architecture—it is still incumbent upon the designer to try to direct the reader down a particular path and thereby create a specific kind of journey. "There's this idea of pacing in a book," says Michael Worthington. "People look at books in two ways: They pick them up and flip through them from back to front and they may stop at a page that catches their interest; the other way is to go from page 1 to 2 to 3, and so on. As the designer, you're trying to control a narrative and also create an overall mood with the design when the viewer is flipping through it."

Brett MacFadden tries to manage this mood by finding and enhancing the connections between images. "The author creates quite a bit of the pacing, but beyond that, you start out with this whole pile of imagery and you look for what sits well next to each other. The majority of the work in these image-heavy books is about dropping things in, resizing them, trying to work it until it holds as a spread." MacFadden consistently finds pacing mechanisms within the material itself. "Sometimes I look for lines in images that will connect them to other images; connecting horizon lines or connecting other elements within images will give me clues. I might match textures, colors, atmospheres. There can be a musical patterning, where you let things fall quiet or bring them to a crescendo. Pacing is essential, and a lot of it is intuitive. Mostly, it's aesthetics and balance. You just go back and see what feels right or feels off."

"One does not need to share all the illusions of the boosters to believe, as I believe," historian Carey McWilliams wrote in 1946, "that the most fantastic city in the world will one day exist in this region: a city embracing the entire region from the mountains to the sea."[1] Although he was boasting about post–World War II Los Angeles, McWilliams's prophesy of growth and prosperity could also be applied to all of California. The state had been a major destination in the vast national migration of Americans who moved during the war in search of well-paid defense work. The whole West Coast, with its massive aircraft and shipbuilding facilities, witnessed remarkable changes, but it was California that profited most from $35 billion in wartime federal funding. After the war, Americans continued to be lured by the state's mild climate and expansive Cold War–related industries. By 1967, California's economy ranked sixth among nations in the world.[2]

These economic and demographic shifts permanently changed the nation's regional balance, giving California newfound status and independence from the East Coast. Benefiting from their exalted position, Californians boldly redefined the American Dream. They popularized then-radical ways of living, from patio houses to automobile-based cities, which were promoted through media such as magazines, movies, and music. High-profile postwar architecture and design initiatives helped raise California lifestyles and their accoutrements to national consciousness. In 1945 the avant-garde magazine Arts + Architecture launched the Case Study House Program, which sponsored the design and construction of a series of modern homes as prototypes for postwar housing. Equally ambitious—yet curiously less celebrated—were the California Design exhibitions, a series of thirteen shows featuring the applied arts and presented primarily at the Pasadena Art Museum between 1954 and 1976. Combining both handcrafted and mass-produced goods, the series sought to highlight and encourage new talent throughout California. New forms, materials, and technologies were showcased as the state's designers and artisans exploited revolutionary innovations in lightweight metals, molded plywood, reinforced concrete, and plastics. Prototypes of innovative furniture and accessories, persuasive harbingers of things to come, were featured in virtually every show. Ultimately, California Design put the Golden State on the national design map.[3]

opposite:
Figure 1.40
Svetozar Radakovich in collaboration with Karl Eckburg, manufactured by Architectural Fiberglass: Double Door; fiberglass, polyurethane foam, wood, 1968 (California Design 10)

below:
Figure 1.41
Douglas Deeds for Architectural Fiberglass, White Bench, fiberglass. Shown with La Gardo Tackett's Ceramic Planter for Architectural Pottery, 1965 (California Design 9)

Groundbreaking fiberglass forms for public places and garden spaces were designed for the company by Douglas Deeds and Elsie Crawford. Deeds's curvaceous, sculptural benches for streets, gardens, airports, and bus stops were exhibited in CD 9 (1965), CD 10 (1968), and CD 11 (1971) (figs. 1.36, 1.37, 1.39, 1.41). Additionally, a Deeds-designed line of futuristic-looking contract furniture, composed of three chairs and two table-ottomans, was shown in CD 10 (fig. 1.38). No less prolific was Elsie Crawford, whose highly imaginative, large-scale garden planters, planter benches, and gracefully fluid Light Column appeared in CD 10 and CD 11 (figs. 1.45, 1.46, 1.47). Designs by Donald Chadwick were also noted for their thoughtful exploitation of the material properties of plastic. Chadwick's prototype Plastic Dining Chair was a highly abstract shape of flowing lines and intersecting curves, whose monolithic construction and exaggerated volumes endowed it with great sculptural presence (fig. 1.42). Similarly, his prototype Side Chair/Dining Chair of bright red molded plastic wedded functional, economic, and ergonomic imperatives

California Design, designed by Brett MacFadden

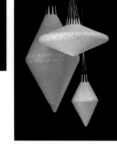

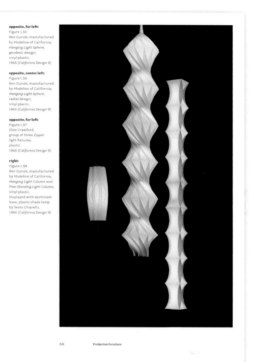

illuminated the way for the next generation of designers to develop new approaches to interior lighting. Although Nelson's lamps were never shown in *California Design*, they were mass-produced by the Herman Miller Company and had become the standard of modernism and new materials by the mid-1950s.

Of the "light sources" showcased in *CD 9* (1965), the pleated geometric, translucent vinyl lamps of Ben Gurule were the obvious standouts (figs. 1.55, 1.56, 1.58). Gurule's intriguing origami-like designs were based on complex patterns derived by joining together a "multiplicity of rectangles," as the catalogue put it, or by echoing geodesic geometry. When illuminated, the creases and folds created shadow patterns that reflected the form's sharp diagonals, giving floor lights and chandeliers the appearance of freestanding or hanging sculptures. The artfulness of Gurule's lamps prompted renowned designer Henry Dreyfus to name him "the Leonardo da Vinci of folded paper."[83] The plasticized paper *Zipper* lights designed by Elsie Crawford were also noteworthy. Their conical, dimensional shapes evoked the language of sculpture, while their interlocking structure—the "zipper"—allowed them to be taken apart and shipped flat (fig. 1.57).

58   **California Design**

59   Production Furniture

---

262   ENJOY THE LENGTH OF THE PROCESS

DAVID **ALBERTSON**

JASON **GODFREY**

"Book design is very civilized," says David Albertson. "It's on a much longer timeline, it tends to require fewer variations in your templating, and you tend to be designing more in a linear way than a multidimensional way." All of which can add up to pleasures akin to planting seeds and having to wait until the spring to see exactly how they'll bloom. "Often you design a book and it's at least six months from when you hand over the files to when you have a book in your hand," Jason Godfrey points out. "In the amount of time that it takes to produce a book, you could have built a house. It's amazing that that's the case. And with book designs, you don't get to see it working until you see the final piece," he notes. "You're never quite sure how it will work out. It can surprise you at the end of the day because of that translation from layout to having the pages you're flipping through. I enjoy that part of the process, that lag and the not quite knowing. I think that's quite a unique experience when you finally get the books in your hand. It feels so great."

California Design, designed by Brett MacFadden

Chapter Eleven:

DESIGNING NEW MEDIA

Comedy Central rebrand, designed by thelab

263

AMANDA **ALTMAN**

ALICIA **JOHNSON**

IT'S ALL ABOUT BRAND BUILDING

While new media offers a new ways to communicate, the essence of what you should be communicating is still all about the brand. "Technology has changed, but the way we see and relate to and interact with the brand has not," notes Amanda Altman of A3 Design, a family-owned design studio. "The rules of branding haven't changed, even though how they're created and displayed has changed."

While designers may love having a whole new box of high-tech tools to play with, customers don't cordon off their favorite brands by media. "The reality is that consumers don't think, 'Oh, this is the brand's digital campaign; this is their print campaign,'" notes Alicia Johnson of theLab, a "media arts" company, and Johnson + Wolverton. "You have to think about the brand, how you want people to feel across the brand, and then bring it all to life across all media." Even though some designers love the screen and others love paper, it's important to stay focused on the message you're trying to convey about your client."

264

ALICIA **JOHNSON**

BRANDS ARE NOW JUDGED BY THE WAY THEY MOVE

While print is beautiful, it is static. You design a logo, make it work in color and black and white, at a reasonable range of sizes, and voila: your creation is complete. In the digital world, "You have behavior that is dynamic," points out Alicia Johnson. "There is the expectation that the logo is going to do something. Will it glow, move, emit sound, change color, tell a story?"

Designers need to consider not just how to bring a logo to life, but what that life says about the brand. "You have to ask yourself how does it behave and what does that tell you about the company," Johnson says. "These things are fundamentally more important in the digital than the print realm because all of that behavior gets translated into the user interface, the site architecture, how a user navigates banner ads, and more. You have to determine how the behavior of the logo communicates the essence and aspirations of the brand."

265

AMANDA **ALTMAN**

YOU'RE ALWAYS COMPETING WITH THE BIG GUYS

Because the digital world allows anyone to be exposed to just about everything, your customer is likely to have different—and much higher—expectations of brands, no matter how large or small the company behind the brand is. If the biggest brand—with the biggest budget—is doing it, customers are going to expect the same level of visual entertainment from even boutique brands. "The younger generation has been inundated with brand messages and marketing since they were born," Amanda Altman says. "It used to be that you didn't see a new product until it was on the shelf." But this is no longer true. "This generation wants the newest and coolest first, and they can sniff that out based on branding. Even small companies have to compete with the Nikes of the world on a visual level because this is what consumers are now used to."

Opposite and above: Rebrand project for Comedy Central by thelab, a media arts company.

266

ADAM **LARSON**

VICTOR **BURTON**

IT'S A FEEDBACK LOOP

Just because the digital realm is an option for all companies and all brands does not mean that it is the best option for every brand. As always, the first step is determining client needs and then deciding if, for example, a website is the appropriate means to fulfill those needs. And how do you get to "website" as an answer? According to Adam Larson of Adam + Company, "When it has to do with monitoring or gathering information."

What is truly unique about the Web is not just its ability to bring designs alive but its ability to offer interactivity with your client's customers and potential customers. "If you need to monitor who is opening things, if you're looking to track activity or solicit input, then you should do something digitally enabled," Larson says. And on the flip side, if you're doing something digital, make sure you build interactivity into it at the outset. Otherwise, you're missing out on the biggest advantage of the medium.

267

ALICIA **JOHNSON**

IF IT'S A SOCIAL PRODUCT, GIVE IT A DIGITAL SOLUTION

New media is about information, but even more, it's about sharing information. These days, when people find something they like, they share it. Even if it's just a ten-second YouTube video featuring a clumsy cat. If enough people share it, you get the ultimate brand win by going viral.

For example, consider the project of rebranding Comedy Central. "The key insight we had about the Comedy Central brand," explains Alicia Johnson, "is that comedy is social. If something

is funny, you want to share it.

And most people share comedy online. They forward the tweet, the post, the video, whatever. This insight meant that we had a digital, an online problem, so we started working on the problem from a digital perspective. All of the subsequent design decisions became influenced by the digital state." Because the digital realm offers, but also demands, so much from designers, understanding which media you're leading with at the outset of the design process is crucial.

Comedy Central rebrand, designed by thelab

268

SPEAK TO THE NEW GENERATION, WITHOUT FORGETTING ABOUT THE LAST GENERATION

ALAN AND AMANDA ALTMAN

It's not enough to understand that people interact with new media differently than print. You also have to understand the way they interact with information itself. "This is the millennial generation," notes Amanda Altman. "You have to take into consideration how they process images, take in information, and shop," she adds.

Conversely, a designer must also be aware of the completely different needs of the late-adopter generation. As Alan Altman, also of A3 Design, points out, "Baby Boomers are tech savvy and open to new ways of communicating, but they weren't born into it. It's a necessity for them."

The differing needs of these two distinct demographic groups have concrete tactical implications for interactive design. "The Millenial generation will click around anywhere, so we can be more unexpected in our navigation and design," says Amanda Altman. "An older audience expects to see the traditional upper navigation; with a younger audience, we can send our message flying across the screen. Depending upon what we do, one audience might be bored but the other might be confused."

Below and opposite: Comedy Central rebrand by theLab

269

ADAM **LARSON**

YOU CAN START TO ASSUME A FEW THINGS

The Internet is no longer a completely new frontier. Everyone from grade-schoolers to your grandma are using it with increasing facility. "Because more and more people are using the Internet," notes Adam Larson, "there is not as much of a learning curve as there used to be." What this means is that designers have a little more real estate to play with and don't have to be quite as directive as they were in the past.

"Screen sizes and resolution are bigger than they used to be," Larson points out. "Scrolling is a learned behavior that people understand now, so we don't have to keep everything 'above the fold.' Not everything has to say, 'click here' or 'download here.' We don't need to clutter everything with instructional text," he continues, "So it's becoming a more flexible medium."

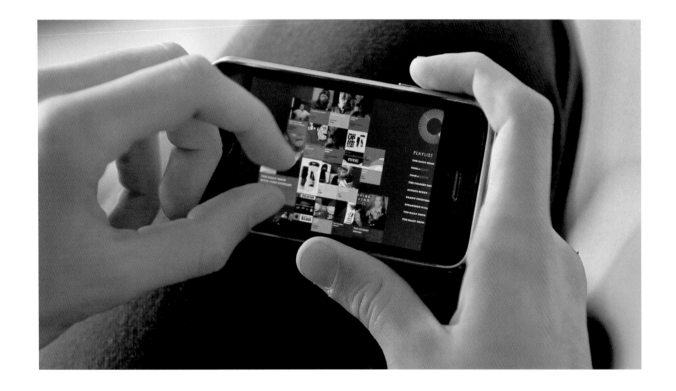

270

CHRISTINE **TAFOYA**

NO MATTER WHAT YOU DESIGN, IT HAS TO WORK DIGITALLY

"Whatever you're creating," says Christine Tafoya of deluxemodern, "you have to keep so many more things in mind." She then helpfully ticks off just a few of the multitude of issues a designer must consider for even a simple logo. "How will it look in print, on business cards, on the Web, how will colors translate to different media, how do we integrate social media, will the font translate to web and print, will it look good as a 100 by 100 pixel square, can it be rearranged and resized . . ." The point is it's not enough for a logo or design to express key brand values and look good doing it; it has to be adaptable to the demands of different media as well.

271

JD HOOGE

DIGITAL DESIGN IS ABOUT VISUALIZING DATA

Data. Messaging. Storytelling. Branding. Whatever you want to call it, design is about connecting people to information. "We are hired to take a lot of complex information and make it look simple," says JD Hooge, creative director at Instrument. "We turn information into something meaningful, visual, and digestible." While this has always been true, even in print, the job becomes more complex—and also more compelling—in the digital realm.

"Visualizing data", as Hooge calls it, also becomes giving data motion, sound, and interactivity. "Interactive visualizations are even more compelling because you can use filters and tools to change the results and uncover more meaning," he says. By allowing designers to engage more senses, more deeply, interactive design allows information to come alive as never before.

Above and opposite: Dear Miss Modern website, designed by Christine Tafoya/Deluxemodern.

Engelbert's Jewelers website, designed by Michelle McCarrick Truett, 484 Design

272 HELP YOUR CLIENTS UNDERSTAND THE ONLINE WORLD

MICHELLE
MCCARRICK TRUETT

Just because your client says they want a website or a Facebook page does not mean they understand the online world and what it can do for them and even more, it does not mean they'll know what to do with a website or Facebook page once they have it. "It's still new to many clients," Michelle McCarrick Truett of 484 Design notes. "People are afraid. They want to work in Word and Powerpoint. You have to encourage them to go in, click around, try stuff."

Also, clients are used to the way print works: print it, distribute it, you're done. They may not realize how much upkeep the online environment requires. Truett oftens gets a client going with a Facebook page or Twitter feed but then has to transition the daily maintenance back to the client. "It's important for the client to do it themselves. You need someone inside, who's sees what's newsworthy, who knows who was promoted. But I have to tell them that it has to be interesting, it has to be updated frequently, that people want to know about you. I have to sit down with them and show them how it works. Some clients don't even know how to upload pictures or an album or videos. Sometimes they'll treat you like you're a kind of tech support, but that's just part of customer service," she concludes.

MIT 150 website design, designed by Adam Larson, Adam&Co.

273

GIVE YOUR CLIENTS TIME TO DIGEST WHAT YOU'RE SHOWING THEM

ALICIA **JOHNSON**

ROBERTA
ROSENBERG

"Very few people are good at seeing things for the first time," notes Alicia Johnson. "A client said to me: 'You guys come in to present work, and you've been living with it for weeks and weeks, and we see it for ten minutes and are supposed to give a response.'" In truth, such expectations are unfair to the client and to the work.

While this advice applies to all kinds of design, it's especially critical in the digital world where there may be many things going on at once. As Roberta Rosenberg of MGP Direct Inc. points out, "People like to look at the pictures. It's easy. Reading text is hard. I learned this working in direct mail. I wouldn't show art first because they'd only look at that and then implode on something like the color. I learned to focus clients on messaging first, and then once we had that settled, we'd focus on the art."

274

DANIEL **SCHUTZSMITH**

MICHELLE **MCCARRICK TRUETT**

AMANDA **ALTMAN**

"MAKING NEW MEDIA STUFF STARTS WITH OLD SCHOOL METHODS"

So says Daniel Schutzsmith of Mark & Phil. "When I started doing web design," he continues, "I was working with people who were traditional designers. We started every design not on the screen but with a sketchpad. We would sketch out everything, drawing out how people would interact with the design." While he is quicker to get to the computer these days, he has not abandoned his sketch pad.

Michelle McCarrick Truett concurs. "I suggest staying away from the computer when you're planning," she advises. "Sit with a pen and paper and sketch it out. This planning portion is the most important. Then go to the computer to do research. But do the intense planning in the beginning. It's like having a blueprint."

Amanda Altman follows a similar process. "We were taught to start with sketching. Don't just hop on a computer. And for Web design this is still critical. Sketch out your site map. Have a clear path of how users will navigate the site. Remember, people have to use it."

275

DOUG **BARTOW**

MAKE SURE YOU'VE GOT A GOOD STORY, FIRST

Whatever brand story you are trying to tell, it should be a natural outgrowth of the brand itself, not the imposition of some technology onto the brand. "We always ask ourselves how we can build a richer media experience into the assets we have," notes Doug Bartow of id29. "We figure we have this video, and these photos, and this information, and we try to figure out how we can get them to interact. This way, you have the basics down and if the technology changes, that doesn't break down the brand story. The bottom line is that your brand story should not be dependent upon the media to tell it."

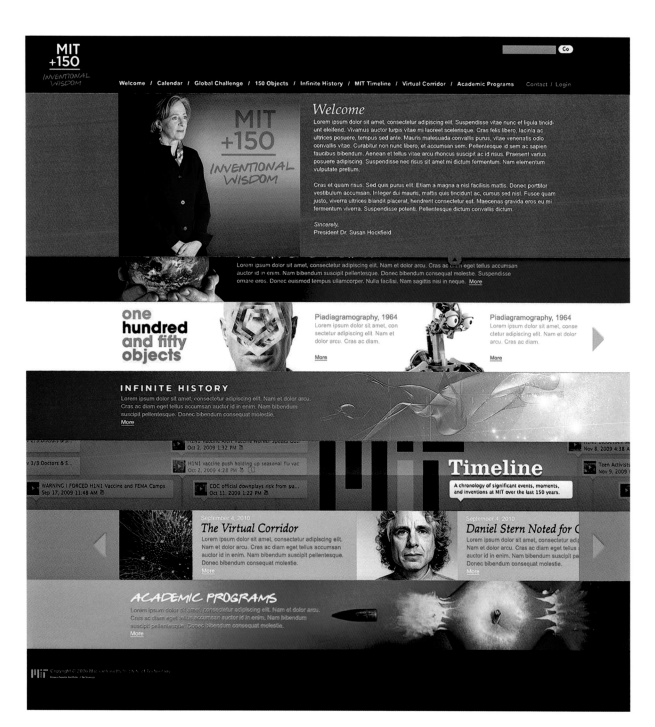

MIT 150 website, designed by Adam Larson at Adam&Co.

276

ALICIA **JOHNSON**

THINK OF NEW MEDIA IN TERMS OF "TALENT"

While it is tempting to load up any client's communications toolbox with every new fangled item a designer can get their hands on, it's important to make sure you're really using the right tool for the job. Alicia Johnson suggests considering each media as if it were a child full of untapped potential. "Think about media the way you think about kids," she says. "Try to figure out what would be the most dazzling use of that kids' talent. Try to figure out how each of those mediums can shine and be important parts of the overall communication." Of course, every designer has a preferred set of tools. But if you bring a video to the table when a postcard would do, it's no good for the client or the video. "Working this way," Johnson adds, "takes the burden off the turf of each media. As a communicator, if you look at all media agnostically, you get much more sparkly communications."

277

DESIGN FOR CHANGE

JD **HOOGE**

MICHELLE
MCCARRICK TRUETT

"Interactive design is completely different from print design," says JD Hooge. "It's like designing a car versus designing a teapot." The biggest difference he and other designers point to is the multitude of issues that have to be taken into consideration, not to mention the technology itself. "A car has thousands of moving parts," Hooge continues. "With interactive, there are so many variables involved, especially multiple viewports with different monitors, different screen sizes, different proportions. And then there's the ever-changing technology behind it all," he adds. As Michelle McCarrick Truett notes, "You're designing for an experience now. Everything is so much more multi-faceted now.

You have to constantly think of where the user going, when they're coming back, integrating social media and video . . ."

What's the first step to managing this brave new world of design? Enjoy it. "All these variables make it more complicated and exciting and fluid," Hooge concludes. Like Hooge, Truett views these variables as just one more chance to do great design. "We have so many more opportunities to lend our talents to different media now. We just have to constantly ask ourselves what we can do to make that experience richer."

Left and below: MIT 150 website design by Adam&Co. with development from Indigo Digital

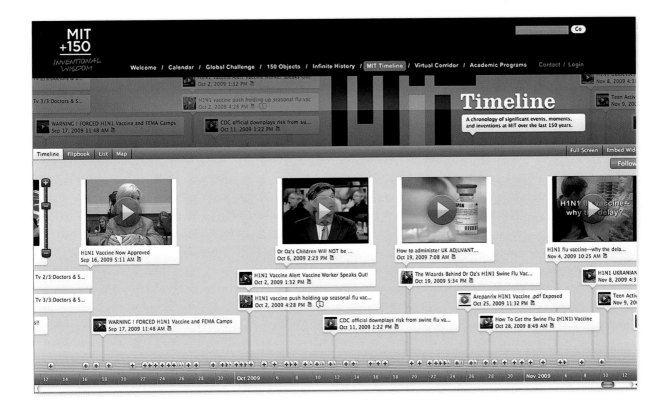

278

ALICIA **JOHNSON**

JUST BECAUSE YOU CAN DOESN'T MEAN YOU SHOULD

Back when websites were first becoming all the rage, designers threw everything they could at them: music, motion, swirling this, and swooping that. The inevitable backlash eventually came as people grew impatient with long load times or sitting through pointless mini movies. Websites calmed down and certain conventions were created that made it easier for people to get directly to the relevant content.

However, as technology evolves, it continues to make more and more possible, and the temptation to load up a digital presence with lots of bells and whistles can be difficult to resist. Alicia Johnson recommends "strategic discipline." She says, "We always think, 'Yeah, we could do that, but does it support the brand; does it serve our objectives?'" And if that mentally mature approach fails, well, there are always the restrictions placed by clocks and wallets. "The one thing that works really well to keep us dialed back is the budget," Johnson laughs. "There is never enough time and money to do everything, so why do something that doesn't serve your aspirations?"

Above and opposite: Nike 6.0 iDNation video trailer designed by Instrument

FILE NAME
NIGEL_MIAMI_SCHOOL_GOOD LINE FISH.mov

TIME CODE
00;00;08;02

PLAYBACK CONTROLS

279

ROBERTA
ROSENBERG

LEARN THE DIFFERENCES IN HOW PEOPLE INTERACT WITH THE ONSCREEN WORLD

The screen is not merely a digital page. Taking a print brochure and posting it online will not get your client results. This is not just because the medium itself is different, but because humans are different when they are using the medium.

Roberta Rosenberg ticks off three key differences: "We read 50 percent slower online than in print. We also respond differently to fonts; while serif fonts are easier to read in print, san serif is easier to read online. And then there's the way the eye tracks, where people look for information." This last consideration is perhaps the most critical for digital designers. "We have conventions of where people look for things on screen, and if you fight that, you've just stopped people in their journey." And if you stop someone in their journey through your site, you can be sure their quickest impulse will be to click off onto someone else's site.

280

ROBERTA
ROSENBERG

DON'T MAKE YOUR USER FEEL STUPID

Of course no designer would overtly try to make the user feel like a dim bulb, but a twenty-something, hipster designer in San Francisco can easily miscalculate how not tech- and pop-culture savvy a more typical person may be.

"The bottom line is the confidence factor," notes Roberta Rosenberg. "When a visitor comes to your site, they should feel confident that they know what to do next." But, the young designer objects, I need to make the site super-hip to convey how super-hip my client is. "The website may be about you and your products and company, but it is for your visitor," Rosenberg counters. "Everything we do is for the comfort of your visitor."

To create this level of comfort, she suggests making navigation so easy, so intuitive, and so obvious that the user doesn't even have to think about it. This does not mean you have to resort to bad design—it just means you shouldn't resort to super subtle or opaque design. Don't use tricky phrases or vernacular in place of known quantities like a button that says "Contact." Don't bury simple functionality beneath layers of design.

"It's like giving a party," she continues. "You're the host, but the whole idea is to keep your guests happy, entertained, and keep them there. When they leave with a smile on their face, then you're happy! You're opening up a relationship with your visitor. It's about making them feel secure and happy and not scaring them away."

281

ROBERTA
ROSENBERG

GIVE PEOPLE WHAT THEY EXPECT

One of the simplest ways to keep visitors on your site and keep them comfortable enough that they'll stay on your site is to fulfill people's expectations of what a site is supposed to look like and how it's supposed to work.

"Work with the conventions of how people expect to interact and relate with your site," says Roberta Rosenberg. "People expect to see obvious navigation. Put the search box where people normally look for it."

And don't give in to the designer cliché of making everything too small. "No matter how big it is, make it a little bigger. Research has shown that if, for example, the search box is small, people won't keep typing in it, even if it expands," she points out, which means they are a lot less likely to find what they're looking for, even if your site offers it. So don't give users an excuse to leave the site. Because given how many sites there are out there, they already have plenty of excuses to move on.

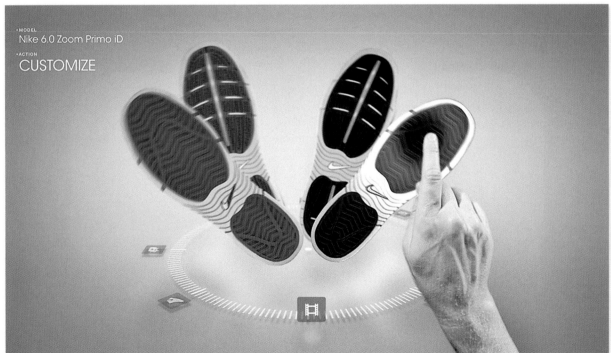

•MODEL
Nike 6.0 Zoom Primo iD

•ACTION
CUSTOMIZE

Nike 6.0 iDNation video trailer, designed by Instrument

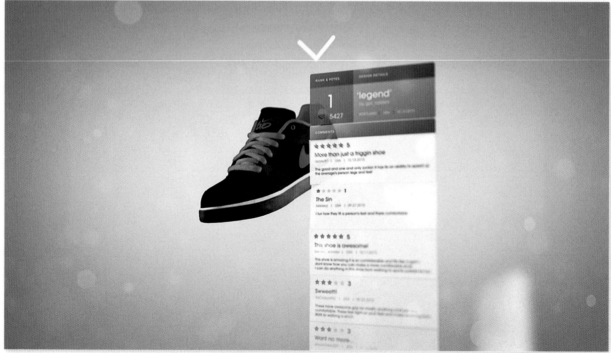

Nike 6.0 iDNation video trailer, designed by Instrument

282

ADAM **LARSON**

DANIEL **SCHUTZSMITH**

CHRISTINE **TAFOYA**

USE TEMPLATES

As the Internet has evolved, it's not just that more and more tools have become available for designers but that these tools have become more and more design-savvy. While templates used to be clunky, limited, and transparently cookie-cutter, they now provide designers with a welcome, pre-fab structure from which to build completely customized sites. "I encourage clients to use WordPress," says Adam Larson. "Platforms like these are becoming more flexible—it's like a printed piece where you have a grid underneath—but they are somewhat template-ized, and that creates consistency."

Daniel Schutzsmith agrees. He prefers Blueprint CSS and 960.gs, but it's for the same reasons. "They're templated grid systems to lay out your website. If you look at the source code for well designed sites, we keep seeing these used over and over again." For Schutzsmith, the real benefit is in what these templates allow him, as a designer, to do. "The beauty is the way that it's put together and how it's provided to designers is that it's not just code but all these different tools. So you could use it for a website, then transpose it to a brochure or to a business card. It's very cool."

For Christine Tafoya of deluxemodern, the benefit of templates accrues directly to her clients: "There are so many gorgeous templates out there," she says. "And many of the sites I've seen that have been done from the ground up don't function as well and are too expensive for many clients." In addition, she likes the fact that templates impose a bit of design discipline. "These are great services. They are a little bit limiting, but that's actually kind of good so people with too much time on their hands don't go a little crazy."

283

DANIEL **SCHUTZSMITH**

JD **HOOGE**

USE PROJECT MANAGEMENT SOFTWARE

One of the most notable differences between interactive and traditional design is often the size of the team and the specialization of the players. Add into this the fact that many team members—and the client—may not live, much less work, in the same office, city, or even state, and you can have a recipe for project management disaster. Fortunately, the Internet has created solutions for problems the Internet created.

"Everyone we work with is spread across the country," explains Daniel Schutzsmith. "We have designers in the Midwest, a publicist in Brooklyn, many are contract workers, our offices are in the Hudson Valley of New York . . . but we've all banded together." And to keep everyone banded together, Schutzsmith has instituted some strong project management structural support.

"We have automatic check-ins, regular conference calls, and an online project management system, Basecamp, so we can track comments and everyone can see what's going on."

JD Hooge manages his teams in similar fashion. "We live by Basecamp," he says. "We are religious about it. Everything we do has to go through Basecamp. It localizes problems and solutions, eliminates long email threads, records the history for each project, and let's everyone get involved."

Of course, Basecamp is just one option of many among online, integrated, interactive project management systems. It doesn't really matter which system you use; just find one that works, use it, and make sure everyone else does too.

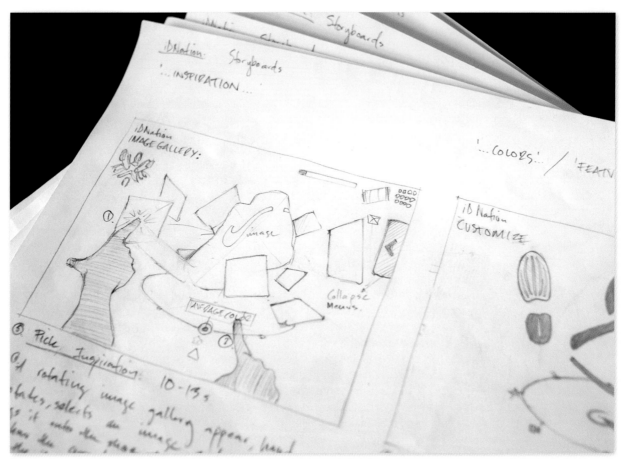

Storyboards developed by JD Hooge of Instrument for Nike campaign

284

JD **HOOGE**

USE WHITEBOARDS

While JD Hooge embraces technology for everything from design to gaming and project management, he is not above using some decidedly old school methods for visualizing what needs to be done in the cyber world. "I really like whiteboards," he says. "We painted two conference rooms' walls with whiteboard paint. We map everything out on those walls. Now, if I don't have a whiteboard, I feel like I'm in shackles."

Fort Schuyler Club website, designed by Michelle McCarrick Truett, 484 Design

---

285 RECOGNIZE THAT WHEN PEOPLE ARE ONLINE, THEY WANT TO "DO" SOMETHING

ROBERTA
ROSENBERG

While print is hardly passive, the activity involved tends to be linear and uni-directional: you offer information and your audience takes it in. Old school direct marketing was about as interactive as it got, with its exhortations to "Call NOW!" Roberta Rosenberg earned her marketing chops in this arena and finds these lessons are very useful in the digital world. "All the things I learned in direct marketing translated smoothly to the online marketplace," she says, "Especially when you want people to do something."

In this way, the online world evens the playing field a bit. Clients want customers to take actions, of course, and when people are in front of their computers or other digital devices, they are primed to do just that. "When people are online, they are looking to do something," Rosenberg says. "They want to buy something, learn something, do something. This is different than advertising." What does this mean for a designer? Recognize that your customers are in the gate, champing at the bit, and ready to run, so make it clear and make it easy for them to take the action that best benefits your client's business.

Lecky Integration website, designed by Michelle McCarrick Truett, 484 Design

286

MICHELLE
MCCARRICK TRUETT

BRAND EVERY PAGE

Maybe this seems obvious, but look around at the Web, and you'll quickly see it's much forgotten. "Of course you have an overall structure," Michelle McCarrick Truett says. "But each page also has to have some branding on it. It has to have some consistency to it." This fundamental maxim isn't just about pounding customers over the head with a brand message. "Consistency equates to comfort and improving someone's experience of the site," Truett explains. And this comfort results in more return on your client's investment. For example, Truett points out that studies have shown the if a visitor clicks on a "Donate Now" button and is taken to a page without branding, donation amounts are less than if the page does have branding.

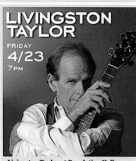

Brown's Brewing Co. homepage, designed by id29

287

DOUG **BARTOW**

REMEMBER THE GRID

While templates are helpful to keep website design contained, there is more to the grid than just guardrails. "When you're designing a site, you have to be coherent," suggests Doug Bartow. "A lot of the techniques of using the grid come into play because you need to have information in places where people will look for it naturally. There's a lot to learn from the grid. A lot of the methodology for information design runs concurrent regardless of the medium."

V-AWARE

HOME | LEARN | NEWS | EVENTS | JOURNAL | ABOUT | FIND A DOCTOR   Search

WELCOME TO V-AWARE.

VASCULAR **SYSTEM** = ARTERIES + VEINS

Millions of Americans suffer from vascular disease. Most do not know that they have it until they require some type of intervention. Prevention and early detection are the keys to a successful outcome. You can make a positive change in your health.

BECOME V-AWARE.

Center for **VASCULAR** AWARENESS

VASCULAR DISEASE= DISORDERS OF THE ARTERIES **+** VEINS

Take the V-Aware Reader Survey
...your opinions and insight are valuable in shaping the future of V-AWARE.

CLICK HERE TO TAKE SURVEY

Vascular Disease can KILL you.
Vascular Disease and Coronary Artery Disease have the same risk factors and are caused by the same disease process.

READ MORE

VAWARE.ORG was created by the Center for Vascular Awareness, a group of dedicated medical professionals whose goal is to help educate the public about the nature, symptoms, treatment, and prevention of vascular disease.

MORE ABOUT US

12 Million People have Peripheral Vascular disease.
Learn ways to decrease your chances of long-term vascular injury.

READ MORE

Patient Story
In 1999, Roseanne, a 60-year-old emergency medical technician (EMT) was driving an ambulance...

READ MORE

SIGN UP TO RECEIVE OUR FREE PDF JOURNAL

Our Mission
The Center for Vascular Awareness was formed to educate the general public regarding the field of vascular medicine and to educate the underserved in an effort to help them help their doctor; to carry on... **READ MORE**

The Center for Vascular Awareness website, designed by id29

288

DOUG **BARTOW**

START WITH A FEW GREAT PAGES

Some designers basically ignore all the glaring differences between Web and print and just start designing in the way they've always done before. "I still have a print mentality in relation to a website," says Doug Bartow. "I don't think of it as 3D. For us, it's always 2D in a different media."

So how does he make the flat design come to life on a screen? "Our approach is basically the same. Designing a brochure or book or billboard is akin to designing a splash page for a website. You really have to grab people's attention quickly. So we storyboard out the site, make a tree, branch, root system, a flow chart of all the pages of the site, and then populate them. You need four or five page designs. Then, it's very scalable. If we can design five great pages, we can make that into a great 100 page site."

Diesel U Music website, designed by Adam Larson, Adam&Co.

289 GIVE EACH PAGE A DISTINCT JOB TO DO

ALAN **ALTMAN**

DANIEL
SCHUTZSMITH

From the very first page, your website should be communicating clearly about why someone should visit and what they should do while visiting. As Alan Altman says, "Create a purpose page so I don't have to figure out what the site's about or who you are." This idea of giving the home page a purpose extends to every other page as well. Because a website is a nonlinear experience and visitors can come—and leave—through any number of doors and windows, each page has to stand on its own with a distinct message.

To deal with this multi-dimensionality, Daniel Schutzsmith breaks down each page into two component parts: "One is the fact of the design, and the other is the objective. You have to make sure these are not disjointed

from one another," he continues. "For design, it's really all about continuity. Whatever is featured on home pages should be featured on internal pages as well. The other side is the objectives. Every single page to your website has a specific objective. For one page, you may want someone to fill out a form; for another, it's to make a donation or to read something. There may be multiple objectives, but there is a specific order in which those objectives should be achieved."

This, after all, is the critical difference between print and online: interactivity. If you don't make the most of the opportunity to get your visitor to interact with you, you've missed the whole point of the online experience.

290

ROBERTA
ROSENBERG

IF IT NEEDS A SKIP BUTTON, SKIP IT

Thankfully, most long, involved, showy—and often forgettable—website introductions have gone the way of the rotary phone. But there are still plenty of them, along with other digital song and dance routines, out there. Roberta Rosenberg offers a simple rule: "If it needs a skip button, take it away." She acknowledges that designers develop these elaborate show-and-tells as an excuse to demonstrate their capabilities, but there are plenty of other venues for that impulse within the context of the site itself. "I know designers want to show their creativity, but really, they're just irritating users."

291

ROBERTA
ROSENBERG

PAY ATTENTION TO READABILITY

When it comes to readability, size does matter. "Make the font bigger so people can read it," Roberta Rosenberg flatly states. "Boomers can't work with 9 point type. It just pisses us off. Make it large enough, without being insulting." Of course, it's not only Boomers who benefit from readable type. And sure, a user can zoom, but why make them work so hard to absorb your message?

Size is not the only consideration when it comes to readability. In general, sans serif faces are more readable on screen. But be careful because this rule does not apply to all san serif faces. Also, text needs to be high contrast for the crisp resolution that is so critical to readability. This is not a recipe for dull design—just an admonition to make sure the content gets to its intended user. The premise is simple: As Rosenberg states, "Don't go just for aesthetics if it means someone is going to have to work hard to read the page."

Diesel U Music website, designed by Adam Larson, Adam&Co.

DIESEL: U:MUSIC

SIGN UP ▶ SIGN IN ▶

ABOUT THE STUPID FOR MUSIC CUP.

- THE CONTEST
- THE PRIZES
- INFO FOR FANS
- INFO FOR BANDS
- THE FINE PRINT

THE CONTEST

Rock legend Frank Zappa commissioned the infamous panty quilt after his 1981 tour. It's made entirely of, you guessed it, panties (and bras) thrown on stage during shows. Stupid, right? And awesome.

The Stupid for Music World Cup award celebrates fans and all the crazy exploits they commit while under the influence of music. Truthfully, a D:U:M band is nothing without stupid fans—rabble-rousers and rebels willing to do anything (or anyone) for the bands they love. The contest is all about what you—real-life music lovers—will do for the love of music. How far you're willing to go will determine how far you get.

HERE'S THE LOWDOWN

At Diesel we're all about screwing with conventions, so unlike most other music awards, the Stupid For Music World Cup is actually only partially rigged.

Sure we'll be handpicking half of the bands that make it into the heats (and you know who you are), but incredibly the rest of you bands have a fair chance of securing a spot in the competition. Seriously, the fans will (for real) determine 32 of the 64 bands chosen to compete.

Regardless of who's sleeping with who, bands still have to enter the contest in order to be either "randomly selected" (wink, wink, nudge, nudge) by Diesel or legitimately propelled to fame, fortune, and promiscuity by an adoring and insanely stupid for music fan base. So that being said, snap to it! If you're a band, create a profile and if you're a fan start acting like one.

NOTE TO FANS: We've spent a ridiculous amount of time devising this elaborate competition all based on your propensity to behave with wild stupid abandon. Please don't make us look bad.

INVITE FANS. ♥

CREATE A PROFILE.

Legal Notice   Powered By sonicbids   Background Band : Anatural   © 2010 Diesel.

DIESEL: U:MUSIC

SIGN UP ▶ SIGN IN ▶

THE MATCHES.

- OVERVIEW
- HEAT 01
- HEAT 02
- HEAT 03
- KNOCKOUT
- QUARTER-FINAL
- SEMI-FINAL
- FINAL
- ALL ENTRIES

QUALIFYING ROUND

Half of the bands that make it into the Stupid For Music World Cup heats will be hand picked (and you know who you are), but the rest of the bands have a fairly honest chance of securing a spot in the Cup. Seriously. The fans will (for real) determine 32 of the 64 bands chosen to compete. Here are the current standings based on fan count...

CURRENT STANDINGS

1-701296 NEXT ▶▶ LAST ▶▶

01

BAND	FANS					♥ 21 FANS
Simon Collins	Linda Joyce	NO IMAGE	NO IMAGE	NO IMAGE		6/10 BUZZ Rock, Canada

02

BAND	FANS					♥ 19 FANS
WESTLAND	samantha	NO IMAGE	kim	Rayanna	Tracey	9/10 BUZZ Rock, USA, Massachusetts

03

BAND	FANS					♥ 7 FANS
Lisha Cash	Leah Leonard Mystie amy				NO IMAGE	0/10 BUZZ Pop, Canada

04

BAND	FANS		♥ 7 FANS

Diesel U Music website, designed by Adam Larson, Adam&Co.

292

ROBERTA
ROSENBERG

FOLLOW THE EYES

While we are all familiar with the standard (to the Western world, at least) upper-left-to-bottom-right pattern of reading the printed page, the eye moves differently on screen. "Eye tracking studies show that we generally look at a site in a rough F pattern," explains Roberta Rosenberg. "So on the top cross of F, put the logo and tag line. The middle horizontal is where the introduction goes; that tells your visitor what you're about, what to expect, and how they'll benefit." Of course, these are guidelines for optimization, not rigid rules.

"The idea is that design should provide intuitive and accessible information points so whoever the visitor is, they can immediately find what they're looking for and go into the site for more information."

293

TELL PEOPLE WHAT TO DO NEXT

ROBERTA
ROSENBERG

The online experience is one of many overlapping and intersecting pathways, as well as the ability to magically jump from one world directly into another. The goal, always, is to get people to stay on your site. In order to achieve this goal, it's important to provide visitors with direction and opportunities to do just that. "Not every visitor is coming to your site with the same urgency of need," notes Roberta Rosenberg. "Some are ready to buy and some are just browsing. You want to make sure that wherever they are in their processes, they will find something relevant."

She likens a website to the window of a retail shop where a variety of items are displayed to entice passersby to come inside to see more. And like a retail shop, you have to make it easy to get inside and easy to browse, with directional signs that get them down the aisles and deeper into the store. "You can't assume people know where to go or what to do next," Rosenberg emphasizes. Use highlights or arrows or color or whatever. Design needs to cue people where to look and what to do next."

Grace Street Floral website, designed by Christine Tafoya, Deluxemodern

Vida Carson Photography website, designed by Christine Tafoya, Deluxemodern

294

ROBERTA **ROSENBERG**

MAKE THE BUTTONS STAND OUT

If you want someone to come into your store, you don't hide the door. The same holds true for the Web, where anything that's clickable is a virtual doorway. "Make the buy buttons big," suggests Roberta Rosenberg. "Make them orange or yellow. Don't make people hunt for it. Make sure it's called something that people understand. Don't be clever; be clear." In other words, don't make it difficult for people to spend money or time with you.

295

ALAN **ALTMAN**

MAKE IT EASY TO GO HOME AGAIN

Digital media is changing the way we consume information. While print is primarily a linear, front to back, one-page-leads-to-the-other experience, websites offer a wide range of entry and exit points. If you want to have any hope of corralling the user's journey, it's critical to create a clear path through the content. And it's no less important to provide some bread crumbs so they can find their way home. As Alan Altman says, "There has to be an easy way to get back to where you started from."

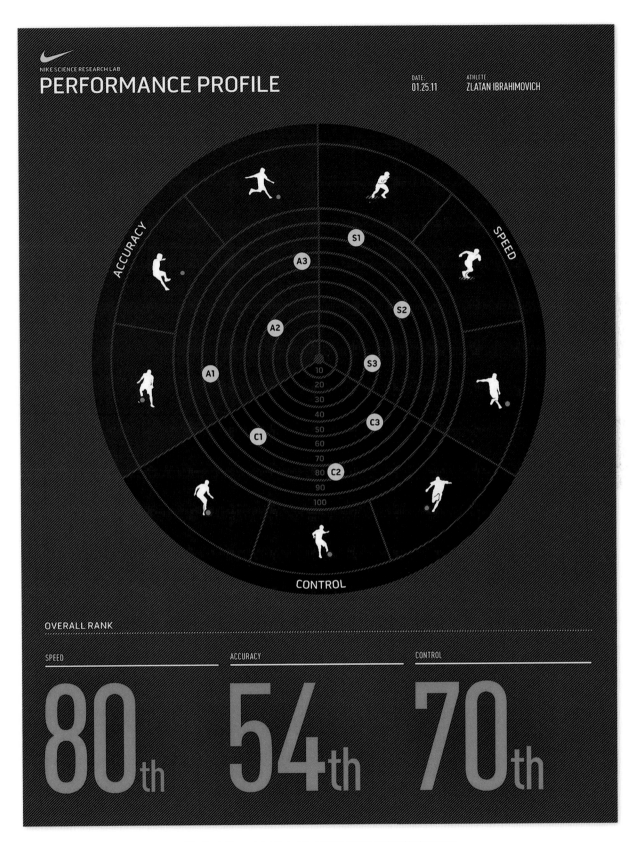

Nike Sports Research Lab Performance Profile website, designed by Instrument

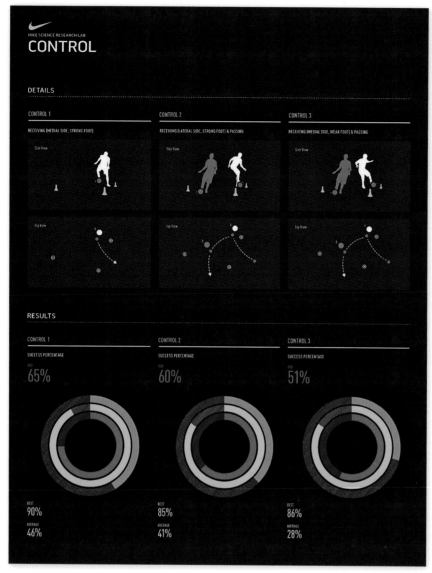

Nike Sports Research Lab Performance Profile website, designed by Instrument

296

MAKE IT EASY TO FIGURE OUT

ADAM **LARSON**

MICHELLE
MCCARRICK TRUETT

Designers often get a bad rap—and too often, deservedly so—for putting tricky and cool design tropes ahead of basic functionality. You have to remember that many, if not most, of your users are not going to understand or value your wacky take on navigation. They're not even going to take the time to dislike it. They're just going to move on to another site. "Even if you have nonstandard navigation," notes Adam Larson, "You should have traditional navigation as well." He points out that

navigation is the means by which a user interacts with your content, so it is not the place to be unclear with directions. "Navigation is the wrapper that holds things together and gets you through the site." As Michelle McCarrick Truett adds, "Always put yourself in the users' position. Ask yourself, 'If I was going through this blind, would I know what to do?'" And would that be true even if I was not someone who grew up with a baby bottle in one hand and an iPhone in the other?

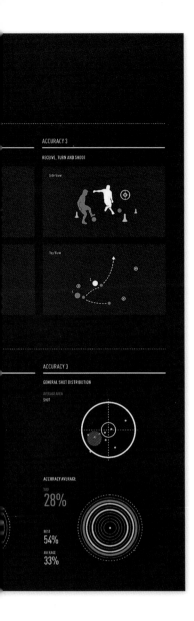

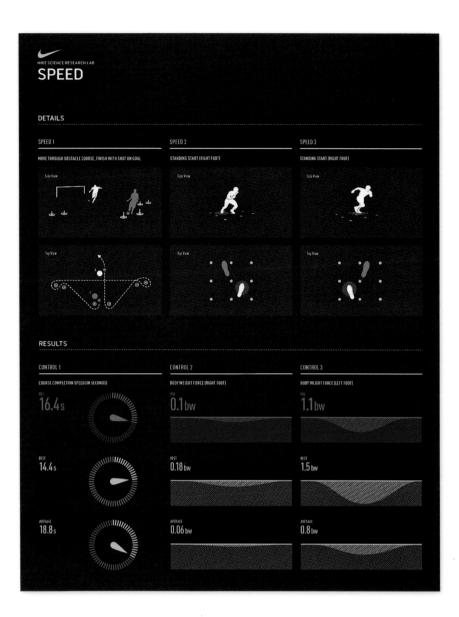

297

MICHELLE
MCCARRICK TRUETT

MAKE IT EASY TO GET IN TOUCH

Here's another obvious but often overlooked point: It's not enough to simply have a contact button on the home page; put them on every page. "People want to do things quickly," Michelle McCarrick Truett points out. "They don't want to search for you. That's why we put the address and contact information on every page." Is it overkill? Not so much. "After all," says Alan Altman, "Getting in touch is the whole point."

298

MICHELLE
MCCARRICK TRUETT

MAKE IT EASY TO KEEP IN TOUCH

If you're doing anything printed, make sure it mentions the website. If you're doing a website, make it easy to get a printed piece. If you're doing anything for a client, make sure you figure out how it all relates to everything else you are doing and might be doing in the future. "The Web is enhancing the printed piece," notes Michelle McCarrick Truett. "And printed pieces should be driving people to the website, where they'll click around and learn more about us. Even if you're doing a postcard, you have to consider how this relates to Web." You also have to consider how it will help get people to the Web.

It is also important to find a way to capture something from your customer whenever possible. This way, you can keep them informed, get back in touch, and begin creating a deeper brand experience. This could be a form for registering for email updates, links to Facebook pages and Twitter feeds, or signing up for special, member's only deals. Or even better, all of the above.

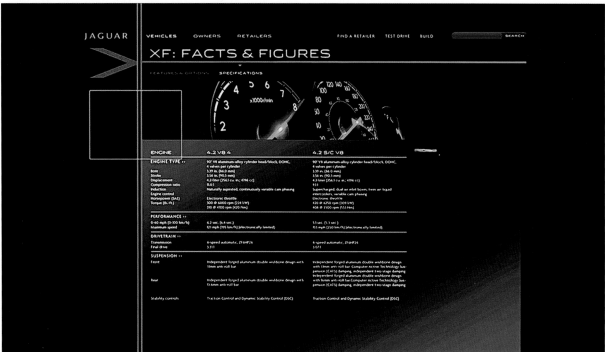

Jaguar online advertising campaign, designed by Alicia Johnson and Hal Wolverton, creative directors for EURO RSCG

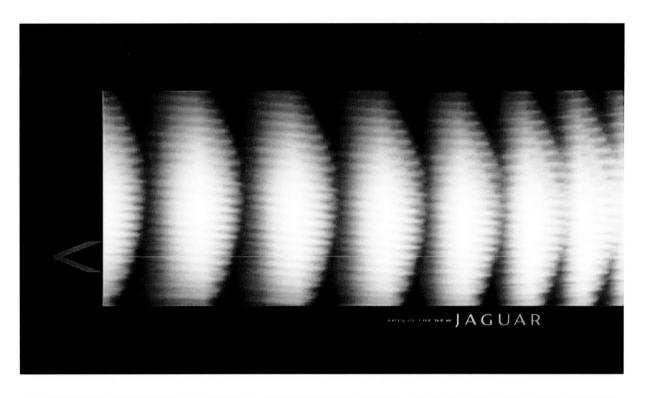

Jaguar online advertising campaign, designed by Alicia Johnson and Hal Wolverton,
creative directors for EURO RSCG

299

ROBERTA
ROSENBERG

KEEP THE IMPORTANT STUFF ABOVE THE FOLD

"If what people can see on the first screen isn't interesting, they won't go anywhere else," notes Roberta Rosenberg. "Online, you have one to two seconds when someone lands on a site to immediately communicate what this page is about so the user can figure out if they're in the right place and if you have what they want." So keep the critical stuff front, center, and right in their face.

300

ALICIA **JOHNSON**

MAKE IT AN AURAL EXPERIENCE

Motion may be the most fundamental thing that sets the digital realm apart from print, but music adds yet another layer to the multi-sensory experience. "When I look at a project, if it's multi-media, I always look at music," says Alicia Johnson. "This is another place where you can communicate at a deep level about the experience of the brand."

301

DANIEL
SCHUTZSMITH

USE CHECKLISTS

While many designers and production people use checklists for print jobs, the complexity and multi-dimensionality of interactive and website design makes these handy, old-school mechanisms even more critical. "We have a project scope worksheet that we use," notes Daniel Schutzsmith. "It's eight pages long and is a list of questions anyone can go through to cover all the bases." In addition to asking strategic questions like, "Who does this matter to?" the list also tackles the basics like, "Who is hosting the site?"

Schutzsmith also recommends a site www. lite.launchlist.net that bills itself as a "one stop website checklist." Built by the Australian group Collapps, which makes "creative apps for web people," Launchlist was created "to help and encourage web designers and developers to check their work before exposing it to the world at large." A straightforward checklist of almost thirty items covers everything from checking for spelling errors to including meta data and ensuring page titles are optimized for search engines. You can even add fields of your own. In this fast changing environment, an easily updateable, online list is a great way to make sure every "i" is dotted, "t" is crossed, and link works.

302

MICHELLE
MCCARRICK TRUETT

CHRISTINE **TAFOYA**

MAKE THE LITTLE STUFF COUNT

One of the wonders and challenges of the digital realm is that the barrier to entry is low. Almost anyone can do it. Download a template for a website or an email marketing campaign, and voila, you're a digital designer.

If a real, educated, experienced graphic designer is smart, he or she can make this plethora of amateur effort work to their advantage. "Even though anyone can use this stuff, you can tell who had a designer touch it and who didn't," insists Michelle McCarrick Truett. "It's really about the basics of spacing and typography, the stuff we learned in freshman year. These things make a huge difference in new media."

Christine Tafoya of deluxemodern concurs. "Professional design always looks professional," she says. "It's about the details a designer adds, that refinement and polish that sets things apart. It's about knowing what works and what doesn't and creating a distinct vibe."

303

MICHELLE
MCCARRICK TRUETT

MAKE SURE EVERYTHING WORKS

Click on every box. Try every link. Fill out forms. Try it on different computers, different devices. Make sure it scales. "It takes twice as much effort as a print project," Michelle McCarrick Truett points out. "It's so easy to forget a link, for example. For every site I do, I create a PDF of the whole thing with lots of notes on it. I review everything, after hours, when it's quiet and I have the silence and time to keep my brain on it. I make sure I'm familiar with how every page works." This extra time and attention may seem onerous, but you avoid it at your peril. Because missing a single detail will send users scurrying away—usually directly to a competitor's site.

304

ALAN **ALTMAN**

USE THE SITE YOURSELF

Ask Alan Altman what the most fundamental, online design must do is and he doesn't hesitate: "You have to use it." This admonition is not just about ensuring the links work. It's more about making sure the entire concept makes sense. "Designers want to take everything they've learned and put it into one big show," Altman notes. Too often, this leads to possibly entertaining but often confusing design overload for your customers. Remember, most online users aren't looking for a show—they just want a pair of jeans to wear Saturday night or some information about how to use their new smart phone.

305

DANIEL
SCHUTZSMITH

AMANDA **ALTMAN**

EVERY WEBSITE IS ACTUALLY MANY WEBSITES

Daniel Schutzsmith calls online design "screen design." And these days, there are many different screens to design for. "You're never just creating a website now," explains Schutzsmith. "You always want to have a CMS, or content management system, so it can be updated. Whatever you design has to be available for multiple platforms; it has to scale and work on different devices. So you're never just making one site; you're always making multiple web sites." When thinking about screens, remember that scalability goes in both directions. "Mobile devices are taking over," notes Amanda Altman. "You have to consider usability in terms of how things look on smaller screens." As smart phones do more, the small screen is only going to gain in importance.

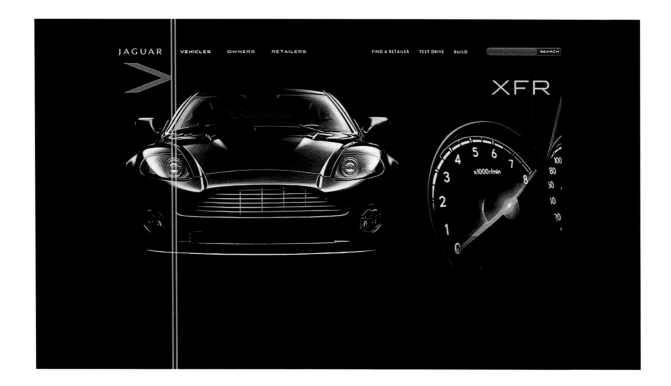

306

ROBERTA
ROSENBERG

DON'T FORGET SEO

Search engine optimization (SEO) may not seem like a designer's job, given that what the engines are searching for is words. But designers decide where words go, and placement is critical to getting up there in rankings. "Search engines give preference to the first two to three paragraphs of text on any given page," says Roberta Rosenberg. "They like to find these paragraphs positioned as high up on the page as possible. Remember, too, that search engines can't 'see' images, so important copy points should be made in text, not the image.

However, if the image is the thing, then make sure a keyphrase-meaty alt-tag is used to describe the image. This is almost as good as the plain text itself." What's another way to ensure excellent SEO? Call in a specialist who can look at the design and give pointers to make sure the crawlers are all over your site.

Opposite and above: Jaguar online advertising campaign by creative directors of EURO RSCG, Alicia Johnson and Hal Wolverton.

307

GET THE DESIGN OUT OF THE WAY

ROBERTA
ROSENBERG

ADAM **LARSON**

It's been said more times than we can count, but it still deserves to be repeated: "Design is an integral part of the message, but it's not the message," is how Roberta Rosenberg puts it. Adam Larson puts it this way: "Design should accommodate the goal but not be the goal."

The point is, too much design can get in the way of the person using the design. As Rosenberg explains, "Good design doesn't call attention to itself. It helps and supports and moves the message forward. It moves people through the message. There are things that designers can do to emphasize something and get a reader to look at something. But good design is supportive of the visitor's experience. It should be invisible to the visitor who just wants to get something done." Design for design's sake is called art. And its place is in a gallery, not a commercial website.

308

REMEMBER, TECHNOLOGY DOES NOT MAKE YOU A BETTER DESIGNER

ALAN **ALTMAN**

MICHELLE
MCCARRICK TRUETT

"Sometimes designers use filters and effects just because they're there," notes Alan Altman. "If you don't have self-control, the technology can actually hinder you." While technology makes it possible to do more, more quickly, it should never be used to prop up weak strategy or to dress up ugly design. After all, technology is still just a tool for expressing the deeper values a designer has to offer their clients, which, according to Michelle McCarrick Truett, is in your ideas. "Your real value is in your thinking and your process," she says.

"Creativity is an internal capability. The tools make it easier and quicker. Youngsters think that facility with the computer makes you special. But the ability to think deeply and communicate well is what makes you a better designer." And she adds, "Also a happier designer with the ability to make more money."

Rough 'N Tumble website, designed by Michelle McCarrick Truett, 484 Design

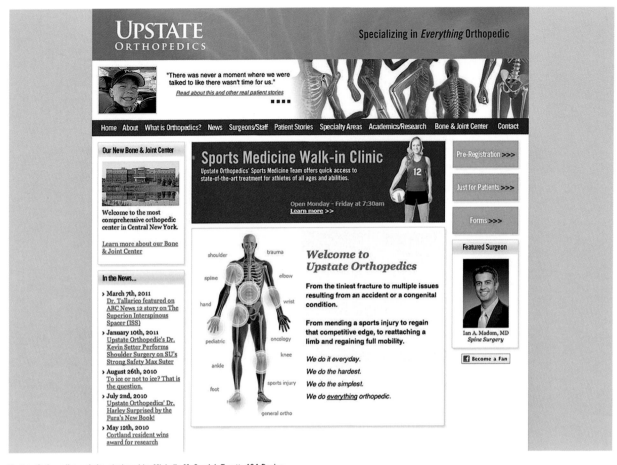

Upstate Orthopedics website, designed by Michelle McCarrick Truett, 484 Design

309

ROBERTA
ROSENBERG

LOOK FOR CONVENTIONS, THEN TWEAK THEM

Every designer worth their salt will spend time checking out a client's competition before designing anything. What you often discover is that everything in a particular industry looks the same. While some of this is certainly design laziness, there are other reasons for this conformity: it helps users understand what they're looking at. Consumers expect bright colors and simple shapes when they're shopping for kids. They expect gray tones and guys in suits when they're looking for a lawyer. If you flipped those conventions around, you'd probably not sell many toys or get any legal business.

"If what we're selling is a commodity," Roberta Rosenberg notes, "We've got to come up with a way to distinguish what we're doing. Is there a way to take a good idea and make it better? Is there an opportunity to be a fresh breeze without being too clever?" Part of a digital designer's job is to make a visitor comfortable while offering some welcome surprises. Rosenberg suggests ". . . taking that convention and tweaking it a little bit so your message is enhanced but not obscured. And the purpose of your visitor is not obscured either."

Berklee School of Music website, designed by Adam Larson, Adam&Co.

310

ALAN AND AMANDA
ALTMAN

DON'T DO IT JUST BECAUSE EVERYONE ELSE IS

"Some clients go overboard with new media," say Amanda Altman. Just because everyone else has it, does not mean that every company needs it. Just because one of your clients uses some cool app on their iPhone, doesn't mean their customers will. "A construction company may not need a twitter feed or a phone app, while a company that appeals to a young audience might want real time notifications about sales," Altman continues.

"Clients will come to us with a list of social media that they want, and we have to advise them that if they're not going to keep up with it, if it's not relevant, then they don't need it. You have to use this stuff strategically." And if you're going to do it, you better do it well. As Alan Altman adds, "If you have it and it's done poorly, you're going to hurt your brand. If you don't stay on top of it, your brand looks like its dead in the water."

311

ALAN **ALTMAN**

DON'T TRY TO DO IT ALL YOURSELF

When so much is possible and so much seems easier than it really is, it can be tempting to try and do too much and do too much of it yourself. "You have to set boundaries for yourself because you can really do everything now," Alan Altman says. Most designers suggest keeping your eye on the design prize and letting the specialists do what they do best. "It's about deciding how much you want to learn without sacrificing some other thing," Altman explains. "We keep our craft focused and let the other experts handle their areas."

Above and opposite: Website design for Berklee School of Music by Adam Larson of Adam&Co.

312

MICHELLE **MCCARRICK TRUETT**

DOUG **BARTOW**

YOUR DEVELOPER IS YOUR FRIEND

Just as great print designers learn how to work with production people and printers so they can uncover ways to use print technology to enhance their design, so digital designers must make it their business to work with the back end geeks who are going to bring their designs to life. "You hear that programmers are a different animal and it's true," says Michelle McCarrick Truett. "But ultimately it's like working with any new vendor. You have to have good communication skills. You have to be perfectly clear, ask how they prefer files, reiterate deadlines, and understand what a programmer does to make it work and try to make things easier for them. When I've faltered on this, the job has suffered."

Doug Bartow agrees and goes on to suggest ways to enhance the collaborative nature of the relationship. "Sometimes we work with a developer and just provide flat art and ask them to build it. Other times, we engage them earlier and ask how we can use technology to make this a richer experience. They have a working knowledge of what's possible and what's a complete pain in the ass. We go to them and say here's what we're thinking, is it possible, and they come back with, yes, but this way is much better. A good developer is a problem solver."

313

ALAN AND AMANDA
ALTMAN

FEED ON THE SPEED

In the digital realm, everything moves and moves faster. First off, there's the design itself. As Amanda Altman says, "The opportunities and possibilities in the digital arena are so exciting. To see an identity animate in front of us, to see it speak, move, change color, it's exciting."

This speed also offers new opportunities for branding. While Amanda points out that all this motion "helps create brand presence," her partner Alan Altman notes that speed also pertains to input from the marketplace. "I like the speed of the way things work," he says. "You introduce a new brand and you don't have to wait months to get feedback. You get feedback on how a brand is doing within hours." And this feedback comes not only fast but from a wider range of sources. "We can communicate everywhere and get opinions everywhere," he adds.

314

DANIEL
SCHUTZSMITH

DO MINI CAMPAIGNS

Don't forget that digital media represents great opportunities not only for your clients but for self-promotion too. Sure, there's always a cool e-card as one way to go. But why not showcase your talents in a more creative, inventive, and hopefully viral way? For example, Daniel Schutzsmith played off the Gulf oil disaster with an "Instant oil spill. We created a little website that allows you to put an oil spill on any other website. It went viral with 1 million hits in a month." That's an awful lot of self-promotion for not a lot of money.

HELLO ♥ DARLING!

DELUXEMODERN DESIGN + DEAR MISS MODERN SHOP

design junkies

website   *shop*   *facebook*   *blog*

Deluxemodern website, designed by Christine Tafoya, Deluxemodern

Moss Fine Floral and Events stationery and website, designed by Christine Tafoya/Deluxemodern

315

JD HOOGE

MICHELLE MCCARRICK TRUETT

IT'S THE "WILD WEST"

"The nature of doing new media is that we don't have rules," says JD Hooge. "We have spaces that we need to stay within. It's like going to the playground and your parents say just stay within these parameters. Within this, you can do whatever you want. You can create your own playground."

The problem and joy of new media is that technology is changing so fast, even if you did have rules, by the time you learned them, they would have changed. And while there are tons of information available on what's happening, new things are happening all the time. Hooge suggests embracing trial and error. "We do a lot of prototyping and we just test things out," he says. "Mostly it's just getting the technology and playing with it. The developers just start digging under the hood."

Of course, this can be an intimidating process. "First off," says Michelle McCarrick Truett, "it's scary. There are always new things to learn and you don't want to put yourself out there as an expert until you've learned. You just have to be brave. You just have to learn it and not be scared to learn it. You don't need to be an expert, but you have to get out there and try stuff," she concludes.

Hooge agrees. "It takes a different kind of person," he says. "You have to embrace a certain amount of uncertainty. Once you accept that, you can make things more flexible; you can expand and contract and flex as needed. It's still kind of the Wild West and will be for a while. People are just making things up, it's constantly changing, and people are trying to innovate and keep up."

Google I/O developer conference website, designed by Instrument

316

DANIEL
SCHUTZSMITH

BUT THE SAME BASIC QUESTIONS APPLY

Even though the medium and technology are different, good digital design is still a response to basic strategic issues. "I ask myself a few specific questions," says Daniel Schutzsmith. "Will it be accessible to the most people possible? In other words, will it work as a digital billboard, on a phone, on a computer? Is it appropriate to the target audience? For example, if we're targeting seniors, we don't need a big mobile campaign. Then there are the technical implications and cost implications: can we do it, do we have to learn it, and can the client afford it?" While these questions are critical to ask on any design project, they are essential in the online milieu where there is even greater temptation—and opportunity—to go overboard and to get in over your head.

317

DANIEL
SCHUTZSMITH

AND THE SAME DESIGN PRINCIPLES APPLY

Even though technology makes it seem that there are infinite possibilities, digital design still demands a designer work with the same foundational tool set. "You're still working with the standard tropes of design—font, color, composition, white space, etc.," says Daniel Schutzsmith. "You can instantly tell when some-one is doing screen-based design who has a traditional graphic design background." And he, for one, thinks that incorporating the rudiments of the craft into the high-tech landscape is the wave of the future. "We are returning to the fundamentals of design in screen-based design. It's a good thing."

Above: Google I/O developer conference website, designed by Instrument

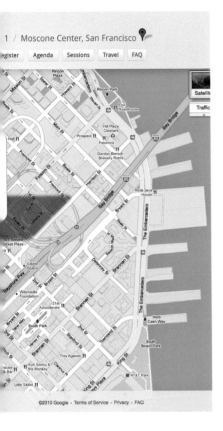

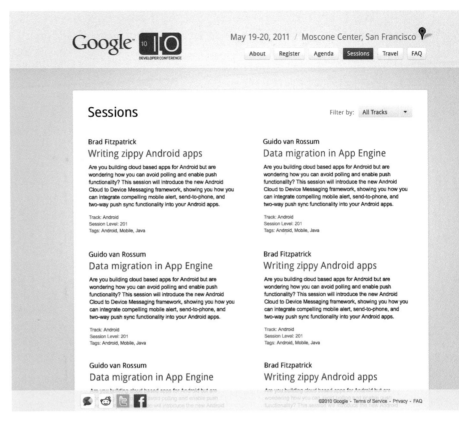

318

ALICIA **JOHNSON**

EMBRACE HOW PRINT DESIGN CAN EFFECT SCREEN DESIGN

"David Carson said 'Print is dead,'" notes Alicia Johnson. "I'd say it's resurrected." Johnson is referring not to paper itself but to transferring what a designer can do on paper to the screen. "This is the same design discipline being expressed in this new medium. We have this extraordinary tool. The things that are awesome about print, things that only print used to be able to do, are now coming to life in this other medium." As object lesson one,

she points to the advent of "The Daily," a daily newspaper for the iPad. "It is so interesting that we now have the technology and the technical capacity with iPads and laptops where we can get high-definition content. It's like a midway step where print, or what we think of as print, which is typeset and static state, is being expressed in this new medium. It's a dazzling opportunity."

319

JD **HOOGE**

LET TECHNOLOGY INFLUENCE THE DESIGN

In the old days, designers didn't need to be computer geeks. Even as computers became standard, they were often considered the tools of production people, the machines that other people used to prep files once the design was done. That way of thinking is no more. "Technology and design include one another now," says JD Hooge. "If you build a multi-touch screen display, it's not the same technology as a website," which means the design has to be different as well.

"I've always though that embracing technology was really important," Hooge says. "I was always creating, designing, and programming. If I know the constraints of the technology, then I know what's possible. When you know the limitations and parameters and strengths of the technology, you can play to those and play within those." And presumably, from that design play comes a much richer user experience and a more relevant brand experience.

320

DOUG **BARTOW**

BEWARE OF BECOMING OUTDATED

At the same time, too much reliance on the latest and greatest technology can leave your designs high and dry when that technology changes. And this is inevitable. "It's easy to get dated," says Doug Bartow, "especially if you use technology as a crutch instead of a design mentality." What's his recommendation? "Don't design for the technology; use the technology to your advantage. It's just a tool. It can be an amazing tool to create interesting and complex environments, but you still need to visually articulate a message and tell a story."

Stills from a series of rich media videos for the seventh Harry Potter release event and website, designed, animated, and produced by id29

modernlove | STYLIZED BOUDOIR PHOTOGRAPHY

home   boudoir   couples boudoir   details   blog   contact us

321

MICHELLE
MCCARRICK TRUETT

ADAM **LARSON**

EMBRACE THE DIGITAL WORLD

"If you're a designer and think you're staying in print land, you're mistaken," says Michelle McCarrick Truett. "You have to learn Web design or else you're stuck."

The transition from print to Web is well underway and only on the increase. "If you're not online, you're not alive," notes Adam Larson, referring to both clients and designers. "We are going to become more and more interrelated with technology. More things will transition off paper and onto screens."

This proclamation, while certainly true, is not a sentence, but an incredible design opportunity. "I approach technology as anything is possible," says Larson. "It opens the world, it makes everything more grand, it opens doors. The only limit is your own knowledge."

Above and opposite: Samples from the Modern Love website designed by Christine Tafoya of Deluxemodern

modern love

STYLIZED PHOTOGRAPHY FOR MODERN LOVERS

WEDDING   BOUDOIR   BLOG

322   LOOK FOR WAYS TO HAVE TECHNOLOGY AND HUMANITY COMMUNICATE MORE CLOSELY

ADAM **LARSON**

JD **HOOGE**

The one thing we can all be sure of is that new technology will keep coming at us. It will open new worlds and change the way we interact with the one we have. For example, Adam Larson points to openFrameworks, a C++ library that has been "designed to assist the creative process by providing a simple and intuitive framework for experimentation." Larson feels that "this language enables all sorts of things. By using projections that you can interact with, it creates experiences. It has connections to street art, street culture, graffiti art, and outdoor performance art. It allows us to start to re-humanize technology, where technology is focused on enhancing rather than replacing human experience. The evolution of design is going way beyond graphics."

For another example of technology becoming more rather than less human, JD Hooge points to the Xbox Kinect, a game and entertainment system that needs no controller; instead, the system reads users' gestures and voice commands for a much more direct human-to-technology interface. "The more you know about what's possible," Hooge says, "the more you come up with concepts that take advantage of what technology makes possible. The more you know about technology, the more you are allowed to wander into places you wouldn't otherwise go."

Or as the developers of openFrameworks point out, "The better tools you have, the better projects you can create."

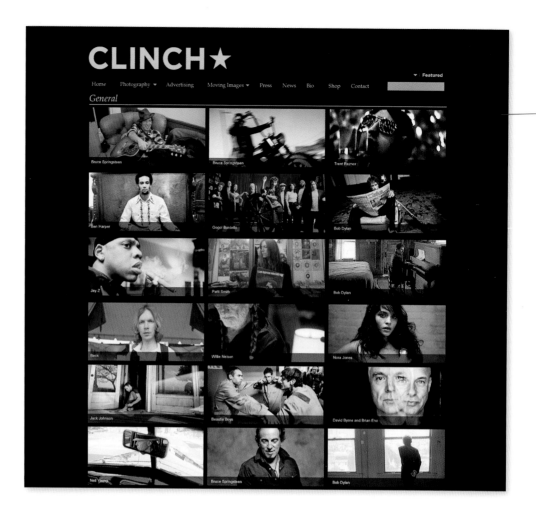

323

JD HOOGE

PLAN FOR AN OVERLOADED FUTURE

Technology has a distinct multiplier effect: an advancement here leads to several advancements there. And because the Internet is an open soapbox, more and more people are finding more and more ways to say more and more things. "There is a pattern developing of everything being distributed to smaller and smaller chunks," observes JD Hooge. "It will be an ongoing challenge to address all these different places where people will be seeing the content being put out there."

This proliferation will be a design challenge not only in sheer quantity but certainly in quality. "There's so much data, period," Hooge says, "people will hit a point where they are overwhelmed with options. That's going to affect the Web because people are so inundated they will pick and choose what kind of content to consume and when and where." A designer's job then becomes increasingly complex, as he or she seeks ways to stand out in the crowd while also helping create ways to make this blizzard of information relevant, interesting, and accessible.

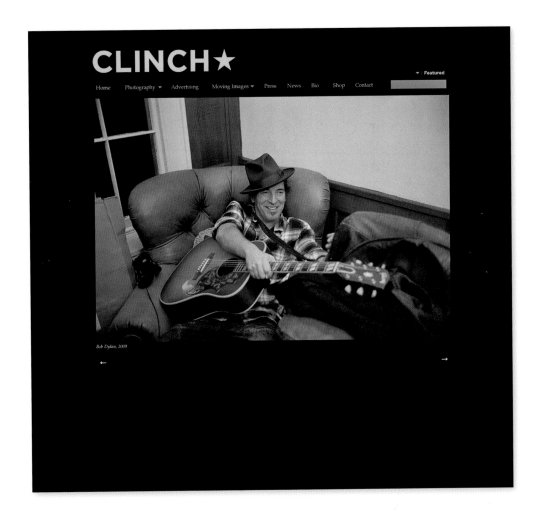

CLINCH★

Home Photography ▼ Advertising Moving Images ▼ Press News Bio Shop Contact

▼ Featured

Bob Dylan, 2009

324

MICHELLE
MCCARRICK TRUETT

THE ONLY CONSTANT IS CHANGE

"While website design entails the same approach to preplanning as print design, you have to dig a lot deeper," notes Michelle McCarrick Truett of 484 Design. "With print, you do the work, and the project goes off to the printer and it's done. With a website, it has no end. It's continually being revised." For these revisions to be meaningful and relevant, rather than wholesale re-dos, it's important to think about the direction the site might go tomorrow, even as you're figuring out how it will look today. As Truett notes, "You have to think about how it will evolve, where people will go, and what they'll do in future revisions."

Opposite and above: Danny Clinch Photography website, designed by Adam Larson of Adam&Co.

325

MICHELLE
MCCARRICK TRUETT

ADAM **LARSON**

DANIEL
SCHUTZSMITH

JD **HOOGE**

TRY TO KEEP UP

The tricks, techniques, and technologies are constantly evolving. There are endless new ways to do new things faster. And if you're working for yourself or in a small shop, staying current can be an even greater challenge. Fortunately, the digital world offers multiple solutions to the very problems it creates.

"When you're working for yourself, you don't have that camaraderie, and you're also not getting tips from people you work with," says Michelle McCarrick Truett. She then turns to ". . . webinars, seminars, and tutorials to keep fresh." Adam Larson uses Google Reader to subscribe to more than 700 resources across the topics of art, design, fashion, and technology. He confesses to "spending a lot more time scrolling than reading," but even a good skim is better than nothing at all. Daniel Schutzsmith is also an avid skimmer. "I skim tons of sources of information and pull up the ones I should pay attention to," he says. JD Hooge also scours the Internet for information about technology and figuring out how things work. "Whatever it is, there are endless amounts of people talking about it online. There's always some strange subculture of people talking about it and giving up tons of information, fortunately."

But Schutzsmith also utilizes some tried-and-true, old-fashioned techniques as well. "Observation is the biggest thing," he says. "Don't stay in your cubby. I go to conferences, and I'm always inspired by the people who are speaking. I've never gone and not taken away at least one big idea I can take away. The big ideas come when you're around other people."

326

ROBERTA
ROSENBERG

REMEMBER, THIS IS TECHNOLOGY IN SERVICE OF SELLING

"At the end of the day, this is all about selling stuff," Roberta Rosenberg says. "To be successful, you have to love selling stuff." 'Nuf said.

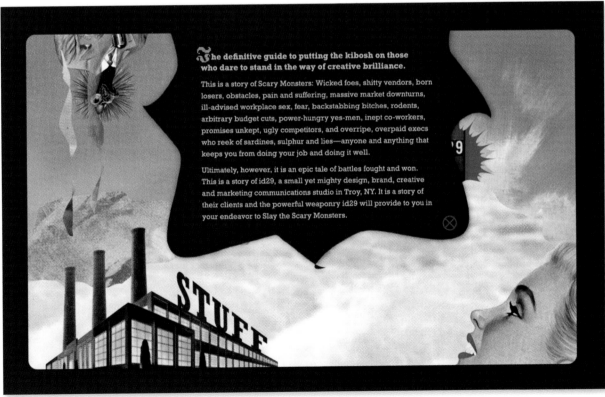

id29's self-promotional website, "Slay the Scary Monsters"

327

IN SPITE OF ALL THE RULES, ACCEPT THAT SCREEN DESIGN IS NOT A STEP-BY-STEP PROCESS

JD **HOOGE**

"I read something by Bruce Mau about how you don't need a patented process," JD Hooge muses. "There are lots of things that have to be done in each project—like planning, concepts, information architecture, visual design, etc.—but it doesn't have to be a linear process. You can start anywhere in that list, and as long as you eventually get to them all, you will be fine. Sometimes it starts with an abstract concept, but sometimes it starts with a visual design idea that leads to a concept. You get the idea."

"Slay the Scary Monsters" id29 self-promotional website

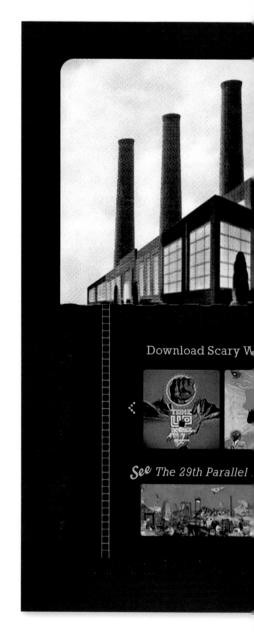

**Slay the
Scary Monsters**

....

The definitive guide to
putting the kibosh on
those who dare to stand in
the way of creative brilliance
and marketing success.
132 pages of awesomesauce.

Download
15.2 MB .PDF

Collect
them all!

UNITED, WE WILL WIN

geddon). 2010

SLAY the
SCARY
MONSTERS

Chapter Twelve

TECHNOLOGY AND DESIGN

328 ACKNOWLEDGE THE VALUE OF THE ANALOG PROCESS

HIDEKI **NAKAJIMA**

Like any comparable design firm anywhere in the world, Hideki Nakajima's office in Tokyo has Macintosh computers. Nakajima himself, however, does not use these machines. He comments, "I cannot use a Macintosh, but there is no problem because the staff can. Just as the invention of the electric guitar and synthesizer gave birth to rock-n-roll and techno music and the invention of the projector gave birth to film, new technology bears new means of expression. I'm trying to seek out the possibilities of new technology." This seemingly contradictory stance, which lauds technology as a catalyst and yet shies away from its use, stands at the center of Nakajima's approach to the process of graphic design.

Nakajima is no Luddite. On the contrary, his work is highly engaged with the way information is processed visually. Rather than impeding creativity, Nakajima feels that technology is a direct result of creativity. He notes, "I think the final state of the development of technology is the human being. For example, robots are improved to become more and more like a human being. Digital processes are inferior to analog. They only enhance design; they cannot replace it. Creativity starts with the human mind and hand."

In his piece "re-cycling," which consists of 40 pieces created for the Japanese design magazine *IDEA* in 2002, Nakajima reconstructed all of his work from the past into refigured designs. Although he calls his work "meaningless," the complex conceptual framework for this series does suggest that the reconfiguration and re-presentation of these highly abstracted images are as useful a process as their initial creation.

The reproduction of images by hand, through photographic or other processes, also influences Nakajima's images. He views computer-aided design as simply another way of treating an image, not more or less significant than other types of technological forms of reproduction. Each kind of reproductive process inserts its own meaning into the image, whether it is in a darkroom or at a copy machine. In fact, it is the fallibility of other technologies (particularly photography) that fascinates Nakajima, and he relishes accidents of color and light that can appear when using these methods.

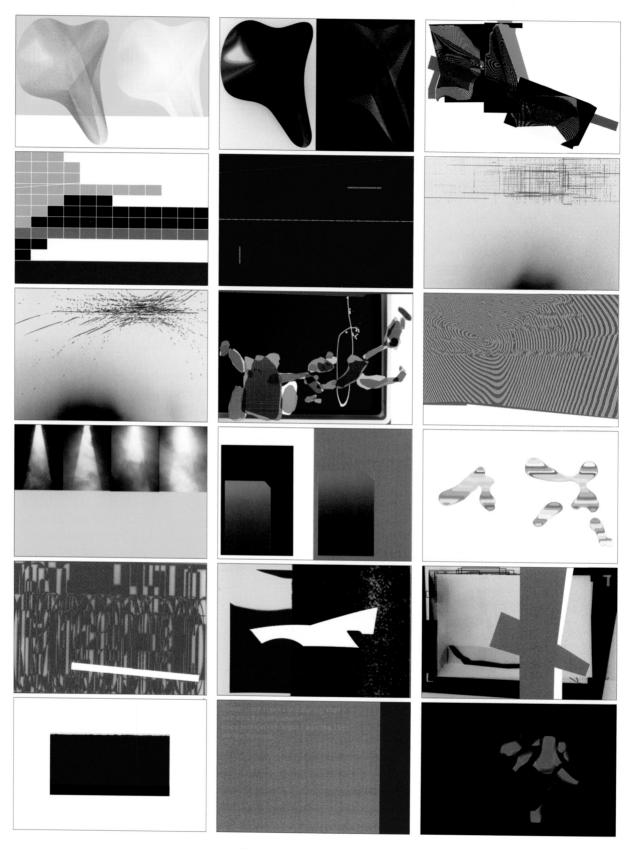

"re-cycling," designed by Hideki Nakajima

A Flock of Words, designed by Why Not Associates

329 USE COMPUTERS TO COMMUNICATE WITH STONE MASONS

WHY NOT ASSOCIATES

As part of a larger project for the small community of Morecambe, Why Not created a 300-yard (274 m) sidewalk out of type, steel, and stone. "A Flock of Words," as the path project is called, was a collaborative project between Why Not Associates, artist Gordon Young, and sculptor Russell Coleman.

"One of the reasons why this project was possible is technology," explains Andy Altmann of Why Not Associates. "I can give a disk to a steel manufacturer, and he can use that disk to cut out all the words using a laser. Also, a quarry can take the same file and sand-blast granite for us. You'd never be able to do this by hand—it would have taken forever, chiseling out all the lettering. Technology is working in strange ways, in antiquated areas. For example, stone masonry is making a comeback, and I find that quite fascinating. It is like learning to print all over again. Stone has a permanence about it that is interesting. To be able to walk over it and past it and around it—it is more interesting than a book."

The pathway, which is over 8.25 feet (2.5 m) wide and just over 350 yards (320 m) long, serves as a connection between the railway station and the seashore.

A Flock of Words, designed by Why Not Associates

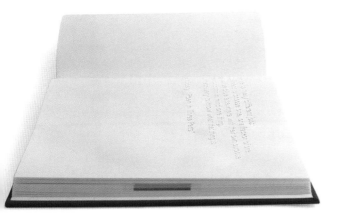
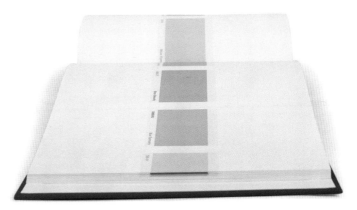

Peter Wegner, Blue, Open Studio CD packaging, designed by Todd Waterbury, Wieden+Kennedy, New York

330

TODD **WATERBURY**

MAKE DESIGN INVISIBLE

Former Wieden+Kennedy Art Director Todd Waterbury frequently collaborates with painter Peter Wegner. Asked by a gallery director to develop what might be called a "Peter Primer," Wegner asked Waterbury to work with him on the project. The final product ended up as a series of thoughts numbered from 1 to 69, each one being a definitive question or declarative idea about Wegner or the world. While reading it, the reader relates each new line to the previous line—each line builds on or subverts the others. Waterbury wanted to show how this pattern leads to a particular way of expanding or contracting the approach that Wegner takes to the world and to his work.

In trying to make the design of the project invisible, Waterbury asked the following questions: Is there a way through language that additional meaning can be given to something that is that simple? Can it be presented in a way that feels more memorable—that is designed but at the same time doesn't feel like design overwhelms the information?

The first thing Waterbury did was to look at the book as a small piece, all white with black text. The layout sequence is that the first statement appears on the bottom edge of the cover. As the reader turns the page, the first line moves up and its place is taken by the next statement, and so forth, each new statement taking

the place of the last, with each preceding one still visible to the reader. Waterbury wanted to express the statements a bit like movie credits, to demonstrate the interrelatedness of each statement but also its individuality. "It is another way of thinking about narrative. I was thinking about it through the form of a book that made use of the medium but tried to bend it a little bit at the same time."

A second example of this kind of "invisible" design is the CD packaging that Waterbury created for a series of recordings entitled *Found*. Russell Davies, the musician who developed the CD, asked friends to record their favorite sounds on cassette tape and then give him the sounds to mix into 16 songs. Waterbury cut a cassette tape in half and sandwiched it between the back of a jewel case and the outer cover. Behind the CD was a gnarled-looking knot of tape. On top was a small bag that contained a booklet with a lost-and-found sticker attached to it. "I tried to make it look like a collection of something you might see blowing in the street, something that had fallen out of someone's wallet or suitcase, that was then reassembled at a lost-and-found department. To me, it understood his intention and executed it in a way that embraced the vernacular, the world of lost and found, but didn't do it in a way that overtook the subject matter," Waterbury notes.

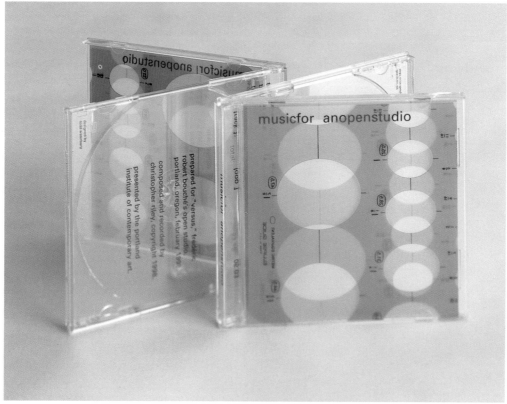

Studio Riley, Music for an Open Studio, designed by Todd Waterbury, Wieden+Kennedy, New York

331

RECOGNIZE THE LIMITS OF DIGITAL TECHNOLOGY FOR CREATIVE WORK

ED **FELLA**

There is a significant disconnect between Ed Fella's teaching and his art. He does not teach the hand-lettering and use of old commercial techniques for which his work is known. "It's not because I don't want to," he notes. "It's just that nobody really wants to learn it. Even my own daughter, who is a graphic designer, never asks me, 'How do you do this lettering?' People want to work with digital technology now. You can't really do anything in the contemporary commercial scene unless you can use the computer to make documents. I can still do what I do because I take my work to a printer, and he scans them in for me, makes the plates. He doesn't even have a camera anymore!"

Announcement Flyer, designed by Ed Fella

Ed Fella contends that now, in his seventies, he is too old to use a computer. When computers first became readily available nearly twenty years ago, he made a conscious decision not to use one because he didn't really do professional work anymore and consequently, didn't need it. "I wanted to explore the work I do, and I thought I'd waste a lot of time doing what the next generation is doing." Despite the fact that he doesn't use a computer, his work has had an important impact on designers who have learned from his unorthodox style. "I don't mind it, that history. If you look at *Meggs's History of Graphic Design*, between "Cranbrook" and "David Carson" is my paragraph. I made a link between that kind of stuff. David Carson went and took it all to the world, whereas in my case it was pretty academic stuff." Ed Fella's work serves as a formal source, which was then adapted by many artists who pushed the boundaries in new media.

When Fella won the Chrysler "Innovation in Design" award (a $10,000 prize), he wanted to do something with the money to improve his technical skills and abilities. He bought himself a video camera but admits to never having actually used it. "I wanted to do some motion stuff, but I never did. My daughter did. I was enticed, but I can't really do it. It's too hard. It's too much effort. I have a hard enough time learning how to do email. I had to hire a student to give me lessons." Although many exciting experiments in font technology were filtered through the unique lens of Ed Fella, he is content to never get himself too involved with technology. He quips sardonically, "Let the next generation do that, make a living doing it. Old guys should get out of the way."

DESIGN FOR THE EVERYDAY

Website page, self-promotion card, designed by Scott Santoro/Worksight

332

WORKSIGHT

LET YOUR SMALL SHOP THRIVE ON HIGH-TEC

The omnipresence of technology means that even a small shop like Worksight needs a website to thrive. Scott Santoro and his partner, Emily, learned to do HTML coding to create their first website in 1997. They soon upgraded to Adobe's GoLive Web development software and continue to educate themselves about the ins and outs of Web technology.

Santoro uses his website for all aspects of his small business operations, from marketing to client interaction to portfolio display. In addition, he has many clients in other cities with whom he communicates over the Internet. Although his shop is small, technological advances have made it easier for him to compete effectively.

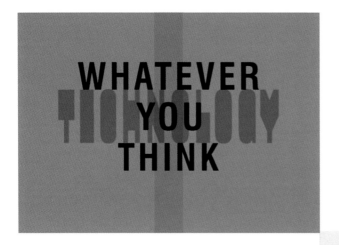

Xbox broadcast advertising, designed by Miles Murray Sorrell FUEL

333

MILES MURRAY SORRELL FUEL

WHATEVER YOU THINK, TECHNOLOGY IS IN CONTROL

Many of the comments made by FUEL about their work remain enigmatic and are, according to the designers, "meant to be subliminal, thought provoking, humorous statements" rather than an obvious description of work habits. In this instance, the sentiment is both paranoid and technophobic, although meant to be read ironically. In its extreme, this sentiment provides a backdrop for a whole intellectual tradition of paranoid technophobes and gives an interesting background to the work that FUEL does, which, like most designers, is highly dependent upon technology for its manifestation. The idea of anyone or anything being "in control" is in itself menacing, and yet what exactly technology is in control of is, in this instance, is not clear. FUEL provides the designer with a habit of mind rather than a habit of practice, abstracting the everyday relationship to technology in order to gain a new perspective on it.

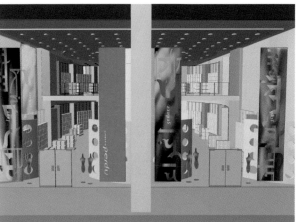

Perdu retail space designs, designed by Chase Design Group

334

REMEMBER THAT TECHNOLOGY SERVES YOU; YOU DO NOT SERVE TECHNOLOGY

CHASE DESIGN GROUP

The Chase Design Group uses the kinds of machines you would expect to see in a contemporary design office and two staff members serve as tech support. Although there are always issues with technology, at the Chase Design Group the tools are almost always working and always getting better.

Rather than seeking out new technology, Margo Chase is lucky to have people around her who tell her what she needs to know.

The Internet has proven to be invaluable to her work as well. "We have a website, of course, which is mainly a brochure, and we use the Internet for research and stock photography. We also buy a lot of supplies and other stuff online. Are we too connected? No. Email is the best invention ever. Technology is a tool, like a pencil. I use both, every day. Technology only helps unless you're lazy. If you're lazy you deserve what you get."

335

USE TECHNOLOGY IN UNEXPECTED WAYS

WHY NOT ASSOCIATES

The same technology that makes it possible for typographers to create new fonts also allows the art of typography to permeate spaces where it might not have previously been an active graphic element.

Why Not worked with frequent collaborator Gordon Young on "The Road to the Isles," a playground at the Auchterarder Community School in Scotland. Andy Altmann of Why Not notes, "As you walk into the playground you see a view looking over the fields and mountains toward the sea. What we wanted to do is to put the view into a map on the floor, so

as you walk toward this view you walk over what you are seeing—the A-roads, the rivers, and the coastline. There are benches made from the letters that spell out the names of the mountains, such as the Gramkind Mountains. We've done all these things on the floor, and we wanted to go up in the air a bit."

Translating typographic elements into materials such as wood and steel is not a new process, but the consistency provided by computerized fabrication systems makes possibilities that were previously unavailable.

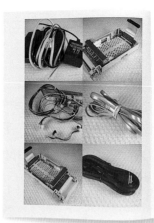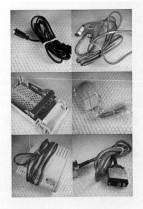

336

RUDY **VANDERLANS**

ZUZANA **LICKO**

WORK WITH EMERGING TECHNOLOGIES

Rudy VaderLans has a utilitarian approach to the use and adoption of technology. When Emigre was started, bitmapped fonts were the only kind of computer font available. FedEx, the Internet, and cell phones didn't exist. VanderLans and Zuzana Licko were still pasting down text galleys with rubber cement. He had never used a computer in his life. When the 128k Mac was first introduced, VanderLans and Licko bought one.

They were challenged to figure out how they could best use this machine with all its short-comings. There was great resistance to the Macintosh in the design community when it first came out. Designers laughed at them for using it. VanderLans and Licko, with a small group of fellow believers, were among the first to try out this new tool. They hooked a video camera to their Mac to capture low-resolution black-and-white still images and made movies with the first video-editing software. They even sold fonts online before the advent of the World Wide Web, long before anybody else did, using bulletin board software.

When you're out on the edge, you run the risk of becoming too focused on making the technology work, and design and ideas start to take a backseat. VanderLans recalls, "Shortly after PostScript was introduced, we found this guy who was able to hook his Mac to a photo setter, allowing us for the first time ever to output high-resolution fonts onto photographic paper. We would drive over to San Francisco with our files on floppy disks and sit there for hours downloading this stuff, never knowing if it would work."

Calling the new technology "impenetrable and expensive," VanderLans now lets the computer take a backseat in his design work. Although he professes to no longer be "chasing the latest gadgets and software," Emigre continues to fuel the imaginations of young designers whose relationship to technology is ever-changing.

Emigre magazine: issue 56 (above), Emigre font catalog (right), designed by Rudy VanderLans

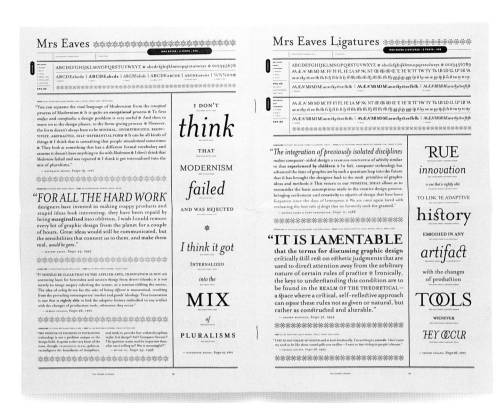

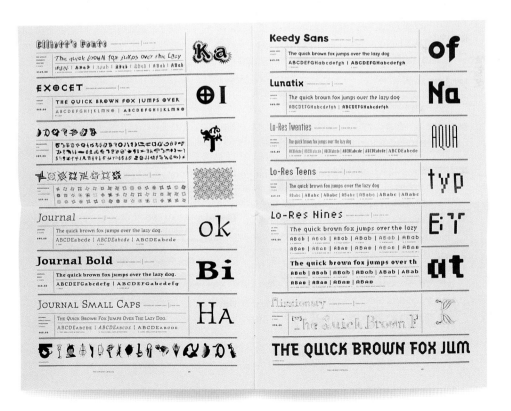

Blue corporate identity, designed by Why Not Associates

337 MAKE FRIENDS WITH PEOPLE WHO KNOW A TECHNOLOGY THAT YOU WANT TO LEARN

WHY NOT ASSOCIATES

The designers at Why Not have been interested in film from the beginning and have slowly built up a relationship with broadcast technology by teaching themselves how to work in this medium. Why Not does a lot of TV work in-house now, and they have developed a small edit facility—"a studio in a little glass box with a very big Mac and lots of hard drives coming off of it," says Andy Altmann.

Why Not has created corporate identities for several video-editing facilities. Because of this work, they have had a lot of contact with the video and film industry—in fact, one of their clients gave them a screen for their video-editing suite. They weren't scared of trying to do it themselves, but if the money is available on a project, they will go to an edit facility. "They obviously know more about it than we do. We hire an After Effects specialist to help us sometimes. He knows all about broadcast qualities and what is expected."

Close contact with experts in allied fields can not only create practical alliances and impromptu education, but it can also expand the capabilities of your design studio.

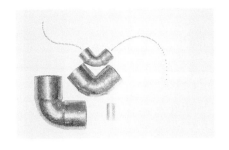

scott w santoro worksight
46 great jones street
new york new york 10012-1162
graphic design services

t 212.777.3558 • f 212.475.9098
www.worksight.com

Self-promotional cards, designed by Scott Santoro/Worksight

338 DEVELOP AN OVERARCHING TECHNOLOGY METAPHOR

WORKSIGHT

Scott Santoro of Worksight has developed a metaphor that informs and deepens all the work he does. "I live on a street that has a construction company, a trucking company, a sandblasting shop, a welder, and a firehouse. It is a very short block and a very active street." The Worksight studio literally sits in a worksite.

Everything that Worksight does derives from an approach that respects the metaphors available to the designer via the industrial world. Worksight's visual language, their point of view, has been a kind of proposition. According to Santoro, plumbing has everything to do with graphic design. "It started out as a joke that I didn't quite believe myself, but the more I looked, the more I found that it would be a great metaphor to use. Plumbing is also my family's trade: my uncles, my father, my cousins—they are all plumbers. I, by contrast, went to art school. Plumbing became a layer, part of my 'everyday' approach that is embedded in there somehow. It is satisfying to have hit upon such an appropriate metaphor, especially one that is flexible enough to allow me to understand design through it."

Santoro uses a pipe connector as an icon to pique the curiosity of people who view his work. Fragments of an industrial world keep reappearing in his designs. "I find that these lunch boxes, wrenches, and pipes convey an honest beauty, a rugged integrity of purpose. And they can be surprisingly architectural or sculptural. I strive to reveal the beauty in the product, and when a company is proud of who it is and what it makes, then it can afford to be honest and direct. An intrinsic approach is more likely to connect with a diverse audience, which includes not just lawyers, teachers, and students but also mechanics, carpenters, and plumbers."

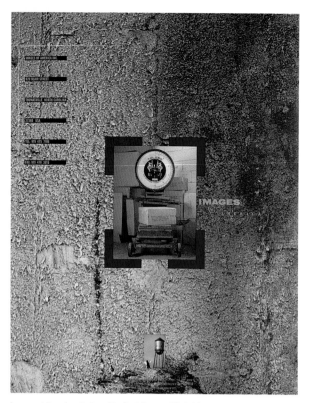

Images of America, designed by Scott Santoro/Worksight

339

WORKSIGHT

IT'S OK TO NOT GO MULTIMEDIA

In the current climate of ubiquitous new technology, deciding to stay within a defined realm of graphic design is not an obvious choice. Scott Santoro, whose work reflects a commitment to a basic constructive aesthetic, understands that the bells and whistles of the new media are not all they're cracked up to be.

At one time, Scott says that he worried his team had missed the boat. "Brand-new, 50-person graphic design studios were opening. Students to whom I had just finished teaching graphic design were starting Web firms and within a half-year had 50 people on staff. I was feeling like I just had a little mom-and-pop shop here, and my student, who had just graduated, had a big staff—it just didn't make sense. Then I realized, I just do what I do. I'm not going to turn this technology away, but I will layer it into what I do and not reinvent myself because of the hype."

"I tend to be a traditional graphic designer. I love to do print; I started in that. One of my professors from Pratt, Charles Goslin, did a presentation for the AIGA. He said, 'I'm content to be a cobbler, cobbling away in my studio, enjoying the craft of the thing as well as the thinking. As far as I'm concerned, just cobbling out stuff is fine with me. If I had a shoe store, I'd be cobbling away at the shoes and enjoying the craft of producing nice pieces.' There is a certain self-satisfaction in that. The flow of the craft of graphic design is really nice."

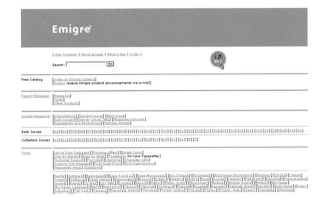

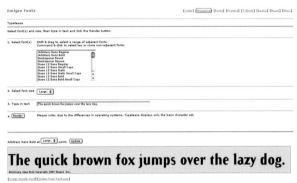

Web pages, designed by Zuzana Licko

340

USE THE COMPUTER AS A BUSINESS TOOL AS WELL AS A CREATIVE TOOL

RUDY **VANDERLANS**

ZUZANA **LICKO**

Although Rudy VanderLans and Zuzana Licko were inspired by computer technology when they founded Emigre, they now use technology primarily as a servant for their business. VanderLans comments, "Our website is listed in all our catalogs, our magazine, and our ads we run in other magazines. Emigre was selling fonts, magazines, T-shirts, and music long before the Internet and the World Wide Web came about. The Web simply made it easier to sell our products, particularly the fonts. Because they are a digital product—meaning they can be bought and sent out on the Web—roughly 80 to 90 percent of our total sales happen online."

Although VanderLans claims that he is not searching out new technology—or at least not at the rate he used to—he does use the computer daily for his work. "I really like how the PDF format has become the standard for transferring and sharing design files. It has made work flow so much more efficiently. And of course, as a type foundry, I'm thrilled by the notion that the format allows people to send and share files without sending and sharing the actual font files."

Chapter Thirteen:

ACHIEVING BALANCE

341

STEVE **GORDON, JR**

DON'T FORGET THE REST OF LIFE

This is perhaps the most important habit of all. It's all about balance. Especially when you're starting out, the temptation is to put everything you've got—time, money, energy, resources—into this new baby called your business. But that's not healthy for you, which means it's not healthy for your business, since your business is simply a product of you and your ideas. Let's speak plainly: The ideal is to work as much as necessary to be able to afford the things that will make life not just livable, but enjoyable. So what good is having the money to have those things if you don't give yourself the time to enjoy them as well?

"'Yeah, but it's not just a job,' you say. 'It's a career. It's my business. It's my future.' This is all true, but if you don't take some time to enjoy today, the future is going to come and go and you will have missed it. One must find a place for work within life, not in spite of or outside of it. After all, life came first."

HOWie Zine 2 "Road Trip" illustration and design by
Steve Gordon, Jr, RDQLUS

North Lawndale College Prep capital campaign materials design, designed by Steve Gordon, Jr, RDQLUS

342

STEVE **GORDON, JR**

ENJOY THE TIME OFF

"Make yourself feel OK with having downtime. Give yourself some minigoals or time frames. Perhaps set aside four hours of your workday for developing new business in some way and then the rest of your day can be spent any way you like."

It will help you feel more focused and productive if you organize your downtime like it's real work time. But let's face it, you can't spend ten hours a day on new business development.

There are not enough leads out there, and you'll burn out and be ineffective at representing yourself. So once you've done something that's productive for the long-term health of your business, do something that's productive for the long-term health of *you*. Go take a hike. Visit your mom. Read a book. Grab that dusty fishing pole. Take a nap. There have undoubtedly been plenty of late nights and weekends spent working; you have to remember that at least some part of downtime can be considered payback.

343

STEVE **GORDON, JR**

GET A LIFE

"Starting your own business can be an all-consuming affair. Especially in the first year when you've had so much to do to get up and running and then to keep up with that first influx of work. There were undoubtedly many nights and weekends devoted to your new baby, your business. In the process, there are friends who have gone uncontacted, books left unread, sock drawers left unsorted, and relatives who've had real babies.

Think back to the days when you left work at someone else's office at the end of the day or week. Did you have a hobby? What about that macramé class you've always wanted to take? How about that girl you met and never got around to asking out? How's that new coffee shop you still haven't tried? If you have some downtime, your best first step might be to look in the mirror and reacquaint yourself with the person you find there."

When I'm weak I draw strength from you
and when you're lost I'll show you how to change your mood
even though we are apart we are each other's destiny

ASCENSION

VNDK8 Freestyle Equipment Co., Ascension apparel artwork, designed by Steve Gordon, Jr, RDQLUS

Sphere magazine, designed by Mark Randall, WorldStudio, Inc. and Worldstudio Foundation

344

MARK **RANDALL**

DEVELOP A SOCIAL AGENDA

The unique integration of Worldstudio, Inc. and the Worldstudio Foundation sets this organization apart. David Sterling and Mark Randall started the foundation before creating their design studio. Their goal was to have a business, but they first wanted to prioritize the mission of the nonprofit organization that became the Worldstudio Foundation. They discovered that it was impossible to merge the interests of a business with their socially active work, so the foundation and Worldstudio, Inc. developed as distinct entities.

The umbrella mission of the foundation is to involve creative professionals in socially and environmentally aware projects. The most overt manifestation of the foundation work is the magazine *Sphere*, which is published approximately once a year and features projects of the foundation as well as global concerns of the foundation. The magazine is a forum for the creative work of Worldstudio and provides ongoing inspiration for the staff of the design studio. It is also the arena in which the cross-pollination between the studio and the foundation occurs.

Specific foundation initiatives include a scholarship program with an emphasis on supporting diversity and support for creative people who build a social agenda into their work in some way. The foundation also has a mentorship program in which creative professionals are paired to work on community-based projects. For example, high school students team up with working graphic designers and artists to create billboards against gun violence, a newspaper on homophobia, or a poster series on tolerance. The end results are displayed in the public arena. Through these programs, high school students are exposed to a variety of career opportunities and are able to learn how they can use the power of creativity to give back to their communities.

Everything that the foundation does nurtures the idea of making artists and designers—whether they be high-school-aged students, college students, or professionals—more socially and environmentally aware and giving them tools, ideas, and inspiration to use their creativity for positive social change.

with more than one million people, has become the largest refugee camp in the world. Emmanuel Rucagoza is the boy on the extreme right.

WISH YOU WEREN'T HERE

Worldstudio foundation

spher9

Wish you were here

Cleared by U.S. Military

Wish you were here...

difference denied...

345 DEVELOP LONG-TERM RELATIONSHIPS WITH NONPROFIT ORGANIZATIONS

STEFAN **SAGMEISTER**

Sagmeister aimed to do about a third of its work for socially relevant causes. In 2002, Sagmeister teamed up with True Majority—a group of 500 business people under the leadership of Ben Cohen, one of the founders of Ben and Jerry's Ice Cream—who had put together a 10-point program to influence national leadership in left-leaning political causes. Some members saw it as a preventative measure against another 9/11; some saw it as a plan for the United States to improve its behavior in the world; some saw it as a group that makes the world a better place. It is a program with very wide goals with some being specific, like paying U.N. dues willingly, and some vast, like trying to solve the problem of world hunger.

Although True Majority didn't get off the ground until late 2002, Sagmeister started working on this project in 2001, doing everything from identity packages and brochures to cars that travel the East Coast, drawing attention to the cause.

At first, Sagmeister worked for True Majority for free, but the workload became so massive that they either had to recommend True Majority to somebody else or get paid for the overhead costs of doing the project. Fortunately, the client was able to afford the reduced rate. Sagmeister stuck with the project because it not only reflected his political values but also allowed him significant creative freedom.

True Majority promotional materials, designed by
Stefan Sagmeister

346

MARK RANDALL

ADDRESS LOCAL, IMMEDIATE NEEDS

Although the Worldstudio Foundation is wholly devoted to the aims of education and empowerment, Worldstudio, Inc. limits its involvement with social causes.

Worldstudio feels a commitment to support community need. Located in New York, Worldstudio was in the thick of the fallout from 9/11. When one of their clients, a business improvement district in New York, asked them to contribute some time on a pro-business, pro-downtown project, they felt compelled to respond and help in the most effective manner they could. Worldstudio created messaging that conveyed a return to life as normal—and not just any life, but a fun-loving life with shopping and going to the theater—in a visual landscape that was devastated and a business climate of severe dislocation and decline. Worldstudio created buttons, banners, posters, and T-shirts, which were very popular and copied widely all over the city. Like Milton Glaser's "I [heart] New York More Than Ever," this campaign shows a team of designers responding to a very local, very fundamental need within their own community. It not only went a long way in providing a visual reminder of hope, but its relevance also gave the designers a sense of satisfaction in being able to help so close to home.

Fight Back NY! post-9/11 economic support campaign, designed by Mark Randall, WorldStudio, Inc.

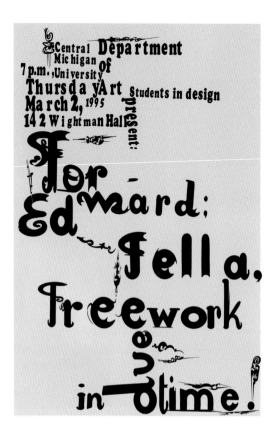

347

ED **FELLA**

USE THE ROBIN HOOD THEORY

Ed Fella worked throughout the seventies for arts organizations in and around Detroit. In addition to designing Detroit Focus Quarterly, a local art magazine, he did thousands of posters on which he would execute his typographic experiments. He contributed his design time as well as the facilities of the shop in which he was working. To get new typefaces, which at that time had to be purchased, he would piggyback the typeface from a paying job onto pro bono jobs. "I'd do a job for a car company for which we'd put on a few lines of type and send it out, so I'd get the type. I'd use the studio facilities. I couldn't have done that work if I didn't have a job. I couldn't be a starving artist and do this pro bono work. I never made a penny on it. Now it costs so little, I never have to pay much for printing."

"My work for nonprofits was entirely based on the fact that I had this big studio at my fingertips. I had the board to do the mechanicals, type, wax, pencils—all of that. I would always give credit to the company I worked at—they didn't mind. It wasn't like I was taking work money away from them. They probably threw more stuff away than I used for the arts organization anyway. I robbed Peter to pay Paul."

Announcement flyer, designed by Ed Fella

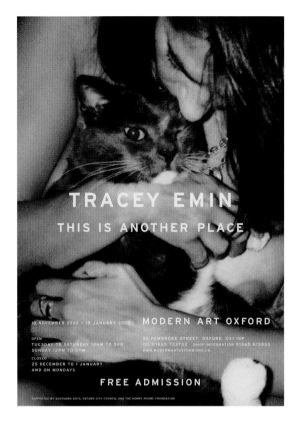

348

MILES MURRAY SORRELL FUEL

MINIMIZE TRAVEL EXPENSES—WORK WITH YOUR NEIGHBORS

Miles Murray Sorrell FUEL worked for the White Cube art gallery in nearby Hoxton Square in London. "The Steven Meisel catalog is just one of the catalogs we have designed for their shows. We started working with Tracey Emin, who lives a few doors down from our studio, through our work with White Cube. We designed the poster and invitation for her New York show and all related material for her Oxford show including poster, leaflets, and catalog. We continue to work with her on major publications of her work," notes Damon Murray.

Tracey Emin poster, Steven Meisel book cover, designed by Miles Murray Sorrell FUEL

349

CREATE HIGHLY VISIBLE AND CULTURALLY CONSEQUENTIAL DESIGN BY WORKING FOR CLIENTS IN EDUCATION AND THE ARTS

JOHN C **JAY**

One of Wieden+Kennedy's clients in Tokyo is the Kumon Learning Institute, which teaches a particular method of learning mathematics and languages. John C Jay notes, "One of the reasons we opened in Japan is to really tie into areas that were socially and culturally significant. One of the great areas of change is the educational system."

As of April 2002, Japanese children no longer had six school days a week. Japanese families suddenly had free time on Saturdays, forever transforming the way that people think about education. Jay notes, "Now that parents have to take responsibility for their children, they're asking, 'What do I do with that extra day?' 'Do I give it to them for free time?' 'Do give them other types of education, in sports or arts?' 'Do I send them to a cram school or a Kumon Institute?' 'What do I do with that day that formerly was used for education?'"

In addition to this massive change in the school week, the Japanese were also experiencing a movement that advocated children's self-sufficiency and free thinking. "Kumon is a great outlet for us to talk about these issues," Jay notes. Any involvement in the change in educational structures is fundamental to the change in Japanese culture.

Wieden+Kennedy also undertook a project with Mori Building, a preeminent builder in Japan, which helped secure their place of status in the art world. Mori Building launched the largest-ever post-war redevelopment of a 28-acre area in Tokyo called Roppongi Hills, which opened in 2003. The centerpiece of this development is a 53-story tower, with the top five floors devoted to the arts. In developing the branding and strategic thinking for Roppongi Hills, Jay knew that the museum and galleries would be an important symbolic and cultural beacon. "Our first assignment was working with Mori Building as strategic planners, as design consultants. One of the first tangible things we did was a mission statement book for everyone who works at Roppongi Hills to help them understand how this city will be different—how and why it is not just a real estate development, what the mission statement of Mr. Mori is, what the goals of building this city are . . . Being involved in the mission statement for the city itself has been a wonderful exercise intellectually, sitting there with the president and talking about the motivations behind this project, how it is going to be different, how it is going to tap into the rest of Tokyo and the rest of the world."

Kumon campaign, designed by John C Jay, Wieden+Kenney, Tokyo

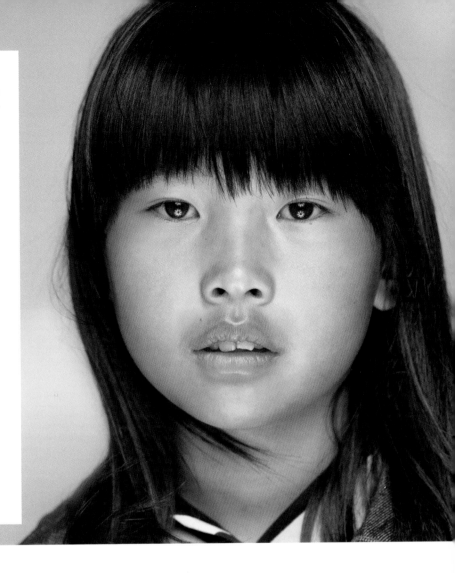

わたしは今、
何を勉強すれば
いいんですか？

この国そして世界は今、多くの問題を抱え、ますます複雑で大変な時代を迎えようとしています。
そんな21世紀をたくましく生きていくために、子どもたちは今こそ「生きる力」を必要としています。
学校だけが子どもの「生きる力」を担うものではないし、そもそも教育は、国、地域、そしてわたしたち自身に
大きく関わる問題であるはずです。子どもは今、何を勉強すればいいのでしょうか。

KUMONは、「高い基礎学力」こそが、
「生きる力」につながると信じています。
わたしたちは、子どもたちが将来どんな道に進む上でも、読解力・数学的分析力・論理的思考力が
必要だと考えています。本を読み、その意味を正確に理解する力であり、いくつかの事例を論理的に組み上げ、
仮説を立てたり解決策を導き出したりする力です。その土台になるのが「読み書き、計算、英語力」の基礎学力です。
KUMONの教室では、子どもたちはこの基礎学力を確実に身につけていきます。

KUMONには確信する学習法があります。
子どもたちから学んだ「個人別学習」と「自学自習」です。
子どもたちは、伸びる機会と方法が等しく与えられるべきだと思います。
そして、それを先生が一方的に「教える」のではなく、子どもが自ら「学びとる」ことが大切なのだと思います。
KUMONは、一斉授業のように同じ学年の子どもに同じことをさせるのではなく、学年の枠を取り払い、
子ども一人ひとりに合った「ちょうどの学習レベル」を「自力」で解き進む、「個人別学習・自学自習」を実践しています。
「教室に新しく入会する生徒には、先ず学力テストをして公文式の何教材の何番から勉強を始めるかをきめます。
 そのきめかたは、生徒がこのあたりから習いたいと思っている内容のところから始めるのではありません。
 この生徒なら五分以内でできるだろうというところから勉強を始めるのです」公文公（くもんとおる・公文式の創始者）
KUMONの教室では、誰もが「100点」の経験をします。
「自分にもできた」という達成感を味わい、「やれば できる」という自信もつく。
人生から逃げない、チャレンジする力はここから生まれるのだとわたしたちは信じています。

KUMONには、つねに進化し続ける「教材」があります。
個人別学習・自学自習を可能にしているのは、スモールステップで構成されたKUMONの教材です。
「生徒たちが勉強しやすいように、段階のゆるやかな自習教材をつくる。多くの生徒たちが勉強してきた
 実例を検討して教材の改訂を進めていく。これをわたしたちは、ずっと続けてきたことになります」公文公
わたしたちが指導事例の研究そして教材改訂を休むことなく続けていけるのは、「なんとしてもこの子を伸ばしたい」
という強い思いからです。だから、KUMONの教材をつくっているのは子どもたちである、ともいえるのです。

KUMONは、親の愛情から始まった教育でした。
公文式教育の原点は、公文公という一人の高校教師が、長男公文毅（くもんたけし）におこなった算数の家庭教育。
どうすればわが子の算数の力を伸ばすことができるか、公文公は無理なく続けられる工夫が必要である、と試行錯誤の末、
子どもが自力で解く教材を、手書きでつくりあげました。息子は自習で問題を解き進み、小学生で微積分の計算へと
進みました。それに合わせて、父親の教材作成や指導法の研究も休みなく進められたのでした。
「悪いのは子どもではない。悪いのは教材であり指導法であり指導者である」公文公
公文式教育の原点ともよべるこの考え方は、第1号の指導者の第1号の生徒への指導の実践から、培われたものでした。

「子どもたちの未来のために」。
今、この時代だからこそ、公文式教育の役割は大きい。そう、確信しています。

KUMONの考えをまとめた小冊子『生きる力〜21世紀の子どもたちのために〜』を読んでください。
教育について、あなたのご意見もお聞かせください。

お申し込み・郵便番号・住所、氏名、年齢、電話番号をお明記の上、下記まで、インターネットや電話でも受け付けております。
〒532-8511 大阪市淀川区西中島5-6-6 日本公文教育研究会「生きる力」編集局
フリーダイヤル 0120-372-100（土・日・祝日を除く、9時30分から17時30分まで）www.kumon.ne.jp
『生きる力』をテーマとした教育雑誌を全国各地で開催しています。入場無料です。開催日時、開催会場、場所、講師など上記ホームページにご案内しています。上記ホームページでご覧いただけます。
※上記のフリーダイヤルでもご案内しています。お気軽にお問い合わせください。皆さまのご来場を心よりお待ちしています。

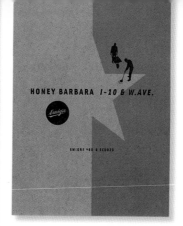

Emigre magazine: issue 60, designed by Rudy VanderLans and Zuzana Licko, Emigre

350 INTEGRATE YOUR POLITICS WITH YOUR CREATION

RUDY **VANDERLANS**

ZUZANA **LICKO**

Rudy VanderLans of Emigre has discovered that doing projects for nonprofit organizations is not the only way to give back to the community. He believes that anyone can be of great service to society by simply considering the impact that daily actions have on society and the environment and acting accordingly. For example, a graphic designer can align himself or herself with clients—and not necessarily nonprofit clients—that contribute in a positive way. VanderLans notes, "If it wasn't for so many exploitative, wasteful, and obscenely unscrupulous businesses, there would hardly be a need for nonprofits because they usually exist to right the many wrongs created by the aforementioned businesses."

Emigre is unique because its designers do not run a service-oriented business—they create their own products. Thus, their responsibilities involve how they use their resources. "I am proud that our catalogs and magazines are often printed on paper with very high recycled content and are often processed chlorine-free, which is much more expensive than nonrecycled paper. This represents a more direct way to support environmental causes than giving money to, let's say, Earth First, or doing pro bono work for them," says VanderLans.

Emigre magazine provided a unique forum for communicating with the public. Emigre feels a degree of responsibility toward their design community, and they take their work seriously. In the magazine, they wrote about design, about the process, and about its effect on culture. "I think it is healthy for graphic design to have this constant probe going on. To look at what motivates designers, to question the work—we can all learn from each other. We're proud of contributing to that in a small way."

Student work, designed by Loan Lam, Worksight

351

WORKSIGHT

TEACH

In economic terms, being an adjunct instructor is a bum deal. The days are long, and the work can be taxing. In emotional terms, it is a labor of love that returns to its practitioner a sense of satisfaction and accomplishment rarely found in other pursuits.

Scott Santoro and his partner Emily have been teaching classes at Pratt for years but they do not do it for the money. "In terms of the output of our little company, it is a lot," Santoro notes. But the payback is enormous.

"One of my students was discussing deconstruction with another professor, and the professor said, 'You should go talk to Scott about that.' So I invited the student over for an hour. We talked, and I showed him work. I think he went away even more confused than when he got here. It is OK though; critical conversations tend to be like that. The great thing for me was that we were both intellectually engaged in the middle of a workday. How many people can claim that during the week?

I see students really take off with their work. Helping to set the wheels in motion for them is wonderful because they come back to you years later with their eyes glowing, so happy to see you, thanking you for helping them with a piece of something—more than just the job of design. That's what makes it worth it."

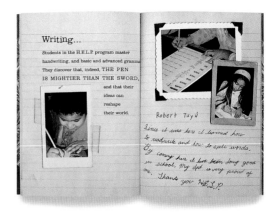

Left and opposite: Hollywood Education and Literacy Project (HELP), designed by the Chase Design Group

352 DON'T FEEL OBLIGATED TO DO CHARITY WORK

CHASE DESIGN GROUP

"I don't believe anyone is obligated to do charity or pro bono work," remarks Margo Chase. "It is a choice that we have the luxury to make because the business is successful enough to be able to give away work and still provide for our staff. If I had to choose between my ability to provide for the people who work here and doing pro bono work, I would choose the staff."

Although she does not believe that designers have any greater responsibility to society and the culture at large than other professionals, the Chase Design Group does work with the Hollywood Education and Literacy Project (HELP) annual fund-raising campaign.

"I strongly believe in supporting literacy education. HELP provides reading instruction to anyone who needs it—old, young, rich, or poor. Everyone's enthusiastic and excited, and they have a terrific success rate. They allow us to bring our own vision to their promotions, so we have a lot of creative freedom. In addition, several friends and a few clients support them, so it's an easy relationship for us."

Two pieces that the firm created recently are part of a continuing series of books about HELP. Chase Design Group mailed these pieces to a list of friends and supporters of HELP in the hopes of raising money, and they have been very successful so far. Each book focuses on a different aspect of HELP. The first piece provides an overview of the program using existing shots of kids and their written testimonials. Chase wanted it to have a handmade, intimate feel—a little like a reading primer or storybook. The second one focuses on a compelling case study involving a child with ADD. Both pieces present HELP's work in a friendly but realistic way, without shouting or banner waving. Chase Design Group felt it was important to capture the personal, one-on-one nature of their teaching and coaching by presenting each piece in an intimate style.

Despite her work with HELP, Chase notes, "I think doing free work is a burden for many small firms who are just scraping by. We are a much larger business now and profitable enough to be able to put resources to work for free when we choose."

I felt I had no way out, and agreed to have him be part of a research study for ADD medication.

"DERANGED"?

"WANDERING CHILD?"

"ATTENTION DEFICIT DISORDER?"

They called him a *wandering child* always day-dreaming. He may suffer from some sort of "Attention Deficit Disorder" the teachers suggested. If you look up the word disorder it means a *disruption; a breach of public peace; a riot; a disregard of system; ill; deranged.* My beautiful child "deranged?"

I did my best to tutor him, but soon Fabian was given evaluations at school. The teachers felt he may fail again.

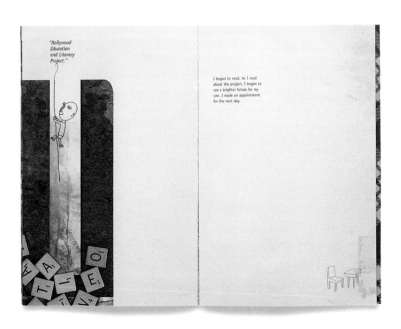

"Hollywood Education and Literacy Project."

I began to read. As I read about the project, I began to see a brighter future for my son. I made an appointment for the next day.

"MY WONDERFUL CHILD"

Amanaka'a newsletter, designed by Scott Santoro/Worksight

353

WORKSIGHT

KEEP IN TOUCH WITH YOUR NONPROFIT CLIENTS

Scott Santoro of Worksight had worked with an organization called Amanaka'a, which supported tribal people in the Amazon region. Santoro helped them create a newsletter every three or four months and designed T-shirts.

The organization ended up folding, in part because they were competing against a much bigger organization—the Rainforest Network—which was started by the musician Sting and had a much more mainstream cachet and popularity. Fortunately for Santoro, many of the people from Amanaka'a followed their political convictions to the Rainforest Network.

Santoro got a call from the Rainforest Network about a possible job. It turned out that they needed an annual report and a calendar and, because of the ties he had forged years before, he was able to show his work at the new organization. They ended up awarding him the project. "They don't pay like a corporation would pay, but they do have a budget. Of course, they will be getting a good deal because they will be getting a ton of energy from me," Santoro says.

Worldstudio capabilities brochure, designed by Scott Santoro/Worksight

354

PARTNER WTH LIKE-MINDED FIRMS

"An average amount of money was involved in this project but an above-average amount of my own interest because my work was for a cause I really believe in. I enjoy working with an organization that has values so near to my own thinking about design and design education," comments Scott Santoro on his collaboration with Worldstudio, Inc.

Worksight and Worldstudio, Inc. collaborated on a project because Scott Santoro knew David Sterling from his old studio, Doublespace. "Cranbrook grads knew about that studio because he and Jane Kostrin were past graduates of the school and were able to create a successful practice in New York City," Santoro says.

While Santoro was on the board of the New York AIGA chapter, he met with Sterling to see how AIGA and Worldstudio might support each other in fostering design education. When Sterling was planning a fund-raising auction

for Worldstudio, Inc., he asked Worksight to contribute a piece, which they did, and it was auctioned for a few hundred dollars. When Sterling and Mark Randall were thinking of bringing another designer in to help reinvent their newsletter and capabilities brochure, they thought of Worksight.

Santoro says, "I was really honored that they asked. I respect and keep all the Worldstudio promotions sent to me over the years and consider their approach to be similar to my own. They aren't afraid of form and enjoy presenting rich text and graphics. We were immediately on the same page. They also hired a good writer, Rachel Kash, as part of the brochure project, which meant that we could build something that both said and read in conceptual harmony."

Developing political alliances can work to the advantage of a designer, particularly when allied organizations share aesthetic styles.

355

USE CLIENT WORK TO COLLABORATE WITH YOUNG, NEW ARTISTS

JOHN C **JAY**

Campaigns for Nike Japan garnered respect and admiration for Wieden+Kennedy, Tokyo, even though they are a relatively young and Western-owned business. Creative director John C Jay cites his company's involvement with the most exciting young artists in Asia and the United States as some of his primary inspirations. He commented that the idea for Presto during its conception had been "the idea behind the shoe itself, the idea of 'instant go,' which encourages young people—and all people—to be physically active, mentally active, socially active, and creatively active."

Jay asked Storm, a.k.a. David Ellis from the Barnstormers in New York, to be the artistic director for the Presto work. "He represents the whole post-graffiti generation of artists who are internationally famous on the street, known around the world to young people," explains Jay. With his help, Wieden+Kennedy chose a young painter, Sasuke, from the Naka Meguro area of Tokyo, as well as a Chinese painter named Frek. They next asked an up-and-coming Japanese DJ to participate. "We assembled everyone in a giant studio in Los Angeles, built

glass walls, and had each painter respond to the others. They painted on top of moving images from Shanghai and Tokyo, responded to the music of DJ Uppercut, and responded to each other, and each one spurred the other one on. It was a three day, nonstop, collaboration of painting and creation."

In addition to the artists, Jay added team members who were experts in motion graphics and digital technology. "We used our knowledge of technology, very much inspired by Presto, very much inspired by Nike's way of working, with their famous R&D labs, always adding technology to our artistic endeavors, and what we helped these painters to do is lift their art off the two-dimensional wall and make it travel in three dimensions throughout the cities in Japan and China. We created a DVD and a two-minute commercial that we aired in Japan." This collaboration not only provided Nike with a truly fresh look, but also helped to elevate up-and-coming artists.

Presto 4, designed by John C Jay, Wieden+Kenney, Tokyo

356

WORKSIGHT

PROVIDE SERVICE TO YOUR DESIGN COMMUNITY

Working with the New York chapter of AIGA allowed Scott Santoro of Worksight to do work that he found really exciting and interesting. He saw his involvement with AIGA as a chance to actually follow though with some of his ideas about lectures he wanted to give and speakers he wanted to see. He was first asked to be on the "Fresh Dialogue" speakers series in 1991, and this opportunity provided the impetus for his involvement. Santoro's board service came out of an interest to create events at which members could extend their understanding of design. "One of the first events that I chaired involved Ed Fella and Massimo Vignelli, not because they were two famous 'celebrity' designers but because they were the two most obsessive-compulsive designers I could think of to pair for what I named 'obsessive-compulsive design,' OCD."

Although it took up a lot of his time, Santoro learned a lot about event management—how to get people to attend events and how to work with a board of directors. Santoro felt the experience was important to his development as a member of a wider design community in New York. "The administrator at the New York chapter was worried about my spending too much time working for the chapter, but I really wanted to put some good time in during my tenure. I knew I was getting something back that I couldn't put a price tag on."

Above and opposite: AIGA New York poster designed by Ed Fella and Scott Santoro/Worksight.

I see graphic design as the organization of information that is semantically correct, syntactically consistent, and pragmatically understandable. I like it to be visually powerful, intellectually elegant, and above all timeless.

OCD

Obsessive-Compulsive Design

Do you clean your work area as well as all of those around you? Is doodling a form of therapy for you? Do these symptoms of the designer's psyche go no further, or can ritualistic thought and behavior be positively channeled into powerful and personal graphic work? **Massimo Vignelli** and **Ed Fella**, two very different, but very driven designers, will present their work, discuss their histories and influences, and reveal the obsessions and compulsions that distinguish their work. **Veronique Vienne** (writer and critique, Communication Arts magazine) will guide us through this introspective evening.

Join Us Wednesday, March 10th, 1999, 7:00pm, Reception 6:30pm

Fashion Institute of Technology, Katie Murphy Amphitheatre, 7th Avenue at 27th Street, NYC. AIGA Members $10.00, AIGA Student Members $5.00, Non-Members $20.00. FIT Students with valid ID Free. For advanced tickets, please fax the names of attendees, credit card number (Amex, MC, or Visa), name and expiration date on card, and contact name along with phone number and e-mail address to 1(6) 212.255.4410, or call 1(4) 212.255.4004.

357

STEFAN **SAGMEISTER**

TAKE SOME TIME OFF

The year before Stefan Sagmeister took time off from client work had been the most successful to date. Business was flowing in, and the then-booming economy had filled their coffers. In addition, the small firm had won many important awards; Sagmeister had gained an international reputation and was invited to speak all over the world.

To-do list, Stefan Sagmeister

The only problem—Sagmeister was bored. The work had become repetitive, and the client demands stifled his flame of creativity. When he was invited to Cranbrook to give a workshop, he observed the students' work and lifestyle. "I actually got rather jealous of all the mature students there being able to spend their entire day just experimenting," says Sagmeister "Then Ed Fella came into the studio and showed me all the notebooks with his freewheeling typographic experiments. That did it. I settled on a date a year in advance, and I called up all my clients."

Sagmeister tried to fill that year with happy experiments. "My work during that time can be summed up by a list of all the things that I felt would be worthwhile exploring but never had the time. This included things as simple as thinking about the whole wide world and my place within it, all the way to more concrete projects, like designing fictitious CD covers under time pressure—doing them in three hours rather than my customary three months—and seeing how that self-imposed restriction changes the process and the result."

Sagmeister spent his time developing a number of what he calls "seed projects" for future collaborations with clients. He comments, "Because my brain has a tendency to follow the well-beaten path, I thought it might be helpful to start a project not from within itself but from an outside departure point, again with the hope of arriving at a different solution."

Sagmeister has learned to approach his design work with a new enthusiasm. "In any case, I got my love for design back, so it was definitely worth it."

358

ERIC **HINES**

UNPLUG FROM THE MATRIX

"Not designing on a machine keeps us creative. Take some time off and find a creative outlet that doesn't involve staring at a computer. Silkscreening, photography, printmaking, and bookbinding all make use of your inner artist and help break creative blocks."

Dan Sidor Photography website, designed by Eric Hines, Honest Bros.

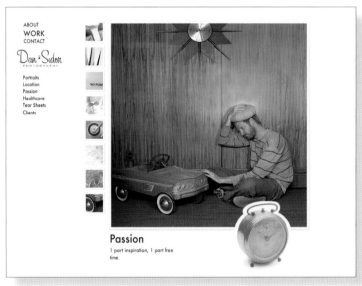

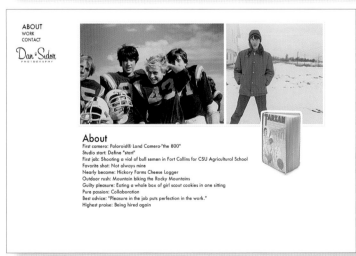

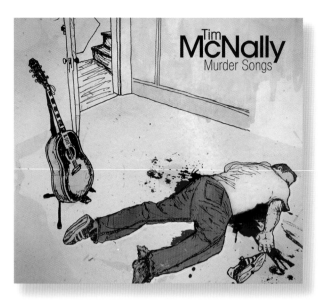

Tim McNally CD package, designed by Keith Bowman, The Design Bureau of Amerika

01 URBAN LEGEND 02 AM RADIO
03 DEFINITELY NOT YOU 04 ANOTHER FACE
05 MURDER SONGS 06 BELIEVE ME
07 CALIFORNIA 08 YOU GOT IT
09 SUICIDE KIDS 10 SINKING FEELING

COVER ARTWORK AND LAYOUT BY
KEITH BOWMAN / THE DESIGN BUREAU OF AMERIKA™
ALL SONGS © TIM MCNALLY 2008 ALL RIGHTS RESERVED

TDBA-PL-002

MURDER SONGS
TIM McNALLY

359

KEITH **BOWMAN**

REANIMATE, REARRANGE, REFRESH

"Another thing I do to stay motivated and fresh is to look at designs that are all around me, posters, package design, billboards, etc. In my mind's eye, I break the design down into geometric shapes and grids. I then try to rearrange the design in my mind to see if I could create a better solution than the finished design. This is a good mental exercise to keep me focused on seeing and understanding grids, as well as hierarchy of the design's message. This can be done at anytime and anywhere without any design tools except your mind. Plus, this is a great trick to stay awake during boring conversations with people you don't like."

Treetop brand campaign poster design by Derek Armstrong, Grill Creative

360

STEVE **GORDON, JR**

BOOST THE SIGNAL

"Update your music constantly. Sound has a profound effect on the brain, our moods, and how we think. You might be in a rut partly because your sound environment has become stale, even though you listen to your favorites and seemingly never tire of them.

You know that feeling you get when you hear a new song and it really strikes a chord with you? A fresh set of tunes on a constant basis helps feed the creative beast."

Treetop brand campaign poster design, Grill Creative

361

DEREK **ARMSTRONG**
MCNEILL

TAP INTO YOUR NONDESIGN CREATIVITY

"Your creative self-worth isn't wrapped up in a brochure you just designed. I've taken letterpress classes, played guitar in a band, and pursued photography as an art form. It all has an indirect beneficial effect on your design work and gives you a creative outlet that doesn't have to be approved by anyone, which is very cathartic."

Modéle Boutique logo adaptation and window graphics, designed by Steve Gordon, Jr, RDQLUS

362

STEVE **GORDON**, JR

YOU OUGHT TO BE IN PICTURES

"There have been times when right in the middle of my day, directly in the middle of a project, when I've become stuck or the idea is stale, I've simply left my home office and gone to see a movie. This is not about putting in a DVD that I have on hand at home but taking in the whole experience of going to a cinema.

There is something about the act of going to the movies that makes us excited and sparks the imagination. Sci-fi and action movies are the best for me because they require a suspension of reality and a boost in imagination. Movies are an art form, so creatives have a natural link to them. It just might stir something up and get your brain unstuck from the doldrums.

There's also the feeling of playing hookie and skipping work that gets the adrenaline flowing a bit more, too. You'll go back to work feeling really refreshed."

363 PROTECT YOUR HEALTH

JENNIFER **WILKERSON**

"It's easy to let yourself get run down, especially if you're juggling clients, kids, working from home, deadlines, making dinner. But it's important to stay healthy so you don't suddenly have to drop out on a project for a few days while you nurse a cold."

Many independents make the choice to work for themselves so they can be home to meet the schoolbus or take some time out during the day to attend their kids' sports events. But some days, it may feel like you're juggling a chain saw, bowling pin, and torch while trying to balance on a high wire. So wash your hands, get your rest, drink some green tea, and ask for an extension on that deadline so you can take care of yourself in addition to taking care of your clients, vendors, kids, dog, cat, and goldfish.

Union College alumni magazine, designed by Jennifer Wilkerson,
Aurora Design

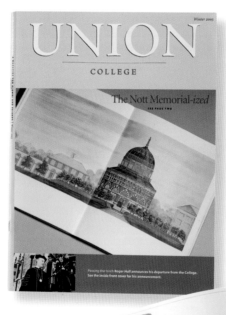

364

JENNIFER **WILKERSON**

PUT "ME" ON YOUR CALENDAR

"When you're working from home—I work in what's supposed to be the dining room—it's easy to get in the habit of always checking your email, picking up the phone anytime it rings, going back to your desk after reading a bedtime story. It's important to carve out personal time and be protective of it. Here's a trick I learned from a freelance work-from-home writer I know. I formally schedule time in my calendar for a swim or yoga class, and if a client wants to plan a conference call or something at that time, I just tell them I'm already booked in another meeting."

Mohawk Fine Papers paper sample book, designed by
Jennifer Wilkerson, Aurora Design

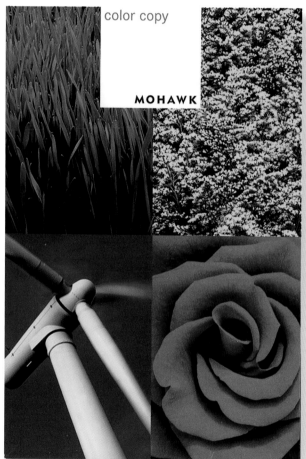

Mohawk Fine Papers paper sample book, designed by Jennifer Wilkerson, Aurora Design

365

STEVE **GORDON, JR**

GET OUTSIDE YOUR COMFORT ZONE

"Let's face it, you got into design because you were good at it. Some art teacher back in 5th grade complimented the scrawls you were doing when you should have been paying attention to the math problems on the board, and you thought, well, this is something I can do! And you've probably been doing something like it ever since, skating by those subject areas where you were a little less confident or those that required a big brain drain. Well, your brain is a muscle, and just like the other ones in your body, sometimes it takes a little pain to get a little gain. Find something really hard and do it. It can be as simple as ignoring the calculator and balancing your checkbook with a pencil and eraser" . . . or as daunting as making a book called *365 Habits of Successful Graphic Designers*.

ABOUT THE AUTHORS

LAUREL SAVILLE
WWW.LAURELSAVILLE.COM

Laurel Saville is the author of many books and articles on design and designers. She is also a corporate communications consultant, brand strategist, and copywriter and the author of numerous essays and short stories along with the award-winning memoir, *Unraveling Anne*, about her mother's life among the artists and hippies of Los Angeles in the 1960s and 1970s, as well as her tragic decline and death.

STEVE GORDON, JR,
WWW.RDQLUS.COM

Steve Gordon, Jr has been a professional graphic designer for more than ten years. He's run the full range of the career path with experience including production design, in-house design, and agency and studio work, and is currently an independent designer and creative consultant under the moniker RDQLUS.

A self-described born creative, Gordon specializes in identity design and branding. As the son of a draftsman, he had dreams of being an architect but found his way into the field of visual communication and graphic design. An avid and self-taught illustrator as a youngster, Gordon still draws on lessons and skills learned and earned as a former graffiti artist.

Steve has been a featured speaker at the HOW Design Conference as well as a member of the HOW Design Conference Advisory Committee. He is a frequent contributor on the "Reflex Blue" podcast at 36point.com, and constantly looks to write and contribute to his local design community, various design publications, blogs, and websites.

JOSHUA BERGER
WWW.JOSHUABERGER.COM

Joshua Berger is a founder and principal of Plazm, an award-winning design studio and publisher of Plazm magazine. He is the winner of Gold Medals from the Portland Design Festival and the Leipzig Book Fair (with John C Jay), and has been recognized by design publications and award shows including the AIGA Annual Show, the Art Directors Club, as well as 2004 and 2008 honorary exhibitions at ZGRAF in Zagreb, Croatia.

SARAH DOUGHER

Sarah Dougher is a composer, writer, musician and educator living in Portland, Oregon. Sarah teaches at Portland State University in the Women, Gender, and Sexuality Studies department and her academic interests focus around gender and popular music and issues related to homeless youth and food security.